Perspectives on Sustainable Resources in America

Roger A. Sedjo, editor

RESOURCES FOR THE FUTURE
Washington, DC, USA

Printed in the United States of America.

An RFF Press book
Published by Resources for the Future
1616 P Street NW
Washington, DC 20036–1400
USA
www.rffpress.org

Library of Congress Cataloging-in-Publication Data

Perspectives on sustainable resources in America / Roger A. Sedjo, editor. — 1st ed.
    p. cm.
  Includes bibliographical references and index.
  ISBN 978-1-933115-62-7 (hardcover : alk. paper) —
  ISBN 978-1-933115-63-4 (pbk. : alk. paper)
    1. Conservation of natural resources—United States. 2. Sustainable development—United States. I. Sedjo, Roger A.
  S930.P47 2008
  333.720973—dc22   2007049704

The paper in this book meets the guidelines for permanence and durability of the Committee on Production Guidelines for Book Longevity of the Council on Library Resources. This book was typeset by Andrea Reider. It was copyedited by Sally Atwater. The cover was designed by Maggie Powell.

The findings, interpretations, and conclusions offered in this publication are those of the contributors. They do not necessarily represent the views of Resources for the Future, its directors, or its officers.

ISBN 978-1-933115-62-7 (cloth)   ISBN 978-1-933115-63-4 (paper)

About Resources for the Future *and* RFF Press

Resources for the Future (RFF) improves environmental and natural resource policymaking worldwide through independent social science research of the highest caliber. Founded in 1952, RFF pioneered the application of economics as a tool for developing more effective policy about the use and conservation of natural resources. Its scholars continue to employ social science methods to analyze critical issues concerning pollution control, energy policy, land and water use, hazardous waste, climate change, biodiversity, and the environmental challenges of developing countries.

RFF Press supports the mission of RFF by publishing book-length works that present a broad range of approaches to the study of natural resources and the environment. Its authors and editors include RFF staff, researchers from the larger academic and policy communities, and journalists. Audiences for publications by RFF Press include all of the participants in the policymaking process—scholars, the media, advocacy groups, NGOs, professionals in business and government, and the public.

Resources for the Future

Contents

Acknowledgments

I WOULD LIKE TO THANK the U.S. Department of Agriculture and the U.S. Army Corps of Engineers for their financial support for the research and writing of this volume, particularly Mark Rey, Under Secretary for Natural Resources and the Environment, USDA, and Douglas MacCleery, of the U.S. Forest Service. In addition, I wish to thank George Dunlop, Deputy Assistant Secretary of the Army for Policy and Legislation, and Robert Pietrowsky, Director, U.S. Army Engineer Institute for Water Resources. In addition, my thanks to John Fedkiw, whose vision and persistence were critical to undertaking this effort, and, whose help with various aspects of this project was invaluable. Both MacCleery and Fedkiw also made substantial contributions to selected chapters. Also, of course, my thanks to the chapter authors for their intellectual work and their patience throughout the process of honing the various chapters. And my thanks to Resources for the Future and particularly its publication staff for their hard work on our behalf. Finally, I wish to thank my wife Ruth for her support throughout.

Roger A. Sedjo

Contributors

Sandra S. Batie is the Elton R. Smith Professor of Food and Agricultural Policy in the Department of Agricultural Economics at Michigan State University. Her research addresses agri-environmental policy design to achieve enhanced environmental quality, particularly with soil and water resources. She also directs a campus wide project called the Sustainable Michigan Endowed Project. She served on an advisory panel of the National Academy of Public Administration addressing the process and design of national environmental indicators. She is currently serving on the National Research Council committee on 21st Century Systems Agriculture.

Jeffrey Chow is a former research associate at Resources for the Future, and is currently pursuing a doctoral degree at the Yale University School of Forestry and Environmental Studies. His research has looked at the economic and ecological drivers of tropical deforestation, as well as the costs of disease control in developing countries, among other topics. He has co-authored articles appearing in *Science* and *The Lancet*.

John Fedkiw is retired from the U.S. Department of Agriculture Office of the Secretary where he served 28 years as a policy advisor and analyst for natural resource and environmental issues and programs. He is a recipient of the President's Meritorious Executive Award and the USDA Distinguished Service Award. He now serves as a volunteer with USDA Forest Service Research Division for resource valuation and use. His book publications include *Managing Multiple Uses on National Forests 1905-1995: A 90-Year Learning Experience*, and *Pathway to Sustainability: Defining the Bounds of Forest Management*.

Dean Lueck is Bartley P. Cardon Professor of Agricultural and Resource Economics, professor of law at the James Rogers College of Law, and co-director of the Program on Economics, Law and the Environment at The University of Arizona. His research focus is on the economics of law, property rights, and organization, and includes projects on agricultural land contracts, conservation easements, systems of property rights in land, right to farm laws, and the behavior of state wildlife agencies.

Douglas MacCleery is a senior policy analyst in the National Forest System, USDA Forest Service in Washington, DC. Between 1981 and 1987, he was deputy assistant secretary for natural resources and the environment in the U.S. Department of Agriculture. His publications include *American Forests: A History of Resiliency and Recovery*, and *Pathway to Sustainability: Defining the Bounds on Forest Management*.

Roger A. Sedjo is a senior fellow and director of the Forest Economics and Policy Program at Resources for the Future (RFF), a position he has held for over twenty-five years. Sedjo has done substantial work on climate change, biodiversity, deforestation, and biofuels. He has authored hundreds of journal articles and book chapters. *Perspectives* is his fifteenth book. His edited books include *The Economics of Forestry*, and *A Vision for the U.S. Forest Service: Goals for Its Next Century*, which received the Best Book Award for 2000 from the Section for Environmental and Natural Resources Administration of the American Society of Public Administration.

Leonard Shabman is a resident scholar at Resources for the Future. Prior to joining RFF he was on the faculty at Virginia Tech where he also served as the director of the Virginia Water Resources Research Center. He is a member of the Water Science and Technology Board of the National Academy of Sciences. His research on water policy and management has been widely published in economics as well as interdisciplinary journals.

Juha Siikamäki is a fellow at Resources for the Future. His research focuses on evaluating the benefits, costs, and cost-effectiveness of environmental policy options, especially those related to biological conservation. He has recently published articles in the *Journal of Environmental Economics and Management* and *Land Economics*.

CHAPTER I

Are America's Resources Sustainable?

Roger A. Sedjo

T HE QUESTION OF HOW society should deal with its natural environment is not new. Biblical directives call for man to "subdue" the earth. Resource management questions go back to the practices of early herders and agriculturists. Primitive attempts at water management systems are often credited with having contributed to the development of social institutions and bureaucracies. An important part of America's resource history is found in the intellectual disputes between Gifford Pinchot and John Muir more than a hundred years ago. Pinchot espoused the "wise use" doctrine of conservation, arguing that resources should be used wisely for the betterment of humankind. Elements of this message carried over to the ethos of the Great Depression. Woody Guthrie, for example, wrote songs lauding the growth of great water development projects with lyrics like "while the water is flowing to the sea, why not let it do a little work for me?" By contrast, Muir embraced notions closer to that of pristine preservation, arguing against resource development that compromised the pristine nature of the resource or resource system.

Toward the latter part of the 19th century, diminishment of the bounty of resources in America became apparent, and resource scarcity pressures became a serious concern. It was largely the wise-use perspective that generated concerns about the sustainability of forests and the water flows that emanated from them, leading to legislation that established the forest reserves in the 1890s and ultimately, in 1905, the National Forest System. Concurrently, the dramatic decline of some wildlife species led to serious restrictions on market hunting and other activities that threatened wildlife. Concerns for pristine values, meanwhile, generated the establishment of an extensive national park system, which is still expanding.

By the latter part of the 20th century some of the earlier concerns had diminished but were replaced by others. The impending timber famine forecast in the

19th century never materialized, and the losses of wildlife habitat had largely abated. Indeed, deer were more numerous than ever, and bald eagles, coyotes, and wolves had made remarkable recoveries. However, increasing population and development made greater demands on many of the country's resources. Although agricultural productivity reduced some pressures on agricultural and forest lands, limited water resources, not only in arid areas of the West but also in parts of the densely populated East, created continued concerns over the future of water adequacy and flows. Finally, even as it was acknowledged that ecosystems were more complex and multifaceted than formerly recognized, concepts of sustainability became more sophisticated, requiring new resource management approaches.

This introductory chapter provides an overview of this volume and its purpose and describes the content, including the limitations, of the chapters that follow.

The Origin of this Book

In 1991 Resources for the Future published *America's Renewable Resources: Historical Trends and Current Challenges*, edited by Kenneth D. Frederick and Roger A. Sedjo. That book provided a collection of chapters by eminent researchers who focused on understanding long-term trends in the condition and capacity of renewable resource systems in America. The current volume can be viewed as a sequel. As in the earlier volume, the approach here involves an examination of the nature and characteristics of an important set of renewable resources, as well as some resource uses. But there are changes: chapters on outdoor recreation and rangeland are not included, for example, while biodiversity is included.

Although this book is intended to present an integrated investigation of selected American resource sectors, each chapter stands alone and can be read independently. Thus, of necessity, there is a certain degree of overlap of concepts and sometimes history in the various chapters. However, the reader will also observe that the authors often approach similar problems differently; no attempt has been made to impose a rigid intellectual structure. Differences in perspective exist among the chapter authors, as indeed they do among resource experts more generally.

New to this volume is a chapter that introduces concepts of resource sustainability. The term has historical antecedents, and unanimity in definitions and applications has not yet been achieved, but the concept has been refined and has gained ascendancy in the past two decades. Sustainability now commonly implies management for a continuous flow of ecosystem services and public goods, as well as private commodity goods and services. Nevertheless, it will become clear in the chapters that the authors do not accept a single, unified concept of sustainability. Some of these differences reflect values; others reflect unique aspects of the different resources.

This book updates the reader on the current situation of some of America's most important renewable natural resources, including biodiversity. Biodiversity is increasingly being viewed as a separate natural resource, and its maintenance and uses have attracted considerable attention (see Simpson et al. 1996). As with the earlier volume, the historical experiences of these resources and resource uses are considered.

Topics examined include the evolving concepts of sustainability, the introduction of policies and legislation, and how the resource has been perceived and the way it is managed. Current challenges in resource management are identified.

The earlier book focused on the productivity of a resource's commodity outputs and the renewability of these outputs. By contrast, this volume gives increased emphasis to a broader array of outputs, many of them public goods, including ecosystem services. Even though the production of many of these noncommodity goods and services is often poorly measured and/or documented and many of these values are not well estimated, there now appears to be widespread recognition and acceptance in the United States that the management of natural resources should consider these outputs.

This volume focuses on the U.S. experience from the past to the present; it is not futuristic and makes no attempt to extrapolate into the future. The future may follow past trends, but trends change and the future may present challenges quite different from those of the past. The impact of humans on earth and resource systems today is different in some ways from that of earlier periods. For example, as the chapter on forests shows, although the area of American forests declined for the first several hundred years after European settlement, the experience of the past hundred years has been quite different. More generally, in much of the world, the earlier trend toward deforestation has been reversed (Kauppi et al. 2006).

An example of an emerging challenge is that of global warming. How will global warming or other future natural or human perturbations increase the challenges to natural resource sustainable management? Almost certainly global warming and other new challenges will occur and the sustainability of many of these systems may be severely tested. However, this volume confines itself to the past and the present and does not try to forecast the effects of new disturbances nor suggest how humans might adapt to prospective future conditions of the resources examined.

Overview

To early European explorers and many later colonists and settlers, the land, forests, wildlife, and water resources of the New World appeared to be wild and essentially unlimited.[1] Until roughly 1800, subduing and harnessing the vast resources of the continent were the concern, not resource sustainability. The importance of food and fiber production made agricultural land a highly desired resource. Some lands were likely more attractive than others by virtue of their location, topography, soils, climate, absence of trees and other impediments to agriculture, access to water and other transport, and so on. From the perspective of farmers, the bountiful forests were more an impediment to cropping and transport than an asset for timber, water flows, or habitat. Wildlife, too, was plentiful throughout much of the country and provided food for both Native Americans and settlers. The area of the continent was so vast that even as land was taken up by the early waves of settlers, others could still homestead sites that were desirable, albeit more remote. Water, plentiful in the East, was less so in the arid West, and indeed the difference in availability resulted in a different basis for water laws (see Chapter 5, this volume).

Even as natural resource scarcity gradually appeared in some regions, the continuing opening of the frontier relieved these pressures on resources generally. Well into the 19th century, in many places forests continued to be viewed largely as an obstruction to development. Water and wildlife had primarily utilitarian value. Particularly before the advent of the railroads in the 1840s, water was used for transport through the early development of canals that complemented river travel. Later, water was dammed and diverted to provide for irrigation and power. Wildlife continued to be a major source of food. Agricultural soils, too, tended to be taken for granted. Soils leached of their fertility or otherwise depleted were often abandoned, particularly in the South, where demanding crops such as tobacco and cotton reduced soil fertility. Indeed, it is the abandonment of these lands by agriculture that allowed the renewal of forests on these lands, largely through natural processes (USDA 1988).

Interestingly, one of the last terrestrial natural resources to come into short supply in the United States was cropland. According to Hayami and Rattan (1985), agricultural land availability did not become a constraint on production until the 1930s. Before that time, all of the agricultural production increases could be attributed to increases in cropping areas. It was at that time that the constraint on new lands for cropping necessitated biological technology—plant improvements via breeding—to allow crop harvests to continue to rise.

Chapter 2, by Sandra Batie, Roger Sedjo, and John Fedkiw, examines the concept of sustainability as it applies to natural resources. Earlier concepts, such as "wise use," are discussed, as is the evolution to modern concepts. The focus is on the sustainability paradigms of resource sufficiency and functional integrity.

Chapters 3 and 4, on forestry and soils, look at these resources from the perspective of the sustainability of the systems and their outputs, both commodity and ecosystem. Chapter 3, by Roger Sedjo and Douglas MacCleery, is historical in orientation. It discusses the history of the American forest from the pre-European period to the first decade of the 21st century. In this context it discusses the evolution of forestry and the concept of sustainability in forest management and observes that in the United States, private forestry has moved toward intensive management on productive lands, while forestry on public lands has a greater focus on nontimber values. The chapter discusses how forest management has gradually been redefined. Earlier concepts, such as the sustained timber yield concept, largely focused on the production of commodity timber; broader multiple-use approaches, developed in the latter part of the 20th century, seek to produce a selected set of outputs, many of which may be environmental goods and services. More recently, an even broader assessment of forest management, especially of public forests, is intended to maintain the "condition of the forest" through the sustainability of forest ecosystems and their provision of ecosystem services.

Chapter 4, by Sandra Batie, addresses the sustainability of U.S. cropland soils. She reviews sustainability concepts and resource sufficiency paradigms that focus on the soil's ability to sustain or enhance crop yields. She notes that in recent years the sustainability concept has been broadened to include ecosystem services, since it has become apparent to scientists that soils perform many functions, including regulation of water quality and flows, nutrient cycling, carbon storage, and other desired services. Since soils contribute to ecosystem stability and hence perform a crucial role in ecosystem functioning, a broader role needs to be assigned to them. The author notes that important research about managing soil for sustainability has been provided to farmers through technical assistance programs. However, she finds little financial incentive for farmers to undertake conservation activities.

Chapter 5, by Leonard Shabman, covers nature's role in supplying water in the form of precipitation, runoff, and storage in lakes and aquifers as well as how water availability is monitored, assessed, and allocated through human management. He notes that current thinking has eliminated the earlier sharp distinction between surface and subsurface water and replaced it with a concept that recognizes that these are often parts of the same system and should be treated in concert. The chapter discusses the development, management, and use of water resources in transportation, hydropower, irrigation, industry, and public water supply. Efforts to address flooding and other hazards through water management are discussed, as are water supply issues, water law, and environmental regulation. The chapter provides a historical perspective on water conservation, naturalness, and sustainable water use. It notes the tension between ecologically sustainable water management and a water management program for human purposes. The author points out that the conflicts among these concepts are largely value driven.

Chapter 6, by Dean Lueck, examines the concepts and conditions of wildlife in the United States, as well as wildlife sustainability since European contact. The chapter explains how wildlife management institutions have affected wildlife populations and how economic forces, in turn, have shaped these institutions. The question is raised as to what distinguishes a wild from a domestic animal, and the chapter offers some innovative suggestions, based in part on the nature of the animal, its range, and difficulties of management control.

Lueck draws from Geoff Heal's (1998, 2000) development of analytical economic rigor to the concept of sustainability. Accepting Heal's notion that the sustainability framework remains an elusive empirical concept, the chapter notes that stocks of natural resources, including wildlife, generate value by providing services beyond those simply derived from resource harvest. This suggests that important values can come from nonconsumptive uses of wildlife, including viewing, genetic information, existence value, and contributions to ecosystem services, such as seed dispersal.

In Chapter 7: Juha Siikamäki and Jeffrey Chow examine biodiversity. Though not traditionally viewed as a natural resource, biodiversity is increasingly treated as such. Also, the condition of a country's biodiversity is commonly believed to be an indicator of the condition and sustainability of its land and water resources. The chapter examines issues of species loss and extinction, which clearly indicate a lack of sustainability in parts of the ecosystem, and also the issue of species recovery, which reflects the resiliency of the system and certainly has implications for long-term sustainability. The chapter provides a comprehensive overview of biodiversity in the United States, including its history, current status, and related policies and legislation. Issues covered include extinctions, species endangerment, threats to biodiversity, and bioprospecting. A useful review of the economics of biodiversity with a discussion of the economic values of biodiversity is included, as well as a discussion of current implementation of the Endangered Species Act.

The chapter spends little time on definitions or philosophical musings. In general, it treats preservation and sustainability as synonyms. In this context wise use implies maintaining adequate stocks of the various components of biodiversity. The chapter concludes that successful strategies to preserve biodiversity likely would examine economic and ecological systems from an integrated perspective, managing human and natural economies as jointly determined systems.

A reading of these chapters makes clear that, at the conceptual level, definitions and concepts of resources sustainability have evolved, and in many cases the details are becoming increasingly well articulated. However, the on-the-ground application of these constructs to real-world management systems can be extremely difficult. Management is directed to achieving some end, whether producing agricultural crops or creating a nature reserve. Trade-offs, however, are pervasive. There are likely to be important trade-offs not only between commodities and pristine resources, but also between different sets of desired ecosystem services flowing from the same natural resource system.

Some Limitations

A criticism of this book might be that it has segmented resources, treating each of them independently and ignoring holistic sustainability. This volume does indeed focus on the parts. Of course, land, forest, agricultural, water, wildlife, and biodiversity are not separate and distinct entities, but rather part of a whole terrestrial system. Changes in one resource system imply changes in the others. More farms often mean fewer forests. Wildlife habitat includes farmland as well as forests. Water is an essential aspect of all the resources examined. Yet it is difficult to judge the whole without some understanding of what is happening to the parts. Indeed, some parts appear to be faring better than others.

Additionally, there is an issue of scale, both spatial and temporal. The concept of sustainability has been applied to a small forest, a species, a landscape, a continent, and the global system. For the survivability of humans as a species, it is the global system that is most critical. Natural resources and resource systems have shown a huge degree of adaptability and resiliency. Biological processes continue to function despite all types of insults, human and nonhuman alike. As the chapters stress, most of these systems are dynamic and continue to change through time. In its long history the earth has undergone huge changes. Continents drift, ice ages come and go, seas rise and fall. Humans are not operating in a static system. For better or worse, humans are dealing with resource systems that are continually changing. In many cases changes are slow and imperceptible, occurring across many generations and often across millennia. But to survive humans must continue to be able to adapt.

Another critique might note the dichotomy apparent in this volume between the concept of sustainability and its application. Nature resource systems are complex. It is sometimes asserted that one cannot manage what is not measured (Binkley 2000). Obviously, not all of the relevant aspects of natural resource systems are yet measurable. Thus, achieving sustainability has been characterized as more of a journey than a destination. Indeed, some have called it a pathway, suggesting that there is a route to be traversed (Fedkiw 2004). But a pathway to where? Ultimately the pathway is the destination, and it must be one that is consistent with the management of resources to meet human needs through time—both commodity needs and the need to protect the natural environment for both amenity and survival purposes.

There are also limitations in the science and in translating science to management systems. Past science has often been shown to be wrong, and this has led to inappropriate resource management. Botkin (1991), for example, has pointed out the limitations and inadequacies of earlier forest yield-and-growth models. Similarly, our notions of wildfire suppression are undergoing radical revisions. Suppression of small forest fires, for example, created problems of fuel buildup, leading to ecologically damaging, catastrophic fires, and may not be consistent with long-term sustainability of forests where fire plays an important regeneration role (O'Laughlin 1996). Additionally, it is difficult to overstate the complexity of applying abstract sustainability concepts to on-the-ground management. It is one thing to say that resources should be managed sustainably, it is another thing to know precisely what needs to be done to achieve this end. Egregious soil erosion, for example, obviously violates the sustainability rule, but the results of other management actions may be more ambiguous. Despite limitations, the chapters reflect our increasing understanding of natural resource systems as well as an understanding of the difficulties of adjusting management to both new science and evolving values.

Finally, there is the issue of large human or natural perturbations. Global warming and other future natural or human perturbations will almost surely complicate sustainable natural resource management. Although this volume makes no attempt to forecast future changes in resource conditions, resource conditions will undoubtedly change, and the nature and sustainability of some of these systems may be severely tested. Perhaps the most comprehensive reviews of such problems have been undertaken by the United Nations Intergovernmental Panel on Climate Change (IPCC), which continues to monitor both the evolving science and possible mitigation and adaptation approaches. Indeed, the editor of this volume has been a contributor to three of the IPCC assessment reports on climate change. The Fourth Assessment Report (IPCC 2007) devotes at least one chapter (Working Group 2, Chapter 5) to examining the implications of global warming on various resources, including forest, agriculture, water, and their productivity and sustainability.

A Basis For Optimism

In 1991, *America's Renewable Resources* was generally optimistic about resource renewability in America (Frederick and Sedjo 1991), based on the positive changes that had occurred, such as the stabilization of the American forest and the partial recovery of many of our wildlife species and rangelands. As this volume shows, the concepts of renewability and sustainability, while related, are clearly different, and no precise comparisons with earlier results are attempted. Nevertheless, it is possible to identify changes that engender optimism about the condition of renewable resources in America. The chapters here suggest that progress has been made at developing social consensus on an appropriate and sustainable balance between commodity outputs and the outputs of ecosystem services. Conflicts between resource users and the environmental community appear to have been substantially reduced over the past two or three decades. For example, the timber wars of the 1980s clearly are over (see Chapter 3). The country has made a de facto decision that the national forests are primarily about not commodities but ecosystem services. Whatever one's view on the legislation and decisions, in a real sense "we are all environmentalists now."

To this observer, it does appear that recently there has been an improved spirit of cooperation in regard to resource management among the private sector, the government, and large components of the environmental community. Conservation easements, which typically involve cooperation between industry and environmentalists, provide one example. As some chapters discuss, certain ecosystem and amenity services and other environmental values of private lands are increasingly protected by environmental easements or trust ownerships. These easements are obtained through voluntary gifts or market purchases by private landowners. Private forestry too has shown a largely voluntary movement toward more sustainable management. Forest certification is now common in American forests that produce the country's industrial wood. Activities to promote wildlife sustainability and broad biodiversity protection have also shown progress. Additionally, the country seems to have accepted the general concept of the protection of endangered species, as reflected in the Endangered Species Act. Although disputes continue in individual cases, the idea of such legislation appears to be broadly accepted, and progress is being made. Delistings are occurring more often. Regarding water resources, another general consensus appears to have been forged. Although engineered structures can help provide society with a host of useful water-related services, it is now agreed that we need to consider the environmental implications of a project and need not build at every opportunity. The values of water are many, and a balance between utilitarian wants and amenity values is required if true sustainability is to be achieved. The soils chapter discusses the progress that is being made on agricultural lands, as well as noting some difficulties. Whether legislation ultimately creates a radical departure from earlier bills by redirecting financial incentives to environmental outputs rather than only commodity outputs remains to be determined. However, an initial articulation of such a new concept demonstrates that thinking in this area has not stagnated. Although contentiousness has not disappeared and sharp differences remain, there are still substantial areas of progress.

Further Thoughts

Our objective in this volume is to provide an update of the current situation of selected natural resources in America, investigate new concepts of resource sustainability, and ask how these concepts may be applied to some of America's natural resources. While exploring the concept of sustainability at some length, this volume does not pretend to provide a final definitive definition of sustainability. It does demonstrate, however, that systems are being put in place to try to achieve some degree of sustainability according to some of the contemporary definitions.

Resource conditions vary over time, as do human demands on the resource. Thus, while today's resource balance is important, tomorrow's could be quite different, either because human demand pressures change or because the ability to supply the resource changes. Technology is an important factor (Simpson 1999). Recent changes in production approaches have been characterized as reflecting the dematerialization of the U.S. economy (Herman et al. 1989). Others note that the United States has moved from an industrial to an information economy. Nanotechnology[2] suggests the possibility of a future where the natural properties of materials can be dramatically altered; this could change the needs for traditional fiber sources. Agricultural technology has changed the productivity of crops, with implications for the amount of farmland required. Future human populations can be projected, but only with large uncertainties. And the demands of future populations are even more unknowable. Thus, sustainability appears to require adhering to a path that is largely unknown, with unanticipated twists and turns. In a world of such uncertainties, flexibility and adaptability become critical.

Notes

1. Recent scholarship suggests that Native peoples prior to European contact had much more intensively affected the resources and environment of the New World than is commonly recognized. See Mann (2005) for a fascinating review. Nevertheless, by the time of European settlement of the Americas in the early 1600s, much of the New World, and particularly the area that is now the United States, had reverted to a wilderness, probably because of huge disease-driven declines in Native populations, and was viewed largely as a limitless wilderness with vast resources.

2. In the "bottom-up" approach of nanotechnology, materials and devices are built from molecular components that assemble themselves chemically using principles of molecular recognition.

References

Binkley, C.S. 2000. Forestry in the New Millennium: Creating a Vision That Fits. In *A Vision for the U.S. Forest Service: Goals for its Next Century*, edited by Roger A. Sedjo. Washington, DC: Resources for the Future.

Botkin, D.B. 1991. *Discordant Harmonies: A New Ecology for the Twenty-first Century*. New York: Oxford University Press.

Fedkiw, J. 2004. Sustainability and the Pathway Hypothesis. In *Pathway to Sustainability: Defining the Bounds on Forest Management*, edited by John Fedkiw, Douglas MacCleery, and V. Alaric Sample. Durham, NC: Forest History Society.

Frederick, K.D., and R.A. Sedjo (eds.). 1991. *America's Renewable Resources: Historical Trends and Current Challenges*. Washington, DC: Resources for the Future.

Hayami, Y., and V.W. Rattan. 1985. *Agricultural Development: An International Perspective*. Baltimore: Johns Hopkins University Press.

Heal, G.M. 1998. *Valuing the Future: Economic Theory and Sustainability*. New York: Columbia University Press.

———. 2000. *Nature and the Marketplace*. Washington, DC: Island Press.

Herman, R., S.A. Ardekani, and J.H. Ausubel. 1989. Dematerialization. In *Technology and Environment*, edited by J.H. Ausubel and H.E. Sladovich. Washington, DC: National Academy Press, 50–69.

Intergovernmental Panel on Climate Change (IPCC). 2007. Food, fibre, forestry and fisheries. Fourth assessment report on climate change. Cambridge, UK: Cambridge University Press.

Kauppi, P.E., J. Fang, and R.A. Sedjo. 2006. Restored Global Forests Improve Carbon Prospects. *Science.*

Mann, C.C. 2005. *1491: New Revelations of the Americas before Columbus.* New York: Knopf.

O'Laughlin, J. 1996. Forest Ecosystem Health Assessment Issues: Definitions, Measurement and Management Implications. *Ecosystem Health* 2(1): 1–12.

Simpson, R.D. 1999. *Productivity in Natural Resource Industries.* Washington, DC: Resources for the Future.

Simpson, R.D., R.A. Sedjo, and J. Reid. 1996. Valuing Biodiversity for Pharmaceutical Research. *Journal of Political Economy* 104(1): 163–85.

U.S. Department of Agriculture (USDA). 1988. *The South's Fourth Forests: Alternatives for the Future.* Forest Resources Report No. 24. Washington, DC: USDA Forest Service.

CHAPTER 2

Sustainability

From Natural Resource Sufficiency to Ecosystem Functional Integrity

Sandra S. Batie, Roger A. Sedjo, and John Fedkiw

SUSTAINABILITY—AS APPLIED TO natural resources—is a concept that has had many meanings and is still evolving. One of the purposes of this book is to trace the evolution of the concept as applied in management. Chapter 1 noted the conflicting claims on the land and its resources through time. Although the "wise use" conservationism of Pinchot, a utilitarian view that stressed sustainable outputs of commodities, was on the ascendancy in the late 19th and early 20th century, it never completely dominated public thought. Nature preserves, wildlife areas, and the maintenance of wilderness that so captivated Muir have always been recognized as having values beyond simple utilitarian wise use. Indeed, it was a preservationist concern for naturalness, uniqueness, and habitat that in 1870 led to the establishment of Yellowstone as the first national park.

A variation of the wise use versus preservation debate is found in the scarcity and growth literature. Humans have wrestled with concepts like sustainability for millennia. For example, Thomas Malthus's 1789 publication, "An Essay on the Principle of Population," argued that population growth would always outrun increases in agriculture production. From this assumption, he concluded that humans were preordained indefinitely to be poor starving creatures—a gloomy interpretation that has contributed toward the characterization of economics as the "dismal science."

In recent years, numerous books have addressed the question of resource scarcity and limitations, with some dismal Malthusian predictions. For example, Meadows et al. (1972) projected huge resource declines before the end of the 20th century. Others have been equally pessimistic; Ehrlich (1968), for example, again blamed population growth. However, another school of thought has been highly optimistic about society's progress and prospects for continuing progress (e.g., Simon and Kahn 1983; Bailey 1995). Still others have taken a somewhat measured view between extreme optimism and pessimism (Barrett and Morse 1963; Simpson et al. 2005).

Today, the concepts of wise-use conservation and simple preservation both appear to have been subsumed by the broader and more dynamic concept of sustainability—that is, sustainability in the context of systems that inevitability change through time. The broad concepts of sustainability incorporate lessons from environmentalism about healthy, well-functioning ecological systems.

Thus, while society still struggles to clarify the concept of sustainability and make it operational within a management context, it is now widely accepted that resource use and conservation must recognize not only those values reflected in markets (such as timber production) and not only nonmarket values (such as preservation of natural resources for recreation and other nonconsumptive uses) but also those nonmarket values associated with ecosystem services (such as the provision of wildlife habitat) (Pearce and Barbier 2000).

Preservation

The concept of nonmarket social values of natural resources has a long history. For example, Krutilla (1967) extended the economic rationale for preservation when he argued that wise-use conservation, which traditionally focused on the efficient use of natural resources for commodity production, ought also to explicitly include public goods, for example, the preservation of unique natural places that can be nonconsumptively used, since they too created economic benefits, albeit nonmarket benefits, to society. This perspective provided a rationale for the commonly used willingness-to-pay criterion, whereby the population is surveyed for their assessment of what they would be willing to pay to preserve a host of nonmarket goods and services, including amenity services and preservation.

Gradually, the concept of nonmarket values has been expanded to encompass more than preservation values. As Pearce and Barbier (2000) note, these values include resource functions, such as "sinks" to receive and assimilate solid, liquid, and gaseous wastes; amenities; biogeochemical cycles that help stabilize climates; nutrients for the growth of living things; the purification of water and air; and information in the form of genetic blueprints and behavioral observations.

An example of this evolution can be illustrated with soil resources. When *America's Renewable Resources* was written in 1991, for example, "soil sustainability" primarily referred to the soil's ability to sustain or enhance crop yields over long time periods (Frederick and Sedjo 1991). As noted in Chapter 4, soil scientists have since extended the concept of sustainable soils beyond crop production to include many other functions. High-quality soils can help maintain water quality, regulate water quantity, prevent water and wind erosion, improve nutrient cycling, buffer global climate changes via carbon sequestration, improve food nutrition and safety, enhance biodiversity, and provide for nonagricultural uses, such as building sites (Jaenicke 1998; Lal et al. 1999; National Research Council 1993; Schjonning et al. 2004).

Similarly, since 1991, much of the attention of public lands forestry has been directed to reorienting forestry management to focus on ecosystem services. For private forests, forest certification attesting to the use of "sustainable" harvesting practices now is widely embraced by environmental groups and producers alike and is becoming quite common in the United States and worldwide (see Chapter 3).

This expansion of sustainability concepts to include the functioning of ecosystems can be seen in related concepts, such as sustainable development. For example, in response to the concerns about the sustainability of the global system, the Brundtland Commission's report *Our Common Future* (WCED 1987) defined sustainable development as "development that meets the needs of the present without compromising the ability of future generations to meet their own needs." Imbedded in this definition is the idea that sustainability requires that all the pieces be preserved somewhere in the system. Also, this definition can be interpreted to include protection of the ecological functions of natural systems. Although the Brundtland Commission definition has been revised and refined by numerous groups, the basic concept has been widely accepted. Its call for a balancing of ecological, social, and economic objectives over time is often considered to be a hallmark of sustainability and even referred to the "triple bottom line" or the "three pillars" of sustainability.

The Three Pillars of Sustainability

The three-pillar approach draws many of its lessons from environmentalism and refers to three dynamically intertwined outcomes and processes (Edwards 2005). *Ecological sustainability* refers to ecosystem functioning and usually involves systematic (as opposed to piecemeal) attention to ecological connections. In addition, it is focused on the possibility of long-term limits to the human–induced impacts that can be sustained by ecosystems as well as the appropriate scale of human activities relative to the amount of resources. *Economic sustainability* focuses on the importance of healthy economies that provide high-quality lives for their citizens. In addition, economic sustainability usually involves the identification of alternative paths of economic development that provide for a more secure future without jeopardizing the long-term ecological sustainability of the natural systems. *Social sustainability* addresses the role of social cohesion and healthy cities and communities as well as an equitable distribution of resources among citizens. It frequently includes a strong orientation to issues of social justice. Figure 2-1 illustrates these concepts as interlocking circles whose intersection represents sustainable outcomes or systems, such as sustainable development.

Sustainability concepts can be specifically applied to natural resources. Smyth and Dumanski (1993), for example, state that sustainable management involves maintaining or enhancing production and services, reducing the level of production risk, protecting the potential of natural resources, and preventing the degradation of soil and water quality, while being economically viable and socially acceptable. Their definition acknowledges that agriculture and forestry provide not just food and fiber but also services, or functions, such as influencing environmental quality and affecting the lives of rural people and the broader society. In addition, it includes the idea that the desirability of such functions is a social decision involving multiple interests.

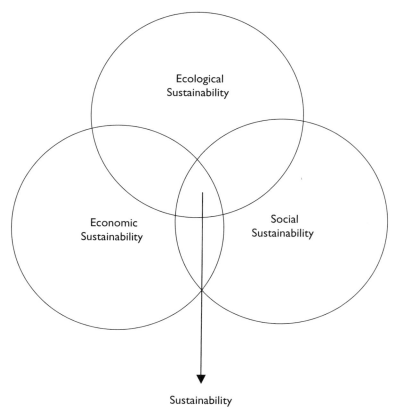

Figure 2-1. *The Three Pillars of Sustainability*

   Nevertheless, statements such as Smyth and Dumanski's are quite general, and though useful in structuring discussions and debate, they are difficult to use in exploring empirical questions. Exactly how the three objectives are to be balanced in particular situations (e.g., what is the appropriate balance, who determines the balance, and on what basis) remains the topic of considerable discussion and debate, both generally and as applied to the management of a specific resource.[1]

   Clearly, sustainability concepts have the potential to dramatically influence how we as a society think about the impact of human activity on the broader environment and on the opportunities available to future generations. How society frames the problems of the sustainability of resource use matters (Thompson 2004). However, there is a significant challenge in making the sustainability concept operational so that it can help answer such questions as how long society can sustain its present use of resources before scarcity or some functional disruption leads to a system breakdown. The next section of this chapter explores the concepts of sustainability in more detail.

Sustainability: The Two-Paradigm Approach

In the past several decades, the expanded concept of the sustainability of resource systems has been explored by many authors (e.g., Batie 1989; Colby 1989; Edwards 2005; Jansson et al. 1994), with many classifications of sustainability. Thompson (2004) concludes that the concepts of sustainability have evolved such that two broad paradigms now characterize discussions: *resource sufficiency* and *functional integrity*.

Resource sufficiency encompasses an approach, common in economics textbooks, that defines sustainability in terms of the ability of manmade capital (e.g., technology), human capital (e.g., knowledge), or social capital (e.g., institutions) to substitute for natural capital (e.g., soil fertility). Resource sufficiency concepts evolved from the earlier discussions of wise use and preservation. The paradigm of functional integrity of systems encompasses many of the nonmarket values that are associated with ecosystem functioning and emerged in the second half of the 20th century to complement the paradigm of resource sufficiency. These two approaches are not mutually exclusive, and there are complementarities between them.

The Resource Sufficiency Paradigm

The resource sufficiency paradigm is concerned with the rate at which a given production or consumption practice depletes a resource. Resource sufficiency implies some measurement of how long certain practices will continue to promote well-being but leaves unanswered whose well-being is enhanced. The variables of interest are usually the historical and current state and trends in use of renewable and nonrenewable resources, as well as various substitutes and complements for resources in providing goods and services

A resource sufficiency approach to defining sustainability views the concept of *substitution* as instrumental to sustainability, particularly ecological and economic sustainability. One way to understand this approach is to think of human activities as utilizing combinations of four types of capital: manmade capital, natural capital, human capital, and social capital to produce goods and services, including ecological services. Symbolically, this relationship can be written as follows:

$$Q = fn\ (Km, Kn, Kh, Ks)$$

Manmade capital, Km, includes technological improvements and equipment. Natural capital, Kn, includes elements of nature, such as renewable and nonrenewable resources; an example is soil productivity. Human capital, Kh, is human labor influenced by human intelligence, education, and skills. Social capital, Ks, is derived from social relationships and includes institutions that are influenced by culture, values, and heritage. This approach recognizes the capacity to substitute one resource for another, but not without limits. Also, within this approach resources are viewed as natural capital that, when combined with human, social, manmade capital, and other types of natural capital, function to produce many services (Q), such as food, fiber, and biomass.

From this perspective, debates about ecological sustainability are seen as addressing the degree of substitutability between the types of capital as well as the desirability of such substitution. For example, consider the use of soils for the production of crops. If manmade capital such as pesticides and fertilizers are seen as appropriate and effective substitutes for the natural productivity of soil, then the argument can be made that our historical management of soils has been sustainable, since crop yields on American soils have increased over the past century. But if manmade capital substitutions are either infeasible or expected to lose effectiveness in the future, then our management of soils is not on a sustainable path for the objective of the production of crops.

The belief that these types of capital easily substitute for one another, and that such substitution is acceptable, is termed a belief in *weak sustainability*. Weak sustainability does not single out the environment for any special treatment; it is simply another form of capital, and it is based on the principle of "perfect substitutability" between the different forms of capital (Turner 1993). Weak sustainability, then, suggests that a system is sustainable if the sum of Km + Kn + Kh + Ks is a constant.

Ed Schuh (1987), an applied economist, succinctly illustrates the concept of weak sustainability with reference to economic sustainability when he refers to the ability of knowledge to substitute for natural resources: "economic development, rather than creating economic scarcity, in its general force, tends to create economic abundance. The reason is obvious ... The engine of economic growth does not lie in physical and natural resources ... but in science and technology—[that is,] knowledge".

Weak sustainability can be contrasted with *strong sustainability*; proponents of strong sustainability argue that natural capital should not decline over time and that future generations have a right to the same amount of natural capital (e.g., soil fertility) as present generations. This viewpoint means that substitutions of manmade capital for natural capital are difficult, inappropriate, and/or unethical and are to be minimized (Daly 1987); that is, Kn should be kept constant. There is also attention given within the strong sustainability framework to the effect of the scale of human impact relative to ecosystem carrying capacity.

Both weak and strong sustainability[2] tend to abstract from a dynamic systems approach, however, in that neither framework addresses whether a system, such as an ecosystem, can reproduce itself over time. Both also fail to consider whether a living system, such as a soil ecosystem, has either resistance to changing function or form when subjected to a disturbance, or resilience to recover functional and structural integrity following a disturbance.

The Functional Integrity Paradigm

The *functional integrity* paradigm focuses on the capacity of a system to reproduce itself over time. Functional integrity refers to whole systems, such as human-dominated ecosystems, and their ability to regenerate themselves. Thompson (2004, 9) writes,

> System level stability manifests itself in social institutions, renewal of soil, water, and genetic resources (including wildlife) and cultural identity ... [It] can be expressed as prudential advice to be cautious about very uncertain risks. It may also be expressed ... as a duty to maintain the integrity of institutions and natural processes ...

In discussing both the resource sufficiency and the functional integrity paradigms, Thompson notes that any framing of the empirical questions about sustainability presupposes a value-laden definition of system borders:

> The broader point here is to illustrate how the definition of system borders involves a value judgment that frames the empirical assessment of sustainability. If one takes the farmer, for granted, one gets one set of borders and a corresponding system that may consist largely of soil, water, and microorganisms; if one asks how the farmers continued involvement can be assured, one is dealing with a very different system, one that may involve banks, loans, and government payments. Which of these perspectives, which way of defining borders is appropriate? My answer to this question is that it depends on what kind of practical problem one is trying to solve … But my view is that the way that we conceptualize a system is deeply value laden, and reflects judgments about what is thought to be problematic, as well as likely guesses about where solutions might lie.[3] (3)

Two important attributes of functional integrity are resiliency and robustness. Both relate to vulnerability. Ecologists generally interpret resilience as the speed at which a system returns to equilibrium following a disturbance (Pimm 1984). Robustness is the ability of a system to resist being dislodged from stability by a disturbance (Holling 1973). Both resilience and robustness relate to the capacity of the system to accommodate disturbances without losing functionality. This capacity, in turn, relates to the concept of adaptiveness: how adaptive is the system to disturbances?

Perrings (2006) explores the connection between economic use and resilience and robustness. This connection is particularly important for the natural resource systems discussed in this book, since economic uses are often a major source of disturbances. Perrings recognizes, however, that the dynamics of a system are often revealed only through its response to external pressures, and definitive measurement of system sustainability can be problematic.

Perrings also notes that sustainable systems can change: "a number of ecological systems are known to exist in multiple stable states, their resilience in each state being dependent on the economic use of the system" (18). Botkin (1991) supports this view, noting that there need not be a unique sustainable path; rather, multiple paths of resource sustainability are possible and indeed may be likely. Thus, a system can change from some earlier predetermined notion of naturalness and still remain both natural and sustainable. Perhaps this conclusion is not so surprising, since over the ages, natural systems have developed an elasticity that allows them to adjust in unique ways to the various disturbances to which they are periodically subjected. The idea of multiple sustainable paths is also consistent with the notion that human values matter and can influence the path to sustainability.

Application to Management: Some Qualifications

Today, with the concept of sustainability on the ascendancy, the normative question of how we in the United States ought to manage our natural resources is being revisited. At one level the obvious answer is we ought to manage them sustainably.

But, indeed, what is sustainability? Thompson (2004) makes clear that it is more than simply the application of science. The very use of the word "ought" should also suggest that this question requires more than a scientific answer. The definition of sustainability requires a societal or stakeholder role (Hagan 2006). Science can describe "what is," and using scientific principles, scientists can predict (more or less successfully) what will happen if this or that management approach is followed. But even if it is accurate, science cannot tell us which management approach to follow until a well-articulated objective is selected. The choice of objectives, while it may be informed by science, is not determined by science.

Management of resources involves a degree of subjectivity. The complexity of resource systems makes the measurement of all the relevant facets and ramifications daunting, particularly when relevant outputs go beyond simple commodities (Boyd 2006). Furthermore, societal values are often difficult to incorporate into an objective measuring system. Indeed, some have argued that sustainability is more a philosophy than a definable, measurable condition of the resource (Flasche 1997).

Even where measurement is possible, measurement alone cannot determine management. Ends need to be determined as well as means. What is the optimal mix of wildlife and timber from a forest? Who determines the societal values attached to various outcomes? In the absence of a well-defined, unambiguous set of societal objectives, agreement on management success is difficult, and not all observers will agree on whether a system is being sustainably managed.

Furthermore, the application of the broad theoretical concepts of sustainability to a management system presents numerous problems. Perhaps most work in the area of applying sustainability concepts to actual management has been done in forestry. This application has been to a large extent an outgrowth of the process that began with the 1992 United Nations Conference on Environment and Development, and the subsequent development of certification schemes to try to ensure that forests are being managed in sustainable ways (see Chapter 3).

In the United States, there has been a two-pronged approach to sustainable forestry. Public lands have seen the development of an "ecosystem management" approach, whereby nontimber values are given a much higher priority than was traditionally the case (see Johnson et al. 1999). For private lands, the approach has been the application of certified management systems (see Fischer et al. 2005). Certification systems use standards against which the management systems and on-the-ground performance are compared.[4] In the developed world, the application of certification systems has generally been viewed as a success in that it has had a positive effect on forest management. However, since a gap between well-managed and sustainably managed remains, the application of abstract concepts of sustainability to on-the-ground management is still often somewhat problematic. Egregious management might readily be recognized as "poor" or "unsustainable," but auditors have acknowledged that identifying sustainability and the management nuances associated with it is sometimes beyond their current auditing capacity (see Sedjo 2004). Even advocates of certification have acknowledged that "scientific data do not yet support a single consensus on definition of biological sustainability, especially given regional variation in ecology ..." (Heaton and Donovan 1996, 55).

Those considerations have led forest certifiers and auditors to recognize a lack of operational content to the term "sustainably managed," and audit organizations have therefore substituted expressions like "well-managed" or "management that is consistent with the standards" of the particular certifying organization.[5]

Some Final Thoughts

Despite the difficulties, particularly in the application of sustainability to management, attempts to move toward some concept of sustainable management have a positive role—a role that emerges from both science and societal values. Some have argued that sustainability should be viewed as more of a pathway than a destination, since neither the science nor societal values show any signs of becoming finalized (see Fedkiw and Cayford 1999; Fedkiw 2004). The approach of this book and its predecessor are similar in that they look at resources from physical, historical, economic, and policy perspectives. What can we say about the physical availability and condition of the resource? How has that changed through time? What policies and institutes have contributed to changes in the resource through time and its improvement or decline?

One indisputable aspect of sustainability is the focus on natural resources as systems that provide a variety of outputs and services, rather than simply commodity outputs. Some have argued that in recent years much of the general discussion about sustainability has become skewed toward ecosystem services, while ignoring the critically important role of resources as commodities. Leonard Shabman (Chapter 5, this volume) points directly to some of the tensions between viewing water as a resource to provide for human needs and viewing sustainability as being essentially one of "naturalness" in watercourses. Many of these same tensions are found with forestry, soils, and wildlife and are touched on in the chapters. Where a resource is capable of producing a mix of several outputs, it is not surprising that differences exist over the relative shares of that mix. There may be no simple, unequivocal definition of sustainability, given the current scientific understanding, our ability to measure, and the evolving social consensus.

Notes

1. Thompson (2004) terms statements such as Smyth and Dumanski's as equating "sustainability" with "good"; that is, the term sustainability is used as a banner on which a number of groups—such as those interested in environment and social justice—can come together. He refers to this definition of sustainability as a "non-substantive use" of the term that is frequently used to link the use of natural resources with social justice, or to make ethical statements on behalf of the environment, resource users, or an economic system.

2. See Turner (1993) for some variations on these definitions. He divides sustainability definitions into four categories: very weak sustainability, weak sustainability, strong sustainability, and very strong sustainability.

3. For the purposes of this volume, the system boundaries of concern will be those that address the resource itself; the contributors do not explore the important connections with the resource users' or rural communities' well-being.

4. Fisheries also are moving toward a type of systematic quota and monitoring system to control harvest levels (see Newell et al. 2002).

5. For example, nowhere in the text of the *Forest Certification Assessment Guide*, a World Wildlife Fund and World Bank (2006) publication, is the term "sustainable" used. Rather the work is called "A Framework for Assessing Credible Forest Certification Systems/Schemes."

References

Bailey, R.G. 1995. *Description of the Ecoregions of the United States.* Washington, DC: USDA Forest Service.

Barrett, H.J., and C. Morse. 1963. *Scarcity and Growth: The Economics of Resources Scarcity.* Baltimore: Johns Hopkins University Press for Resources for the Future.

Batie, S.S. 1989. Sustainable Development: Challenges to the Profession of Agricultural Economics. *American Journal of Agricultural Economics* 71(5): 1083–101.

Botkin, D.B. 1991. *Discordant Harmonies: A New Ecology for the Twenty-first Century.* New York: Oxford University Press.

Boyd, J. 2006. The Nonmarket Benefits of Nature: What Should be Counted. In *Resources,* http://www.rff.org/rff/Documents/RFF-Resources-162_GreenGDP.pdf (accessed February 20, 2007).

Colby, M.E. 1989. The evolution of paradigms of environmental management in development. Strategic Planning and Review Discussion Paper 1. Washington, DC: World Bank.

Daly, H.E. 1987. The Economic Growth Debate: What Some Economists Have Learned But Many Have Not. *Journal of Environmental Economics and Management* 14(4): 323-36.

Edwards, A. 2005. *The Sustainability Revolution: Portrait of a Paradigm Shift.* Gabriola, BC: New Society Publishers.

Ehrlich, P. 1968. *The Population Bomb.* New York: Sierra Club/Ballantine Books.

Fedkiw, J. 2004. Sustainability and the Pathway Hypothesis. In *Pathway to Sustainability: Defining the Bounds on Forest Management,* edited by J. Fedkiw, D. MacCleery, and V.A. Sample. Durham, NC: Forest History Society, 7–24.

Fedkiw, J., and J.A. Cayford. 1999. Forest Management: A Dynamic and Evolving Profession. *Forestry Chronicle* 75(2): 213–18.

Fischer, C., F. Aguilar, P. Jawahar, and R. Sedjo. 2005. Forest Certification: Toward Common Standards. Discussion Paper 05-10. Washington, DC: Resources for the Future.

Flasche, F. 1997. Presentation to the Second International Forest Policy Forum. Solsona, Spain, March 12.

Frederick, K.D., and R.A. Sedjo (eds.). 1991. *America's Renewable Resources: Historical Trends and Current Challenges.* Washington, DC: Resources for the Future.

Hagan, J. 2006. Biodiversity Indicators for Sustainability Forestry. *Journal of Forestry* 104(4) (May-June): 203-10.

Heaton, K., and R. Donovan. 1996. Forest Assessment. In *Certification of Forest Products: Issues and Perspectives,* edited by Virgilio M. Vana. Washington, DC: Island Press.

Holling, C.S. 1973. Resilience and Stability of Ecological Systems. *Annual Review of Ecology and Systematics* 4:1-23.

Jaenicke, E.C. 1998. *From the Ground Up: Exploring Soil Quality's Contribution to Environmental Health.* Policy Studies Report 10. Greenbelt, MD: Henry A. Wallace Institute for Alternative Agriculture.

Jansson, A.M., M. Hammer, C. Folke, and R. Costanza (eds.). 1994. *Investing in Natural Capital: The Ecological Economics Approach to Sustainability.* Washington, DC: Island Press.

Johnson, N.C., A.J. Malk, R.C. Szaro, and W.T. Sexton. 1999. *Ecosystem Stewardship,* vol. 1. Oxford: Elsevier Science.

Krutilla, J.V. 1967. Conservation Revisited. *American Economic Review* 56: 777–86.

Lal, R., D. Mokma, and B. Lowery. 1999. Relation between Soil Quality and Erosion. In *Soil Quality and Soil Erosion,* edited by Rattan Lal. Boca Raton, FL: CRC Press, 237–58.

Malthus, T.R. 1789. *An Essay on the Principle of Population*. London; J. Johnson.

Meadows, D.H., D.L. Meadows, J. Randers, and W.W. Behrens III. 1972. *Limits to Growth: A Report for the Club of Rome's Project on the Predicament of Mankind*. Washington, DC: Earth Island.

National Research Council. 1993. *Soil and Water Quality: An Agenda for Agriculture*. Washington, DC: National Academy of Sciences.

Newell, R., J. Sanchirico, and S. Kerr. 2002. Fishing Quota Markets. Discussion Paper 2002-20. Washington, DC: Resources for the Future.

Pearce, D., and E.B. Barbier. 2000. *Blueprint for a Sustainable Economy*. London: Earthscan Publications.

Perrings, C. 2006. Ecological Economics after the Millennium Ecosystem Assessment. *International Journal of Ecological Economics and Statistics* 6: 8-22.

Pimm, S.L. 1984. The Complexity and Stability of Ecosystems. *Nature* 307: 321–26.

Schjonning, P., S. Elmholt, and B.T. Christensen (eds.). 2004. *Managing Soil Quality: Challenges in Modern Agriculture*. Cambridge: CABI Publishing.

Schuh, G.E. 1987. Some Thoughts on Economic Development, Sustainability, and the Environment. In *Sustainability Issues in Agricultural Development: Proceedings of the Seventh Agriculture Symposium*, edited by T.J. David and I.A. Schirmer. Washington, DC: World Bank, 614–19.

Sedjo, R.A. 2004. Challenges to Sustainable Forestry: Management and Economics. In *Forest Futures*, edited by J. Bowersox III and K. Abeese. New York: Rowman and Littlefield, 68–83.

Simon, J., and H. Kahn (eds.). 1983. *The Resourceful Earth*. Oxford: Basil Blackwell Publisher.

Simpson, R.D., M.A. Toman, and R.U. Ayers (eds.). 2005. *Scarcity and Growth Revisited: Natural Resources and the Environment in the New Millennium*. Washington, DC: Resources for the Future.

Smyth, A.J., and J. Dumanski. 1993. *FESLM: An International Framework for Evaluating Sustainable Land Management*. World Resources Reports 73. Rome: UN Food and Agriculture Organization.

Thompson, P.B. 2004. Sustainability: What It Is and What It Is Not. Unpublished manuscript, Department of Philosophy, Michigan State University, East Lansing.

Turner, R.K. 1993. Sustainability: Principles and Practice. In *Sustainable Environmental Economics and Management*, edited by R.K. Turner. New York: Belhaven Press, 3–36.

World Commission on Environment and Development (WCED). 1987. *Our Common Future*. Oxford: Oxford University Press.

World Wildlife Fund and World Bank. 2006. *Forest Certification Assessment Guide*. Washington, DC: Bank Global Forest Alliance.

CHAPTER 3

Sustainable Forests in America?

Roger A. Sedjo and Douglas MacCleery

MORE THAN 15 YEARS AGO, *America's Renewable Resources* (Frederick and Sedjo 1991) examined the historical trends and current challenges then facing U.S. resource managers. The chapter on forests characterized them as "resilient and serviceable." Despite having been subjected to a wide array of abuses and destructive uses, U.S. forest area had been stable for almost a century. Indeed, the growing stock of American forests expanded for the entire second half of the 1900s, a time during which systematic forest inventories were undertaken, even as these forests provided fully one-quarter of the world's wood harvested for industrial purposes. And through this period, the forests continued to supply the American people with bountiful recreational and environmental goods and services.

Once disturbed—whether by logging or natural phenomena such as ice storm or fire—a forest will almost always be renewed naturally if not prevented from doing so. Management actions, however, can facilitate renewability. The renewability of forest cover, however, does not guarantee sustainability of the previous forest condition or type. The new forest can be quite different from the one it replaced. Not only do stands of pioneer tree species provide habitat for different kinds of wildlife than an old-growth forest, but the species mix of the new forest can be very different than that of the old as the forest moves toward maturity. In fact, the traditional notion of forests taking part in a recurring cycle has been seriously challenged (Botkin 1991). So, in a technical sense, renewability, which implies that some of the parts remain, need not be sustainability, which requires that all of the parts be retained. Although new forests need not replicate their predecessors, at least somewhere in the broad national or regional forest system all of the parts should be retained. This chapter explores both the concept of forest sustainability and its application to the historical experience and current condition of America's forests.

The first section considers the general question of sustainability in the context of various systems of forest management. The second section presents a brief his-

22

tory of American forests, from the time when they were considered inexhaustible to modern concerns about their sustainability. The third section looks at the role of the private sector in conserving forests and promoting sustainability. Recent issues addressed include certification, and contemporary changes in forest ownership, which may have a bearing on sustainability. The final section examines American forests from the perspective of some concepts of sustainability.

Sustainability

Since the early 1990s there has been enormous interest, both domestically and internationally, in "forest sustainability" in its various dimensions. Although the terminology used to describe the concept has evolved over the decades, the concept is not new. It emerged as a national issue in the United States in the late 1800s and led to a number of policy responses, including the establishment of the USDA Forest Service. It emerged again as a part of the 1970s environmental movement and prompted federal laws addressing air and water pollution, endangered species, federal land management, and the environment generally.

The Evolving Concept of Forest Sustainability

Sustaining the natural resources and ecosystem services needed to ensure the well-being of human communities has been a challenge dating back thousands of years. As resource depletion became apparent, communities often took steps to conserve and sustain them. Indeed, the science and practice of forestry were born of concerns for the continuing maintenance of forests, and the discipline continues to evolve as human conditions and attitudes change (Floyd et al. 2001).

The challenges of forest sustainability are complex because forests themselves are complex ecological systems that supply both products needed by humans (such as lumber, fuel, and nontimber products like medicines) and ecosystem services (such as providing clean water, soil conservation, watershed protection, and biological diversity, and mitigating climate change through trees' ability to use and store atmospheric carbon, a cause of climate change, as well as spiritual and recreational values.

Forest sustainability today encompasses several dimensions. One dimension focuses on meeting society's need for timber products, now and in the future – the commodity issue. Especially since the 1970s, timber production has increasingly used an agricultural model, growing trees on plantations, like crops. Such a production system can be stable geographically over time, or it can shift as costs of production and transportation change. In fact, we are seeing that shift today as wood production in the United States increasingly shifts from natural to planted forests and, most recently, fast-growing plantations in the South. In this case, although the overall production system for forest products may be sustainable, production from individual forests may vary. A second dimension of sustainability concerns important environmental services, mostly nonmarket and highly localized. Examples are healthy watersheds producing clean water and habitats that support local, or endemic, species. This system is immobile and tends to require forests that are stationary, persistent, and sustainable by site. A third dimension of forest sustainability involves global public environmental goods, such as regional or global biodiversity[1] and especially carbon sequestration. Since carbon sequestration in biomass is provided by most forests, the service need not be site-specific. However, if the focus is on biodiversity, site becomes important.

Those dimensions of forest sustainability, and the types of forests needed to achieve them, are not necessarily mutually exclusive but in some circumstances may be. In some cases many of the outputs can be provided by a single forest. Society has an interest in a forest system regionally, nationally, and globally that produces all these sets of outputs. However, it may not require sustaining each individual forest on a continuous basis.

So what is sustainable forestry? Certainly, sustainability goes beyond the narrow meaning of renewability.[2] Acceptably balancing and meeting ecological, social, and economic objectives over time is often considered a hallmark of sustainability. But exactly how ecological, social, and economic objectives are to be balanced in particular situations, who makes such decisions, and on what basis, remains the topic of considerable discussion and debate.

Sustainable forestry is, at least in part, a philosophy or conceptual framework as to how forests should be cared for as much as it is a definable condition of the forest or a set of acceptable management practices. Although management is often oriented toward future forest conditions, uncertainties about the long-term effects of management still abound (Botkin 1991).

Is the concept of sustainability operational? That is, would we know a forest under sustainable management if we saw one? Webster defines *management* as "judicious use of means to accomplish an end." Management requires the identification of an end or an objective so that success (or failure) of the management can be unambiguously recognized. Within this context, sustainable forestry management must refer to a system in which all of the parts and all of the functions are maintained indefinitely in a way that provides acceptable environmental, social, and environmental results. Because of the complex parameters of sustainability and the spatial and extended time frames involved in assessing them, this is not easy to determine. It is particularly problematic to assess how management of a particular forest property relates to sustainability at larger landscape scales. A snapshot view of a single forest obviously is inadequate to determine sustainability through time.

Since forests are dynamic entities, the concept of sustainability in forestry must apply to some type of process over time. But is there a social consensus as to which changes over time are consistent with sustainability and which are not? Have we identified and are we actually measuring the relevant factors that allow us to assess progress toward sustainability? Do we have the political and institutional mechanisms in place to respond to needed adjustments at relevant spatial scales? As of today, even though considerable progress is being made on each of these questions, it is difficult to answer in the definitive affirmative on any of them.

As noted in Chapter 2 of this book, any meaningful and operational concept of sustainable forestry must have at least two dimensions. First, sustainability is a dynamic concept. As others have indicated, sustainability is a journey, not a destination; that is, it is more an ongoing process than a specific final result. Second, sustainability is a system concept, and so it applies to the system as a whole but need not necessarily involve each unit of the system. Thus, as we examine the individual forest unit, its condition will not necessarily say anything about the sustainability of the broad system as a whole. In a regional, national, or global sense, sustainable forestry relates to the functioning of that whole system and not necessarily to any individual component or part.

The broad scale is critical. Realistically, it is the sustainability of the system at large landscape scales and over time that is most important to humankind. Thus, the concept need not be so inflexible as to preclude land-use changes at some scales at some times, including conversion to nonforest uses (Sedjo 2005). The critical issue is not whether an individual piece of land produces a specific array of outputs over time, but rather, whether the system as a whole can continue to produce the full range of outputs. Two essential elements of achieving this objective are identifying the ecological, social, and environmental indicators of sustainability and having a monitoring system that will track them consistently and objectively over time.

The challenges to forest sustainability can come in several forms. First, forest sustainability can be threatened by large-scale forestland conversion to other uses. European settlement and agricultural practices—converting forests to pastures and fields—eliminated forests on some large areas.[3] Second, certain impacts can change the fundamental character of the forest. One example is forest fragmentation caused by disturbances, such as agriculture, some types of logging, intense wildfires, or development. Another example is intensive wood production, where large areas of forest are never allowed to develop the age and structure needed for some types of wildlife species and biodiversity values.[4] Introduced species can also cause the loss of critical native species. The American chestnut, which once dominated much of the eastern forests of America, has been all but eliminated by an exotic fungus introduced at the beginning of the 20th century.

Although the concept of sustainability is now a widely shared public ethic, what it means in any particular situation and context can vary widely. And that meaning may change over the years as society changes its preferences for the specific forest values, uses, and objectives it seeks to sustain over time. To paraphrase Marion Clawson (1975), when considering whether a particular management approach will result in sustainable forests, one should ask the underlying questions, "Sustainable for whom?" "Sustainable for what?" and "Over what time frame and spatial scales?" Once those several questions are addressed, the meaning of *sustainability* in a particular context can be refined. But specificity may invite disagreement. Maintaining a social consensus on the value of sustainability may well require that we not ask too many questions as to what it really means.

Approaches to Sustainable Forest Management

As demands on forests have increased over the centuries, various approaches to their use have evolved. The earliest and the longest-running approach has been timber foraging. Indeed, one could question whether foraging is management at all. As human demands increased, management techniques were developed, including sustained-yield forestry, multiple-use management, and in recent years, ecosystem management.

All of these management approaches can be maintained over long periods of time under the right circumstances. All are being practiced somewhere in the world.

Timber Foraging. Foraging for timber is perhaps the most common approach globally. In what is now the eastern United States, aboriginal people and later the early European settlers practiced shifting agriculture, combined with timber and wildlife foraging for fuel, forest products, and wild game. Although foraging can be a sustainable approach when human population is low and forests are abundant relative to human demands, as human population and demands increase, it requires more and more land area and can evolve into unsustainable resource depletion. As U.S. population and demands rose dramatically in the 19th century, the epicenter of logging moved first from New England to the Great Lakes States, then to the Southeast, and later to the West Coast, where only the Pacific Ocean proved an effective barrier to further westward movement of the logging industry.

One policy response to the shifting nature of logging in the 19th century was the establishment of public timber reserves toward the end of the century, which became the National Forest System. The overriding objective of the management of these lands was to protect and maintain the forest reserves while allowing them to maintain watercourses and provide timber for the future needs of the population.

Sustained-Yield Forestry. The concept of sustained (or sustainable) sustainable-yield timber harvesting developed in European forestry with the objective of equating forest harvest with forest growth. In 1804, 180 years before the Brundtland Commission, G.L. Hartig, head of the Prussian Forest Administration, stated that the objective of managing forests was to "utilize them to the greatest possible extent, but still in a way that future generations will have at least as much benefit as the living generation" (Schmutzenhofer 1992).

In the United States, sustained-yield forestry was advocated as a response to the "cut and run" logging practices of the 19th century. Wood production is the primary objective (but not necessarily the only one), and the goal is to produce a relatively even flow of wood from a given forest over the long term. Protecting and maintaining nontimber objectives and environmental services, such as clean water and game populations, is consistent with sustained-yield management, although doing so may reduce the yield of timber that otherwise might be produced.

This system has been applied to both naturally regenerated and planted forests. A determination of a maximum annual or periodic allowable cut is usually made, often with a management objective of creating a forest containing a relatively even distribution of age classes, with the oldest stands harvested on an annual or periodic basis. Such forest management systems are common around the world.

Systems approximating this are commonly practiced in private forestry in the United States, both within industrial forestry, where a company harvests a portion of its forest annually, and among some smaller forest products entities, with harvests being followed by new plantings in a repetitive cycle system akin to cropping.

Multiple-Use Management. All forests can produce a wide array of potentially desirable outputs, ranging from timber to environmental services, recreation, and amenities. Even without purposeful management, some outputs and values will be produced incidentally.

As public demands for nontimber forest outputs and values increase, sustained-yield forest management often transitions to purposely managing forests for a variety of objectives and values. Often referred to as *multiple-use management*, this approach is normally applied to public lands where management specifically seeks to produce a broad range of outputs and services over time.

The Society of American Foresters has defined multiple use as "any practice of forestry fulfilling two or more objectives of management" and says that "multiple uses may be integrated at one site or segregated from each other" (Helms 1998). Just because a forest provides multiple benefits does not mean that multiple-use management is being applied, however; there must be a conscious effort to influence the mix of goods and services being produced. Neither is it possible or desirable to manage all areas of a forest for all uses. In addition to the uses and values purposefully managed for, various "incidental" uses may also occur, as when reseeding for timber production helps prevent soil erosion and the young regrowth provides habitat for ruffed grouse.

In 1960 multiple use became the official management approach for the national forests with the passage of the Multiple-Use Sustained-Yield Act. Multiple use on public lands is often implemented by allocating different portions of a forest to exclusive, primary, secondary, and general use zones. At low levels of resource demand, most lands tend to be included in the general use category. As demands increase, zoning is utilized to reduce conflicts among less compatible uses and to target investments toward increasing the capacity of the land to meet the preferred uses. The zoning or land allocation question on public lands is a political issue that often becomes highly contentious. Three common points of debate are (1) who should make the land allocation decisions (agency administrators or elected political leaders) and on what basis; (2) how the input of stakeholders should be considered; and (3) how often and by what means initial decisions should be revisited and revised.

The National Forest Management Act of 1976 and the 1982 Forest Service forest planning regulations called for the national forests to produce a mix of market and nonmarket outputs. Haigh and Krutilla (1978) argued that the legislation also called for an approach that would maximize the social value (discounted net present value) of the social benefits of the forest, both market and nonmarket, through time.[5] To meet this objective requires estimating the economic and social values to be used in the determination of the optimal mix of outputs. Bowes and Krutilla (1989) developed planning approaches intended to achieve this optimization. Nevertheless, the idea of economic optimization failed to win consensus, and it has been largely ignored in favor of a more politically oriented stakeholder-driven approach. As a practical matter, several factors limit our ability to apply the strictly economic approach. One is the inability to quantify the production function for some jointly produced goods and services. Another is our inability to readily value jointly produced goods and services not exchanged in markets. As stated by Kirkland (1987), "Despite ingenious attempts to devise them, there are no satisfactory common yardsticks for measuring commercial and non-commercial returns. Commercial returns are measurable in the marketplace. Non-commercial returns defy simple measures ..."

Although using a stakeholder-driven, political process for determining the mix of outputs on public lands remains the preferred method, that approach has its own limitations. For federally managed forests, weighting local as opposed to national stakeholder viewpoints—that is, the preferences of "communities of place" versus the desires of "communities of interest"—has thus far proven exceedingly difficult. Persuasive arguments can be offered in support of contrasting positions.[6] Unfortunately, the inability to resolve this issue, and others, has left national forest managers in an untenable situation and opened the door to continuing controversy.

Ecosystem Management. As public controversy over the management of federal lands escalated, a new management paradigm emerged in the 1990s: "ecosystem management," also sometimes referred to as "an ecological approach" to management.[7] It now applies to many publicly owned forests in the United States: the Forest Service adopted ecosystem management as a guiding philosophy for managing the national forests in 1992,[8] and the Bureau of Land Management adopted an ecological approach to managing the lands it administers in 1994. In many respects ecosystem management, where practiced on public lands, can be viewed as a shift toward a more biological orientation and away from an economic maximizing perspective.

At one level, ecosystem management is viewed as simply an alternative management tool for achieving the legally mandated multiple-use outputs identified in the legislation. In this case, the management concepts would be broad ecosystem concepts. Tilman and Polasky (2005) characterize ecosystem management as emphasizing an array of ecosystem services and moving away from a focus on a single management objective. They note, however, that "incomplete knowledge of ecosystem function and the difficulty of providing proper incentives to landowners impede meaningful ecosystem management."

At another level, however, ecosystem management is viewed as a means for identifying additional ends: the condition of the ecosystem becomes another output of interest, beyond specific commodity or amenity outputs.[9] When the condition of the forest becomes an end in itself, the objectives of management shift from specific multiple-use outputs to managing the forest for some condition, as an end in itself. Is the forest an asset to produce outputs or is the forest condition per se the principal objective? Sustainable forestry implies both maintaining outputs and maintaining the condition of the forest.

MacCleery and Le Master (1999) stress the changed objectives of ecosystem management. They note that "ecosystem management has greatly expanded the objectives for which federal lands are purposely managed." Moreover, they continue,

> the effect has been a substantial deemphasis on the role of federal lands in producing commodity outputs. The focus of multiple-use sustained yield has tended to be on resource outputs or "flows," whereas ecosystem management places relatively more emphasis on ecosystem "states" and "conditions." A corollary to this view is that resource outputs under ecosystem management

are often a consequence of achieving biodiversity or other ecosystem-centered objectives, rather than explicit objectives in their own right.[10]

Sedjo (1996, *26*) makes a similar observation but notes the practice difficulties:

Ecosystem management replaces the traditional objectives of public forest management ... with a somewhat nebulous "desired forest condition." However, that concept is not operationally useful in the absence of specific dimensions of that desired condition. In many cases, the objective of ecosystem management appears to be simply the practice of an ecosystem management approach: the means and the ends have merged.

Operationally, managing for the difficult-to-define and difficult-to-measure goal of ecosystem condition can be a serious problem. Clark Binkley (2000), former Dean of the Forestry Faculty at the University of British Columbia, has observed that it is widely recognized that one cannot manage what one cannot measure. If true, how then can the success of ecosystem management be measured? How is the achievement of the desired forest condition to be objectively assessed? Who should determine what set of forest attributes provide the ideal condition? In a political setting where interest groups vie to achieve their objectives, someone will be left unhappy. Ultimately, political decisions that respond to the various interest groups are made, which try to capture the social consensus of the time, are likely to be required for public lands.

Third-Party Forest Certification and Sustainability. Forest certification is one of the most significant developments in forest management in the United States, and indeed over much of the developed world, in the past two decades. The idea of forest certification originally arose from concerns in the 1980s about rapid deforestation, particularly the loss of rainforest in the Amazon and illegal logging of tropical hardwoods. Led by nongovernmental organizations, such as the World Wildlife Fund, forest certification for wood products emerged in the 1990s as a response and an alternative to timber boycott campaigns. Certification programs developed guidelines for responsible forest management, including logging, and then certified the wood as harvested from properly managed forests, in some cases providing a quality logo on the wood product. For corporations, forest managers, and landowners who want to demonstrate responsible forest management, certification is a tool that promises market access or a competitive advantage. For governments, it is a "soft" policy instrument that voluntarily shifts the determination of criteria, largely for private lands, to nongovernmental agencies. Private certifiers make the determination of adequacy of management to promote environmentally sound practices through demand-side responses (Stevens et al. 1998; Eba Atyi and Simula 2002). Certification seeks to assure consumers and others that the forest products they purchase have been grown, harvested, and processed in ways that meet environmental standards.

Although the original objective was to conserve forests in developing countries, certification programs overwhelmingly have certified management practices in developed countries, with less than 5 percent of all forests certified globally currently located in tropical countries. Reasons often cited for the low levels of certification in the tropics include (1) inadequate capacity to implement sustainable forest management[11]; and (2) the costs of instituting sustainable forest management, including a lack of willingness by the market to provide a premium for certified products (Eba Atyi and Simula 2002).

What distinguishes certification from existing government regulatory approaches of forest management practices is that it is private rather than governmental and it is voluntary. The driving rationale for private forest owners to participate is that it provides the promise of a positive market incentive for sustainable forest management, rather than sanctions for violations. Although price premiums are rare, access to markets and commercial "good will" is often facilitated by certification (Cashore et al. 2004).

U.S. Forests

A Brief History of American Forests

The United States has a vast forest estate covering different regions and comprising different forest types. The precolonial forest estate has been estimated at 950 million acres, excluding Alaska (Clawson 1979). Although the area probably was roughly stable, the forests did not lack dynamism; perturbations and disturbances are an intrinsic part of almost all forest systems. Precolonial disturbances included disease, insect infestations, windthrow, fire, and the effects of indigenous peoples (including agricultural clearing and use of fire), often in combination.

Conditions before European Settlement. The popular image of precolonial North America is that of a pristine wilderness continent barely influenced by human action, with indigenous peoples who lived in the forests and on the grasslands but did little to affect either. During the past two decades, scholars have challenged that popular image (e.g. Williams 1989; Butzer 1990; Denevan 1992; Blackburn and Anderson 1993; Mann 2005). It is now generally accepted that when Columbus arrived, many areas east of the Mississippi River were heavily populated by agricultural societies. Forest clearing for agriculture was widespread, as was prescribed use of fire. Using fire, native peoples caused major changes to the nature of the forest and the forest ecosystem. The use of frequent fires as a management tool to clear saplings and brush, promote grasses, and open areas for both transport and cropping resulted in a forest ecosystem that was substantially different from what it would have been in the absence of human impact.

European Settlement. Initially, the effect of European contact was a substantial reduction in human impacts in North America, lasting for two centuries or more. Diseases for which the Europeans had acquired relative immunity, such as smallpox, measles, diphtheria, and influenza, created massive mortality in American Indian communities. Many areas likely suffered 80 to 95 percent losses (Dobyns 1983). During the colonial period from 1600 to 1780, the European American population rose slowly and people tended to cluster adjacent to the Atlantic coast

and the major rivers flowing into it. Even so, local shortages of timber and deple-
tions of game populations occurred. Early efforts to conserve forests and wildlife
are reflected in local laws and restrictions on the taking of game species (Trefethen
1975; Williams 1989). These were relatively limited attempts to constrain the use
of resources to ensure their permanence—what we now call sustainability.

Forest clearing was prevalent during the early years of European American history. The arriving European settlers remarked at the abundance of forests, the
countless streams, and the apparently unlimited land (Hawke 1988). The challenge
was to clear the forests and establish permanent agriculture. Little thought was
given to future renewal of the converted forestland. The problem from the perspective of the early settlers was too many forests, not too few (Hawke 1988;
Williams 1989; Sedjo 1991). With forests covering much of the continent, forest
regeneration and reforestation were a low social and economic priority. Forest
clearing accomplished two objectives: it made land available for agriculture while
providing plentiful construction materials and fuelwood.

The Westward Expansion. By the mid-1800s the impacts of European Americans were increasing substantially as populations expanded and large areas of forestland were converted to agriculture. The U.S. population, which in 1800 was 5
million, by 1850 had risen to 23.2 million. By 1900 it reached 76 million. During
the second half of the 19th century, the U.S. population rose in absolute numbers
10 times more than it had in the two centuries from 1600 to 1800. The rising population began to put significant pressures on U.S. forests, wildlife, and other natural
resources.

Initially, the population was predominantly rural. After 1850, however, the
United States began to change from a rural, agrarian society to one increasingly
urban and industrialized. Between 1850 and 1900, the population of the nation's
cities increased at twice the rate of the general population. The demand for wood
for construction jumped, as did the need for agricultural lands required to feed the
growing number of people. Crop yields per acre were stagnant throughout the 19th
and well into the 20th century. Because of this, farm clearing increased at about
the same rate as the growth in population. Between 1850 and 1900, the area of
cropland increased four times, from 76 million to 319 million acres (Fedkiw 1989).
In the 60 years from 1850 to 1910, American farmers cleared more forest for agriculture than the total amount that had been cleared in the previous 250 years of
settlement—about 190 million acres (Williams 1989)—at an average rate of 13.5
square miles per day every day (Figure 3-1).

To meet the needs of a rapidly growing population, houses, barns, and fences were
being constructed at a dramatic rate. Logging and sawmilling increasingly began to
be organized as large-scale industrial operations. Lumber production rose more than
eight times between 1850 and 1910, from 5.4 billion to 44.5 billion board feet annually, or more than twice the rate of population growth (U.S. Department of Commerce 1975). For the first time, consumers and the forests upon which they
depended for their natural resources began to be separated by hundreds of miles.

Vast areas of the Midwest were logged, and often relogged. The tree limbs, tops,
and other debris that remained after logging were often burned in the belief that

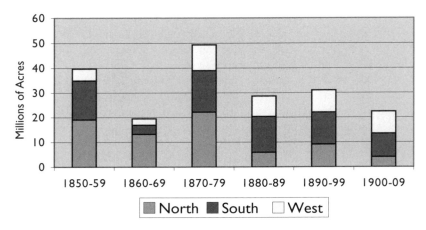

Figure 3-1. *Farm Clearing of Forest, 1850–1910*

Source: Williams 1989.

the logged areas could be converted to cropland or improved pasture. These uncontrolled slash fires burned more or less continually, and when weather conditions were right, they sometimes spread into massive wildfires, causing property damage and loss of human life. Repeated wildfires also killed residual trees and seedlings left after logging and created tens of millions of acres of what came to be called cutovers or stumplands, which remained idle, unstocked, or poorly stocked with desirable tree species for decades (Williams 1989).

The heyday of forest clearing varied by region. The clearing of the upper Great Lakes States ended about 1910, when the bulk of the desirable timber was gone (Hansen 1980). In the South, timber production remained high into the 1920s and beyond, and cropland abandonment was slow (Figure 3-2). Due to the land's specialization in tobacco and cotton, crops unique to the South, abandonment was not significant until the Great Depression and the post–World War II periods. Farther west, the settlers found a somewhat different situation: much of the forest was on arid mountain slopes that were not particularly conducive to eastern-style cropping. Forestland conversion for agriculture and development took place in the valleys, and other forests were cleared for extensive livestock grazing or left to regenerate through natural processes.

The First U.S. Conservation Movement. By the latter part of the 19th century, the rapid clearing of forests was increasingly being viewed as evidence of excessive and short-sighted exploitation. During the settlement period, Americans were, in effect, focused on transforming their natural capital, in the form of land and forests, into economic, social, agricultural, and transportation capital and infrastructure. Although that was considered a socially desirable outcome at the time, the environmental effects of this transformation—the substantial reduction in forest area, the degradation of many of the forests that remained, the depletion of many wildlife

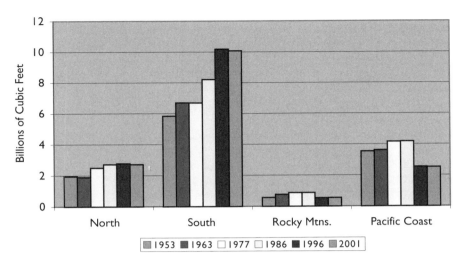

Figure 3-2. *Trends in Timber Removals by Region, 1953-2001*

Sources: Forest Resources of the United States 1997; USDA Forest Service 1997; Forest Resources of the United States 2002; and USDA Forest Service 2004.

populations and species, as well as destructive wildfires and accelerated soil erosion from farms and forests—provoked a social reaction (Trefethen 1975; Williams 1989).

The rapidly declining forest, wildlife, and other environmental conditions of the late 19th century provided the impetus for the first national conservation movement. In an expression of concern typical of early conservationists, I.A. Lapham, in an 1867 report on the depletion of forests in Wisconsin, stated

> a country destitute of forests as well as one entirely covered with them is only suited for the condition of a barbarous or semi-barbarous people ... It is only where a due proportion between the cultivated land and the forest is maintained that man can attain and enjoy his highest civilization (Williams 1989, 373).

Lapham's concern that things had gotten out of balance was a common theme of early conservationists, such as George Perkins Marsh, and reflected their conviction that appropriate and strategic adjustments had to be made—a crucial element of the pathway to sustainability process as described in Chapter 2.

The emergence of the conservation movement at the end of the 19th century caused a major paradigm shift for resource use and management. The conservation policy framework that was put into place included the following:

- closing the public domain to further private land disposal and reserving the remaining public lands for protection and management in national forests, national parks, and national wildlife refuges;

- promoting and encouraging the protection of forests and grasslands, regardless of their ownership, from wildfire, insects, and disease;

- improving the art and science of natural resource management and promoting the more efficient utilization of raw materials;

- improving the management and productivity of agricultural lands and forests (70 percent of the latter were privately owned) through research and technical and financial assistance; and

- adopting and enforcing federal and state wildlife conservation laws.

In addition to the conservation policies described above, several fortuitous events combined in the early 1900s to substantially reduce human pressures on forests and wildlife. One was plant breeding and the consequent spectacular increase in agricultural productivity, which after the 1930s rose at a rate greater than that of population growth (Hayami and Rattan 1985). Others were the conversion from fuelwood to fossil fuels and the shift from draft animals to internal combustion engines. These trends reduced human pressures on forests and allowed pastures to revert to forest or to be used as cropland. As the area of cropland stabilized, so did the area of forests. Today the United States has about the same area of cropland and forest it had in 1920 (Figure 3-3).

The policy changes that were put in place, along with conversion to fossil fuels and other fortuitous events, changed profoundly the nature of human impacts on forests and other land resources. The United States also had the benefit of a relatively stable and resilient political and social infrastructure, as well as the economic prosperity to make needed changes.

U.S. Federal Lands and Forests: A Legacy of the 1900s Conservation Movement. Concerns over the long-term future of natural lands and forests led to the

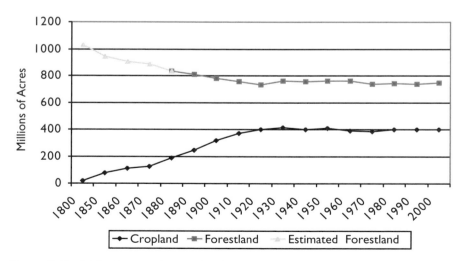

Figure 3-3. *U.S. Crop and Forestland Area, 1950–1980*

Source: Fedkiw 1989.

creation of protected areas and forest preserves. Yellowstone was set aside in 1870 as the world's first national park. Although concerns persisted beyond the simple preservation of unusual and unique sites. In response, various presidents, from Benjamin Harrison to Teddy Roosevelt, administratively set aside portions of the public land as permanent forest reservations.

The nation's first forest reserves were created in 1891 with the withdrawal from the public domain of certain federal lands. A few years later, in 1897, Congress passed the Organic Act, which provided for protection and management authority for the forest reserves. This act mandated the permanent forest reserve to (1) secure favorable conditions of water flows and (2) furnish a continuous supply of timber for the use and necessities of the people of the United States.

By 1900, about 70 percent of the total area of productive forests in the United States had already been transferred into private ownership. It was widely assumed that, given the long time frames associated with growing trees plus the relatively low timber prices, once the original forest capital was removed, private landowners would not make the necessary investment in forest management to ensure future supplies of timber. Therefore, publicly managed forest reserves were needed to secure a long-term supply of timber for the U.S. economy.

From 1896 to 1910, the area of forest reserves (which became national forests) rose from 18 million to 168 million acres. In 1905 the U.S. Forest Service was created to manage these forests. What was to be produced from the National Forest System was straightforward: water and timber. And the beneficiaries were well-defined: the people of the United States. Of course, the creation of a permanent reserve implied some elements of forest sustainability. Because production of timber—viewed as a crop—was one of the Forest Service's primary functions, the agency was placed not in the Department of Lands (later the Department of the Interior), which had been overseeing these lands, primarily for disposal, but rather in the Department of Agriculture.

Today the National Forest System consists of 192 million acres, three-quarters of which is forested land. This area constitutes about 8 percent of the land area, 20 percent of the forest area, and 29.4 percent of the federal lands of the United States.

U.S. Forest Management before World War II. By 1920, the total forest estate had decreased from roughly 1 billion acres at the time of European settlement to about 750 million acres and since that time has remained roughly the same. The vast bulk of U.S. timber production prior to World War II came from private lands. Most of this timber was harvested in the timber foraging mode described earlier in this chapter. The Great Depression placed tremendous pressures on the forest products industry, as it did on other industries. More intensive management of forests would need to wait for more prosperous times.

During the early years of the Forest Service, roughly from 1905 until the post–World War II era, its role consisted of relatively simple custodial management: keeping poachers out, occasionally allowing for harvest of some timber for local use, minimizing disturbances of the watersheds, and making sure that forest regeneration eventually occurred after a harvest. There was an informal national policy not to harvest significant volumes of national forest timber in competition with private forest landowners, especially during the Depression years (Steen 1976). Overgrazing by millions of sheep and cattle was a serious problem in the national forests. A major focus for land managers was reducing livestock numbers to the carrying capacity of the land. The Forest Service provided for recreation, wildlife habitat, and other uses as well (Fedkiw 1998).

The Forest Service also focused on forestry research, which included, importantly, research related to improving wood utilization and better forest management for timber production. During the Great Depression federal conservation and public works programs were set up to provide jobs for the unemployed, who worked to reduce soil erosion, plant trees, restore watersheds, suppress fires, and construct campgrounds, buildings, and other facilities on national forests, national parks, and rangelands (Fedkiw 1998). The Civilian Conservation Corps took up reforestation, soil conservation, and facilities construction; the Tennessee Valley Authority handled watershed restoration, hydrodam construction, and rural electrification and development; and the Soil Conservation Service[12] provided technical and financial assistance to farmers to reduce soil erosion.

Authorized in 1911 by the Weeks Act, acquisition through purchase of forest land in the eastern United States expanded greatly during the Depression years. By 1945, when land acquisition substantially slowed, more than 20 million acres of depleted farmsteads and cutover and burned-over woodlands had been incorporated into the eastern national forests.

These were relatively easy times for the Forest Service. It had broad support among the American people (a remarkably favorable article appeared in *Newsweek* in 1952) and it was even viewed as a paradigm of organizational structure in the classic book *The Forest Ranger* (Kaufman 1960), which has been used in the public policy programs of universities around the country.

Rising Resource Demands after World War II. After a decade of the Great Depression and five years of war, America's housing stock was inadequate to meet the needs of its growing and increasingly affluent population. The building boom of the post–World War II period saw demand and resource prices rising.

The housing boom of the 1950s ended the Forest Service's role as a custodial manager and saw the onset of a period of active management with ever-increasing harvest levels (Steen 1976; Clawson 1983). Road access to national forests and Bureau of Land Management lands had improved by the late 1940s, and many of the more accessible private lands had been logged to provide timber for the war effort. Federal timber sale levels increased from 2 billion to 4 billion board feet in the late 1940s to 11 billion to 14 billion board feet in the 1960s and beyond. By the 1960s, federal forests were meeting more than 15 percent of the nation's total consumption of wood volume and more than 28 percent of its consumption of softwood sawtimber, the primary source of lumber and plywood for housing (USDA FS 2002a; USDA FS 2004b).

That substantial increase in federal timber harvest not only met the critical national need for timber, it also took pressure off private forestlands, many of which had been heavily cut to meet the war effort (Fedkiw 1998). Timber harvests also gave the Forest Service additional justification for firefighting activities: increasingly valuable timber could be protected through fire suppression and then logged for profitable use. Timber production provided an economic rationale for fire suppression.

The postwar boom was just the type of situation for which the Forest Service had been waiting. Since the early 1900s, the Forest Service had predicted severe timber famines, but as yet no famine had arrived. During the 1950s, however, real prices for timber were rising more rapidly than for most other natural resources. Some of the increase reflected relative scarcity, but general inflation was another factor. In any case, rising timber prices provided the opportunity to use national forest harvests to help dampen this increase and achieve the objective of providing a continuous supply of timber for the United States.

The forest industry also responded to the postwar boom by increasing output. In fact, the industry was in many respects more forward-looking than the Forest Service. The forest industry realized that although it held huge supplies of old-growth, these stands would not last forever. Its continued existence as an industry and as individual companies was dependent upon a secure source of resources into the future, and it moved in this direction through aggressive planting and management programs.

Where disturbances had taken place, the American forests of the early 20th century were regenerating much more rapidly than expected by those who had feared a timber famine (Clawson 1979). Disturbance, whether by wildfire, infestation, or logging, was not fatal. Nevertheless, it was questionable whether natural processes alone could generate the wood supplies that would be required in America's future. In the 1930s, the forest industry began to experiment seriously with reforestation and tree planting, expanding on earlier reforestation research and practical experience by the Forest Service. The first commercial tree farms in the United States were established in the early 1940s.

In 1950, during the midst of the postwar boom, a timber company press release shows that the company anticipated the coming changes in forestry: "The supply of logs during the next thirty years will come largely from old growth timber with a gradually increasing amount from new growth. Beginning about 1980 the yield from old growth will diminish rapidly and the yield from new growth will be proportionally increased" (Smyth 2003, *43*). For the timber industry, planting began in earnest in the late 1950s, and by the 1980s, more than 1 million acres of new industrial forest was being planted each year, approximately 3 million seedlings per day—a level of planting that has persisted (Figure 3-4).

Much of the earlier reforestation was natural regeneration as forests overran abandoned agricultural lands. Subsequently, tree planting, virtually all in native conifers, occurred on logged-over forests and also on lands recently abandoned by agriculture. Additionally, the industry moved aggressively to establish tree-breeding programs, and intensive research was undertaken on planting, spacing, thinning, and other productivity-increasing management activities.

The 1950s also witnessed a substantial increase in demand for other uses, outputs, and values from the federal lands. National forest recreation visitation increased from about 5 million in the early 1920s to 18 million in 1946, 93 million in 1960, and 233 million in 1975. National park visitation increased from 50 million in 1950 to 72 million by 1960, and the Bureau of Land Management counts went from a few million visits just after WW II to 50 million by 1980. Visitation at state, county, and municipal parks rose even more rapidly than that on federal lands (DPC 1988).

The Effect of the 1960s and 1970s Environmental Movement. The increased uses of federal lands began to be reflected legislatively in the 1960s. The Multiple-Use Sustained Yield Act of 1960 provided that national forests be managed for a variety of uses and values, including outdoor recreation, wildlife, timber, rangeland grazing, and watershed protection. Although some management of this type was already occurring, the law codified those objectives. Other actions followed, including the 1968 the Wild and Scenic Rivers Act, the 1968 National Trails System Act, and the 1964 establishment of the Land and Water Conservation Fund.

The 1960s was also a time of growing public controversy over timber-harvesting practices on federal lands. Clear-cutting, the removal of essentially all trees in a stand, became a particularly controversial practice, with the Bitterroot National Forest in Montana and the Monongahela National Forest in West Virginia receiving national attention. These controversies led Congress to recommend guidelines for the application of clear-cutting on federal lands (Fedkiw 1998).

A growing segment of the public began seeking statutory protection for maintaining federal lands in their "natural" condition. The Wilderness Act, which passed in 1964, provided for the designation of significant areas of federal land in their natural and "untrammeled" condition.[13] Most commodity uses were prohibited from these areas. In 1975, legislation was passed to allow designating wilderness in the East.

The legislation of the 1960s and 1970s set the stage for later conflicts over the use and management of public national forest lands. On one hand, the possible uses of these lands—timber, water protection, recreation, wildlife, and forage—were codified in the Multiple-Use Sustained-Yield Act of 1960 and again in the 1976 National Forest Management Act (NFMA) and 1976 Federal Land Policy and Management Act. On the other, the Wilderness Act of 1964 provided for the creation of separate wilderness reserves under which most commercial uses of the national forests were prohibited.

The growing environmental awareness of the 1960s, which had coalesced over such issues as clear-cutting on the national forests, expanded into a general concern over the deterioration of air and water quality and a perceived lack of attention to the environmental and health effects of industrialization. Rachel Carson's *Silent Spring* galvanized public concern over pesticide use. Earth Day 1970 was successful in raising public awareness of environmental issues generally. Congress responded to these concerns by passing the Clean Air Act of 1970, the Clean Water Act of 1972, the National Environmental Policy Act (NEPA) of 1970, amendments to the Federal Insecticide, Fungicide, and Rodenticide Act, the Toxic Substances Control Act of 1976, the Endangered Species Act (ESA) of 1973, and laws aimed at protecting wetlands.

Changes in the U.S. Forest Sector since 1970

Traditionally, forestland has been categorized as public or private. Public forestlands include federal, state, and local government forestlands. The environmental legislation of the 1970s had a profound influence on the use and management of public lands, both federal and nonfederal, and less direct but no less consequential effects on private forestland.[14]

Changes in Public Forest Management

NEPA and ESA gave new opportunities and standing for individuals and groups to challenge national forest management practices in court based on environmental and biodiversity issues. The lack of consensus over how the national forests should be managed has resulted in the imposition of ever more detailed environmental assessment requirements, a tedious appeals process, continuing litigation, and a series of court decisions that created management gridlock.[15] It has been argued that during the 1990s the dominance of multiple-use management in effect shifted to a focus on biodiversity, a use not explicitly recognized in NFMA but consistent with the overall Forest Service mission. In oral comments at a Senate committee hearing, Former Chief Jack Ward Thomas (1994) suggested that the net effect of the administrative and legal challenges to national forest plans has been to make protection of biodiversity the overriding goal of federal lands in the United States: "That de facto policy has simply evolved through the interaction of laws, regulations, court cases, and expedient administrative direction. This de facto policy, I believe, is the very crux of the raging debate over the levels of commodity production that can be expected from federal lands."

Harvest levels were cut dramatically, from 10 billion to 11 billion board feet in 1988 to 2 billion board feet by 2000. These federal timber harvest reductions began in the administration of the first President Bush and continued through the Clinton administration, and low levels of harvest were maintained through the two terms of President George W. Bush that followed. Much of the timber harvest activities that remain are designed to maintain or restore ecological conditions, such as thinning to reduce the risk of uncharacteristically intense wildfires, and salvage and rehabilitation of forests damaged by wildfires.

If the debates of the 1970s and 1980s were truly timber wars, then the environmentalists have won. Today, the National Forest System is providing only a very small fraction of the nation's industrial wood, about 2 percent, and this is unlikely to increase much, regardless of which political party is in power. The challenge for the Forest Service will be finding a mission for the management of the national forests for the 21st century that will capture the aspirations of the American people (Sedjo 2000a).

Changed Perceptions of the Forest Service. After its first half-century of existence, the Forest Service generally was looked upon as a stunning success—an agency known for high morale, a strong sense of purpose, and administrative excellence (Kaufman 1960). Forty years later, at the end of the 20th century, the reputation of the Forest Service was in disarray (e.g., Nelson 2000). The major divisive issues were articulated by Clawson (1975) in his book *Forests for Whom and for What*. Who are the beneficiaries of national forest management, and specifically, what is to be the objective of management? Although the Forest Service's role appeared to have been well articulated in law more than 100 years ago, the role has evolved.

The question of what is to be produced in the national forests has been reasonably clear, at least as found in the legislation, but how the mix of resources on individual areas is determined and how national and local stakeholders' preferences are weighed have been left to the judgment of the federal land manager. Forest Service judgments have left the agency open to second-guessing and legal challenge. Furthermore, when the National Forest Management Act added wilderness to the list of legally required objectives, the complexity of management increased markedly, as did attempts by interest groups to pressure the Forest Service and Congress to provide more of their preferred outputs.

In response to increasing demands and controversy, the Forest Service has struggled to develop ever more elaborate means to assess stakeholder preferences and make the decisionmaking process more transparent. In the 1970s, in response to environmental laws, particularly NEPA and NFMA, this took the form of a "rational planning model," under which the agency would solicit input from diverse publics on issues to be addressed and on the management options the agency had prepared to address them. The agency then decided how best to weigh this stakeholder input in reaching a decision. In retrospect, because many did not trust the federal agency's judgments on such matters, that premise was optimistic. The shift in power from resource-dependent local communities to national and regional special-interest groups has also left many forest-based communities with a sense of powerlessness to influence their own future (Lee 1994). More recently, a new agency role has emerged in which the Forest Service and other agencies encourage competing interests to sit down and "reason together" in the same room to find ways to accommodate their diverse objectives collectively.

Problems and questions remain, however. For one thing, the incentive to engage in collaborative decisionmaking can be discouraged by the prospect of postdecisional administrative appeals and litigation processes. Moreover, balancing local versus national interests in the use and management of federal lands is a particularly intractable issue.

It is no wonder, then, that in its early years, when the mission was timber, water, and custodial maintenance of the forest asset, the Forest Service could carry out its mandate with relative ease. As the management task became much more complex, given the changing political climate and the absence of clear guidance regarding the precise mix of outputs, the system faltered and then failed. So serious have been the weaknesses of the system that for decades there have been calls for organizational and institutional changes that would improve the management of National Forest System lands (Sedjo 2000a). These suggestions include privatization (Clawson 1983), management transfer to environmentalists (Baden and Stroup 1981), various types of decentralization (O'Toole 1988; Nelson 1995; Forest Options Group 2000), and the creation of corporations utilizing trust-type instruments (Fairfax 2000). Some of these alternative organizational arrangements focused on economic efficiency criteria and others on new governance arrangements. Given the absence of either fundamental changes or reforms, some have questioned whether the Forest Service as we know it can survive (O'Toole 1997; Fairfax 2000; Nelson 2000; Sedjo 2000b).

If it is true, as Jack Ward Thomas (1994) suggests, that protection of biodiversity is now the de facto goal of federal land management, the task may become somewhat less complex than the multiple objectives of multiple-use management. If the objective becomes the unambiguous production of biodiversity, the pressures and concerns for other outputs abate, and achievement of the objective would be more feasible. However, as noted in the discussion below, the appropriate management regime to achieve biological diversity amenities is likely to be highly controversial. A confounding element today is the changed nature of the forest because of fire suppression.

Back to the Future for Public Forests? At the beginning of the 21st century, the demands on the National Forest System have come full circle: from a system that provided modest amounts of timber in the early 20th century, to one that provided substantial timber in the middle and latter parts of the century, to one that once again provides only modest amounts of timber. The original rationale for creating the National Forest System was that the private sector was rapidly drawing down the private stock of timber with little regard for future needs. The forest reserves were viewed as a public insurance policy against that eventuality. They were envisioned as a sustainable forest system—one that would produce timber while providing watershed protection. Although this assumption seemed reasonable at the time, it has now been found to be invalid. Because of rising real prices for wood products and a tax and related institutional situation that encouraged investments in timber-growing practices, private forests now account for 92 percent of the U.S. timber harvest while also providing high levels of watershed protection. Yet the role of private lands in growing timber as a crop, not just harvesting nature's accumulated bounty, really did not emerge until after World War II, when the forest products industry finally began to plant and manage intensive forests.

Over the roughly 100 years during which the Forest Service has been the guardian of the forests, it has gone through a series of management modes. Former Forest Service Chief R. Max Peterson makes the following observation:"that the emphasis on the various purposes changes from time to time is clearly shown in the activities of the 1920s, 30s, 40s, and 50s …" (Peterson 2000, *196*). In the 1930s, the national forests provided employment, in the 1940s timber and war materiel, in the 1950s lumber for the postwar housing boom, and during the 1960s, 1970s, and 1980s wilderness and the reestablishment of wildlife populations, particularly in the East. This view is consistent with that of Clawson (1983), who notes an evolution from custodial management during the first half of the 20th century to a timber production focus that was modified to multiple use, with the emphasis gradually shifting to noncommodity uses.

Changes in Private Forest Management

Private forests include industrial ownerships, defined as forestland held by firms owning wood-processing facilities, and nonindustrial forest ownerships, which include farm forest holdings, small timberland ownerships, and a host of other private forest-owning entities. In 2002, the majority of the nation's forestland, 57 percent, was in the private sector, with about 51 percent of all U.S. forestland owned by nonindustrial owners (Table 3-1).

The management objectives of private forest landowners vary considerably. Industry owners and other owners, such as those with large forest estates, normally are strongly oriented toward financial gain and wood production. The most productive timberlands tend to be owned by industry and are concentrated in the South, Northeast, and Pacific Coast. With only 12 percent of U.S. productive, nonreserved forestland, the forest industry produces 29 percent of domestic timber harvest volume. As would be expected, industrial forests tend to be managed on relatively short rotations, using high-yielding species of trees, usually conifers.

Nonindustrial private forest (NIPF) owners are a heterogeneous group, with the only common characteristic being they do not own wood-processing facilities. NIPF landowners own 51 percent of U.S. forestland and produce 63 percent of domestic timber harvest volume. Most NIPF forestland is in the eastern United States. Although this group is the major supplier of industrial wood in the United States, it also includes many farm forests and land belonging to nonresident owners, many having little interest in traditional forestry. NIPF landowners in the United States number about 10 million, but about 70 percent of NIPF forestland is held by the approximately 700,000 landowners who own large forest tracts of 100 acres or more. For this group, timber production is often a primary objective. For others, especially those with smaller holdings, forestland is held primarily for its wildlife, recreational, or environmental amenities. At the end of the 20th century, 92 percent of U.S. timber production came from the private sector, with roughly two-thirds of this coming from nonindustrial private forests (Table 3-1).

The 1970s environmental legislation that affected management of federal lands has also had some effects on private forests. In fact, federal and other public lands have sometimes been treated as "reservoirs" of biodiversity—their management for endangered and threatened species allowing for less restrictive use of adjacent private lands than might otherwise have occurred (Babbitt 1994).

Effects of the legislation on private forests include (1) restrictions on the flexibility of private landowners to drain forested wetlands to increase site productivity for commercial tree species; (2) requirements to implement best management practices to meet federal and state water quality goals; (3) requirements to protect habitats of endangered and threatened species; (4) pesticide use restrictions; and (5) limitations on the use of prescribed burning to protect air quality. With the exception of enforcement of the Endangered Species Act, state and local governments are the primary enforcement authorities for federal, state, and local environmental laws affecting private lands. It is not clear how much the increased level of federal and state regulation may be affecting private sector investments in forest management activities.

One recent issue for private forestry is the role of planted forests and intensively managed plantations. A second issue concerns the changing structure of private forestland ownership. Finally, there is the question of the voluntary certification of private forestlands and management practices.

The Transition to Intensive Management of Plantation Forests. The latter part of the 20th century marked the beginning of a major transition in the source of U.S. wood products—a transition that has yet to run its course. Humans made a similar transition in agriculture when, over a period of thousands of years, they

Table 3-1. *U.S. Forest Area, Ownership, and Timber Harvests, 2002*

Ownership category	All forestland Area (million acres)	All forestland Percentage	Productive, nonreserved forestland Area (million acres)	Productive, nonreserved forestland Percentage	Timber removals Billion cu. ft./ year	Timber removals Percentage
Private						
Forest industry	66.4	8.9	59.0	11.6	4.61	29.1
Nonindustrial	383.4	51.2	304.4	59.8	9.95	62.9
Subtotal, private	429.8	57.4	363.4	71.4	14.55	92.0
Public						
Federal						
Forest Service	148.5	19.8	94.7	18.6	0.34	2.1
BLM	44.1	5.9	18.1	3.6	0.15	0.9
Other federal	53.9	7.2	5.2	1.0	0.11	0.7
Subtotal	246.4	32.9	118.1	23.2	0.60	3.8
State and local						
State	63.1	8.4	19.2	3.8	0.55	3.5
County, municipal	9.6	1.3	8.2	1.6	0.12	0.8
Subtotal, public	72.7	9.7	27.4	5.4	0.67	4.2
Total, all owners	319.2	42.6	145.4	28.6	1.27	8.0
	748.9	100.0	508.9	100.0	15.82	100.0

Sources: USDA Forest Service 2004b (Tables 1, 10, and 35).
Note: Private nonindustrial ownership includes Indian Trust Lands administered by the Bureau of Indian Affairs. Timber removal figures for BLM, other federal, and state and local categories are estimates.
Note: Numbers in columns may not add to totals due to rounding.

moved from a foraging and hunting mode of obtaining food to modern cropping and livestock raising. So too in the latter half of the 20th century, forestry changed from a primitive gathering of the forest bounty created solely by nature (logging of old-growth) to the science of tree growing (silviculture): like grains, trees have become a crop, to be planted, tended, and harvested. With this approach, trees can be grown faster and desirable individuals chosen and bred to have the traits demanded by society. And this can be done in many cases at a cost lower than traditional logging.

Although tree planting was practiced by the Forest Service and other public entities during the Depression of the 1930s and later, it was in the latter part of the 20th century that tree planting began in earnest, largely in the private sector. In recent decades tree planting has regularly exceeded 2 million acres annually, with the private sector accounting for roughly 87 percent of the tree planting in the United States—about 45 percent by the forest industry and 42 percent by nonindustrial owners (Figure 3-4).

Such changes need not imply that most natural forests are about to be replaced by tree farms. Rather, intensive management means that huge volumes of wood can be produced from relatively small amounts of land. The vast majority of the U.S.

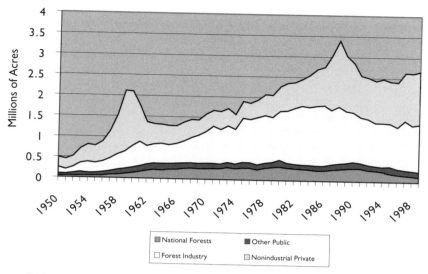

Figure 3-4. *Tree Planting in the United States, 1950–1999*

Source: Moulton and Hernandez 1999.

forest remains natural, brought about by natural processes, including natural regeneration after disasters, such as wildfire or windthrow. In the West, some 96 percent of the area is natural, and in the East, planted forests account for only about 7.4 percent of the total forest area (USDA FS 2004b), most of this in the Southeast.

In recent decades most of the planting has been done by the private sector, on both industrial and nonindustrial lands. The area of forest planted annually rose from about 500,000 acres in the early 1950s to almost 3.5 million acres in 1990 (Figure 3-4). Since that time, it has stabilized at a rate of roughly 2.3 million acres annually. On those sites, the use of improved seed stock and the application of intensive management improve biological growth and tend to reduce the harvest age. One of the implications of increased biological productivity is the need for less land for production.

The rationale for planting commercial forests is simple: the increased productivity and profitability that arise from the careful selection of sites, species, and improved stock (Sedjo 1983). Over the past half-century U.S. timber harvests have begun to reflect this increased planting, and harvest costs in real terms have declined because of site selection (Sedjo 1997). In the 1980s only about 2 percent of softwood harvests came from plantations. In 1995, that had increased to 19 percent. By 2050 plantations are expected to constitute about 54 percent of the softwood timber harvested, yet those plantations will occupy less than 15 percent of U.S. forestland (USDA FS 2000, Chapter 3).

Some have argued that the increased productivity of the private sector, achieved in large part through plantations of improved trees, has spared more natural forest area, particularly in the national forests, for other purposes. And it is this effect that allows environmentalists to maintain that the national forests ought to be set aside for biodiversity and ecological purposes.

Changes in U.S. and North American Industrial Ownerships. The structure of the U.S. forest industry has begun to change markedly in recent years. One recent trend is the apparent divesture of domestic forestlands owned by large, vertically integrated forest products corporations. According to one estimate based on Securities and Exchange Commission filings, the corporate sector as a whole divested itself of close to 30 million acres in the 25 years up to 2005. Today, timber investment management organizations (TIMOs) are estimated to hold about 10 million acres of timberland in the United States, more than any of the multinational forest products companies. TIMOs are partnerships of institutional investors who manage for returns on timberland assets. Throughout the forest industry, there has been a long and ongoing discussion regarding the optimal amount of timberland that a firm should own. The issue usually revolves around having a secure timber supply for the mill and the proportion of wood from nearby markets to the mill's own source of timber.

Reasons for the changing forest holdings might include attempts to rationalize overall forest holdings, attempts to dispose of low-productivity sites and sites whose unique environmental values jeopardize future harvest, tax considerations, the belief that land prices are high and provide a good opportunity for liquidations, and lack of confidence in the long-term competitive position of certain forest sites. In the past, forestland sales were often to other corporations, so the overall industrial land holdings did not change much. In the past 25 years, however, there has been a net transfer of about one-half of ownership out of the industry.

A method to rationalize forest holdings chosen by some corporations has been to change their entire business structure from, for example, a corporation to a trust. Alternative ownership forms include the TIMOs and the master limited partnerships. Also, many corporations are becoming real estate investment trusts (REITs). None of these forms allow processing facilities, such as mills, and thus ownership of processing facilities must be detached from forest ownership. A critical advantage of the new forms is found in the tax structure, which imposes lower taxes on trust-owned timber operations.

Overall, some domestic firms are trying to select and rationalize their timberland holdings to best position themselves for the changing economic and regulatory environment. In some cases they are identifying those domestic forestlands that are deemed most critical by virtue of their location to mills and potential productivity. Then they are gradually disposing of forestlands deemed less critical over the longer term, including those that are likely to be lost to development. Even as firms are reducing their holdings of domestic forestlands, however, some of them are increasing their forestland holdings in high-productivity sites abroad.[16]

Certification of Private Forest Management. Industrial forest firms, those that process as well as grow industrial wood, are obviously interested in management objectives that relate to profitability, usually over the long run. Typically, private management is constrained by both formal regulations and self-imposed environmental constraints associated with an implied social contract to do business in the United States. Such self-imposed constraints usually are designed to reduce the risk of off-site damages, which could lead to lawsuits, and visual blemishes, which could cause poor public relations.

Recently, voluntary certification, provided by a third party, has been added to the collection of approaches to demonstrate conformance to acceptable environmental performance standards.[17] Several national and international certification schemes have developed standards to address the operation of the forestry industry, promising benefits to all stakeholders. The premise is that the environment will benefit from better forestry practices, and forest products firms will receive higher prices for their product, assuming that consumers express a preference for certified "green" wood.

Certification criteria and procedures generally are established by a certifying organization, often in cooperation with corporations, nonprofit organizations, nongovernmental organizations, or other stakeholders. The certifying body sets performance-based or management-based guidelines to be followed by those seeking its certification—companies, individual landowners, or national, state, or community forests. Private organizations accredited by the certifier determine whether applicants meet the requirements. These third-party auditors[18] conduct on-site visits to examine internal plans, document field evidence for a given practice, interview personnel in the organization or community, review compliance records or internal monitoring, and conduct independent assessment and investigation (Sample et al. 2003).

A major worldwide forest certifying organization is the Forest Stewardship Council.[19] In the United States the dominant forest certifier is the Sustainable Forestry Initiative (Table 3-2). It was developed by the American Forest and Paper Association,[20] which requires all its industry members to agree to work toward a concept of sustainable forestry, even if they are not formally certified.

Forest certification auditing is still in its infancy, and sometimes clarity in what is being measured is lacking. This is particularly true when the certification standard addresses social issues, in addition to the more customary forest management issues like ecological, biological, and economic goals. However, even certification focused on forest management can have ambiguities. Early on, forests were certified as "sustainably managed." More recently, however, forests are being certified as "well managed" or "managed to standards" of the certifying organizations. This change seems to imply a recognition that sustainability in a broad sense encompasses more than individual forest properties and therefore must be evaluated at larger landscape scales. Some differences occur even within a particular standards-setting organization. Perhaps this is not surprising—one certifier, the Forest Stewardship Council, recognized that a single, global standard was not sensible and has created local teams to develop regionally specific standards.[21]

A major issue of certification is incentives for forest owners to become certified. As long as certification is voluntary, a forest firm must weigh the advantages of certification against those of remaining uncertified. Forest certification involves

Table 3-2. *Certified Forest Area in North America, 2005*

Certifier	Area (million acres)
Sustainable Forestry Initiative	129.0
Forest Stewardship Council	27.6
American Tree Farm System	29.0

Sources: Wilent 2005; American Tree Farm System, http://www.treefarmsystem.org/cms/pages/29.html (accessed February 24, 2007).

some increase in management costs in all cases. In a 1997 study of U.S. forests, Abt and Murray (Sedjo et al. 1998) estimated that about 50 percent of the current domestic harvest could meet Forest Stewardship Council certification standards at a cost increase of 10 percent or less. However, the remaining 50 percent would incur costs above 10 percent. In addition, if raw wood from sustainable forests is going to be converted to ecolabeled products, additional costs are incurred to maintain the chain of custody to processing facilities and retail markets.

A major incentive for certification has been the hope and expectation that the wood market is willing to pay a premium for certified wood. Certified, ecolabeled products would be viewed as more desirable, at least by some subset of consumers, and thus could bring a price premium in the market. It is the price premium that would give owners a direct financial incentive to incur the additional costs associated with certifiable management.

The experience is not encouraging so far on the question of the price premium for certified products. Several studies have suggested that consumers' willingness to pay higher prices is limited when lower-priced, noncertified substitutes are available. Although the price premium rarely occurs (Sedjo and Swallow 2002), many producers may still participate either for altruistic reasons or to generate public goodwill. Some major forest products companies regard certification as a cost of doing business. There is some evidence that TIMOs and the other newer classes of forest ownership appear less willing to incur the costs of certification than traditional industrial landowners (Irland 2005).

Preliminary evidence suggests that certification has improved the management of forests on which it has been applied (Mater et al. 2002). Certification of large numbers of forest properties could have a measurable positive effect on forest management.[22] But since it focuses on the management practices of individual forest properties, certification has a limited capability to address sustainability issues arising at larger landscape scales.

To date, nonindustrial private landowners have not become certified in large numbers, although they are required to meet certain standards if their wood is to be intermingled in mill processing with wood that is certified. Similarly, certification has been little utilized by national forest and other federal land management agencies.

Private Forests and Conservation. An ongoing concern for forest sustainability has been the condition of private forestlands in the United States. When forests are viewed solely as a source of timber, landowners may be tempted to "cut and run."[23]

However, as concerns about the nonmarket values of the forest have increased, such an approach has become increasingly unacceptable. One solution is for governments, federal and state, to impose regulations on private forestlands. Indeed, this has been done directly, via state forest practices legislation, and indirectly, through federal legislation such as the Endangered Species Act. But if private forestry declines as a viable economic operation, as it has in Maine (Irland 2006) and some other areas, or as development and other alternative land uses become increasingly attractive (Wear and Greis 2002), forestland could increasingly be converted to other uses. In fact, such conversions are already occurring. In recent decades some 20 million acres of former forestland has changed to other uses, although total forestland area has remained essentially stable because agricultural and other land uses have been converted to forest (Alig et al. 2003).

A view that is gaining ascendancy is the need for "working" forests—that is, forests that continue to be managed and harvested for timber production, not necessarily intensively, to ensure that large areas of land remain in forest. In Wisconsin, for example, the state has developed a graduated land tax system. If a private owner has a forest management plan that includes harvesting, land taxes are reduced. Further tax reductions are possible if the owner allows access for certain recreational purposes, such as bird watching.

Another approach is the use of a conservation easement, a covenant on the land title that limits the uses to which the land can be put. An easement conveys with the title in perpetuity, thereby constraining the future use of the land. Conservation groups have recently been active in purchasing forestlands from industry and have been major users of this instrument. They purchase the land, affix environmental easements to protect its environmental values, and then sell most of it to entities that continue to operating working forests. The nature of the easements can vary from highly restrictive to only moderately so.

A recent example is the sale of large areas of timberland by International Paper Company to The Nature Conservancy and the Conservation Fund. Many of these lands, in turn, were sold to entities such as TIMOs, which will manage them for timber with only modest management restrictions: the conservation easements included a provision that limited the types of land uses and precluded conversion for development. For other lands with unique natural features, the easements were more restrictive in the allowable types of management and land changes, or the land was kept by the environmental group. The Nature Conservancy, for example, has acquired 9 million acres of environmentally sensitive land for wildlife and biodiversity objectives and manages more than 1,500 reserves.

When such acquisitions involve purchases of land, the environmental organization needs financing to pay the market price of the forestland with unrestricted use. The affixing of an environmental easement then reduces the market value of the property, since some of the financial options for the land have been precluded. Thus the sale price is generally lower than the initial purchase price, and the difference is paid by the environmental group and its financial supporters.

New Directions in Private Forestry. The combination of forest certification, advantageous tax treatment, and conservation easements may constitute a fundamental change in the way private forests are managed and regulated. Although certification is sometimes applied to public forests, the initial intent is that these voluntary certification programs can supplement government regulation, particularly on private lands. Government regulation has been the usual approach to achieving an acceptable level of environmental protection of private forests. What distinguishes certification from previous rule-based approaches to improving forest management practices is that it is private rather than governmental, it is voluntary, and it depends on market incentives for sustainable forest management rather than sanctions for violations (Cashore et al. 2004).

Advantageous land tax treatment at the local and state level gives private owners incentives to maintain land in forest, even if it is marginally productive for industrial wood. The reduced taxes collected by state and local authorities in return for management plans and public environmental services reflect the enjoyment of those services by the local public as well as the jobs created by working forests. Environmental easements provide an opportunity for the public to participate in forest management decisionmaking without requiring vast sums of money for the fee-simple purchase of huge forest areas. Associated with these easements are a series of environmental services that are, in fact, financed not by government but by the environmental community.

U.S. Forests Today

Over the past century, the total forest area of the United States has remained essentially constant (Figure 3-2), but forest cover changes by region have been considerable. After 1907, both the South and the West experienced significant forest cover reductions, while the North experienced substantial increases. This reflects continuing adjustments in agriculture and development, not unlike the regeneration of New England forests beginning in the mid-1800s, when agricultural lands were abandoned because of the development of agriculture in the Midwest, the rail transport of cheap agricultural products to eastern markets, and the subsequent decline in agriculture in the less fertile Northeast. At the same time parts of the southern forests continued to be converted into agricultural use well into the latter part of the 20th century. The forest recovery in New England was later repeated in parts of the South, where cotton and tobacco fields were abandoned beginning before the Great Depression era of the 1930s and continuing through the postwar boom of the 1950s.

The extent of forestland depends not only on the land but also on the density or volume of the forest. In the United States, the forest inventory—that is, the growing stock volume of forest—increased by almost 40 percent between 1953 and 2002 (USDA FS 2004b). Part of this increase can be attributed to the success in suppressing wildfire. Thus, despite major commercial logging activities, conversion to development, and forest mortality of many types, the volume of the forest increased steadily over the latter half of the 20th century.

Shifts in Supply and Demand for Timber. The United States has been the world's leading producer of industrial wood for many years and currently produces more than one-quarter of the world's total raw industrial wood. The source of this production has always been predominantly the private sector, but with declining harvests from the national forests and the public sector, timber production from the private sector has risen. In the early post–World War II period, harvests on the national forests increased rapidly from their low, prewar level until by the late 1970s they accounted for about 16 percent of total U.S. harvests, with other public forest harvests amounting to almost another 8 percent (Clawson 1979). However, these shares fell dramatically in later years as national forest harvests declined (Figure 3-5) and the private sector moved to fill some of the gap. In recent years about 30 percent of the U.S. harvest has been provided by the timber industry, and more than 60 percent comes from private nonindustrial forests (Table 3-1).

Despite the decline in timber production from the national forests, U.S. wood products consumption has remained essentially constant as increased private harvests partially replaced the decline in harvests from the national forests, with the difference made up mostly from increased softwood lumber imports from Canada and increased harvests from private forestlands in the United States. For example,

- Since 1990, softwood lumber imports from Canada have risen from 12 billion to more than 18 billion board feet, increasing from 27 to 36 percent of U.S. softwood lumber consumption. Much of the increase in Canadian lumber imports has come from old-growth boreal forests.

- Harvesting on private lands in the southern United States also increased after the reduction of federal timber in the West. Between 1986 and 2001, timber harvests from U.S. private lands increased from 13.2 billion to 14.6 billion cubic feet.

- The 1990s saw a shift in timber production from the West, with its dominance of federal forests, to the South and North, where the forests are predominantly

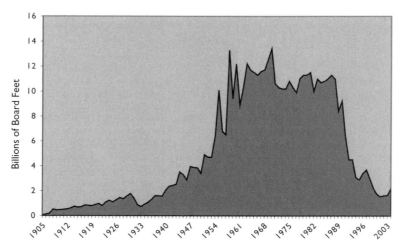

Figure 3-5. *National Forest Timber Sales, 1905–2003*

Source: National Forest System Timber Cut and Sold Reports.

privately owned. Thus, overall U.S. timber production has remained largely unchanged despite the very large reduction in national forest harvests.

Today, Americans are using more timber than at any time in U.S. history and are also consuming more natural resources per capita than any other nation.[24] Since the first Earth Day, in 1970, the average family size in the United States has dropped by 16 percent, yet the average size of a new single-family house has increased by 50 percent. U.S. forests comprise a wide array of forest types and conditions in several ownerships. Some 504 million acres, or 67 percent, of the total U.S. forestland area is classed as timberland[25] (USDA FS 2004a). Ownership consists of industrial, private nonindustrial, private investor forest ownership (TIMOs), as well as public ownerships at the local, state, and federal levels.

Forest Fires. Forest health is the subject of considerable attention. Most agree that the Forest Service has a major responsibility for forest health, particularly on national forestlands, but has not yet fulfilled this function very effectively. Well before the fires of recent summers, Sampson (1993) and Clark and Sampson (1995) argued that large portions of the national forests were in poor condition. Clark and Sampson (1995, 5) characterized the situation as follows: "The concern for forests today is not simply that trees will die from bugs and disease—it is that entire forest systems are so far out of normal ecological range that virtually every element in the system is affected, and may be at risk."

In fact, it is the dramatic reduction of forest fires that has led to many of the current forest health problems (Nelson 2000). Significant reductions in ecosystem fire in many parts of the West occurred in the 1870s and 1880s, predating modern fire control by more than half a century. The change was associated with the elimination of burning by Native Americans and the introduction of large numbers of livestock, which changed fuel dynamics and often prepared a mineral seedbed for forest regeneration. Modern fire control, which became increasingly effective in reducing the area burned by wildfire after 1930 (Figure 3-6), certainly exacerbated the problem.

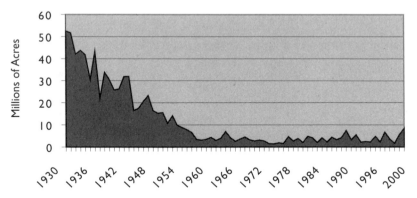

Figure 3-6. *U.S. Wildfire Trends, Area Burned, 1930–2000*

Source: Wildland Fire Statistics, Fire and Aviation Management, USDA Forest Service.

But eliminating fire control is not the solution. We need to continue to suppress *unwanted* wildfires. The problem is that in the West, the Forest Service and other federal agencies did not distinguish between destructive and beneficial wildfires[26] and failed to recognize the need for more thinning and use of prescribed fire.

Many argue that at least some minimum degree of human management is desirable to reduce the risk of uncharacteristically intense wildfires and restore ecological processes and conditions. Some intervention now is being recognized within the National Park System, which previously had prohibited such types of management.

Urbanization. The forestland estate has been relatively stable since the 1920s, but today this situation may be changing. Private forests are being converted to suburban and residential development at an unprecedented rate, and this urbanization can contribute to forest fragmentation (Radeloff et al. 2005). In the Southern Forest Resources Assessment, the Forest Service identified urbanization as a primary cause of forest loss in the South and expected the trend to increase (Wear and Greis 2002). Nationally, the Forest Service projects that total forest area in the United States will decrease by approximately 23 million acres by 2050, a 3 percent reduction from the 1997 forest area. Industrial timberland is projected to decrease by 3 percent by 2050, and nonindustrial private timberland by 4.4 percent (Alig et al. 2003).

As urban dwellers move to rural areas, political opposition to timber harvesting often increases. Other effects of conversion of forest to residential development include accelerated erosion, fragmentation of wildlife habitat, increased energy usage, and demands for more police and social services. In addition, these growing "wildland-urban interface" areas are increasingly at risk from wildfire. Whereas forest and agriculture lands have ebbed and flowed over the years, urbanization is essentially a one-way process. In urbanization, the timber industry and environmentalists—traditional adversaries—are finding common cause. But only time will tell whether the social will and institutional tools exist to deal with it in a meaningful way.

U.S. Sustainability Performance

The concept of sustainable development as defined by the Brundtland Commission (WCED 1987) has become a cornerstone of discussions of sustainability. The commission defined sustainable development as "development that meets the needs of the present without compromising the ability of future generations to meet their own needs." Note that this broad definition describes a continuing process rather than the static maintenance of some existing condition or state. Also, the definition is results oriented. It doesn't stress maintaining any particular state but rather maintaining the system's ability, or flexibility, to allow the future to address its needs.

Taking that definition to America's forests implies that forestland needs to be managed to produce the full range of current forest outputs without compromising its ability to produce those outputs in the future. It also implies the commitment to identify and then measure those factors associated with sustainability at appropriate landscape scales (national, regional, and local) and over time. We will discuss later how well America's management of its forests appears to be meeting these objectives.

Measuring Sustainability

Building on the Brundtland concept, attempts have been made to develop a detailed approach for assessing sustainability for forests. The beginnings of the process came out of the 1992 UN Conference on Environment and Development (the "Earth Summit") in Rio de Janeiro and the Rio Declaration (1992) on forest principles. However, at that time there was little agreement on how to characterize or assess forest sustainability. Subsequently, in 1993, the United States committed to a national goal of sustainable forest management following the Forest Principles, with the objective of contributing to the management, conservation, and sustainable development of forests and providing for their multiple and complementary functions and uses. In 1995, as part of the Montreal Process, the United States and other countries[27] engaged in discussions that resulted in the adoption of a set of criteria and indicators (C&I). The C&I are intended to provide a common understanding of essential components of sustainable forest management and a common framework for describing, assessing, and evaluating a country's progress toward this goal at the national level.[28]

The Montreal Process C&I consist of 7 criteria and 67 indicators:

- conservation of biological diversity (9 indicators);

- maintenance of productive capacity of forest ecosystems (5 indicators);

- maintenance of forest ecosystem health and vitality (3 indicators);

- conservation and maintenance of soil and water resources (8 indicators);

- maintenance of forest contribution to global carbon cycles (3 indicators);

- maintenance and enhancement of long-term multiple socioeconomic benefits to meet the needs of societies (19 indicators); and

- a legal, institutional, and economic framework for forest conservation and sustainable management (20 indicators).

Each Montreal Process country was expected to seek to measure the indicators and develop a country-level report summarizing the results.

In 2003, as part of a series of international assessments involving other countries that are signatories to the Montreal Protocol, the U.S. Forest Service conducted an analysis of the sustainability of American forests using available data on the condition of forests in the United States and applying the C&I approach endorsed by the Montreal Process (USDA FS 2004a). The *National Report on Sustainable Forests—2003*[29] was an attempt to provide a quantitative assessment of the state of the American forests. The report also identified data gaps and made recommendation for next steps to improve the collection of useful data.

The approach of the report follows the definition of sustainability given by the Brundtland Commission and views sustainability as a journey, "an ongoing dynamic process rather than a static condition." Sustainability entails concurrent attention to three spheres of activity: environment, the economy, and society. It requires environmental foundations to support economies and societies, economic performance for the sake of social well-being and environmental conservation, and social institutions that help foster both the economy and the environment (USDA FS 2003, *85*).

Not surprisingly, the results were somewhat mixed.[30] For example, the section on Criterion 2, maintenance of productive capacity of forest ecosystems, listed positive results:

- Although the area of forestland fell sharply in the latter part of the 19th century and early 20th century, since about 1920 the forest area has been approximately unchanged, at about 750 million acres.

- Growth has exceeded removals throughout the 1952–2001 period, on both public and private lands. Harvests constitute about 65 percent of forest growth in recent years.

- Because of this, the total volume of forest growing stock has increased in every region over the 1953–2002 period. Nationally, the volume of standing timber increased by 40 percent since 1953; in the eastern United States, it has almost doubled.

- Tree planting in the United States increased substantially over the period in the South and West but declined in the North. Tree planting peaked in the late 1980s and has stabilized at about 2.3 million acres annually.

- Protected areas in the United States are estimated to cover about 154 million acres, or 7 percent of the land area. Of this, 106 million acres of forestland (14 percent of all forestland) is protected.

Negative results were also listed:

- At least 20 percent of the nation's forestland has "diminished biological components" indicative of changes in fundamental ecological processes. This may suggest poor forest health.

- There are indications of soil and water problems in more than 10 percent of the forests of each major region.

- Portions of some forest-associated taxa (species) are at risk of becoming extinct.

- Fire can be either too frequent or too rare because of excessive controls and has had some detrimental affects on forest health.

Finally, the report found one inconclusive result: Forest fragmentation, although often cited as a problem, was not analyzed because analysis of fragmentation data is very dependent on scale, and the data were insufficient to permit a meaningful analysis.

Although many of the figures in the *National Report on Sustainable Forests—2003* are snapshots of current conditions and may be too aggregated to forecast the future condition of American forests, they generally do suggest a growing, expanding forest estate not subject to excessive harvesting pressure. The level of tree planting suggests that investments are being made in future forests. Environmental and health issues do arise, however, for a substantial area of forestland. It should be noted that such national figures can hide significant trends—for example, diminishing areas of rare or ecologically important forest types or conditions.

An Assessment

The *National Report on Sustainable Forests—2003* states that an unequivocal interpretation of the trends of the nine indicators is difficult; nevertheless, some general comments are offered.

Biological diversity. The report observes that forest habitats generally appear to be stable over recent decades, suggesting that forests are being used in a manner that is sustainable in the long term. It notes, however, that portions of some forest-associated species are at risk of becoming extinct, suggesting that elements of forest habitats are becoming lost or used in ways that are incompatible with maintaining the species composition of forest ecosystems.

Maintenance of productive capacity of forest ecosystems. This criterion specifically addresses the capacity of the forest to produce extractive goods and services. The report suggests that despite gaps and interpretation difficulties, with the land area stable and the growing stock volume and productivity rising, the productive capacity for timber production is favorable. Although major gaps in monitoring nontimber forest products have made analyses largely anecdotal, the evidence, such as it is, is generally consistent with the maintenance of productive capacity.

Forest ecosystem health. The report notes that healthy forests are essential for maintaining biodiversity, productivity, soil and water, carbon cycles, and socioeconomic benefits. The introduction of nonnative pests has had wide-ranging negative effects on forest health. In addition, native pests and air pollution have contributed to forest health difficulties, and urban sprawl affects millions of acres of forest. Finally, fire, which can be either too frequent or too rare because of excessive controls, can have and has had some detrimental effects on forest health. An overall appraisal, however, is not made.

Soil and water. In general, undisturbed forests are associated with low levels of soil compaction and with high levels of water yield and quality. Although nationally summarized statistics are not available, it is known that many forest areas are managed specifically to serve in a protective capacity for soil and water. However, there are indications of soil and water problems in more than 10 percent of the forests of each major region.

Carbon cycles. This criterion relates to the increasing atmospheric concentrations of certain types of gases—greenhouse gases—that contribute to the warming of the planet. Forests have large amounts of carbon in their vegetation, especially trees and soils. Thus, trees can serve as a vehicle for the mitigation of the buildup of atmospheric carbon. In recent decades, substantial amounts of carbon have been sequestered in the forest, although the annual amount of sequestration is declining. Currently, forests and forest products sequester about 12 percent of gross U.S. greenhouse gas emissions.

Socioeconomic benefits. These benefits are indicated by various aspects of supply, demand, investment, and utility related to America's needs. Included are production and consumption of wood products, forest-related tourism and recreation, and other forest amenities, including spiritual values, investment in forest management and processing, employment, and so forth.

It is clear that American forests provide many types of benefits. Some, such as wood production and employment and recreational visits, can be measured. Others, such as the value of a tourism or recreation experience, are more difficult to assess. Hence, the study concludes that overall socioeconomic benefits are difficult to measure.

Legal, institutional, and economic framework. The issue here is whether the legal framework for forest sustainability includes the body of laws and customs adequate to maintain the sustainability of the forest. The report does not provide a definitive answer, perhaps because of the difficulty of quantifying legal and institutional frameworks using the numerical indicator approach taken by the national assessment.

The report showed that although the data available for assessing American forests generally present positive results, the results are not uniform. Also, there are numerous areas where the relevant data were either sketchy or unavailable. Many of the data needed for a comprehensive evaluation of the criteria and indicators are absent or have not been gathered consistently. For other indicators, we do not really know how to measure them or have not reached a consensus on how they should be measured. The report concluded that of 67 indicators (Irland 2005),

- for 8, data are consistent and suitable;

- for 39, data are inconsistent nationally (and thus difficult to aggregate), out of date, or not measured frequently enough;

- for 11, data are of "questionable usefulness"; and

- for 9, the results are based on modeling only.

Perhaps more importantly, the report demurs on judging how well the various criteria have been met in practice. The authors of the report probably were wise not to attempt a judgment. However, the question arises, how much information is needed to permit a definitive judgment? A related issue is subjectivity: when do we know enough to make a really definitive judgment about something as loosely defined as the necessary legal and institutional framework for forest sustainability? This problem is not unique to the particular criterion or to the United States. Other signatories to the Montreal Protocol going through this same exercise have encountered similar difficulties.

Overall, the good news is that U.S. forests have maintained their essential size and productivity over almost the past 100 years. By many of the criteria, one could argue that American forests are doing quite well. The difficulties that do appear seem to be largely localized and relate to changes in the uses of the forest and indeed to changes in the forests themselves as forests expand in some parts of the United States while declining elsewhere. A large portion of the negative features are related to forest health. Invasive species, disease, and problems with fire, in some case exacerbated by the suppression of fire in earlier periods, are major sources of the negative trends in the relevant criteria and indicators.

The attempt to apply the criteria and indicators of the Montreal Process to real forests shows the conceptual and practice difficulties involved. However, it is a start, and it provides a basis for the more careful development of the conceptual tools to ensure that they are operational—that is, one can determine when the criteria are met and when they are not—and that sufficient data exist to determine their empirical validity.

Today there is an ongoing effort among the Montreal Process countries to use the lessons learned to improve future assessments. In furtherance of this, the Forest Service assembled external groups to assess the process and make recommendations on how it might be improved and made more useful, including revising or amending indicators to make them more meaningful and measurable. But it appears likely that many of these data gaps will remain when the next national sustainability report is prepared, in 2010. Finally, it should be noted that the 2003 national sustainability report has nothing to say about the effects of domestic consumption of forest resources on the forests of nations that supply wood products to the U.S. economy.[31]

Summary and Conclusions

In *America's Renewable Resources* (Frederick and Sedjo 1991) the subject was renewability. A mere 15 years later the issue has become forest sustainability. This is a more difficult concept than renewability, embodying strong philosophical and value components. Recognizing the elusiveness of precision in that term and the larger spatial and temporal scales needed for its assessment, most certifying organizations now certify not for a "sustainable" forest but for a "well-managed" forest, or they certify that the forest has met certain standards.

Nevertheless, sustainability implies certain types of management behavior in caring for the land and its future condition. It is said that sustainability implies that even when humans cause a disturbance, they should be sure to "keep all of the parts" so that, following Brundtland, "the needs of the present are met without compromising the ability of future generation to meet their own needs." Thus, maintaining representative ecosystems and biodiversity is important. However, forests are inherently dynamic, and as demonstrated by Botkin (1991), forest systems do not simply recycle through time in a highly predictable fashion but may sometimes respond to disturbances in an unexpected manner.

Confounding difficulties are invasive species and climate cycles, both largely unavoidable. Thus, there may be new components to the forest today that were not there 1,000 years ago or even 50 years ago. The course of forest development and growth may be altered permanently. Nevertheless, it seems clear that in the past century the America forest system reached a type of "steady state" in total land area within the context of a dynamic system. As demonstrated in the *National Report on Sustainable Forests*, the forest area has remained largely intact over almost the past 100 years. Although there have been some changes at the margins—that is, some forestland has been converted to agriculture while some cropland has reverted to forest—the vast bulk of the area in forest today was in forest in 1920. A variety of technical and institutional factors have contributed to the recovery of U.S. forests since 1900, including increasing agricultural productivity, well-defined and stable land tenure and land rights systems, and strong markets for forest products that discourage conversion to nonforest land uses.[32]

As management of federal forestland moves away from timber production toward protection and biodiversity, the disturbances in these forests are likely to be less caused by logging and extractive activities and more driven by "natural" forces. Whether this approach will contribute to the sustainability of the entire American forest system or lead to increased levels of uncharacteristically intense wildfires and related forest health concerns is a question that remains for the future.

Modern forestry practices are providing more timber from less area. In the future, the country may want private forests to provide additional ecosystem services. The emergence of certification and environmental easements may provide the tools to achieve that end.

In summary, the concept of forest management has been evolving, driven by changing values, technical change, and legislation. Cut-and-run logging gave way to sustained-yield forestry, which in turn was replaced by multiple-use forestry, at least on many U.S. public lands. Recent years have seen a movement toward ecosystem approaches and sustainable forestry. This evolution of forest management ideals is occurring not only in the United States but also in many other countries. This continuing evolution leads us to conclude with the observation of Sayer and Maginnis (2005, *191*) when looking at forest globally: "There is no single approach to the management of forest ecosystems, but multiple approaches ... will need to be adapted and applied pragmatically in each situation."

Notes

1. For a detailed discussion of forest management and biodiversity, see NCSSF (2005).

2. Webster's defines renewable with respect to natural resources as "capable of being replaced by natural ecological cycles or sound management practices." Most biological resources are considered renewable, as are some energy resources, such as wind, hydropower, biomass, and geothermal.

3. During the 60-year period between 1850 and 1910, U.S. forests were being converted to agricultural uses at an average rate of 13.5 square miles per day (Williams 1989).

4. This is not a particular problem for individual forest ownerships, but it may be if most or all forests in a region are managed under short-rotation silvicultural regimes.

5. The 1982 National Forest Management Act regulations defined net public benefits as "an expression used to signify the overall long-term value to the nation of all outputs and positive effects (benefits) less all associated inputs and negative effects (costs) whether they can be quan-

titatively valued or not. Net public benefits are measured by both quantitative and qualitative criteria rather than a single measure or index. The maximization of net public benefits to be derived from management of units of the National Forest System is consistent with the principles of multiple use and sustained yield."

6. For a discussion of the arguments giving more weight to local viewpoints, see Gray et al. (2001). For a discussion of some counterarguments, see Harmon (1998).

7. The Society of American Foresters (1993) has described ecosystem management as follows: "Ecosystem management attempts to maintain the complex processes, pathways and interdependencies intact, and functioning well, over long periods of time. The essence of maintaining ecosystem integrity is to retain the health and resilience of systems so they can accommodate short-term stresses and adapt to long-term change. The key elements include: maintenance of biological diversity and soil fertility; conservation of genetic variation and its dispersal; and through evolution, future biological diversity … Maintenance of these ecological processes and properties sets the bounds within which specific ecosystem management objectives (including sustained-yield of products) can be pursued."

8. For more insight into these events, see Steen (2000).

9. See Sedjo (1996).

10. This discussion is contained in *Ecosystem Stewardship: A Common Reference for Ecosystem Management* (Sexton et al. 1999), which was intended to be a definitive intellectual base for ecosystem management as practiced by U.S. federal agencies.

11. "Inadequate capacity" includes (1) lack of proper legal frameworks and the ability to enforce forest and environmental laws; (2) inability to conduct forest inventory and assessment; (3) lack of knowledge or ability among public forest services, rural communities, and private landowners; (4) inability to implement reduced-impact logging; (5) inability to protect the nonmarket values and services of forests; and (6) failure to constructively involve local communities and indigenous groups.

12. This agency is now the Natural Resources Conservation Service.

13. Few areas in North America are truly "untrammeled"—that is, unaffected by human action. Most areas, even those now designated as national parks and wilderness areas, were affected by the activities of American Indians, especially burning and hunting. With the reduction of natural and human-set fires, many of these protected areas today are much different ecologically than they were in precolonial times. And many continue to move toward conditions unlike any that existed in the past.

14. These laws affect not just federal land management. ESA, the Clean Water and Clean Air acts, the Federal Insecticide, Fungicide, and Rodenticide Act, and several other laws are also applicable to private lands.

15. A report by the USDA Forest Service (2002b) contains a detailed discussion of how process requirements are adversely affecting the Forest Service. It found that overlapping procedural requirements, procedural redundancy, and multiple layers of interagency coordination contribute to inefficiencies in decisionmaking.

16. Weyerhaeuser Company has recently acquired major forest plantation lands in Uruguay, and Stora-Enso, a Nordic firm, has acquired the rights to 500,000 hectares of land for tree plantations in southern China. Both firms are disposing of some of their forest holdings elsewhere.

17. Earlier approaches, such as the American Tree Farm system, go back several decades.

18. Examples of third-party auditing enterprises include SmartWood and Scientific Certification Systems for the Forest Stewardship Council; and PricewaterhouseCooper, Bioforest Technologies, Interforest/Arthur Andersen, and The Plum Line for the Sustainable Forestry Initiative standards. Some auditors, such as Société Générale de Surveillance, offer certification audits for the Forest Stewardship Council, the Sustainable Forestry Initiative, and the Private Enterprise Forest Certification.

19. Information on the Forest Stewardship Council can be viewed at http://www.fscoax.org/principal.htm.

20. Information on the Sustainable Forestry Initiative can be found at http://www.afandpa.org/Content/NavigationMenu/Environment_and_Recycling/SFI/SFI.htm.

21. A report comparing the Forest Stewardship Council and the Private Enterprise Forest Certification systems on pilot areas in Nordic countries can be found at www.nordicforestry.org.

22. See Swallow and Sedjo (2000) for an assessment of the likely overall effects.

23. Of course, many private owners maintain forests for a variety of purposes, including wildlife and environmental amenities, beyond simply timber production.

24. On a per-capita basis, the United States consumes twice the volume of wood products as other developed countries and four times that of the average for the rest of the world (Brooks 1993).

25. *Timberland* is defined as productive forestland not withdrawn from timber production by statute or regulation.

26. These have been called "prescribed natural fires" and are now called "fire use" fires.

27. The Montreal Process countries are Argentina, Australia, Canada, Chile, China, Japan, Korea, Mexico, New Zealand, Russia, the United States, and Uruguay. For more information, see http://www.mpci.org/home_e.html.

28. Several other C&I efforts are also going on around the world, but the Montreal Process seems to be the most advanced.

29. First Approximation Report, 1997: htpp://www.fs.fed.US/global/pubs/links/report/candi.htm.

30. For a number of stakeholder comments, see htpp://www.sustainableforests.net/perspectives/index.php. For a particularly critical view, see the comments of Irland (2005, 2006).

31. For another assessment of indicators of forest sustainability, see the work of the Heinz Center, at http//www.heinzctr.org/ecosystems.

32. The real price of lumber (adjusted for inflation) has risen steadily since 1800, increasing four times since 1900 (Howard 1999), while the real prices of most competing materials were declining. Since the 1970s, the real price for lumber has fluctuated, but the trend has generally been flat. Weak agricultural commodity prices have also encouraged the reversion of cropland and pasture to forest.

References

Alig, Ralph J., Andrew J. Plantinga, Soeun Ahn, and Jeffrey D. Kline. 2003. Land Use Changes Involving Forestry in the United States: 1952 to 1997, with Projections to 2050. General Technical Report PNW-GTR-587. Portland, OR: USDA Forest Service, Pacific Northwest Research Station.

Babbitt, Bruce. 1994. The Endangered Species Act and "Takings": A Call for Innovation within the Terms of the Act. *Environmental Law* 24(2): 355–67.

Baden, John, and Richard Stroup. 1981. Saving the Wilderness. *Reason* July: 28–36.

Binkley, C. S. 2000. Forest in the New Millennium: Creating a Vision that Fits, in *A Vision for the U.S. Forest Service: Goals for its Next Century*, edited by R.A. Sedjo, Washington, DC: Resources for the Future.

Blackburn, T.C., and Kat Anderson (eds.). 1993. *Before the Wilderness: Environmental Management by Native Californians*. Menlo Park, CA: Ballena Press.

Botkin, Daniel. 1991. *Discordant Harmonies: A New Ecology for the 21st Century*. New York: Oxford University Press.

Bowes, Michael, and John V. Krutilla. 1989. *Multiple-use Management: The Economics of Public Forestlands*. Washington, DC: Resources for the Future.

Brooks, David J. 1993. U.S. Forests in a Global Context. General Technical Report RM-228. USDA Forest Service. Available at http://svinet2.fs.fed.us/pl/rpa/93rpa/93pub.htm.

Butzer, Karl W. 1990. The Indian Legacy in the American Landscape. In *The Making of the American Landscape*, edited by M.P. Conzen. Boston: Unwin Hyman, 27–50.

Cashore, Benjamin, Graeme Auld, and Deanna Newsome. 2004. *Governing Through Markets: Forest Certification and the Emergence of Non-state Authority*. New Haven: Yale University Press.

Clark, Lance, and R. Neil Sampson. 1995. *Forest Ecosystem Health in the Inland West: A Science and Policy Reader*. Washington, DC: Forest Policy Center, American Forests.

Clawson, Marion. 1975. *Forests for Whom and for What?* Baltimore: Johns Hopkins University Press and Resources for the Future.

————. 1979. Forests in the Long Sweep of American History. *Science* 15: 1168–74.

————. 1983. *The Federal Lands Revised.* Washington, DC: Resources for the Future.

Denevan, William M. 1992. The Pristine Myth: The Landscape of the Americas in 1492. *Annals of the Association of American Geographers* 82(3): 369–85.

Dobyns, Henry F. 1983. Their Number Become Thinned: Native American Population Dynamics in Eastern North America. Knoxville: University of Tennessee Press.

Domestic Policy Council (DPC). 1988. *Outdoor Recreation in a Nation of Communities: Action Plan for Americans Outdoors.* Washington, DC: Task Force on Outdoor Recreation Resources.

Eba Atyi, R., and Markku Simula. 2002. Forest Certification: Pending Challenges for Tropical Timber. Technical Series No. 19. Yokohama, Japan: International Tropical Timber Organization.

Fairfax, Sally. 2000. State Trust Lands Management: A Promising New Application for the Forest Service. In *A Vision for the U.S. Forest Service: Goals for its Next Century,* edited by Roger A. Sedjo, 105–142. Washington, DC: Resources for the Future.

Fedkiw, John. 1989. The Evolving Use and Management of the Nation's Forests, Grasslands, Croplands, and Related Resources. General Technical Report RM-175. Washington, DC: USDA Forest Service.

————. 1998. *Managing Multiple Uses on National Forests, 1905–1995: A 90-year Learning Experience and It Isn't Finished Yet.* Washington, DC: USDA Forest Service.

Floyd, Donald W., Sarah L. Vonhof, and Heather E. Seyfang. 2001. Forest Sustainability: A Discussion Guide for Professional Resource Managers. *Journal of Forestry* 99(2): 8–28.

Forest Options Group. 2000. Second Century Report: Options for the Forest Service's Second Century. Report of the Forest Options Group. Available at http://www.ti.org/2c.html.

Frederick, Kenneth D., and Roger A. Sedjo (eds.) 1991. *America's Renewable Resources: Historical Trends and Current Challenges.* Washington, DC: Resources for the Future.

Gray, George, Larry Fisher, and Lynn Jungwirth. 2001. An Introduction to Community-based Ecosystem Management. In *Understanding Community-based Forest Ecosystem Management,* edited by George Gray, Maia Enzer, and Jonathon Kuzel. Washington, DC: Haworth Press and American Forests, 25–34.

Haigh, J., and John V. Krutilla. 1978. An Integrated Approach to National Forest Management. *Environmental Law* 8(2): 383.

Hansen, Henry L. 1980. The Lakes States Region. In *Regional Silviculture of the United States,* edited by John W. Barrett. New York: John Wiley and Sons, 67–106.

Harmon, W. 1998. A Conversation with Michael McClosky. *The Compass* (Fall). Available at http://consensus.fsu.edu/epp/hammers.html.

Hawke, David F. 1988. *Everyday Life in Early America.* New York: Harper & Row.

Hayami, Yujiro, and Vernon W. Rattan. 1985. *Agricultural Development: An International Perspective.* Baltimore: Johns Hopkins Press.

Helms, John A. (ed). 1998. *The Dictionary of Forestry.* Bethesda, MD: Society of American Foresters.

Howard, James L. 1999. U.S. Timber Production, Trade, Consumption, and Price Statistics: 1965 to 1999. Madison: Forest Products Laboratory.

Irland, Lloyd. 2005. U.S. Forest Ownership: Historic and Global Perspective. Starker Lecture, October 27, Oregon State University, Corvallis.

————. 2006. Manomet Report. Available at http://www.eurekalert.org/pub_releases/2006-01/mcfc-mrs011106.php (accessed November 4, 2005).

Kaufman, Herbert. 2005 (1960). *The Forest Ranger* (rev. ed). Washington, DC: Resources for the Future.

Kirkland, Andrew. 1987. The Rise and Fall of Multiple Use Management in New Zealand. Excerpted from *Financial Management Systems for Multiple Use Forest Management, a New Zealand Case Study.* Presentation to Workshop for Multiple Use Forest Management, Albury, New South Wales, New Zealand, November 1–6.

Lee, Robert G. 1994. *Broken Trust, Broken Land: Freeing Ourselves from the War over the Environment.* Wilsonville, OR: Book Partners.

MacCleery, Douglas, and Dennis Le Master. 1999. The Historical Foundation and Evolving Context for Natural Resource Management on Federal Lands. In *Ecological Stewardship: A Common Reference for Ecosystem Management,* edited by William T. Sexton, Robert C. Szaro, Nels C. Johnson, and A.J. Malk. Oxford: Elsevier Science, 517–556.

Mann, Charles C. 2005. *1491: New Revelations of the Americas Before Columbus*. New York: Knopf.

Mater, C., A. Sample, and W. Price. 2002. Certification Assessments on Public and University Lands: A Field-based Comparative Evaluation of the Forest Stewardship Council and the Sustainability Forestry Initiative. Washington, DC: Pinchot Institute for Conservation.

Moulton, R. J. and G. Hernandez. 2000. *Tree Planting in the United States—1998*. Tree Planters' Notes 49(2):23–36.

National Commission on Science for Sustainable Forestry (NCSSF). 2005. *Science, Biodiversity, and Sustainable Forestry: A Findings Report of the National Council on Science for Sustainable Forestry*. Washington, DC: NCSSF.

Nelson. Robert H. 1995. *Public Lands and Private Rights*. Lanham, MD: Rowman & Littlefield.

———. 2000. *A Burning Issue: A Case for Abolishing the U.S. Forest Service*, Lanham, MD: Rowman & Littlefield.

Newsweek. 1952. Fabulous Bear, Famous Service Fight Annual Billion Dollar Fire. June 2, 50–54.

O'Toole, Randal. 1988. *Reforming the Forest Service*. Washington, DC: Island Press.

———. 1997. Expect the Forest Service To Be Slowly Emasculated. *Seattle Times*, May 7, 12.

Peterson, R. Max 2000. Discussion. In *A Vision for the U.S. Forest Service,* edited by Roger A. Sedjo. Washington, DC: Resources for the Future, 191–204.

Pyne, Stephen J. 1982. *Fire in America: A Cultural History of Wildland and Rural Fire*. Princeton: Princeton University Press.

Radeloff, V.C., R.B. Hammer, and S.I. Stewart. 2005. Rural and Suburban Sprawl in the U.S. Midwest from 1940 to 2000 and Its Relation to Forest Fragmentation. *Conservation Biology* 19(3): 793-805.

Rio Declaration on Environment and Development. 1992. Statement of principles on forests. Available at http://habitat.igc.org/agenda21/forest.htm (accessed February 22, 2007).

Sample, V.A., W. Price, and C. M. Mater. 2003. Certification on Public and University Lands: Evaluations of FSC and SFI by the Forest Managers. *Journal of Forestry* 101(8): 21–25.

Sampson, R. Neil. 1993. Assessing Forest Ecosystem Health in the Inland West. Report of Forest Policy Center workshop, November 14–19, Sun Valley, ID. Washington, DC: American Forests.

Sayer, Jeffery A., and Stuart Maginnis. 2005. *Forests in Landscapes: Ecosystem Approaches to Sustainability*, edited by Jeffrey A., Sayer and Stewart Maginnis. London, The Earthscan Forestry Library.

Schmutzenhofer, Hans. 1992. IUFRO's Birthday. *IUFRO News* 21/1: 2–3.

Sedjo, Roger A. 1983. *The Comparative Economics of Plantation Forestry: A Global Assessment*. Baltimore: Johns Hopkins University Press and Resources for the Future.

———. 1991. Forest Resources: Resilient and Serviceable. In *America's Renewable Resources: Historical Trends and Current Challenges*, edited by Kenneth D. Frederick and Roger A. Sedjo. Washington, DC: Resources for the Future, 81–120.

———. 1996. Toward an Operational Approach to Public Lands Ecosystem Management. *Journal of Forestry* 94(8): 24–27.

———. 1997. Land Use Change and Innovation in U.S. Forestry. In *Productivity in Natural Resource Industries,* edited by R. David Simpson. Washington, DC: Resources for the Future, 141–74.

———. 2000a. *A Vision for the U.S. Forest Service: Goals for Its Next Century*. Washington, DC: Resources for the Future.

———. 2000b. Does the Forest Service Have a Future? *Regulation* 23(1): 51–55.

———. 2005. Sustainable Forestry in a World of Specialization and Trade. In *Sustainability, Institutions, and Natural Resources: Institutions for Sustainable Forest Management*, edited by Shashi Kant and R. Albert Berry. Dordrecht, The Netherlands: Springer, 211–32.

Sedjo, Roger A., and Stephen K. Swallow. 2002. Voluntary Eco-labeling and the Price Premium. *Land Economics* 87(2): 272–84.

Sedjo, Roger A., Alberto Goetzl, and Steveron O. Moffat. 1998. *Sustainability in Temperate Forests*. Washington, DC: Resources for the Future.

Sexton, W.T., Robert C. Szaro, Nels C. Johnson, and A.J. Milk. 1999. *Ecological Stewardship: A Common Reference for Ecosystem Management*. Oxford: Elsevier Science.

Smyth, Arthur V. 2003. *Millcoma: Biography of a Pacific Northwestern Forest*. Durham, NC: Forest History Society.

Society of American Foresters (SAF). 1993. Taskforce report on sustaining long-term forest health and Productivity. Cited in D.W. Floyd (ed.), 1999, *Forest of Discord: Options for Governing our National Forests and Federal Public Lands*, 19–20. Bethesda, MD: SAF.

Steen, Harold K. 1976. *The U.S. Forest Service: A History*. Seattle: University of Washington Press.

———. 2000. Traditional Forestry Hits the Wall: Excerpt of Interview with F. Dale Robertson. *Forest History Today* Spring: 2–7.

Stevens, J., M. Ahmad, and S. Ruddell. 1998. Forest Products Certification: A Survey of Manufacturers. *Forest Products Journal* 48(6): 43–49.

Swallow, Stephen K., and Roger A. Sedjo. 2000. Eco-labeling Consequences in a General Equilibrium Framework: A Graphical Assessment. *Land Economics* 78(1): 28–36.

Thomas, Jack W. 1994. Oral remarks before the Subcommittee on Agricultural Research, Conservation, Forestry, and General Legislation, Committee on Agriculture, United States Senate, concerning the health and productivity of the fire-adapted forests of the Western United States. August 29.

———. 1996. Challenges to Achieving Sustainable Forests in NFMA. In *Proceedings of a National Conference on the National Forest Management Act in a Changing Society, 1976–1996*, edited by K. Norman Johnson and Margaret A. Shannon. Draft review, December 10, 1997.

Thompson, D.Q., and R.H. Smith. 1970. The Forest Primeval in the Northeast—A Great Myth? *Proceedings of the Annual Tall Timbers Fire Ecology Conference* 10(1970): 255–65.

Tilman, D., and Stephen Polasky. 2005. Ecosystem Goods and Services and their Limits: The Roles of Biological Diversity and Management Practices. In *Scarcity and Growth Revisited*, edited by R. David Simpson, Michael A. Toman, and Robert U. Ayers. Washington, DC: Resources for the Future, 78–97.

Trefethen, J.B. 1975. *An American Crusade for Wildlife*. New York: Winchester Press and the Boone and Crockett Club.

U.S. Department of Commerce. 1975. Historical Statistics of the United States from Colonial Times to 1970. Bicentennial edition, Part 1. Washington, DC: Bureau of the Census.

U.S. Department of Agriculture Forest Service (USDA FS). 2000. 2000 RPA Assessment of Forest and Range Lands. Available at http://www.fs.fed.us/pl/rpa/rpaasses.pdf (accessed November 4, 2005).

———. 2002a. U.S. Timber Production, Trade, Consumption, and Price Statistics. Research Paper FPL-RP-615. Madison: Forest Products Laboratory.

———. 2002b. *The Process Predicament: How Statutory, Regulatory, and Administrative Factors Affect National Forest Management*. Washington, DC: USDA Forest Service.

———. 2003. An Analysis of the Timber Situation in the United States: 1952 to 2050. Portland, OR: USDA Forest Service, Pacific Northwest Research Station.

———. 2004a. *National Report on Sustainable Forests—2003*. FS-766, February. Available at http://www.fs.fed.us/research/sustain/ (accessed October 7, 2005).

———. 2004b. Forest Resources of the United States, 2002. GTR-NC-241. St. Paul: USDA Forest Service, North Central Research Station.

Wear, David N., and John G. Greis. 2002. Southern Forest Resource Assessment. Asheville, NC: USDA Forest Service, Southern Research Station.

White, R. 1975. Indian Land Use and Environmental Change: Island County, Washington: A Case Study. *Arizona and the West* 17: 327–38.

Wilent, Steve. 2005. Is Forest Certification Good for Forestry? *The Forestry Source* 10(8): 2–3.

Williams, Michael. 1989. *Americans and their Forests: An Historical Geography*. New York: Cambridge University Press.

World Commission on Environment and Development (WCED). 1987. *Our Common Future*. Oxford: Oxford University Press.

CHAPTER 4

The Sustainability of U.S. Cropland Soils

Sandra S. Batie

MORE THAN 60 PERCENT of the 2.3 billion acres of land in the United States is in private ownership. Of this acreage, approximately 20 percent (442 million acres) is in cropland and 26 percent (587 million acres) is in permanent grassland pasture and range (Lubowski et al. 2006). The farms and ranches are managed by less than 2 percent of the population (Vesterby and Krupa 2001). The management of cropland soils not only influences food and fiber production but can also have a major impact on the quality of U.S. air and water, including such seemingly remote resources as shellfish beds in marine estuaries and global climate conditions. Thus, whether the current use of these agricultural soils is sustainable in the long run is worthy of close examination.

However, sustainability is a concept that has many meanings, and the definition has evolved over time. At one time, *soil sustainability* primarily referred to the soil's ability to sustain or enhance crop yields over long periods (Frederick and Sedjo 1990). Thus, factors that influenced soil productivity, such as the basic fertility of the soil resource, as well as substitutes and complements for natural fertility, such as fertilizers, farm management techniques, and the availability of hybrid crops tailored for certain soils and climates, were examined closely. Recently, soil scientists have extended the concept of sustainable soils beyond crop production to include many other functions. High-quality soils can help maintain water quality, regulate water quantity, prevent water and wind erosion, improve nutrient cycling, buffer global climate changes via carbon sequestration, improve food nutrition and safety, enhance biodiversity and provide for nonagricultural uses, such as building sites (National Research Council 1993; Jaenicke 1998; Lal 1999; Schjonning et al. 2004).

More generally, high-quality soils can maintain ecosystem stability by buffering the negative impacts of human activities, and they play a crucial role in ecosystem functioning and the provision of food. The importance of these functions is why society should care about the sustainability of soils: society's well-being depends on high-quality soils, and human activities affect soil quality.

Soils differ in their inherent capacity to function because of such characteristics as texture, structure, and fertility. This inherent soil quality is captured within soil capability classification systems, which rank soils according to their suitability for cultivation. Soil quality can also be influenced by management over time. Dynamic soil quality changes are the result of past or current land uses.

This chapter focuses on those cropland soils owned within the private sector and does not address public rangelands or forest soils. It includes attention to the history of soil management as well as policy influences on that history.

The Sustainability of Soils

The many functions of soil complicate the investigation of the question of the sustainability of U.S. soils. Not only is there disagreement about the soil's ability to provide various functions, there is also disagreement about how these functions relate to sustainability and which management practices are harmful to soil quality.

The disagreements emerge, in part, because of scientific uncertainties. More agreement on appropriate social choices may emerge once there is more certainty and knowledge about the interactions of soils and the quality of air, water, food, and fiber. However, some disagreement will remain because of differing values about the use of soils. People will differ, for example, about what they consider the ideal type of agriculture, the appropriate distribution of ownership of farms, or the wildlife or plant species that warrant trade-offs with crop production to ensure their survival. As Campbell et al. (1995) note, the classification of sustainability requires some "judgment criteria" as to what is ecologically, politically, socially, and economically acceptable. Although decisions about the use of soils can be informed by scientific knowledge, most decisions are fundamentally questions of social choice and not science.[1] Thus, it may be relatively easy to obtain some public consensus on a goal for the use of agricultural soils to ensure that society benefits broadly, not only from the production of food and fiber but also from the maintenance and restoration of ecosystem services. However, serious disagreements and political debates may remain about whether today's agriculture is on the right path to that goal in the long run.

Chapter 2 in this volume introduced the sustainability paradigms of resource sufficiency and functional integrity. An exploration of these two paradigms—with the assumption of either weak or strong sustainability—will illustrate these disagreements. The exploration will also demonstrate how differing paradigm frameworks will influence answers to the question of whether society's use of croplands soils is sustainable.

Resource Sufficiency and Weak Sustainability

The resource sufficiency paradigm is concerned with the rate at which society depletes resources. In addition, a resource sufficiency argument presupposes an objective. Historically, the concern with respect to the U.S. cropland soils has been whether they can continue to produce food and fiber over time at affordable costs. Advocates of a resource sufficiency paradigm, many of whom have a belief in weak sustainability, tend to argue that U.S. soil resources have been sustainable in that they have provided food and fiber at declining consumer cost over a long period of time.

The evidence for this argument is found in the impressive story of American agricultural productivity (Gardner 2002). Whereas most sectors of the U.S. economy grow with increased use of inputs, agricultural output in 2002 was 2.6 times as high as it was in 1948 despite a decline in purchased inputs, such as capital, land, labor, and materials (Ball 2005). Labor in agriculture, in particular, has contracted dramatically, with a significant reduction in the number of workers per acre of production (Schjonning et al. 2004). Specifically, at the beginning of the 20th century, almost 40 percent of the U S. labor force lived on farms. By the end of the century, this number had contracted to less than 2 percent (Gardner 2002).

Similarly, cropland used for crops, idled, or in pasture, which peaked shortly after World War II, has since decreased steadily (Vesterby and Krupa 2001). Today the number of harvested cropland acres—303 million acres—is actually less than the 330 million harvested cropland acres in 1910, yet these croplands are producing vastly more food and fiber (USDA 1980, 2002). Yields per acre have grown since 1935 at a rate of 2.1 percent per year (Gardner 2002). For example, from 1900 to 1999, U.S. corn yields have risen steadily, even though the land dedicated to corn acreage peaked in 1917 (USDA 2002). Many other U.S. crops have similar records of growth in yields per acre.

That dramatic productivity growth, according to applied economist Bruce Gardner (2002, *343*), was the result of four major drivers:

> (1) the development and diffusion of new agricultural technologies; (2) the expansion and commercialization of agricultural commodity markets; (3) the integration of farm people into the post–World War II period, especially through increased participation in the non-farm labor market; and (4) government policies, of three distinct types—(a) regulatory institutions that began to be introduced in the first decade of the twentieth century; (b) public investment in infrastructure (irrigation, transport, communication, research, education); and (c) the commodity programs introduced in the 1930s.

Resource sufficiency arguments frequently focus on Gardner's first driver of agricultural productivity growth—the development and diffusion of new agricultural technologies. These arguments emphasize how the use of technologies (i.e., manmade capital) and improved management skills (i.e., human capital) have more than compensated for any loss of natural fertility of soils (i.e., natural capital). One major technological advance was hybridized corn, which was introduced in the 1930s and widely used after World War II. By 1960, almost 96 percent of the U.S. corn crop was seeded with hybrids, with attendant increases in aggregate corn production and yields (Cochrane 1979).

Another important technology is the use of fertilizer to enhance natural soil fertility. Nitrogen in the soil is a limiting factor in food and fiber production. Although there is considerable nitrogen in air, its conversion into soil nitrates by soil bacteria is not sufficient for high crop yields over time. Indeed, the early historical records of the United States make clear that farmers expected "soil exhaustion" as a natural consequence of their farming, which they could only partially offset by the planting and plowing under of clover or by the addition of manure. Insufficient soil fertility seriously reduced crop yields, and in many cases farmers abandoned their exhausted lands and moved on to new fields (Rasmussen 1982). For example, in reference to southern agriculture in the early 1700s and early 1800s, Gray (1933, *446*) wrote, "planters bought land as they might buy a wagon—with the expectation of wearing it out ... Especially in the rolling piedmont lands [of the Southern states], the planting of corn and cotton ... hastened erosion, leaving the hillsides gullied and bare."

The process of declining soil fertility was halted when inexpensive commercial nitrogen fertilizers became widely available following World War II. Nitrogen-based fertilizer enhanced natural soil fertility and substituted for losses in soil fertility from continual production and erosive processes. As Gardner (2002, *22*) notes,

> During and after World War II fertilizer use took off, sustained at a rate of [an increase of] 4½ percent annually for the forty years between 1940 and 1980. One reason is that improved seeds and irrigation made crops more responsive to larger doses of nutrients. Another [reason] is the decline over time in the real price of fertilizer caused by innovations in manufacturing inorganic fertilizers.

Innovations—many of which came from agricultural experiment stations and colleges of agriculture in land-grant universities—accelerated productivity growth. For example, significant yield dividends resulted from the substitution of new plant varieties bred to have a greater capacity to consume nutrients from the soil. When coupled with commercial fertilizers and the almost universal use of pesticides after World War II, yields rose. Innovations in information and marketing technology also facilitated farmers' adoption of new production methods (Gardner 2002).

Those trends were both induced and supported by complementary government farm agricultural policies. An example is the large public investments in infrastructure development, such as the development of water resources for irrigation. The application of water to arid soils vastly improved their ability to provide food and fiber. As a direct result of these taxpayer-supported programs, farmlands receiving subsidized irrigation grew to almost 40 million acres by 1970 (Pavelis 1978; Cochrane 1979). Today, U.S. irrigated land exceeds 55 million acres (USDA 2002).

The result, over the past century, has been surplus production of food and fiber—enough to meet domestic demand accompanied by substantial growth in agricultural exports. The population of the United States grew from 75 million in 1900 to 296 million in 2005 (U.S. Department of Commerce 2005), and in 2005, agricultural exports were a record $62.4 billion (Schweikhardt and Batie 2006). Thus, fewer farmers, using no more acreage than they did at the beginning of the century, are producing enough food and fiber to meet the current domestic and international market demands—both of which are significantly larger than those in the 1900s. Furthermore, this growth has been accompanied by a decline in the average percentage of disposable income spent by U.S. consumers for food. For example, in 1950, the average percentage of disposable income spent on food—both food at home and away from home—was 20.6 percent. By 2004, this amount was 9.4 percent (ERS 2005a).[2]

Thus, advocates of a resource sufficiency concept of sustainability can point to the substitution of manmade, human, and social capital for the natural capital of soil fertility as well as to historical evidence supporting the conclusion that the use of U.S. cropland soil has been sustainable. Their assumption is that in the future, as in the past, investments in research and development will continue to yield the necessary knowledge and technologies to overcome any threats to soil sustainability.

Soil Erosion. Resource sufficiency arguments have also been applied to analyze the importance of soil erosion. Soil erosion is a natural process and is not considered a problem if the rate at which soil erodes is less than the rate at which soil is renewed. That is, soil is a renewable resource that can regenerate with the decay of natural plant cover or with certain farming techniques, such as plowing cover crops into the soil. One Illinois study showed that a farm, if managed to do so, could regenerate as much as 12 tons of soil per acre per year (Bartelli 1980), although most farms are not managed to regenerate the maximum amount of soil possible. One can compare regeneration rates, however, with a common standard for maximum sustainable soil loss of 5 tons per acre per year. On average, on U.S. croplands, a soil loss of 5 tons per acre per year translates into a net loss of 1 inch of soil every 30 years, or 1 foot of soil every 360 years (Larson 1981). Whether any net soil loss rate is a social concern depends, as is discussed in the following sections of this chapter, on whether the soils can continue to be productive at reasonable costs as well as on off-farm environmental impacts and the societal values for productivity.

When lands are covered by grasses and trees, the rate of soil erosion is slow and there can be a net regeneration of soil. But when natural vegetation is replaced with crops, unless careful management is followed to regenerate soil, net erosion rates that remove inches of soil over time can result. That is, the hydrologic response to rain and snowfall is accelerated on croplands, and water flow concentrates in a few paths on the field, leading to accelerated water-caused erosion rates. This erosion occurs as thin sheets of soil removed (interrill[3] erosion), as channel incisions (rill erosion), and as gullies in the soil surface (gully erosion). With erosion, nutrient flux through the system increases, and soils are "mined" of both organic matter and nutrients (Vache et al. 2002). Rill and gully erosion are easily observed, but a casual observer may not be aware of interrill erosion. For example, even a farm losing the large amount of 40 tons of soil per acre per year from its fields is losing only about 4 inches of soil every 15 years—or one quarter of an inch annually (Batie 1983).

In addition, erosion can also result from wind blowing over nonvegetated croplands. If rainfall or irrigation is inadequate, the exposed soil becomes dry, light, and powdery. When winds blow across such fields, detached soil particles become airborne and create dust storms. The most infamous episodes of wind erosion in the United States were the "black blizzards" of the 1930s. The so-called dust bowl of that decade was caused by farmers who plowed up the Great Plains in pursuit of high wheat prices in the first quarter of the 20th century. When the already arid plains were subjected to a serious, prolonged drought in the 1930s, there was nothing to protect the plowed soils from the wind's scouring effects.

Soil erosion affects the productivity of soil in many ways and can cause off-farm damage as well as on-farm impacts. Both soil eroded from the fields and soil deposited elsewhere on the farm can alter the inherent properties of soil, such as fertility, and damage crops. A common problem is that soil erosion can reduce the depth of the rooting zone that is favorable for plants, such that roots of crops reach the subsoils, which are less hospitable to plant growth. These same subsoils can be more prone to compaction and less able to absorb water in a manner that makes water available to the crops. Erosion can also move soil around on a field, from higher locations to lower ones—sometimes depositing sediment on and thereby smothering young seedlings, or depositing eroded soil downslope in a field. Frequently, these downslope soils are already quite fertile and thus the deposited soil adds nothing to their productivity but leaves hillsides without fertile topsoils (American Farmland Trust 1984). Furthermore, the lighter, nutrient-rich organic particles are more likely to be carried the farthest, leaving the fields and polluting waterways and lakes.

Soil erosion was a serious public concern in the first half of the 20th century in the United States. In response, a temporary agency, the Soil Erosion Service, was created in 1933. It was made a permanent agency within the Department of Agriculture the next year and renamed the Soil Conservation Service; it has since been renamed again and is now known as the Natural Resources Conservation Service (NRCS) (Batie 1983). The results of the efforts of this agency and other public entities, such as the cooperative extension service at land-grant universities, meant that by the 1960s, erosion losses had been greatly reduced from the conditions of the 1930s (Held and Clawson 1965).

Soil Erosion Data. In the late 1970s and early 1980s, data on erosion rates became available as a result of the congressionally mandated Natural Resources Inventory (NRI). In 1977 and 1982, as part of the NRI, researchers collected data on factors that would influence wind and water erosion. They used equations to estimate potential wind and soil erosion rates across the nation's croplands and rangelands.[4] The resulting estimated national soil erosion losses from croplands totaled 2 billion tons per year. One of the main conclusions of this massive data collection and analysis was that only a small proportion of the nation's croplands accounted for a large proportion of the total erosion. Only 5 percent of land eroded at rates in excess of 11 tons per acre, but these lands accounted for more than 52 percent of all the interrill and rill erosion estimated by the 1977 NRI (American Farmland Trust 1984).

Using the National Resources Inventory, NRCS estimated erosion rates (interrill, rill, and wind) on croplands from 1982 to 2001. Gully erosion was not included in the estimates. One finding was that erosion has been significantly reduced. In the aggregate, soil erosion declined from 3.1 billion tons per year in 1982 to 1.8 billion tons in 2001. Interrill and rill erosion declined almost 41 percent, and wind erosion declined by 43 percent (NRCS 2003). In tons per acre, sheet and rill erosion declined from 4 tons per acre in 1982 to 2.7 tons per acre in 2001; wind erosion dropped from 3.3 tons to 2.1 tons per acre per year. Furthermore, between

1982 and 2001, cropland acreage eroding at excess rates dropped by almost 40 percent (a total decline of 170 million acres to the 2001 level of 104 million acres) (NRCS 2003). Much of the highest annual value of soil lost to erosion is found in the upper portion of the Mississippi River basin.

Erosion, Resource Sufficiency, and Weak Sustainability. Many of the reports based on the 1977 and 1982 NRI results clearly used a resource sufficiency paradigm as their analytical framework. Furthermore, these reports demonstrate a belief in what is termed weak sustainability—that is, that the substitution of one type of capital for another (e.g., manmade for natural) is possible and acceptable (see Chapter 2, this volume). Larson et al. (1983), for example, estimated the effects of erosion on potential soil productivity for selected areas of the country by simulating soil erosion from the rates reported in the 1977 NRI data and calculated changes in a productivity index for 25, 50, and 100 years. For corn yields in the Midwest, they found that erosion explained about 71 percent of any variations in corn yields over these long time periods, with the severity of losses increasing with the slope of the fields. Total productivity losses on slopes less than 6 percent, however, were estimated to be small—less than 2 percent—because the method used by Larson and his colleagues assumed that fertilizers would always be available, affordable, and effective to offset erosion-induced loss of nutrients or nutrient-holding capacity (American Farmland Trust 1984).

Trimble and Crosson (2000, *248*) write in reference to similar studies,

> Studies of on-farm productivity effects based on 1982 NRI cropland erosion rates indicated that if those rates continue for 100 years, crop yields (output per hectare) would be reduced by only 2 to 4 percent (Pierce et al. 1984). These results indicate that the productivity effects of soil erosion are not significant enough to justify increased federal outlays to reduce the erosion …

That conclusion—that soil erosion rates are not significant enough to justify increased federal outlays—is based on the assumption that future generations are interested not so much in the productivity of the soil as in keeping the costs of producing adequate food and fiber constant. Crosson (1983) suggests that policy should be based on a "constant cost criterion of intergenerational equity," where losses of soil productivity are acceptable only if there are compensating increases in the quantity or productivity of other resources for production of food and fiber.

The resource sufficiency argument for cropland soils' ability to produce food and fiber assumes the substitutability of other resources, particularly fertilizers, for soil fertility. There are also resource sufficiency arguments focusing on the use of management skills and technologies to reduce erosion rates. For example, the 1997 NRI found that, nationally, erosion on cropland, including cropland idled in response to the Conservation Reserve Program, had been reduced by 38 percent from 1982 levels (Claassen et al. 2001). The resource sufficiency argument is that the reduction in erosion resulted from improved farm management motivated by the perceived need to lower erosion rates and protect soil productivity. The argument continues that these improvements provide further evidence of the sustainability of farmers' use of cropland soils.

Resource Sufficiency and Strong Sustainability

If the resource sufficiency argument is combined with a belief in the strong sustainability principle (i.e., substitutions of one type of capital for another are difficult and perhaps unacceptable), a more pessimistic assessment of the sustainability of U.S. soils emerges. The advocates for this perspective are less sanguine about the availability and affordability of substitutes for soil. For example, one concern is the future availability of cropland as it continues to be converted to noncropland uses (Crosson 1986). Another concern relates to the affordability of resources and addresses the role of relatively inexpensive energy in intensive, technology-dependent agriculture: Will energy resources remain affordable? An additional concern is whether technology can continue to substitute for losses in soil fertility.

Cropland Availability. A concern that reflects a strong sustainability belief is that of the long-term adequacy of agricultural land in the United States (Sampson 1981; Crosson 1982). For example, the American Farmland Trust study (Sorenson et al. 1997) reported that although the U.S. population grew by about 17 percent from 1982 to 1997, the area of urbanized land grew at about 47 percent—much of it at the expense of high-productivity cropland. Most discussions focus on the adequacy of high-quality land to meet the future demands for food and fiber, but recent terrorist events have also added the concern about maintaining enough domestic cropland capacity to reduce U.S. dependency on imports of food and fiber.

The evidence is strong, however, that the U.S. supply of food will be greater than the demand for food for some time to come. Fewer farmers produce more food on less land than in the past because of substitutions of other types of capital for cropland soil fertility. Various studies and analyses have shown that current land-use changes do not represent threats to the nation's total food production (NRCS 2001).

Nevertheless, advocates of strong sustainability continue to articulate this concern for several reasons. One is that focusing on adequate supplies of food in the near future is too myopic—they advocate a much longer time span. They are concerned that croplands near the cities are those being developed into nonagricultural uses, and that reversal of these developments is politically difficult and expensive. These advocates note that some excellent farmland is threatened by development (see, e.g., Nizeyimana et al. 2001).

Another concern involves specialty crops. Much of the specialty fruit and vegetable production occurs in Florida and California, which are experiencing the most rapid rates of land development in the country (Norris and Deaton 2001). An American Farmland Trust study (Sorenson et al. 1997) estimates that 86 percent of U.S. fruits and vegetables are produced in urban-influenced areas. Although the farmers in these areas may have benefited from close access to large population centers, competition for both land and water for urban and industrial uses is strong. These specialty production areas have substantially contracted because of urban development.

Expensive Inputs: Energy and Irrigation Water. Another concern that reflects a strong sustainability belief is the availability and cost of energy. For example, groundwater pumping for irrigation depends on energy prices that are low, relative to crop revenues. Concern that irrigation water will become scarce and expensive can be illustrated by a case study of the Ogallala aquifer. This aquifer supports agricultural activity in parts of Colorado, Kansas, Nebraska, New Mexico, Oklahoma, South Dakota, Texas, and Wyoming. The aquifer is enormous—it underlies an area of almost 220,000 square miles (Kneese 1986)—and it accounts for approximately one-third of the groundwater withdrawn for agricultural irrigation in the United States (ERS 2005b). The water is used to produce corn, wheat, cotton, alfalfa, and soybeans; some of these crops are used to support about 40 percent of the U.S. supply of feedlot beef (ERS 2005b). Although rates of drawdown and recharge of the aquifer differ from one locale to another, the overall withdrawal of groundwater greatly exceeds recharges. In effect, the Ogallala aquifer is a nonrenewable resource, similar to a coal mine. Thus, the current pumping of groundwater for irrigation is permanently depleting groundwater quantities available for future uses (Kneese 1986).

A strong sustainability concern, then, is that the drawdown of the resource will be so great that it will become too expensive to pump this water for agricultural purposes and then the Plains agriculture will have to return to lower-yielding, dryland farming. Already, some farmers in Texas have suspended the use of irrigation with groundwater because of its expense relative to the value of the crops grown.

A related strong sustainability concern is absolute scarcity—that the drawdown of the Ogallala aquifer will be so drastic that little water will be available for agricultural uses regardless of farmers' willingness to pay the energy costs for pumping. These concerns suggest that society's current cropland use of the Great Plains soils may not be sustainable to the extent that they rely on affordable irrigation obtained by pumping the Ogallala aquifer.

Erosion. The resource sufficiency advocates who hold an assumption of strong sustainability place less faith in the substitutability of resources over time than do those who hold an assumption of weak sustainability. For example, with reference to soil productivity, Larson et al. (1983) note that there are both replaceable and irreplaceable losses. A replaceable loss is nutrients lost in eroded soils; an irreplaceable loss might be the loss of water-holding capacity due to a decrease in soil depth from erosion. Similarly, Walker and Young (1986, 25) partition yield declines from erosion damage into two components, reparable damage and residual damage:

> Reparable damage is usually associated with loss of soil fertility from erosion and is that portion of the yield decline from erosion that can be restored by increasing organic matter, fertilizer, or other inputs. After economically optimal input adjustments, there will usually be residual yield damage due to deterioration in the soil environment. Reduced moisture infiltration and retention capacity, diminished rooting zone, and impaired soil structure cause residual damage to yields that cannot be remedied economically.

Thus, the advocates of strong sustainability point to the difficulty or impossibility of substitution of manmade and human capital for natural capital. They advocate a more cautious use of soil resources.

Resource Sufficiency Debates

Those who use the resource sufficiency paradigm and who also assume weak sustainability relationships have a response to the assumptions of strong sustainability. They argue that scarcity should result in higher market prices, which will not only lead to conservation of scarce resources but also induce a search for more abundant substitutes as well as the technology appropriate to their exploitation. Thus, if the availability of cropland is a constraint in a region, more resources will be dedicated to developing new land-saving technology appropriate to the region's soils and climate (Crosson 1986, 1990). Similarly, high energy prices will induce farmers to seek less energy-intensive technologies, adopt water-conserving irrigation practices, or shift from irrigated farming to dry-land farming (Crosson 1979). The advocates of weak sustainability point to a long history of such responses to scarcity that have kept natural resources prices from increasing over the long run. This perspective on the role of scarcity translates into less concern about limits to growth posed by any scarcity of physical resources, such as soil and water.

The advocates of strong sustainability counter that argument with their own. For example, Walker and Young (1986) examined whether technological progress in northwest wheat production was motivated by a concern about losses due to erosion and determined that it was not induced specifically by such a concern. They conclude that much of the yield-enhancing technical progress in agriculture has not offset erosion damage but has actually intensified it. They note

> Concluding categorically that technology offsets erosion damage because of a positive yield trend over time is a naïve view based on an assumption that yield enhancement is due to technological change induced by concerns over erosion … . Another way of viewing this conclusion is that the cost of erosion damage is likely to increase in the future. (*44*)

In addition, advocates of strong sustainability point out (1) that there are many difficulties—physical and political—in obtaining substitutes and (2) that escalating prices of food and fiber are undesirable. They have less faith in the role of technology to solve these types of scarcity in the long run, in part because they focus on the unintended but negative impacts of such technologies. Though not necessarily anti-technology, they are concerned about the type and appropriateness of the technologies as well as whether society will invest in the appropriate technology research in a timely fashion (Ervin and Schmitz 1996). They point out, for example, that some crops, such as rice, appear to have reached technological plateaus, as their yields have not increased for the past several decades, and therefore increasing yields over time are not guaranteed (Clay 2004).

Resource sufficiency arguments are mainly about limits to growth; these arguments have been going on for centuries. For example, in 1798, Thomas Malthus published *An Essay on the Principle of Population*, in which he predicted that the human population would outrun its food supply, leading to a decrease in food per capita and starvation. The prediction was based on a belief in the insufficiency of land for food production. Malthus argued that the food supply could grow only at an arithmetic rate, whereas human populations grew geometrically. Thus, the availability of food would necessarily be inadequate for the needs of a growing population. What Malthus failed to foresee was that agricultural technologies would allow food supply to also grow at geometric rates, vastly reducing the land base needed for agricultural production as well as keeping food prices low.

The resource sufficiency argument continues to this day, and many authors draw on it to make predictions or explain past events. Some predictions, like that of Malthus, have not become a reality. Ecologist Paul Ehrlich, for example, incorrectly predicted massive overpopulation of the globe by the 1970s in his book *The Population Bomb* (1968). On the other hand, geographer Jared Diamond's (2005) *Collapse: How Societies Choose to Fail or Succeed* appears to offer a credible explanation for the collapse of Easter Island society as a result of massive deforestation of the island by the 1600s.

Arguments for weak and for strong sustainability—when used within the resource sufficiency paradigm—can be compared with the more systems-oriented, dynamic approach of the functional integrity paradigm. This paradigm is more recent and draws many of its lessons from post–World War II environmentalism and the rise of ecological sciences.

Functional Integrity and Sustainability

In the past few decades, particularly because of trends in agriculture, many people have not found the resource sufficiency arguments compelling and instead lean more toward a strong sustainability assumption within a different paradigm. The functional integrity paradigm views agriculture as embedded in a larger ecological system. An ecosystem encompasses the functional links between soil, water, and air. Functional integrity frameworks consider the management of soil—not from a single-resource, single-species management approach, but rather from multiple management approaches that involve the composition, structure, and function of the entire ecosystem (CEQ 1993).

Advocates of the functional integrity paradigm point to evidence that, in the past century, U.S. agriculture has become a large-scale, high-input sector that is dependent, in the main, on mono cropping techniques and concentrated animal production. These changes in agriculture have shifted public concern from productivity to ecological sustainability.[5]

With respect to these concerns, Clay (2004, 6) notes,

> … environmental problems caused by such production systems perpetuate and intensify earlier agricultural impacts. The most damage is caused by habitat conversion (and the corresponding loss of biodiversity and ecosystem functions), soil erosion and degradation and pollution (from fertilizers and pesticides). These impacts are not new. They result from the expansion of agriculture into natural habitats, shortened or eliminated fallow cycles, adoption of double and even triple cropping schemes, introduction of faster maturing and higher yielding varieties, and of heavy machinery that causes soil compaction. In addition, the consolidation of smaller farms into huge operations, salinization of soil resulting from improper irrigation practices, use of agrochemicals, inefficient use of large quantities of water and conse-

quent creation of more effluents from farming systems also contribute to increasing levels of environmental degradation. These negative impacts raise serious questions about the long-term sustainability of high-input, intensive agriculture.

The functional integrity framework suggests that physical resources pose real limits to growth. However, the concern is not so much that society will run out of fertile soils but that the environment cannot assimilate all the waste products and provide adequate biodiversity (Soule and Piper 1992; McNeely and Scherr 2003). More generally, there is concern about the dynamic and interconnected nature of ecosystem functions and about the unintended but detrimental impacts of human activities on ecosystem functioning (Batie 1992). Goodman (1997, *190–191*), for example, argues, "Ecological principles should dominate how we think about agriculture ... Our objective must be productive agrosystems that operate in concert with natural systems rather than simplifying or degrading them."

Ecologists point to many instances in which such unintended impacts have been the result of some human activity. One example is the conversion of cropland to urban uses and an attendant loss of unique soil types (Amundson et al. 2003). Such soils may provide unique terrestrial biotic diversity of importance to rare and endangered plants or may be a source of new pharmaceuticals, such as antibiotics. Other examples of negative agri-ecological relationships include the conversion of environmentally significant wetlands or forests to agricultural uses, and the algal blooms in estuaries caused by excessive nitrogen fertilizer applications to soils upstream.

Soil management in the Mississippi River drainage basin, for example, is important for the health of the Gulf of Mexico. The gulf's hypoxic zone, about the size of Connecticut, is found off the mouth of the Mississippi River. The zone is characterized by dissolved oxygen levels too low to sustain animal life. The evidence indicates that a significant cause of the hypoxia can be attributed to nitrogen fertilizers from croplands in the Mississippi River watershed. These nitrate-nitrogen concentrations and fluxes in the Mississippi River basin increased dramatically after the 1950s, when nitrogen fertilizers came into widespread use (Mitsch et al. 2001). Because more than 52 percent of U.S. farm receipts are derived from agriculture in the Mississippi River basin, and the basin is so huge—covering over 41 percent of the contiguous United States (CAST 1999), solving the problem by reducing nitrogen fertilizer use is challenging.

That example illustrates that agriculture can be a major contributor to a serious environmental problem, but agriculture can also be perceived, within a functional integrity paradigm and with different management systems, as supplying high-quality environmental services, such as environmental amenities, including open space (Norris and Deaton 2001; Batie 2003).[6]

Soil Quality Functions. The functional integrity paradigm gives more consideration to the capacity of soils to meet a broader set of social objectives than just crop yields. Not only can high-quality soils promote plant growth, they can also regulate and partition infiltration and water runoff in watersheds, mitigate the damages of global emissions of greenhouse gases, regulate air and water quality, and maintain ecosystem stability and resilience by buffering and filtering natural and artificial wastes and potential pollutants (NRC 1993; Heimlich 2003).

Thus, one question about whether our use of soils is sustainable is, Will soils continue to be able to provide a broad range of functions? Within this broader view of functional integrity, soil is seen as a living subsystem of ecological systems. This new frame of reference has led to scientific exploration of the concept of *soil quality* (see Box 4-1).

The very use of the word quality implies a value judgment about the importance of various functions (Schjonning et al. 2004). That is, it assumes a social objective, such as the production of food or fiber, the provision of wildlife habitat, or the protection of water quality.

Box 4-1. Soil Quality and Its Functions

The concept of soil quality has had its own evolution, and there are many definitions (NRC 1993; Karlen et al. 2004). For the purposes of this chapter, however, the definition of soil quality provided by the Soil Science Society of America is a reasonable one: "Soil quality is the capacity of a specific kind of soil to function, within natural or managed ecosystem boundaries, to sustain plant and animal productivity, maintain or enhance water and air quality and support human health and habitation" (Allan et al. 1995; Karlen et al. 1997). Thus, the concept is more encompassing than the concept of soil productivity in that it includes environmental impacts; chemical, physical, and biological properties; soil uses; human health (Karlen et al. 2004); and land settlement patterns. Important soil quality attributes are texture, structure, bulk density, rooting depth, permeability, water storage capacity, carbon content, organic matter, biological activity, pH, and electrical conductivity (NRC 1993; Bird et al. 1998).

High-quality soils provide stability to agricultural soil systems, where stability can be expressed as either resistance or resilience (or both). *Resistance* is the ability of the soil system to resist changing in either function or form when subjected to a disturbance, such as a severe flood (Schjonning et al. 2004). *Resilience* refers to the capacity of the soil system to recover functional and structural integrity following a disturbance (Schjonning et al. 2004). Physical disturbances (e.g., tillage) degrade soil through erosion and compaction; chemical disturbances (e.g., pesticides) degrade soil via toxification, salinization, or acidification; and biological disturbances (e.g., monocropping) reduce organic matter, carbon, and the activity and diversity of soil fauna (NRC 1993). The quality of the soil can be a major factor in determining the ability of the soil to sustain its functions over long periods despite disturbances, including human activities.

Although most researchers agree that degradation of natural resources, such as water, is closely related to a loss in soil quality, there is disagreement about how the concept of soil quality can be made operational for improved soil management. One particular conflict involves the utility and validity of developing and deploying soil quality indices (see, e.g., Singer and Ewing 2000; Singer and Sojka 2001; Delgado and Cox 2003; Karlen et al. 2003; Letey et al. 2003). There is general agreement on the importance of managing soils to obtain those soil properties that both improve productivity and protect the environment.

High-quality soils not only supply sufficient water and nutrients for crops, they can also store, degrade, or immobilize nitrogen, phosphorus, pesticides, and other potential pollutants, such as sewage and manure (NRC 1993). High-quality soils also provide biological, chemical, and physical processes that buffer environmental changes in water quality and air quality (Lal and Pierce 1991). This buffering regulates water conservation and storage and resists wind and water erosion, limiting the unwanted "leaking" of soil and nutrients from the farm to nearby water bodies (Carter et al.1997; Swift 1997; Lal 1999; Lal et al. 1999; Jordon 2002). In addition, high-quality soils store atmospheric carbon, reduce air pollution by dust, and reduce the need for pesticides and fertilizers (Janeicke 1998).

Jordon (2002, *156*) notes that high-quality soils result from a partnership of plants with soil biota:

> At heart, the biological creation of high-quality soil results from a partnership between plants and inhabitants of the soil around their roots (the soil biota); this partnership has been called "biotic regulation" of the soil (Swift and Anderson 1993; Perry 1995) … Plants also cultivate soil biota by controlling soil temperature, moisture, and other environmental qualities. In return, the soil biota collectively supply many benefits to the plant, thereby supporting its growth. This growth allows the plant, in turn, to provide an increasing flow of resources to the soil biota. In this way, plants and soil biota are linked together in a relationship of mutual support (although interlopers such as parasitic organisms that cause soil-borne plant diseases can enter the scene).

Thus, soil microbial activity appears to be primarily governed by organic matter diversity rather than just organic matter quantity (NRC 1993), and it benefits from diversity of crops, either within a field or over time in a rotation (Harwood 1993). Therefore, agricultural systems, whether conventional or alternative, can be managed to maintain and enhance soil quality, although conscious management decisions are necessary on a continuing basis. In particular, rotations that are properly managed over time for their impact on soil biota appear to be the key to the management for soil biota (Harwood 1993; Cavigelli et al. 1998).

Degradation of Soil Quality. Soil quality can be degraded from physical, chemical, and biological sources. Physical threats to soil quality include soil erosion and compaction. Chemical threats include acidification, salinization, and reduced biological activity due to toxification from pesticides and excessive fertilization (NRC 1993). For example, even when fertilizers are applied according to recommendations based on soil tests, studies suggest that, over several crop seasons, the crops rarely use half of the applied nutrients (Andow and Davis 1989; Harwood 1993). The result of excess nutrient applications can be contamination of the groundwater or the surface water or volatilization of chemicals into the air.

Biological degradation is also important in sustaining soils and in combating plant pests and diseases (Doran et al. 1996). However, currently, little is known about how agricultural activities can alter soil's biological properties and how such changes affect soil functioning (Heimlich 2003). It is known that soil organisms contribute to the maintenance of soil quality and control many critical processes, such as decomposition of plant residue and organic material, nitrogen fixation, and nutrient availability (Kennedy and Papendick 1995).

Modern agricultural practices—the production of only a few species of crops, the separation of crops from livestock production, and limited rotations—run counter to the natural tendency for more diversity that can result in high-quality soils. Conventional systems, Harwood (1993, *49–50*) writes,

> lead, more often than not, to a decrease in soil quality, as indicated by the soil's ability to infiltrate and hold water, to maintain particle structure for optimal root habitat, and to hold and recycle nutrients. Less-than-optimal soil quality raises production costs in the long term, lowers production potential, and accentuates production variability.

Slowing, stopping, and reversing these degradation processes can improve soil quality and the ability of soil to function. However, depending on many factors, rebuilding soil with various management practices or natural processes can take decades to centuries (Lal et al. 1999). Also, improvements in soil quality alone will not be sufficient to improve, for example, water quality (Figure 4-1), if such factors as excessive pesticide applications cause runoff and delivery to surface waters (NRC 1993).

Erosion and Functional Integrity Paradigm. The functional integrity framework views soil not as a single resource but as part of a functioning ecosystem. Soil degradations, such as increased compaction or reduced soil depth from erosion, that lead to increased runoff of nutrients, pesticides, and sediments can ultimately impact water quality.

Soil erosion, in particular, can lead to biological degradation that translates into reduced biological activity, reduced waste degradation, and ultimately a decline in organic matter content. If farming practices damage the biotic regulation of the soil and destroy its structure, the soil can lose functions, such as water-holding capacity, thereby increasing water runoff and leaching to groundwater while reducing the soil's potential for abundant crop production. The extent to which this reduction happens depends on the specific soil properties, such as soil resilience. Soil resilience, in turn, is influenced by such factors as rooting depth, topsoil thickness, soil organic carbon content, plant available water capacity, and available nutrient capacity (Lal et al. 1999).

In addition to examining the relationship between soil quality and crop yields, the functional integrity framework draws attention to the function of soil quality in protecting or harming watershed ecosystems. For example, sediment, nutrients, pesticides, salts, and pathogens (from manure) are major pollutants of U.S. waters (Waters 1995; Claassen et al. 2001). Of these, sediment is consistently singled out as overshadowing other pollutants in the extensiveness of its impact and its total economic and ecological effects (see Box 4-2).

Control of erosion is best achieved when the farming operation is thought of as a system and soils are viewed as providing a range of ecosystem functions to the landscape (Cavigelli et al. 1998). This systems view is termed *field crop ecology*, a part of agricultural ecology. Field crop ecology studies the interactions among the many biological, environmental, and management factors that can influence soil functioning. The functional integrity framework leads to recognition that these interactions occur in a changing environment and that it is impossible to change one

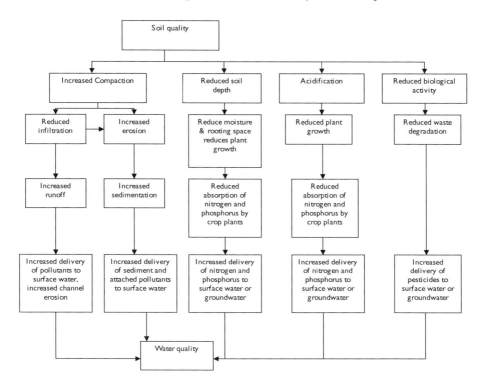

Figure 4-1. *How Soil Quality Affects Water Quality*

Source: NRC 1993.

Box 4-2. Siltation and U.S. Fisheries

Excessive siltation is a major adverse factor on the health of U.S. fisheries because it destroys fish habitat (Waters 1995). Sediment can coat fish eggs and larvae and bury streambeds under deposited layers, smothering and killing many benthic invertebrates and fauna on which fish populations depend. As Waters (1995, *169*) notes, "… in the last half century, excessive sediment of anthropogenic origin has caused enormous damages to streams throughout North America … . Most extensive damage to streams has been in the agricultural Midwest and Southeast, where warm water streams have been severely degraded by excessive sediment."

Agricultural croplands are the principal source of these sediments (U.S. EPA 1990). Surface erosion can result from poor cultivation techniques (such as fall plowing or up-and-down-slope plowing), poor soil quality, poor ground cover, and plowing frequently flooded croplands, combined with the lack of streambank protection (e.g., buffer strips). Controlling sediment delivery to U.S. waters requires that erosion from fields be reduced either on the fields or by intercepting and retaining the sediment after it leaves the fields but before it enters the water body. However, in many cases there may be extremely long "lag times" before changes in upland erosion levels result in significantly reduced sediments in water bodies because of "legacy" sediments from past deposition.

aspect of a farming system without affecting its other aspects. A systems viewpoint suggests integrating ecological management into farming systems in a way that recognizes these complex biological connections, including the connections with the health of the crop, the health of the nearby water bodies, and the profitability of the farm (Bird et al. 1998).

Sustainability Concepts: Conclusions

To this point, the discussion in this chapter has shown that sustainability as a concept does not refer to a unique, identifiable outcome. Making the concept of sustainability operational requires many value-laden choices. First, use of the concept requires a choice of objectives for society's use of soils. Are we interested in soils as part of overall ecological functioning or only for the production of food and fiber? Second, there are many social choices involved in the pursuit of each objective— such as how much substitution of fertilizers or other manmade capital is acceptable and appropriate. Other societal choices involve what costs and risks we are willing to bear. Are we willing to invest in reducing erosion rates as a conservative option to reduce the possibility of future regrets, even when the current economic situation suggests that such a strategy appears not to be cost-effective? Do we want to assume that in the future there will be affordable, acceptable technological advances that will ameliorate any damages from our current use of soil?

Rather than trying to identify sustainable outcomes, we might better ask ourselves whether society is investing in those affordable management systems and processes that improve the probability of desired outcomes, such as the provision of many high-quality soil functions. The remainder of this chapter will explore the factors that influence the quality of U.S. cropland soils, including institutional influences. These factors determine how we currently manage our soil resources and draw conclusions about whether our use of cropland soils is sustainable as well as how we might improve our management of cropland soils in the future.

Soil Management: Factors That Influence the Quality of Soils

The soil quality concept provides a way to explore the factors that influence the health and functioning of U.S. cropland soils within a functional integrity framework. As Figure 4-2 illustrates, soil and landscape conditions, under the influence of climatic regimes and when coupled with farm management systems, result in soils of various qualities. The choice of farm management systems can be influenced by a variety of institutions, particularly public policies. The quality of the soil is a major factor in its ability to perform a multitude of functions, such as providing the physical, chemical, and biological processes for plants to grow; storing, regulating, and partitioning water flow through the environment; and buffering environmental change by providing for the decomposition of organic wastes, nitrates, pesticides, and other potential pollutants (NRC 1993). However, how highly each of these functions is valued is a social decision. Let us explore each of these factors in more detail.

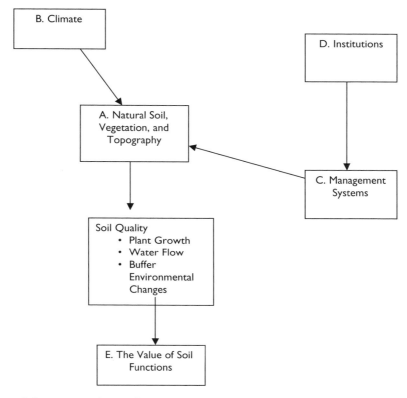

Figure 4-2. *Factors that Influence Soil Functions*

Natural Soil and Landscape Conditions

The productivity of the soils to sustain plant and animal productivity is influenced by a host of factors, including the water balance of the soil; the temperature regime of the soil and its surroundings, such as the length of the frost-free growing season; the chemical properties of the soils, such as acidity, available nutrients, and presence of toxic elements; and the physical properties of the soil, such as stoniness, depth, and texture (Swader 1980). Soil quality is influenced by the same factors as soil productivity and can be enhanced or degraded by human activities.

Cropland soils vary across the United States, ranging from poorly drained to very dry, from sandy to clayey, from acid to alkaline, and from shallow to deep. Topography can also determine the choice of crops. High mountain areas are usually in noncultivated uses; whereas the flatter land of the Midwest, with its rich soils, is excellent for growing many crops.

All other things being equal, land is better for crops if it is nearly level, with just enough slope for good drainage. About 45 percent of the cropland used in the United States falls into this category. Only 10 percent of U.S. cropland exceeds slopes of 12 percent. This figure is not surprising, since it is expensive, difficult, and even dangerous to plant and harvest steeply sloping areas. Yet even gently sloping land erodes or can otherwise be degraded. In the central Corn Belt, erosion from slopes of 2 to 4 percent is estimated to be 2.6 times greater than from slopes of 0 to 2 percent (Batie 1983).

Under a system devised by the Natural Resources Conservation Service, soils can be grouped into eight land capability classes. Soil classes I and II are generally higher quality soils well suited for frequent cultivation. Classes III and IV, while arable, have severe limitations for most common crops, and soils in classes IV–VIII are not suitable for crops. Figure 4-3 summarizes these classifications. A state like Illinois, where 85 percent of the soil is in classes I, II, and III, is better suited for crops than is Nevada, where only 6 percent of the soil is so classified.

Another way to characterize the quality of cropland is whether it is considered prime farmland. The characterization is based on physical and morphological soil characteristics, such as depth of the water table in relationship to the root zone, moisture-holding capacity, degree of salinity, permeability, frequency of flooding, soil temperature, erodibility, and soil acidity (Heimlich 2003). Prime lands are those that are the most suitable for growing crops because they have the appropriate growing season, soil quality, and moisture conditions. Prime farmlands total about 222 million acres (Heimlich 2003).

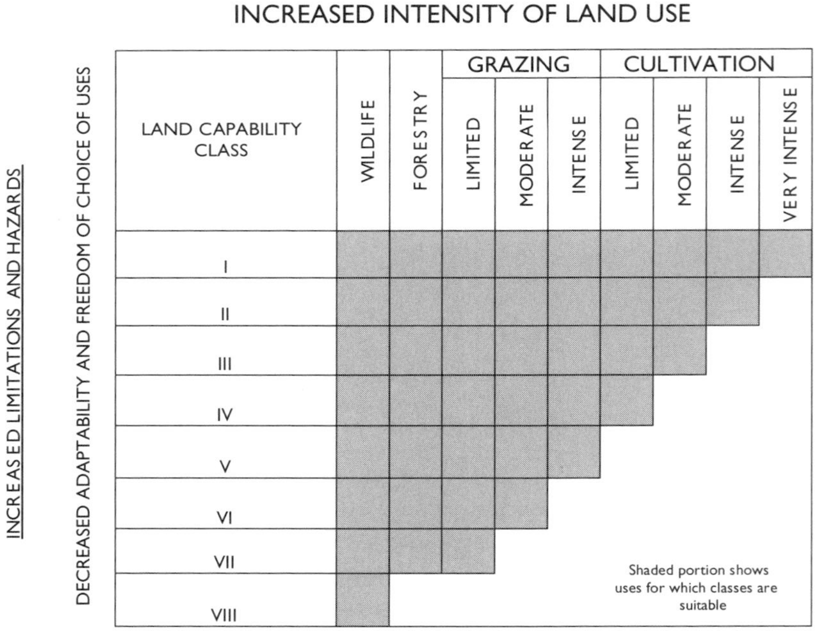

INCREASED INTENSITY OF LAND USE

LAND CAPABILITY CLASS	WILDLIFE	FORESTRY	GRAZING			CULTIVATION			
			LIMITED	MODERATE	INTENSE	LIMITED	MODERATE	INTENSE	VERY INTENSE
I	▓	▓	▓	▓	▓	▓	▓	▓	▓
II	▓	▓	▓	▓	▓	▓	▓	▓	
III	▓	▓	▓	▓	▓	▓	▓		
IV	▓	▓	▓	▓	▓	▓			
V	▓	▓	▓	▓	▓				
VI	▓	▓	▓	▓					
VII	▓	▓	▓						
VIII	▓								

(Left axis: INCREASED LIMITATIONS AND HAZARDS; DECREASED ADAPTABILITY AND FREEDOM OF CHOICE OF USES)

Shaded portion shows uses for which classes are suitable

Figure 4-3. *Soil Capability Classifications*

Source: N.C. Brady and H.O. Buckman (1974).

Interestingly, these prime farmlands are not necessarily the lands that earn the highest dollar values per acre. High-value acres tend to be concentrated on the coasts—where high-valued fruits and vegetables as well as livestock production tend to take place. Intensive livestock production accounts for some of the highest values per acre, and it requires major imports of feed from other regions and countries.

Climate

Not only are soil types and topography diverse across the United States, so is the climate. The annual precipitation in the United States varies widely across the country. Total precipitation is only part of the story, however. Rainfall varies substantially, not only in amount but also in intensity. The rainfall in the Pacific Northwest region can be substantial, averaging more than 37 inches a year, but the rain, for the most part, falls slowly and softly. In contrast, southeastern rainstorms can be intense, falling hard. Thus the potential for erosive rainstorms is far more severe in the Southeast than in the Northwest.

But potential erosion is not actual erosion. Actual erosion depends on the type and amount of vegetation covering the land during periods of heavy rains. In the Corn Belt, for example, rains frequently occur in June, when the land has been plowed and planted but the plants have not yet matured enough to provide protection for the soil. In the South, rains occur more frequently in the winter months, when the land may be protected by wintertime cover crops. Thus, rain-induced erosion may be worse in many parts of the Corn Belt than in much of the South, despite the latter's heavier rainfall. In arid areas of the West, serious water erosion may occur because there is not enough rainfall through the year to establish plants as groundcover for the infrequent rainstorms that do occur.

The location of wind erosion is different from that of water erosion. Winds tend to be most severe in the Great Plains, especially Oklahoma, Kansas, northwestern Texas, and Colorado.

Management can ameliorate some cropping limitations due to climate. Dry soils can be irrigated, for example, and wet soils can be drained, as in the case of areas that were previously wetlands, such as much of the acreage in Florida and Michigan.

Management Systems

Erosion, compaction, salinization, acidification, and toxic chemical pollution can degrade soil quality, but prudent management can enhance and raise the value of the functions provided by high-quality soils. Farmers affect the soil by their choices of crops, tillage systems, fertilizer rates, crop rotations, grazing intensity, manure applications, pesticide use, and residue-management choices (Hrubovcak et al. 1999).

Basic guidelines to improve soil quality include conserving soil organic matter, minimizing soil erosion, substituting renewable for nonrenewable resources, and using management practices that coexist with nature (Doran et al. 1999). Table 4-1 shows how some of the important soil and environmental indicators are affected by certain agricultural practices. Practices consistent with these guidelines include

Table 4-1. *Key Soil and Environmental Indicators as Influenced by Agricultural Management Practices*

Soil or Environmental Indicator	General Trend/change	Long-term Agricultural Practices Affecting the Indicator
Soil organic matter	Increase	Continuous cropping with well-managed crop residue, zero or minimum tillage, legume-based and other crop rotations, legume plowdown (green manure), cover crops, forages
	Decrease	Excessive tillage, summer fallow, crop residue removed or burned
Microbial biomass and biology diversity	Increase or decrease	Same as for soil organic matter
Soil aggregate stability	Increase	Conservation tillage, maintenance of crop residue, forages and legumes in crop rotations
	Decrease	Same as for soil organic matter decrease
Hydraulic conductivity	Increase	Reduced and zero tillage, maintenance of crop residue, forages and legumes in crop rotations – degree and extent of change vary with different practices
	Decrease	Same as for soil organic matter decrease
Soil depth/rooting volume	Increase	Conservation tillage and forage-based crop rotations should reduce erosion and allow soil-forming factors to maintain and rehabilitate topsoils
	Decrease	Excessive tillage, summer fallow cropping system, and crop residue removal or burning are the main agricultural practices that subject soil to serious wind and water erosion, resulting in topsoil removal
Water quality	Positive or negative?	Data are lacking on how soil water quality is affected by different agricultural practices; in general, zero or minimum tillage, forage-based cropping systems, and maintenance of crop residue reduce surface runoff and soil loss to water streams; excessive use of herbicides and fertilizers may result in deterioration of water quality

Note: Additional indicators include soil pH, water-holding capacity, bulk density, and nutrient retention capacity. However, they are affected, to a large extent, by factors such as soil organic matter, aggregate size distribution, and stability. These factors are listed in the table.

Source: Arshad 1996; unpublished data as edited in Doran et al. 1999.

the addition of organic matter from crop residue, manure, and other sources; the avoidance of excessive tillage; the prevention of compaction of soil; the careful management of fertilizers and pesticides; the increased use of groundcovers; and increased plant diversity (Doran et al. 1999; NRCS 2005). However, the specific effects on soil quality of such practices vary by soil type, seasonal weather patterns, and landscape topography.

Why Do Farmers Farm the Way They Do? Farmers make decisions, like other people, based not only on their subjective beliefs about the probable outcomes of contemplated actions, but also on the purpose of their farming, their understanding of the link between their farming practices and environmental quality, and the value they place on environmental quality improvements (McCown 2005). These "mental models" about their farming are influenced, in varying degrees, by their own experiences, the experiences of others, and the information they acquire. The mental models allow farmers to selectively perceive and interpret their situations. One result is considerable variation within the farming community as to the value of adopting practices compatible with conservation. Some farmers' mental models may lead to management practices that degrade cropland soils; those of other farmers may lead to practices that protect soil quality.

Farmers may not be managing their soils for quality because of missing information. That is, they may not be familiar with or understand the concepts of high-quality soils and conservation management systems, they may not believe in the concept, or they may not understand that they are degrading their soils with their production practices. McCallister and Nowak (1999) found, for example, that although farmers understand the relationships between surface soil characteristics and crop productivity, they tend not to have a good understanding of the whole-soil mechanisms that influence long-term soil quality for sustainable crop productivity. They are also less aware of the implications of their management on groundwater, surface water, and air quality (Letey et al. 2003). The researchers conclude that farmers' overall knowledge of soil could be much improved.

In addition, even if they understand how their practices affect their soils, farmers may feel they cannot afford the system changes necessary to improve their management. Or they are confronted with incentives that encourage practices contrary to maintaining high soil quality (Nowak 1992; NRC 1993). These perverse incentives can come from such things as requirements in supply contracts, bank loan requirements, and lease conditions.

Still other factors affect the use of conservation management practices. Operators of small farms who have off-farm employment may be less likely to change practices or use practices that take more time (Lambert et al. 2006). On the other hand, operators of larger farms, those who have college degrees, those who receive commodity program payments, and those who frequently seek professional advice about their farming (e.g., from university or government agency personnel) are more likely to use conservation practices that may be more management- and time-intensive (Lambert et al. 2006).

Another reason why all farmers do not already manage their farms and ranches to protect and build high-quality soils is that, while there are markets for food and fiber products, there are almost none to compensate a farmer or rancher for high-quality soils and resulting functions. So unless farmers see a strong link between these functions and the revenue they receive from their harvests (Claassen et al. 2003; Lambert et al. 2006), they tend not to adopt conservation management practices. This strong link is missing for off-farm environmental impacts that stem from on-farm use of soils. The "missing market" means that, without sufficient countervailing forces, farmers have few incentives to enhance soil quality (Batie 2001). The lack of incentives is one reason for conservation programs that provide cost-sharing to encourage the use of conservation practices.

Farmers tend to differentially adopt conservation practices based on three separate groupings: standard practices, decision aids, and management-intensive practices (Lambert et al. 2006). *Standard practices* such as conservation tillage, crop rotation, and the use of insect- and herbicide-resistant plants, have high adoption rates, whereas adoption rates decline for the use of *decision aids,* such as soil testing, integrative pest management (e.g., pest scouting), and mapping. *Management-intensive practices*, such as nutrient and pest management programs and variable-rate applications of nutrients and pesticides, require the farmer to gather and consider field-level information and use new farming techniques. Although these management-intensive practices have the potential to increase profits, the farmer must invest considerable time in learning how to implement them. The adoption rates for these practices are lower than for the decision aids and are more likely to be adopted primarily by the operators of large farms (Lambert et al. 2006).

Depending on how they are implemented, all of those conservation practices can assist in maintaining soil quality and reducing erosion rates. For example, crop rotation can interrupt the life cycle of some pests, reduce fertilizer and chemical inputs, and reduce soil erosion. However, soil quality is best protected and enhanced by leaving crop residue on the field, tilling minimally, and including legumes that are plowed back into the soil as green manures in crop rotations. In addition, soil quality can be improved if cover crops protect the soil during the winter, and if nutrient management is synchronized with actual plant uptake throughout the year (Doran et al. 1999). This type of soil management is knowledge-intensive and is unique to the climate, soil type, and soil environmental factors, such as nutrient availability, water content, temperature, and aeration (Doran et al. 1999). Some farmers invest in learning and using this knowledge; others do not (see Box 4-3).

Institutions

Producers do not make decisions in a vacuum. They are influenced not only by financial forces and personal motivations, but also by numerous local, state, federal, and international policies. These policies might be directed at environmental goals (e.g., air, water, or grazing lands quality), they might involve infrastructure (e.g., road, sewer, or fiber optic locations), or they might be macroeconomic (e.g., tax or labor policies) (Batie 2001). Public and private policies that influence producers' decisions include environmental regulations, liability rules, tax incentives, trans-

Box 4-3. Who Participates in Conservation?

Recent research finds that the role of conservation programs in influencing conservation practices decisions varies by the type of practice, the farm's cost structure, the farmer's skills, and the goals for the household. Adoption rates also differ by type of farm and farmer characteristics, for standard practices, decision aids, and management-intensive practices. Conclusions from a study by Lambert et al. (2006) include the following:

- Conservation practices that require little specialized knowledge and skill (such as variable-rate application of inputs) and cost the farmer little in forgone profits are widely used.

- Structures compatible with continued crop production, such as filter strips, appeal to farmers with large operations that receive more in federal commodity program payments than in conservation payments.

- Farm program recipients are more likely to adopt conservation practices than farms growing nonprogram crops.

- Close to 40 percent of corn farmers practice conservation tillage, but fewer than 20 percent practice nitrogen management.

- About 75 percent of the commercial farms with sales of $250,000 or more participate in farm commodity programs, slightly more than 20 percent use management-intensive practices, but only 19 percent receive conservation payments.

- Small farms whose operators report they are retired are more likely to participate in land retirement programs, such as the Conservation Reserve Program; more than 25 percent of such retirees report having planted whole fields of grasses.

- Very few farms (less than 10 percent) report wildlife enhancement practices.

- Different types of farms use land retirement and working-land practices.

portation policies, antitrust legislation, credit availability, intellectual property rights, disaster payments, education and research, crop insurance policies, international and domestic trading rules, and private contracts.[7]

Collectively, these influences can be termed institutions. They are the "rules of the game" that influence individual behavior. As Pierre Crosson (1990) notes, sustainability requires appropriate management systems, but their adoption by farmers and ranchers is influenced by incentives provided by institutions. For example, a farmer might be influenced in her choice of a management system by religious beliefs, a farm organization's advice, or by governmental policies. Federal agricultural or energy policies can provide strong financial incentives to plant certain crops or use certain management systems.

Some agricultural programs can provide incentives to improve soil quality. For example, if a farmer received taxpayer dollar from a federal conservation program to help him build a properly designed manure storage facility: the result could be improved management of manure applications and enhanced soil quality on his fields. Improved manure management can improve the soil organic matter content and thus the moisture-holding capacity of the soil. The result can be soils that are more conducive to plant growth and less likely to erode or have high surface runoff (NRC 1993).

Other programs can work against the protection of soils. For example, federal crop insurance can result in "adverse selection," where farmers with the highest risk of losses benefit the most from subsidized premiums. The program can therefore encourage farming in flood-prone areas or on fragile soils in marginal locations, or it can shift production from less intensive to more intensive uses (Wu 1999). An example is agricultural production in the Minnesota River floodplain: here, periodic floods wash away soils, fertilizers, pesticides, and crops and agricultural production forestalls wetlands restoration projects, yet insurance is available to compensate for production losses (Grunwald 1999).

Discussing the influence of all the institutions on producers' use of soils is beyond the scope of this chapter. For the purposes of illustration, the influences of agricultural policies, environmental regulations, and private contracts and other initiatives will be discussed in more depth.

The Farm Bill[8]. One of the major institutional forces influencing U.S. agriculture has been the Farm Bill. The Farm Bill is reenacted every four to five years by the U.S. Congress; it contains significant funding and provides payments to farmers, directly or indirectly, for the production of major commodity crops, such as cotton, rice, corn, wheat, and soybeans. There are also specialty programs for dairy and sugar. The Farm Bill contains the provisions for conservation programs that authorize cost-sharing of expenses with producers for certain conservation practices.

Conservation programs have been included within the Farm Bill since the inception of the Farm Bill in the 1930s. However, although soil conservation programs have always been intertwined with commodity programs, the commodity programs have been dominant (Doering 2000). Historically, conservation program budgets have been funded at a fraction of commodity program budgets. Also, in 2000, about 85 percent of the Department of Agriculture conservation budget was spent on land retirement assistance, and only 15 percent was for treatment on working acres (SWCS 2000).

However, the 2002 Farm Bill, The Farm Security and Rural Investment Act, authorized a significant increase in funding for conservation programs. Funding was increased to $13 billion, double that of the earlier Bill (Claassen 2003). Conservation has become more central to farm policy and, in the future, can be expected to receive a growing portion of Farm Bill funding.

The reason for the intertwining of commodity and conservation programs dates to the 1930s. Because of the combined effect of the Great Depression and a severe drought across the Plains, the 1930s was a period of great social upheaval. The Depression was exceptionally severe in the farm sector. In the 1930s, more than 26 percent of the nation's population was farmers. From 1929 to 1932, the index of prices received by farmers fell 56 percent, and the net income of agriculture fell 70 percent (Paarlberg 1981). This decline came at a time when there was no public welfare, no unemployment insurance, and no food stamps (Batie 1983). The federal government had little or no involvement in agriculture, since the national goal was to tame and exploit land, not to protect it (Batie and Healy 1980; Trimble 1985).

At the height of the Depression, in 1934, severe dust storms rolled across the Great Plains, causing a mass exodus of more than a quarter of a million people (Egan 2006). These storms carried soil from the plowed fields of the Plains all the way to the Atlantic Ocean. The Dust Bowl at its peak covered some 100 million acres, with an epicenter in the southern Great Plains (see Box 4-4; Egan 2006).

Box 4-4. Dust Storms in the 1930s

As one author describes a dust storm in the Dust Bowl:

> On May 9, 1934, a flock of whirlwinds started up in the northern prairies, in the Dakotas, and eastern Montana ... The sun at midmorning turned orange and looked swollen. The sky seems as if it were matted by a window screen. The next day, a mass of dust-filled clouds marched east, picking up strength as they found the jet stream winds, moving toward the population centers. By the time this black front hit Illinois and Ohio, the formations had merged into what looked to pilots like a solid block of airborne dirt. Planes had to fly fifteen thousand feet to get above it, and when they finally topped out at their ceiling, the pilots described the storm in apocalyptic terms. Carrying three tons of dust for every American alive, the formation moved over the Midwest. It covered Chicago at night, dumping an estimated six thousand tons, the dust slinking down walls as if every home and every office had sprung a leak. By morning, the dust fell like snow over Boston and Scranton, and then New York slipped under partial darkness. Now the storm was measured as 1,800 miles wide, a great rectangle of dust from the Great Plains to the Atlantic, weighing 350 million tons. In Manhattan, the streetlights came on at midday and cars used their headlights to drive (Egan 2006, *150–151*).

These twin forces—the Great Depression and the Dust Bowl—energized a new concept: that government should have responsibility for the economy. This concept was institutionalized in the New Deal of President Franklin D. Roosevelt's administration. One policy response was the Soil Conservation Act, which declared that the United States was "to provide permanently for the control and prevention of soil erosion and thereby, to preserve natural resources, control floods, prevent impairment of reservoirs, and maintain the navigability of rivers and harbors, protect public health, public lands, and relieve unemployment" (Batie 1983, 4).

Another policy vehicle to implement the New Deal was the Agricultural Adjustment Act of 1933, which was designed to increase the purchasing power of farmers and the consumption of manufactured goods. Because many policymakers thought the farm problem was caused by overproduction, farmers were paid to take crops out of production (Batie 1985). However, in 1936, the Supreme Court found the Agricultural Adjustment Act of 1933 unconstitutional. In an effort to pay farmers to limit production despite the Court's ruling, Congress amended the Soil Conservation Act to become the Soil Conservation and Domestic Allotment Act of 1936 (Kramer and Batie 1985). This act provided a legal avenue for farmers to be paid for reducing "soil-depleting crops," which were also the crops that were in surplus. Thus, two objectives—soil conservation and farm income support—became intertwined and have remained intertwined throughout a procession of Farm Bills, from 1936 to the present.

Starting in the 1930s, some farmers were paid to place land in "conservation reserves" and retire them from crop production. The policy purpose was both to limit supply of agricultural products (and thus raise prices of these products while reducing budgetary outlays) and to protect soil from wind and water erosion (Ervin et al. 1998; Ribaudo and Caswell 1999). Because the dominant program goal was to improve farm income, those who implemented the programs paid scant attention to whether the retired lands actually needed protection from wind and water erosion. Indeed, until 1985, the taxpayer cost-shared conservation investments were often directed at revenue-enhancing on-farm activities, such as subsidized irrigation, the liming or fertilizing of soils, or the draining of wetlands. Furthermore, conservation payments have always included payments for the retirement of croplands—regardless of the cost-effectiveness of these investments for conservation purposes.

When crop prices were high, the Farm Bill tended to encourage farmers to return retired land to crop production, negating wind and water erosion protection on these lands. In the 1950s, for example, the Farm Bill authorized a "soil bank" to set aside lands from production and plant them in grasses and trees. But in 1972, an export boom occurred, brought on in part by a change in how commodity farmers were paid, from price supports to target prices. This policy made U.S. agricultural products more competitive in world markets. In response to the agricultural export boom, the soil bank payments ended, and farmers were urged to plant "fencerow to fencerow."

After 1985, however, conservation programs became more tailored to environmental problems, and each Farm Bill since 1985 has paid increasing attention to environmental issues (see Box 4-5).

Farm Bill commodity programs have had a strong influence on the choice and geography of crops as well as management practices (NRC 1993). The 1936 policy decision to pay producers of only some commodities—corn, cotton, soybeans, and wheat—created incentives for farmers to plant those crops and maximize the number of bushels per acre. Although recent Farm Bills have attempted to modify some of these incentives, they nonetheless remain influential. The incentive to maximize production discourages appropriately managed rotations, which would help achieve the high soil microbial activity in soil that is necessary for high-quality soils (Harwood 1993). Furthermore, the program crops are those that are more soil eroding (Reichelderfer 1985).

The policy of rewarding producers for high yields of commodity crops may have also led to more intensive methods, such as using large volumes of pesticides and fertilizers. Also, the incentive to maximize bushels results in producers' removing natural habitat, such as fencerows, hedgerows, or ponds, to make more room for crop production. The less diverse landscape has reduced wildlife habitat from what would have been the case with more diverse farming operations (Soule and Piper 1992; Sandiford-Rossmiller 1997).

Not all the incentives for intensive agriculture were created by the Farm Bill, however. Only some cropland acreage receives commodity program payments.

Box 4-5. Farm Bill Environmental Programs

Conservation programs have been almost entirely voluntary, on the assumption that farmers are land stewards who require only some financial and technical assistance to conserve soils. Moreover, since agricultural lands are in private ownership, there is a bias toward compensating farmers for any changes in land management that the public asks of them. Of the many current voluntary conservation programs, three large ones are the Conservation Reserve Program, the Environmental Quality Incentives Program, and the Conservation Security Program.

When the export boom of the 1970s ended and agricultural prices fell, a new federal land conservation initiative was authorized within the 1985 Farm Bill, the Conservation Reserve Program (Hummon and Casey 2004). This program makes yearly payments to farmers who voluntarily retire croplands for 10 to 15 years. Like earlier programs, it has multiple objectives, which reduces its effectiveness as a soil conservation and water quality protection program (Claassen et al. 2001). Since 1996, farmers have had the option of using the payments to develop riparian buffers and other working-land conservation practices. By 2004, nearly 35 million acres had been enrolled in the program, at a cost of $1.8 billion (USDA 2005).

In 1997, the Conservation Reserve Enhancement Program provided the possibility of a federal-state partnership to target farmlands in specific geographic areas for retirement as part of the Conservation Reserve Program. Nearly 600,000 acres had been enrolled in this program by 2004 (USDA 2005).

The Environmental Quality Incentives Program is an environmentally oriented program authorized in the 1996 Farm Bill; its focus is working land. Although the objective is to encourage producers, including livestock producers, to adopt practices that reduce agri-environmental problems, it does not correlate well with the location of such problems (Day 2000). The multiple objectives of conservation programs dilute the cost-effectiveness of this program when it is judged only as a conservation and environmental program, but it has helped nearly 46,500 farmers and ranchers change practices and improve their environmental performance (USDA 2005).

The Conservation Security Program was authorized in the 2002 Farm Bill. Unlike the Conservation Reserve Program, which retires cropland, this program is designed to reward ongoing stewardship efforts on working land while providing incentives for farmers to adopt additional conservation practices. Unlike the Environmental Quality Incentives Program, it can reimburse farmers for existing conservation practices. In 2004, the first year of the program, 2,200 farmers received $35 million for conservation practices on roughly 2 million acres of working land (USDA 2005). By 2005, 15,000 farmers had received $146 million for practices on 12.1 million acres (NRCS 2005). In 2006, an additional 4,323 farmers participated and were paid $49.6 million (NRCS 2007).

Commercial farms that grow differentiated products, such as fruits and vegetables, do not receive Farm Bill subsidies, but many of them rely on intensive use of pesticides and fungicides. The reason for such high agrichemical use stems, in part, from consumer demand for unblemished produce, as well as a desire by the producer to keep yields per acre high. These farms can have low soil quality and thus "leaky" borders, such that some of the applied farm chemicals leach to groundwater, run off to surface water, or volatize (NRC 1993). However, on a national basis, noncommodity crops occupy relatively small amounts of acreage;

commodity crops receive an estimate 65 percent of total agrichemical applications (Fleming 1987).

Environmental Regulations. U.S. agriculture has been exempt from most environmental regulations. Much of the explanation for this exemption is found in the history of the Farm Bill. The current Farm Bill retains its roots to the 1930s New Deal period with its intellectual base of the Progressive movement. The Progressive conservation leaders of the early 20th century, such as Theodore Roosevelt, Gifford Pinchot, and Frank Newell, articulated a basic rationale for federal public sector involvement in the market economy, including the agricultural sector: that government should assist in the management of the natural resource base because resources were the source of national material welfare. Thus, the government's role was placing public lands into private ownership while promoting the development of agriculture. The result was not only the original Farm Bill, but also programs to develop water resources for flood control, irrigation, agricultural transportation, and low-cost energy, as well as subsidized railway transportation.

The Progressive Era was a time when most Americans had strong faith that science would lead to human betterment. Products of science were generally accepted as positive contributions to human welfare. The stage was thus set for modern scientific agriculture directed at enhancing productivity and improving farm profitability (Ervin et al. 1998). Until 1985, scant attention was paid to any indirect impacts from the use of scientific products.

For decades, the Farm Bill and related New Deal programs remained intact and essentially immune from major criticism because they reflected the Progressive values shared by most Americans. Federal soil conservation programs policies were almost exclusively guided by these values until the 1980s, even though public attitudes began to embrace the principles of environmentalism starting after World War II (Hays 1975).

The most fundamental divergence between environmentalism and progressive conservation beliefs was the view of the human relationship to nature:

> The traditional [Progressive conservation] viewpoint saw people (often the farmer) as managers of nature extracting a bounty to support the continued material prosperity of the nation—a not surprising attitude to emerge from an agrarian economy and a depression. To the environmentalist, the manipulation of nature by people for solely material gain was unethical. The blending of this ethical argument with the argument that human survival depended upon a harmonious relationship with the natural world had a widespread impact on public thought.
>
> The environmentalist viewpoint went beyond the argument that the nation's drive for material welfare was creating some undesirable side effects from an otherwise desirable industrial production system. These critics raised basic questions about the system itself and the economic arrangements that perpetuated it (Batie et al. 1986, *137*).

Thus, the rise of environmentalism led to the scrutiny of the federal New Deal policies that undergirded agriculture. There were also profound changes in the sector from the 1930s to the post–World War II period that fueled criticisms as well. First, the economic health of the farm sector improved dramatically, particularly for larger farms. Since the large farmers had wealth and income that exceeded that of most Americans, the historical objective of enhancing farm income was increasingly questioned.

Second, coupled with economic changes were the revolutionary technological and scientific changes that made U.S. agriculture so productive. Whereas the commercial farmer of the 1930s was likely to rely on the mule for power and prayer for rain, modern farmers were outfitted with expensive and powerful tractors, irrigation systems, and other purchased inputs, such as improved genetic stock, herbicides, pesticides, and fertilizers. However, with these technological advances came unintended impacts on water quality, air quality, and biodiversity (Ervin et al. 1998).

Starting in 1985, the Farm Bill made some adjustments in response to criticisms, such as requiring producers to meet a minimum level of acceptable farming practices to be eligible for farm income support payments. This requirement is termed cross-compliance in Farm Bills. Subsidies for draining wetlands or plowing fragile soils were replaced with penalties. In addition, attention was given to reducing on-farm soil erosion to reduce the threat to off-farm water quality.

But some of the more restrictive environmentally oriented modifications of the Farm Bill have been met with inertia and hostility by some farmers (and their representatives) who have benefited from the past Farm Bill subsidies. As a result, such modifications have been frequently diluted in their implementation and have not always been well targeted to environmental problems (Batie 2001). Thus, many of the basic philosophical premises of the original 1936 Farm Bill remain largely intact in current legislation.

Criticisms of both the commodity and the conservation programs continue. For example, Craig Cox (2005, 9), director of the Soil and Water Conservation Society, identifies the following shortcomings of the existing conservation programs:

- Farm management practices are out-of-date and unsuited for environmental management.

- The cost-share model of existing conservation programs does not work well because most benefits from desired farm management changes are off-farm.

- Paying for practices is a weak link to improved environmental performance.

- Targeting to obtain the most environmental improvements per taxpayer dollar is weak.

- Perverse incentives reward "bad actors" (i.e., producers who cause degradation of ecosystem functioning) more than "good actors."

Political discussions today concern redirecting the conservation programs so that they are better targeted to achieve improvements in environmental quality. The Conservation Security Program is one model of such a redirection toward "green payments" programs. However, many problems—mostly political—remain in designing green programs to enhance soil and water quality (Lynch and Batie 2005; Batie 2006).

Some of those who strongly criticized the agriculture sector and its use of the soil resources have turned to non–Farm Bill vehicles, such as environmental regulation, to influence producers' choice of practices and farm systems. Whereas current Farm Bill programs assume that farmers hold the property rights to the uses of their cropland and therefore should be paid for any desired changes in conservation management, much of the environmental legislation reflects a "polluter pays" philosophy. That is, if farmers are harming (rather than providing) public benefits, they should be required (via regulation) to make amends (improvements) at their own expense. This viewpoint is reflected in some of the recent regulatory requirements of farmers, including the protection of water quality from pollution from confined-animal feeding operations, the protection of endangered species on private lands, and the protection of children's diets from pesticide contamination (Ervin et al. 1998).

Environmentally oriented regulations influence some producers' use of soil. For example, the Federal Clean Water Act applies to the larger confined-animal feeding operations and requires farmers to acquire a permit to operate so as to minimize discharges of pollutants into waters. A condition of the permit is that the producer manages the spreading of manure on soils to levels that reduce potential runoff—something that can also improve soil quality. Similarly, the Food Protection Act requires that special consideration be given to the exposure of children to pesticide residues. In consequence, producers of fruits and vegetables in particular have adopted management tools such as integrated pest management (IPM). IPM involves scouting to determine whether pest damage is at "economic thresholds" that warrant action and relying as much as possible on natural predators in lieu of chemical pesticides. The reduction of the use of pesticides can improve soil quality (Doran et al. 1996).

Federal and state regulatory influences on producers are increasing, but implementation and enforcement vary across the states. Furthermore, the agricultural sector in general continues to be granted many exemptions from regulations that affect nonagricultural firms. For example, the Clean Water Act applies only to large, confined-animal feeding operations, exempting much of the nonpoint pollution from other agricultural sources (Ervin et al. 1998).

Because of changing public attitudes, the purposes and implementation of the Farm Bill, including its conservation and environmental programs, are often the subject of debate. Some draw their lessons from Progressive conservation concepts and the resource sufficiency paradigm, and others approach the issues from environmentalism and the functional integrity paradigm. Should farmers be subsidized to protect soil functioning and other public benefits, or be penalized if they harm them? The answer is ultimately a political choice, but with few exceptions, federal policymakers have favored voluntary and subsidized approaches for agricultural conservation and environmental objectives (Batie 2001).

Private Initiatives. In response to public interest in the environmental attributes of agricultural products and the environmental impacts of production processes, the number of business-led initiatives addressing agri-environmental, animal welfare, and food safety concerns has increased. Sometimes, the motivation for private initiatives emanates from demand-pull forces; that is, the farm and ranch firms position themselves in retail markets, such as those for sustainable and organic foods. In other cases, the motivation appears to be compliance-push forces; that is, the retail sector requires, through contracts, that their food suppliers participate in environmental, food safety, or animal welfare programs to reduce their liability to regulations or lawsuits (Batie 1997; Batie and Ervin 1998).

An example is the Gerber Company. The baby food company has strict production protocols that its suppliers must follow to ensure food safety. This is part of an accelerating trend in which retailers and wholesalers are influencing not only *what* is produced on America's croplands, but also *how* it is produced (Batie 1997). As more farmers face more supply chain requirements that require different soil management techniques, they will be adopting new soil management systems to comply.

Value of Soil Functions

It is a societal choice as to what value to assign to varying qualities of soil functions. History demonstrates that the U.S. public's attitude about agriculture and its use of resources can and do change over time. Whereas the Progressive-Era concepts of conservation and wise use of the soil resource for the production of food and fiber dominated much of the 20th century, today cropland increasingly has value as part of agro-ecosystems. There are many reasons for this change in values, such as the rise of the environmental movement, increased knowledge about the interactions and linkages in ecological systems, and Americans' rising incomes, which bring more political demands for environmental quality.

Conclusions: The Sustainability of U.S. Cropland Soils

This chapter's brief exploration of factors that influence soil quality demonstrates the complexity of making changes to improve the functioning of U.S. cropland soils. Farmers encounter various qualities of soils in diverse landscapes subject to differing climatic conditions. Farmers also are influenced in their choice of practices, crops, and farm management systems by a host of institutional incentives—both positive and negative—as well as their own beliefs and financial situations. That diversity means that knowledge and policies need to be tailored to the farmer's situation and resources to achieve improved soil quality.

However, this chapter also has documented that protection of the functional integrity of soils has not, to date, been a goal for many farmers or policymakers. What then can we conclude about whether the United States can be said to be on a sustainable path with respect to its management of soils?

The historical evidence suggests that as a direct result of the work of the Natural Resources Conservation Service and other institutions, such as the land-grant universities, the United States has made important contributions in managing soil for sustainability by improving farmers' knowledge and management skills as well as by providing cost-sharing and technical assistance (see, e.g., Claassen 2004). There have been significant improvements in our knowledge of soils and the best management techniques for using them. However, barriers have kept many farmers from using this knowledge and implementing these practices. And although farms of all sizes have adopted some management practices that provide environmental benefits while improving profitability—largely without financial assistance from conservation programs—producers have little incentive to adopt those practices that entail substantial net financial and time costs. However, conservation programs until very recently have been quite modest, and overall participation rates have been low, in part because of the limited funds. For example, in 2004 only about 15 percent of farms received conservation payments (Claassen 2007). The conservation programs have been hampered by congressionally mandated requirements to support farm income broadly and limit the targeting of conservation programs to obtain the most environment improvements. Regulatory programs, meanwhile, have not yet focused on agriculture, and thus we do not see significant reductions in agri-environmental problems, in the aggregate.

Nevertheless, when viewed through the narrow lens of resource sufficiency of soils for the provision of food and fiber at reasonable cost, one can conclude that the use of U.S. cropland soils has been sustainable. That is, U.S. agriculture has more than kept up with demands for food and fiber. Absent major system breakdowns, such as a serious crop disease, devastating climate change, or absolute shortages of crucial inputs, U.S. agriculture should be able to maintain adequate production of food and fiber in the future.

When viewed from a functional integrity framework, however, much remains to be done. Data show that poor agricultural practices are the primary cause of impairments in surface water nationwide. Despite the policy focus on erosion through the decades, sediment remains a major problem in waterways—along with agricultural pesticides and nutrients. As a result, many are dissatisfied with both farmers' use of soils and traditional conservation programs and are not convinced that the use of U.S. soils is sustainable.

Are U.S. cropland soils sustainable? The answer, in part, lies in the answers to be related issues: which functions does society desire from its agricultural soils, and is soil sustainability a unique outcome or a process of improving soil quality functioning? If sustainability is a process, then the answer to whether U.S. cropland soils are sustainable may well be the following:

> U.S. agricultural use of soils and the policies influencing their use appear to be in transition. The older framework of resource sufficiency appears to slowly being replaced with that of functional integrity. There is considerable inertia in the institutions that influence farmers' use of cropland soils. However, functional integrity questions are being raised—in both the scientific and the political world, and information about both the positive and the negative effects of various soil management systems is accumulating rapidly. Policy reform is under discussion. Thus, even if functional integrity is the metric for sustainability performance, we can still say that we have now embarked on a path to sustainability.

History teaches us that our ability to make transitions—like managing our soil resources to maintain their functional integrity—is well within our abilities. Cox (2005) suggests that to improve farmers' management of soils, we must translate current scientific knowledge into soil, water, and air quality planning tools, invest in the science of incentives, and invest in the science of institutions. He notes, "The really big question for the research agenda lay within the integration of social and environmental policy" (10). Conservation programs can be redesigned to better reflect the science associated with obtaining functional integrity and provide expert information on functional integrity to the farming community. Achieving sustainable functional integrity for agricultural systems will also require reforming agricultural policies to better protect soil quality. Some might argue that achieving functional integrity will also require some institutional redesign so that clear, enforceable property rights to the use of the environment are established. Such rights would imply that the public can require environmental stewardship from farmers and induce greater public and private investments in conservation technologies and practices.

Notes

1. However, researchers can help identify the trade-offs between achievements of social objectives that result from decisions.

2. Nevertheless, there are wide disparities in food security in the United States. The Economic Research Service of the U.S. Department of Agriculture (Nord et al. 2004), for example, estimates that because of low incomes, 10.5 percent of U.S. households are food insecure in that they did not have enough access to food at all times for an active, healthy life for all household members. This figure means that about 11 million U.S. households are considered food insecure.

3. Interrill erosion is sometimes referred to as sheet erosion.

4. Trimble and Crosson (2000) note that the use of equations and models within the NRI to estimate potential erosion tends to overestimate erosion rates and tons of deposited soil. They advocate more actual field testing of the modeled relationships. On the other hand, Pierce (1991) notes that these same estimates do not account for productivity losses from gully and ephemeral erosion, sedimentation, or reduced water availability. A National Research Council 1993 study, *Soil and Water Quality: An Agenda for Agriculture*, also reports that predicted erosion and yield losses do not account for other factors that degrade soils, such as compaction, salinization, and acidification.

5. These concerns extend to concerns about the economic and social sustainability of agriculture, but these issues will not be addressed in this chapter. However, it is this framing of functional integrity—that addresses ecological, economic, and social system functioning—that underlies much of the interest in the sustainable agriculture movement, also termed alternative agriculture (Jackson and Jackson 2002). These interests can trace their intellectual heritage to such early conservationists as Aldo Leopold and his concern for land ethics and the "biotic community" (Leopold 1949).

6. For example, when the public is asked about any concerns they have regarding the loss of croplands, many report that the loss of environmental and natural amenities ranks equal to or higher than the loss of agricultural production (e.g., Kline and Wichelns 1996; Rosenberger 1998; and Hellerstein et al. 2002.)

7. For a discussion of these and other policies that influence farming decisions, see Gardner (2002).

8. The next two sections of this chapter draw from Batie (1983, 1985) and Batie et al. (1986).

References

Allan, D.L., D.C. Adriano, D.F. Bezdicek, R.G. Cline, D.C. Coleman, J.W. Doran, J. Haberen, R.G. Harris, A.S.R. Juo, M.J. Mausbach, G.A. Peterson, G.E. Schuman, M.J. Singer, and D. L. Karlan. 1995. Soil Society of America Statement on Soil Quality. In *Agronomy News*. June. Madison, WI: Agronomy Society of America.

American Farmland Trust. 1984. *Soil Conservation in America: What Do We Have to Lose?* Washington, DC: American Farmland Trust.

Amundson, R., Y. Guo, and P. Gong. 2003. Soil Diversity and Land Use in the United States. *Ecosystems* 6: 470–82.

Andow, D.A., and D.P. Davis. 1989. The Ecological Role of Biodiversity in Agro-Ecosystems. *Agriculture, Ecosystems, and Environment* 74: 19–31.

Ball, E. 2005. Ag Productivity Drives Output Growth. *Amber Waves* June. Economic Research Service. Washington, DC: U.S. Department of Agriculture. www.ers.usda/AmberWaves/June05/Findinfs/AgProductivity.htm.

Bartelli, L. 1980. Soil Development Deterioration and Regeneration. Paper presented at Soil Transformation and Productivity Workshop, National Research Council, Washington, DC, October 16–17.

Batie, S.S. 1983. *Soil Erosion: Crisis in America's Croplands?* Washington, DC: Conservation Foundation.

———. 1985. Soil Conservation in the 1980s: A Historical Perspective. *Agricultural History* 59(2): 107–23.

———. 1992. Sustainable Development: Concepts and Strategies. In *Sustainable Agricultural Development: The Role of International Cooperation,* edited by G.H. Peters, B.F. Stanton, and G.J. Tyler. Proceedings of 21st International Conference of Agricultural Economists, Tokyo, August 22–29, 1991. Dartmouth: University of Oxford, 391–402.

———. 1997. Environmental Issues, Policy, and the Food Industry. In *Food Industry and Government Linkages,* edited by Bill Schroder and Tim L. Wallace. Boston: Kluwer Academic Publishers.

———. 2001. Public Programs and Conservation on Private Lands. Paper prepared for Private Lands, Public Benefits: A Policy Summit on Working Lands Conservation, National Governors' Association, Washington, DC.

———. 2003. The Multifunctional Attributes of Northeastern Agriculture: A Research Agenda. *Agricultural and Resource Economics Review* 32(1): 1–8.

———. 2006. Green payments and the next Farm Bill. Paper presented at Farm Foundation Bennett Roundtable, Phoenix, AZ, January 5–7.

Batie, S.S., and D.E. Ervin. 1998. Will Business-led Environmental Initiatives Grow in Agriculture? *Choices* (4th Qtr): 4–10.

Batie, S.S., and R.G. Healy (eds.) 1980. *The Future of American Agriculture as a strategic Resource.* Washington, DC: Conservation Foundation.

Batie, S.S., L.A. Shabman, and R. Kramer. 1986. U.S. agriculture and natural resource Policy: Past and Future. In *The Future of the North America Granary: Politics, Economics, and Resource Constraints in North American Agriculture,* edited by C. Ford Runge. Ames: Iowa State University Press, 132–48.

Bird, G.W., M. Berney, and M.A. Cavigelli. 1998. Soil Ecology. In *Michigan Field Crop Ecology: Managing Biological Processes for Productivity and Environmental Quality,* edited by M.A. Cavigelli, S.R. Doering, L.K. Probyn, and R.R. Harwood. Extension Bulletin E-2646. East Lansing: Michigan State University, 12–16.

Buckman, N., and B. Buckman. 1974. *The Nature and Property of Soils.* Macmillian Publishing Co.

Campbell, C.L., W.W. Heck, D.A. Nether, M.J. Munster, and D.J. Hoag. 1995. Biophysical Measurement of the Sustainability of Temperate Agriculture. In *Defining and Measuring Sustainability: The Biophysical Foundations,* edited by M. Munasinghe and W. Shearer. Washington, DC: World Bank, 251–73.

Carter, M.R., E.G. Gregorich, D.W. Anderson, J.W. Doran, H.H. Janzen, and F.J. Pierce. 1997. Concepts of Soil Quality and Their Significance. In *Soil Quality for Crop Production and Ecosystem Health: Developments in Soil Science,* edited by E.G. Gregorich and M.R. Carter. Amsterdam: Elsevier, 1–19.

Cavigelli, M.A., S.R. Doering, L.K. Probyn, and R.R. Harwood (eds.) 1998. *Michigan Field Crop Ecology: Managing Biological Processes for Productivity and Environmental Quality.* Extension Bulletin E-2646. East Lansing: Michigan State University.

Claassen, R. 2003. Emphasis Shifts in U.S. Agri-environmental Policy. *Amber Waves* November. Economic Research Service. Washington, DC: U.S. Department of Agriculture.

———. 2004. Have Conservation Compliance Incentives Reduced Soil Erosion? *Amber Waves* June. Economic Research Service. Washington, DC: U.S. Department of Agriculture.

———. 2007. Green Payments: Can Income and Conservation Payments Be Combined? *Amber Waves* February. Economic Research Service. Washington, DC: U.S. Department of Agriculture.

Claassen, R., L. Hansen, M. Peters, V. Breneman, M. Weinberg, A. Catteneo, P. Feather, D. Gadsby, D. Hellerstein, J. Hopkins, P. Johnston, M. Morehart, and M. Smith. 2001. *Agri-environmental Policy at the Crossroads: Guidepost to a Changing Landscape.* Agricultural Economic Report 794. Economic Research Service. Washington, DC: U.S. Department of Agriculture.

Claassen, R., K. Wiebe, and L. Hansen. 2003. Farmers' choices and the role of economic indicators in the development of soil conservation policy. Presentation at OECD expert meeting on soil erosion indicators, Rome, March 25–28.

Clay, J. 2004. *World Agriculture and the Environment.* Washington, DC: Island Press.

Cochrane, W.W. 1979. *The Development of American Agriculture: A Historical Analysis.* Minneapolis: University of Minnesota Press.

Council for Agricultural Science and Technology (CAST). 1999. *Gulf of Mexico Hypoxia: Land and Sea Interactions.* Task Force Report 134, Ames, IA.

Council on Environmental Quality (CEQ). 1993. *Environmental quality. Twenty-fourth Annual Report.* Washington, DC: Executive Office of the President of the United States.

Cox, C. 2005. Building the Scientific Basis for Green Payments—Agro-environmental Research Priorities: What Do We Need to Know? In *Building the Scientific Basis for Green Payments,* edited by Sarah Lynch and Sandra S. Batie. Washington, DC: World Wildlife Fund, 8–11.

Crosson, P.R. 1979. Agricultural Land Use: A Technological and Energy Perspective. In *Farmland, Food, and the Future,* edited by Max Schnepf. Ankeny, IA: Soil Conservation Society of America, 99–111.

———. 1982. *The Cropland Crisis: Myth or Reality?* Baltimore: John Hopkins Press and Resources for the Future.

———, with A.T. Stout. 1983. *Productivity Effects of Cropland Erosion in the United States.* Washington, DC: Resources for the Future.

———. 1986. Land Resource Constraints in the North American Granary. In *The Future of the North America Granary: Politics, Economics, and Resource Constraints in North American Agriculture,* edited by C. Ford Runge. Ames: Iowa State University Press, 149–62.

———. 1990. Cropland and Soils: Past Performance and Policy Challenges. In *America's Renewable Resources: Historical Trends and Current Challenges,* edited by K.D. Frederick and R.A. Sedjo. Washington, DC: Resources for the Future, 169–203.

Day, E. 2000. Analysis of resource shifts of the Agricultural Conservation Program and the Environmental Quality Incentive Program allocation. Unpublished paper. DeKalb, IL: American Farmland Trust.

Delgado, J.A., and C.A. Cox. 2003. Soil Quality: Similar Goals, but Different Pathways. *Journal of Soil and Water Conservation* 58(4): 170.

Diamond, J. 2005. *Collapse: How Societies Choose to Fail or Succeed.* London: Viking Press.

Doering, O. III, 2000. Where Do We Want to Go with Farm Subsidies? *Conservation Voices* April/May: 4.

Doran, J.W., M. Sarrantonio, and R. Janke. 1996. *Agricultural Resources and Environmental Indicators.* Chapter 4.2, Strategies to promote soil quality and health. U.S. Department of Agriculture. Natural Resources Conservation Service. Washington, DC. http://www.ers.usda.gov/publications/arei/ah722/arei4_2/AREI4_2soilmgmt.pdf.

Doran, J.W., A.J. Jones, M.A. Arshad, and J.E. Gilley. 1999. Determinants of Soil Quality and Health. In *Soil Quality and Soil Erosion,* edited by R. Lal. Ankeny, IA: Soil and Water Conservation Society, 17–39.

Economic Research Service (ERS). 2005a. Food CPI, Price and Expenditures: Food Expenditures by Families and Individuals as a Share of Disposable Personal Income. Washington, DC: U.S.

Department of Agriculture. http://www.ers.usda.gov/Briefing/CPIFoodAndExpenditures/ Data/table7.htm (accessed May 25, 2006).

————. 2005b. Agricultural Chemicals and Production Technology: Sustainability and Production Systems. Washington, DC: U.S. Department of Agriculture. http://www.ers.usda.gov/Briefing/ AgChemicals/Sustainability.htm (accessed May 25, 2006).

Egan, T. 2006. *The Worst Hard Time: The Untold Story of Those Who Survived the Great American Dust Bowl.* New York: Houghton Mifflin Co.

Ehrlich, P. 1968. *The Population Bomb.* New York: Ballantine Books.

Ervin, D.E., and A. Schmitz. 1996. A New Era of Environmental Management in Agriculture. *American Journal of Agricultural Economics* 78(5): 1198–206.

Ervin, D.E., C.F. Runge, E.A. Graffy, W.E. Anthony, S.S. Batie, P. Faeth, T. Penny, and T. Warman. 1998. Agriculture and the Environment: A New Strategic Vision. *Environment* 40(6): 8–15, 35–40.

Fleming, M.H. 1987. Agricultural Chemicals in Groundwater: Preventing Contamination by Removing Barriers Against Low-input Farm Management. *American Journal of Alternative Agriculture* 2: 124–30.

Frederick, K.D., and R.A. Sedjo (eds.) 1990. *America's Renewable Resources: Historical Trends and Current Challenges.* Washington, DC: Resources for the Future.

Gardner, B.L. 2002. *American Agriculture in the Twentieth Century: How It Flourished and What It Cost.* Cambridge, MA: Harvard University Press.

Goodman, R. 1997. Ensuring the Scientific Foundations for Agriculture's Future. In *Visions of American Agriculture,* edited by William Lockeretz. Ames: Iowa State University Press, 187–204.

Gray, L.C. 1933. *History of Agriculture in the Southern United States to 1860* (vols. 1, 2). Publication 430. Washington, DC: Carnegie Institute of Washington.

Grunwald, M. 1999. Sowing Resentment over Crop Insurance. *Washington Post Weekly Edition,* November 15, 29.

Harwood, R.R. 1993. Managing the Living Soil for Human Well-being. In *Environment and Agriculture: Rethinking Development Issues for the 21st Century.* Proceedings of Symposium in Honor of Robert D. Havener, May 5–6, Winrock International, Morrilton, AR, 48–59.

Hays, S.P. 1975. *Conservation and the Gospel of Efficiency: The Progressive Conservation Movement, 1890–1920.* New York: Atheneum.

Heimlich, R. 2003. *Agricultural Resources and Environmental Indicators, 2003.* Agricultural Handbook AH722. Economic Research Service. Washington, DC: U.S. Department of Agriculture.

Held, R.B., and M. Clawson. 1965. *Soil Conservation in Perspective.* Baltimore: Johns Hopkins University Press.

Hellerstein, D., C. Nickerson, J. Cooper, P. Feather, D. Gadsby, D. Mullarkey, A. Tegene, and C. Barnard. 2002. *Farmland Protection: The Role of Public Preferences for Rural Amenities.* Report AE 815. Economic Research Service. Washington, DC: U.S. Department of Agriculture.

Hrubovcak, J., U. Vasavada, and J.E. Aldy. 1999. *Green Technologies for a More Sustainable Agriculture.* Agricultural Information Bulletin 752. Economic Research Service. Washington, DC: U.S. Department of Agriculture.

Hummon, L., and F. Casey. 2004. *Status and Trends in Federal Resource Conservation Incentive Programs: 1996–2001.* Washington, DC: Defenders of Wildlife.

Jackson, D.L., and L.L. Jackson (eds.) 2002. *The Farm as Natural Habitat: Reconnecting Food Systems with Ecosystems.* Washington, DC: Island Press.

Jaenicke, E.C. 1998. *From the Ground Up: Exploring Soil Quality's Contribution to Environmental Health.* Policy Studies Report 10. Greenbelt, MD: Henry A. Wallace Institute for Alternative Agriculture.

Jordon, N.R. 2002. Sustaining Production with Biodiversity. In *The Farm as Natural Habitat: Reconnecting Food Systems with Ecosystems,* edited by Dana L. Jackson and Laura L. Jackson. Washington, DC: Island Press, 155–68.

Karlen, D.L., M.J. Mausbach, J.W. Doran, R.G. Cline, R. F. Harris, and G.E. Schuman. 1997. Soil Quality: A Concept, Definition, and a Framework of Evaluation. *Soil Science Society of America Journal* 61: 4–10.

Karlen, D.L., J.W. Doran, B.J. Weinhold, and S.S. Andrews. 2003. Soil Quality: Humankind's Foundation for Survival. *Journal of Soil and Water Conservation* 58(4): 171–79.

Karlen, D.L., S.S. Andrews, and B.J. Wienhold. 2004. Soil Quality, Fertility, and Health—Historical Context, Status, and Perspectives. In *Managing Soil Quality: Challenges in Modern Agriculture,* edited by P. Schjonning, S. Elmholt, and B.T. Christensen. Cambridge, MA: CABI Publishing, 17–33.

Kennedy, A.C., and R.I. Papendick. 1995. Microbial Characteristics of Soil Quality. *Journal of Soil and Water Conservation* 50 (November-December): 243.

Kline, J., and D. Wichelns. 1996. Public Preferences and Farmland Preservation Programs. *Land Economics* 72(4): 538–49.

Kneese, A. 1986. Water Resources Constraints: The Case of the Ogallala Aquifer. In *The Future of the North American Granary: Politics, Economics, and Resource Constraints in North American Agriculture,* edited by C.F. Runge. Ames: Iowa State University Press, 163–70.

Kramer, R.A., and S.S. Batie. 1985. The Cross-compliance Concept in Agricultural Programs: The New Deal to the Present. *Agricultural History* 59 (April): 30719.

Lal, R. (ed.). 1999. *Soil Quality and Soil Erosion.* Soil and Water Conservation Society. Boca Raton, FL: CRC Press.

Lal, R., and F.J. Pierce. 1991. The Vanishing Resource. In *Soil Management for Sustainability,* edited by R. Lal and F. Pierce. Ankeny, IA: Soil and Water Conservation Society of America, 1–5.

Lal, R., D.L. Mokema, and B. Lowery. 1999. Relation Between Soil Quality and Erosion. In *Soil Quality and Soil Erosion,* edited by Rattan Lal. Soil and Water Conservation Society. Boca Raton, FL: CRC Press, 237–58.

Lambert, D., P. Sullivan, R. Claassen, and L. Foreman. 2006. *Conservation-Compatible Practices and Programs: Who Participates?* ERR-14. Economic Research Service. Washington, DC: U.S. Department of Agriculture.

Larson, W.E. 1981. Protecting the Soil Resource Base. *Journal of Soil and Water Conservation* 36(1): 13–16.

Larson, W.E., F.J. Pierce, and R.H. Dowdy. 1983. The Threat of Soil Erosion to Long-Term Soil Erosion in the United States. *Science* 219: 458–65.

Leopold, A. 1949. *A Sand County Almanac.* New York: Ballantine Books.

Letey, J., R.E. Sojka, D.R. Upchurch, D.K. Cassel, K.R. Olson, W.A. Payne, S.E. Petrie, G.H. Price, R.J. Reginato, H.D. Scott, P.J. Smethurst, and G.B. Triplett. 2003. Deficiencies in the Soil Quality Concept and Its Application. *Journal of Soil and Water Conservation* 58(4): 180–87.

Lubowski, R.N., M. Vesterby, S. Bucholtz, A. Baez, and M. J. Roberts. 2006. *Major Uses of Land in the United States, 2002.* EIB-14. Economic Research Service. Washington, DC: U.S. Department of Agriculture.

Lynch, S., and S.S. Batie (eds.) 2005. *Building the Scientific Basis for Green Payments.* Washington, DC: World Wildlife Fund.

Malthus, T.R. 1798. *An Essay on the Principle of Population.* London: J. Johnson.

McCallister, R., and P. Nowak. 1999. Whole-soil Knowledge and Management: A Foundation of Soil Quality. In *Soil Quality and Soil Erosion,* edited by Rattan Lal. Ankeny, IA: Soil and Water Conservation Society, 173–94.

McCown, R.L. 2005. New Thinking about Farmer Decision Maker. In *The Farmer's Decision: Balancing Economic Agriculture Production with Environmental Quality,* edited by Jerry L. Hatfield. Ankeny, IA: Soil and Water Conservation Society, 11–44.

McNeely, J.A., and S.J. Scherr. 2003. *Ecoagriculture: Strategies to Feed the World and Save Biodiversity.* Washington, DC: Island Press.

Mitsch, W.J., J.W. Day Jr., J.W. Gilliam, P.M. Groffman, D.L. Hey, G.W. Randall, and N. Wang. 2001. Reducing Nitrogen Loading to the Gulf of Mexico from the Mississippi River Basin: Strategies to Counter a Persistent Ecological Problem. *BioScience* 51(5): 373–88.

National Research Council (NRC). 1993. *Soil and Water Quality: An Agenda for Agriculture.* Washington, DC: National Academy of Sciences.

Natural Resources Conservation Service (NRCS). 2001. 1997 National Resources Inventory Summary Report. 1997 National Resource Inventory. Washington, DC: U.S. Department of Agriculture. http://www.nhq.nrcs.usda.gov/NRI/1997/summary_report/original/contents.html (accessed March 15, 2006).

———. 2003. National Resources Inventory: 2001 Annual NRI. Soil Erosion. Washington, DC: U.S. Department of Agriculture. http://www.nrcs.usda.gov/Technical/land/nri01/ (accessed March 25, 2006).

————. 2005. Soil Quality Concepts. Washington, DC: U.S. Department of Agriculture. http://soils.usda.gov/sqi/concepts/index.html (accessed November 4, 2005).

————. 2007. Conservation Security Program: FY 2006 Contracts Approved by State. www.nrcs.usda.gov/programs/csp (accessed February 26, 2007).

Nizeyimana, E.L, G.W. Peterson, M.L. Imhoff, H.R. Sinclair Jr., S.W. Waltman, D.S. Reed-Margetan, E.R. Levine, and J.M. Russo. 2001. Assessing the Impact of Land Conservation to Urban Uses on Soils with Different Productivity Levels in the USA. *Soil Science Society of America Journal* 65: 391–402.

Nord, M., M. Andrews, and S. Carlson. 2004. *Household Food Security in the United States. 2003.* Food Assistance and Nutrition Research Report 42. Economic Research Service. Washington, DC: U.S. Department of Agriculture.

Norris, P., and B.J. Deaton. 2001. *Understanding the Demand for Farmland Preservation: Implications for Michigan Policies.* Staff Paper 2001-18. Department of Agricultural Economics. East Lansing: Michigan State University.

Nowak, P. 1992. Why Farmers Adopt Production Technology. *Journal of Soil and Water Conservation* 47: 14–16.

Paarlberg, D. 1981. Effects of New Deal Farm Programs on the Agricultural Agenda a Half Century Later and Prospects for the Future. *Journal of Agricultural Economics* 65: 1163–67.

Pavelis, G.A. 1978. *Natural Resource Capital Stocks: Measurement and Significance for U.S. Agriculture Since 1900.* Economics, Statistics, and Cooperative Service, U.S. Department of Agriculture. Washington, DC: Government Printing Office.

Perry, D.A. 1995. Self-organizing Systems Across Scale. *Trends in Ecology and Evolution* 10: 241–44.

Pierce, F.J. 1991. Erosion Productivity Impact Prediction. In *Soil Management for Sustainability,* edited by R. Lal and F.J. Pierce. Ankeny, IA: Soil and Water Conservation Society, 53–83.

Pierce, F.J., R.H. Dowdy, W.E. Larson, and W.A.P. Graham. 1984. Soil Productivity in the Cornbelt: An Assessment of Erosion's Long Term Effects. *Journal of Soil and Water Conservation* 39: 131–38.

Rasmussen, W.D. 1982. History of Soil Conservation: Institutions and Incentives. In *Soil Conservation Policies, Institutions and Incentives,* edited by H.G. Halcrow, Earl O. Heady, and M. L. Cotner. Ankeny, IA: Soil Conservation Society of America, 3–10.

Reichelderfer, K. 1985. *Do USDA Farm Program Participants Contribute to Soil Erosion?* Agricultural Economics Report 532. Economic Research Service. Washington, DC: U.S. Department of Agriculture.

Ribaudo, M., and M. Caswell. 1999. In *Flexible Incentives for the Adoption of Environmental Technologies in Agriculture,* edited by Frank Casey, Andrew Schmitz, Scott Swinton, and David Zilberman. Boston: Kluwer Academic Publishers, 7–26.

Rosenberger, R.S. 1998. Public Preferences Regarding the Goals of Farmland Preservation Programs: Comment. *Land Economics* 74: 557–65.

Sampson, R.N. 1981. *Farmland or Wasteland: A Time to Choose.* Emmaus, PA: Rodale Press.

Sandiford-Rossmiller, F. 1997. Environmental Issues in Agriculture and Rural Areas. In *Searching for Common Ground: European Union Enlargement and Agricultural Policy,* edited by K. Hathaway and E. Hathaway. Agricultural Policy and Economic Development Series. Rome: Food and Agriculture Organization, 91–108.

Schjonning, P., S. Elmholt, and B.T. Christensen (eds.). 2004. *Managing Soil Quality: Challenges in Modern Agriculture.* Cambridge, MA: CABI Publishing.

Schweikhardt, D., and S.S. Batie. 2006. Trade and Policy Outlook. In *2006 Annual Agricultural Outlook,* edited by Hilker. Staff Paper 2006-11. Department of Agricultural Economics. East Lansing: Michigan State University, 2–4.

Singer, M.J., and S.A. Ewing. 2000. Soil Quality. In *Handbook of Soil Science,* edited by M. Summer. Boca Raton, FL: CRC Press, 271–98.

Singer, M.J., and R.E. Sojka. 2001. Soil Quality. In *Yearbook of Science.* New York: McGraw Hill, 312–14.

Soil and Water Conservation Society (SWCS). 2000. *Reforming the Farm Bill: Ideas from the Grassroots.* Seeking Common Ground for Conservation: An Agricultural Conservation Policy Project. Ankeny, IA.

Sorensen, A.A., R.P. Greene, and K. Russ. 1997. *Farming on the Edge.* American Farmland Trust. Northern Illinois University.

Soule, J.D., and J.K. Piper. 1992. *Farming in Nature's Image: An Ecological Approach to Agriculture.* Washington, DC: Island Press.

Swader, F.N. 1980. Soil Productivity and the Future of American Agriculture. In *The Future of American Agriculture as a Strategic Resource,* edited by S.S. Batie and R.G. Healy. Washington, DC: Conservation Foundation, 79–116.

Swift, M.J. 1997. Biological Management of Soil Fertility as a Component of Sustainable Agriculture: Perspective and Prospects with Particular Reference to Tropical Regions. In *Soil Ecology in Sustainable Agricultural Systems,* edited by L. Brussard and R. Ferra-Cerrato. Boca Raton, FL: CRC Press, 137–57.

Swift, M.J., and J.M. Anderson. 1993. Biodiversity and Ecosystem Function in Agricultural Systems. In *Biodiversity and Ecosystem Function,* edited by E.D. Schultz and H.A. Mooney. Berlin: Springer-Verlag, 15–41.

Trimble, S.W. 1985. Perspectives on the History of Soil Erosion Control in the Eastern United States. *Agricultural History* 59(2): 162–80.

Trimble, S.W., and P. Crosson. 2000. U.S. Soil Erosion Rates—Myth and Reality. *Science* 289 (5477): 248–50.

U.S. Department of Agriculture (USDA). 1980. Economics, Statistics, and Cooperative Service. *Changes in Farm Production and Efficiency, 1978.* Statistical Bulletin No. 628: Washington, DC.

———. 2002. National Agricultural Statistics Service. 2002 Census of Agriculture. http://www.nass.usda.gov/Census_of_Agriculture/ (accessed March 15, 2006).

———. 2005. Johanns Lauds Voluntary Conservation on Private Lands. Farm Service Agency Newsroom Release 0115.05, April 4. http://www.fsa.usda.gov/pas/FullStory.asp?StoryID=2108 (accessed March 15, 2006).

U.S. Department of Commerce. 2005. Nation's Population Approaches 298 Million on New Year's Day. U.S. Census. http://www.census.gov/Press-Release/www/releases/archives/population/006142.html (accessed March 17, 2006).

U.S. Environmental Protection Agency (U.S. EPA). 1990. National Water Quality Inventory. 1988 Report to Congress. EPA-440-4-90-003. Office of Water. Washington, DC.

Vache, K., J.M. Eilers, and M. Santelmann. 2002. Water Quality Modeling of Alternative Agricultural Scenarios in the U.S. Corn Belt. *Journal of the American Water Resources Association* 36(5): 1101–17.

Vesterby, M., and K.S. Krupa. 2001. *Major Uses of Land in the United States, 1997.* Statistical Bulletin 973. Resource Economics Division, Economic Research Service. Washington, DC: U.S. Department of Agriculture.

Walker, D.J., and D.L. Young. 1986. Assessing Soil Erosion Productivity Damage. In *Soil Conservation: Assessing the National Resources Inventory* (vol. II). National Research Council. Washington, DC: National Academy Press, 21–62.

Waters, T.F. 1995. *Sediment in Streams: Sources, Biological Effects and Control.* Monograph 7. Bethesda, MD: American Fisheries Society.

Wu, J. 1999. Crop Insurance, Acreage Decisions, and Nonpoint-Source Pollution. *American Journal of Agricultural Economics* 81: 305–20.

CHAPTER 5

Water Resources Management and the Challenge of Sustainability

Leonard Shabman

WATER IS NEEDED to produce things people value, whether for manufacturing automobiles, growing lettuce and strawberries, ensuring greener lawns and full swimming pools, or for automated dishwashing to save time and improve household sanitation.[1] And water provides for more than material comforts. In art, music, and literature, water in the landscape is a symbol of pleasure and inspiration. Water is the focus of even the least wild places—Japanese gardens and Las Vegas hotel fountains. Rivers, lakes, and reservoirs behind dams are at the center of many recreation experiences. To secure all these uses of water, significant public and private investments have been made to control and manage the flows of water in rivers and lakes and into estuaries. Dams create reservoirs that store rainfall and snowmelt from wet times to provide water during dry times. Pipelines and canals move water over long distances. Wells are drilled and water is pumped to the surface and used in homes and on farms.

Water availability and the adequacy of the nation's water supply infrastructure to serve those many uses is a long standing national concern (Select Committee 1961; Wollman and Bonem 1971; U.S. WRC 1978; U.S. GAO 1982). Recently, Congress requested a review of "the future of water availability for the nation [because] water is vital to the needs of growing communities, agriculture, energy production, and critical ecosystems" (USGS 2002; Barlow et al. 2004). The Executive Office of the President (Subcommittee on Water Availability and Quality 2004) and the U.S. Department of the Interior (2005) recently issued reports on future water availability. A report from the National Research Council (2001c, v) concludes,

In this new century, the United States will be challenged to provide sufficient quantities of high-quality water to its growing population. Water is a limiting resource for human well-being and social development, and projections of population growth as well as changing social values suggest that demands for this resource will increase significantly. These projections have fueled concerns among the public and water resources professionals alike about the adequacy of future water supplies, the sustainability and restoration of aquatic ecosystems, and the viability of our current water resource research programs and our institutional and physical water resource infrastructures.

Contemporary statements of concern about the adequacy of the water supply frequently include the term *sustainability*. A collaboration of federal and state agencies that has proposed principles for water management calls itself the Sustainable Water Resources Roundtable (Heinz 2004). Scholarly articles that call for sustainable water use cite the Brundtland Commission principles—that the laws and regulations governing water use and management must serve the welfare of future as well as present generations (Loucks et al. 2000). A century ago Gifford Pinchot, a leader of the Progressive conservation movement, expressed a similar concern for the future when defining resource (including water) conservation. One of the great contributions of the conservation idea, he said, was that it "added to the worn and well known phrase 'the greatest good for the greatest number', the additional words 'for the longest time'" (Nash 1968, *61*).

For much of the 20th century, conservation of water to meet the needs of present and future generations meant dams to capture water that would otherwise flow to the sea, and levees and channels to direct river flows. These structures would control floods, maintain consistent channel depths for navigation, and allow agriculture to flourish and great cities to be built in arid areas. However, the word *sustainability*, as often applied to water resources management, is a call for fundamentally different management goals, policies, and investment strategies than those advanced by the Progressives. Sustainable water management means that existing water control structures will be managed differently—in some cases even be removed—and withdrawals of water from streams and lakes will be minimized wherever possible to return at least some natural variability to river flows.[2]

This paper provides the technical and historical background for understanding how the theme of sustainable water use challenges the nation's longstanding approach to water management. The next section is briefly reviews basic hydrologic principles, water availability, and water use—necessary background for the sections that follow on the nation's water development history, the meaning of sustainable water use, and the implications for future water management.

Nature's Water Supply

Annual precipitation for the nation averages nearly 30 inches. Although two-thirds evaporates or is quickly transpired by grasslands, forests, and crops, the remaining one-third, 1,400 billion gallons per day (bgd) for an average year, runs off the land into streams, rivers, and lakes and percolates into the ground (Frederick 1991). To put this volume of water into perspective, for the year 2000, U.S. water withdrawals from surface water for all uses were about 260 bgd (Hutson et al. 2004), or about 20 percent of average daily runoff. Of course, precipitation and runoff vary greatly across regions and across time within regions. Average annual precipitation ranges from more than 54 inches in the Gulf Coast states of Mississippi, Louisiana, and Alabama to 9 inches in Nevada. Annual runoff can vary over great distances (arid West to humid East) but also may differ over smaller areas (west slope and east slope of the Rocky Mountains) or in urban versus rural areas in a single eastern county. Within any region and across regions, runoff varies with soil type, topography, temperature, vegetation, and land use. Precipitation and runoff also vary greatly between years and within a year. In Florida, flows are highest in the summer and early fall, when rainfall is the heaviest, and then taper off for extended periods. In northern California, much of the precipitation arrives as snow in the mountains, and the heaviest runoff is from spring snowmelt. Regions with substantial precipitation may receive that water in a few large tropical storms in the summer and early fall (NRC 1999b).

Water science describes this variability among regions and across time by comparing the water available in watersheds. A watershed (also called a river basin or drainage basin) is an area of land that catches precipitation that then drains or seeps into wetlands, streams, rivers, lakes, and aquifers. Watershed boundaries are defined by choosing a location in a stream or river and then tracing the runoff that arrives from all land upstream of that point. Depending on the downstream measurement location, watershed sizes range from large river systems to areas of just a few acres. Small streams discharge into larger ones and then into the nation's major rivers, so smaller watersheds are always nested within larger ones. A standardized identification system for watersheds recognizes this nesting of smaller units inside larger ones (NRC 1999b).

Stream gauges measure the flow at fixed locations in watersheds, and a plot of measured stream flow is reported as a hydrograph. A plot of average daily flows over a year describes the annual variability of available water. A hydrograph that reports average monthly flow will show that there are wetter and drier months throughout the year. Another hydrograph will show that even the driest month can have high flows in some years and even the wettest months may have occasional low-flow periods (NRC 2004b).

Stream flows in a watershed depend not only on runoff but also on each stream's connection to underlying aquifers—subsurface areas of sand, gravel, and soil that are saturated with water. Aquifers are characterized by how readily they recharge and discharge. Confined aquifers are overlain by relatively impermeable materials. In confined aquifers, recharge from the surface has effectively ceased, and its water is "stock," just like in a coal mine: pumping from that storage is identical to mining a coal deposit. Unconfined aquifers are sufficiently permeable to accept water that percolates from above or enters laterally from rivers and lakes (recharge); they can then release water over time to surface sources (discharge). Water in an unconfined aquifer is linked to the water flowing in the lakes and streams to which it is connected. However, the movement of water between surface and groundwater locations does not follow surface watershed boundaries, and the understanding of these movements is still developing (Alley et al. 2002). Freshwater stored in aquifers within 2,500 feet of the earth's surface is equivalent to more than 50 years of the annual renewable supply of 1,400 bgd (Frederick 1991).

Water Use

The freshwater on the surface and in aquifers serves people in many ways. *Water withdrawal use* means removing water from a stream, lake, or aquifer for use in households, public and commercial facilities, agricultural production, and manufacturing. Some of the withdrawn water may be returned to the same watershed after its use in homes, business, and industry. For example, at the large watershed scale, water withdrawn for use in the upper Mississippi River is returned to the streams, modestly diminished in quantity, to be used many times over as the river flows to the Gulf of Mexico. *Consumptive water use* is, with reference to the point of withdrawal, water that is lost to evaporation and transpiration, incorporated into a product and shipped out of the watershed, or discharged to a different watershed or groundwater aquifer. Consumptive use of water denies others in the same watershed the use of that water and can alter seasonal and interannual stream flows. Most water uses are not highly consumptive, the exception being irrigation. Of course, when withdrawn water is transferred out of a watershed of any size, the withdrawal is a fully consumptive water use from the perspective of people in the watershed of origin. Water has long been transferred from the Colorado River to California cities, where it is used and then discharged to local streams from wastewater treatment plants or used to recharge aquifers used for water supply (NRC 1999b). The transferred water is a fully consumptive use of water in the Colorado River watershed, even though the water is reused in California. Water transfers and consumptive use may not be the result of intent or design. In the Ipswitch River basin in northeastern Massachusetts, groundwater is withdrawn and used in that area and then sent to a wastewater treatment plant that does not discharge back to streams in the Ipswitch watershed. The result is that the groundwater withdrawal use diminishes both the aquifer storage in the original area as well as stream flows in that same area, which effectively makes the groundwater withdrawal a consumptive use of the Ipswitch River water (USGS 2002, *24*).

For the year 2000, total U.S withdrawals of freshwater for all uses were 345 billion gallons per day, of which 76 percent was from surface water (Hutson et al. 2004).[3] About 39 percent of the 345 bgd was withdrawn from surface water by fossil fuel and nuclear power plants to make steam to drive turbines that generate electricity, and less than 1 percent of that volume was consumed by electricity production. Freshwater withdrawals for electric power generation are concentrated in the eastern half of the nation. Farm irrigation and some other applications, such as watering golf courses and parks, account for 40 percent of the 345 bgd of freshwater withdrawals. Of those irrigation withdrawals, 86 percent occurred in the 17 conterminous western states, with the four states of California, Idaho, Colorado, and Nebraska accounting for one-half of that amount.

Consumptive water use in irrigation depends on the region, crop, and irrigation technology used. For example, irrigation withdrawals in California and the Pacific Northwest were about the same, but consumptive use was 40 percent of withdrawals in the Pacific Northwest and 80 percent in California (Brown 1999). Although only 15 percent of the nation's cropland is irrigated, those lands generate much of the value in agricultural sales. In some areas water is used to support production of vegetable and fruit crops to supply fresh produce in the winter months. These crops have a high market value. Irrigation water is also used to flood pastures for hay crops and grazing, which yield low economic returns to farmers and ranchers. Nationally, 58 percent of irrigation water was taken from surface water and the rest from groundwater. Irrigation has the greatest potential to conflict with other water uses not only because irrigation withdrawal is highly consumptive but also because the use peaks when stream flow is at its lowest seasonal level. In areas were groundwater and surface water connections are significant, pumping of groundwater for irrigation can directly alter the watershed hydrograph (patterns and volume of stream flow) and surface water available to other users.

The remaining withdrawals were for public water supply, industrial production, and miscellaneous other uses. During 2000, about 85 percent of the population in the United States was served by municipal water utilities (public water supply) that deliver water used inside households and for outdoor uses such as lawn watering. Other customers for municipal water utilities are commercial establishments and public uses, such as fire protection and street cleaning. Municipal water utilities withdrew about 12 percent of all water in 2000, with surface water providing 60 percent of all withdrawals for that use. Industrial water uses include cooling of materials and equipment in processes such as steelmaking, and incorporation of water into products, as in producing beverages and canning agricultural products. Less than 8 percent of all withdrawals are for industrial and other purposes. Industrial water withdrawals can be locally significant and highly consumptive in a small area, as when water is used for production of soft drinks or beer. As a general rule, states located along and east of the Mississippi River have been the main users of water for industrial purposes, Texas being the geographic exception.

The year 2000 total freshwater withdrawal of 345 bgd total was twice the volume of water withdrawn in 1950 (175 bgd). Of note is that in 1980, freshwater withdrawals peaked at 373 bgd and then fell to the year 2000 amount, even as population increased by about 25 percent and economic activity as measured by gross domestic product more than tripled. Water withdrawals for thermoelectric power production and industrial uses mimic this trend. Withdrawals for these uses increased after 1950, and the water, once used, was discharged at a higher temperature than the surrounding stream or contained other pollutants. Withdrawal use fell when regulations to limit the discharge of heated water and pollutants encouraged recirculation and water reuse to avoid the costs of treating wastewater (Osborn et al. 1986; Brown 1999).

Withdrawals for irrigation use rose until 1980 and then fell. Irrigation water use grew by more than 68 percent from 1950 to 1980 as the total number of irrigated acres increased from 25,000 to 58,000 with the expansion of irrigation in the western states. The decline in irrigation water use after 1980 was caused, depending on the region of the country, by changes in crops grown, advances in irrigation water use efficiency, or higher energy costs that made pumping and distribution of water too expensive relative to the value of the crops being produced (Gollehon and Quinby 2006).

Withdrawals for public supply are an exception to declining water withdrawals. The amount of water withdrawn by municipal water utilities more than tripled between 1950 and 2000, paralleling increases in total population and increases in the population served by public suppliers. Of note is that withdrawals per person served increased from 1960 to 1990, possibly because of more frequent outdoor water uses like swimming pools and lawn watering, especially in arid areas (Brown 1999). However, between 1990 and 2000 the upward trend in per-person use ceased as public water utilities expanded efforts to limit water through a combination of pricing, regulatory, and consumer education programs. Nonetheless, public water supply withdrawals will continue to grow in areas where population growth is increasing—in coastal areas, in the arid states of the West (Anderson and Woosley 2005), and in the suburbs surrounding older cities.

Water to serve these many uses comes from the natural supply, but variability in runoff among regions and over time makes natural runoff an unreliable water source. Dams create reservoirs that ensure a reliable water supply between seasons and across years. Pipelines and canals move the stored water as well as water running in rivers across boundaries of small watersheds to centers of population and economic activity. Dams are operated to regulate the flow of water downstream, both by releasing stored water in dry seasons and by capturing water during high-flow periods to provide flood protection to lands located downstream of the dam site. The storage and release patterns that are the result of dam operations, as well as the movement of water into and out of watersheds, make noticeable changes in watershed hydrographs across the nation (Collier et al. 1996).

Like reservoirs, aquifers are storage facilities. Measures of aquifer storage capacity, and the amount of water in storage at any time, are made using mathematical models of the subsurface soils and surface water and groundwater interactions, combined with measurements of water levels in monitoring wells and other data (USGS 2002). Accessing water in aquifer storage requires pumping the water to the surface after constructing a well to the top of the aquifer. The amount of pumping required depends on the artesian pressures that force water toward the surface through the well. Water pumped from aquifer storage usually diminishes an aquifer's discharge to surface waters and reduces surface flows. However, in some places or at certain times, pumping might increase the rate of recharge from surface streams, and that might lower the stream flow. In coastal areas, pumping can cause saline water to flow toward the aquifer, and saltwater intrusion might reduce the value of the aquifer as a freshwater storage source. The relationship between pumping and the movement of water between an unconfined aquifer and surface water can be quite complex (Alley et al. 2002). As a general matter, if there is a constant pumping rate, the pattern of recharge and discharge will, as before the pumping began, be affected by rainfall, runoff, and an aquifer's connections to the surface water network.

An important exception to the relationship between pumping, surface water, and the aquifer is when the water is being pumped from a confined aquifer. In a confined aquifer, recharge has effectively ceased, and pumping water is the same as mining a fixed supply, such as an oil field. This situation characterizes groundwater used for irrigation over the southern portions of the Ogallala aquifer in the high Plains area. Past decades of pumping into thousands of wells has led to declining water levels, the need to drill ever-deeper wells, and greater electricity costs for pumping water to the surface. Combined with a general decline in the profitability of U.S. agriculture, higher costs to obtain water slowed and then reversed the increase in irrigated acreage and water use in the region (USGS 2002; Gollehon and Quinby 2006). Looking to the future, importing surface or groundwater is costly, and the cost may not be justified by the low market value of the crops now being irrigated. Innovative programs to encourage reduced water use and the sharing of the fixed supply will emerge. In Kansas, individuals with rights to use certain amounts of water can "deposit" water they do not plan to use for an upcoming year in a water bank in exchange for payment or other compensation from other persons who want to use that water. However, the other user can have only 90 percent of the water that is deposited (Central Kansas Water Bank Association 2007). Over the long term, there may need to be changes in acres irrigated, perhaps with replacement by perennial grasses and other cover crops that are suited to the region's precipitation pattern.

River flows as modified by dams and channels support *in-stream water uses* as well as water withdrawal uses. In-stream water users do not need to take water out of the stream, river, or lake to realize its benefit. The first in-stream water uses were power generation and barge navigation—uses that remain significant today. Hydropower facilities generate electricity by using the energy of flowing water to drive turbines. Approximately 10 percent of the nation's electricity is produced in this manner, and in the Pacific Northwest, hydroelectric facilities provide an even greater share of total power production. Barge transportation uses nine-foot-deep navigation channels (maintained by dredging), a system of locks, and flow releases from reservoirs. In 2003 barges on the inland waterways network carried 610 million tons of bulk cargo, such as grains, coal, and petroleum products. The waterways remain an important part of the nation's transportation system, although overall traffic has not increased in recent years and some segments of the system have limited traffic (U.S. Army Corps of Engineers 2007).

Finally, in-stream flows in rivers and lakes support recreational uses of water and provide fish and wildlife habitat. In addition, for decades some minimum level of flow has been maintained to assimilate the degradable wastes discharged to rivers and lakes. Water releases from reservoir storage have been justified to secure water flow and temperature needs of desired recreational fish, such as trout, as well as for waste assimilation. "Environmental flows" are increasingly recognized as a valued in-stream water use, and as we will see below, ensuring environmental flows is a central premise of sustainable water management.

Conservation, Water Development and Sustainable Water Use

At the beginning of the 20th century, leaders of the Progressive conservation movement argued that scientific management of natural resources, including water, was the foundation for national social and economic progress. The dams, channels, canals, levees, and pumps that control the flows of the nation's rivers are a legacy of that movement and are the context for understanding how contemporary definitions of sustainable water use challenge the water conservation tradition.

Water Conservation and Water Project Development

The Progressive Era conservation leaders wanted to prevent what they understood to be the waste of natural resources and ensure that the nation's natural wealth remained adequate for future generations. Gifford Pinchot (1865–1946) argued for extending the availability of fossil fuel resources by using the renewable resource of water to provide electric power. "Conservation," he proclaimed, "stands emphatically for the development and use of water-power now, without delay" (Nash 1968, 59). Early hydroelectric power development began at small dams that relied on the available flow of the river. However, the ability to generate power varied with daily and seasonal river flows, whereas the market value of generated power is determined in part by the availability of power on a reliable basis and at peak demand times. The market value of reliability justified the cost of building dams that could store water when demand was low and release water for power production during low river flow and at times of peak hourly or daily demand. Over the years, single dams and systems of multiple dams were built by public and private entities either solely for hydroelectric power or as part of storage projects that served multiple water uses.

Pinchot also argued for an aggressive program to develop river navigation: conservation, he said, "stands for the immediate construction of navigable waterways under a broad and comprehensive plan as assistants to the railroads. More coal and iron are required to move a ton of freight by rail than by water, three to one" (Nash 1968, 59). The 1898 report of the Inland Waterways Commission combined two Progressive Era concerns, ensuring future resource adequacy and countering the monopoly power of railroads, into an influential endorsement of a federal program to build locks and dredge rivers to maintain channel depths suitable for barge transportation (Holmes 1972).

Even earlier, in middle 19th century, the Swamplands Act represented a national commitment to reclamation of wetlands by drainage to support agricultural production—a commitment that was later supported with federal tax policies and cash subsidies for construction of major canals. The results have been impressive: many of the most productive agricultural lands throughout the Midwest, the lower Mississippi River delta and along the eastern coastal plain into Florida were once wet and poorly drained (Kramer and Shabman 1993). The Homestead Act of 1862 turned over vast amounts of what was then publicly owned land to private citizens who had only to work the land to claim ownership. Homesteading states included what is now Florida and ranged across the delta region into the Midwest and to the west coast, leaving only Texas outside the reach of the act. In places where land was too wet, the provisions of the Swamplands Act and other programs to support land drainage were employed make the land productive.

However, much of the public land was too dry to support settlement. Land reclamation therefore meant irrigation of arid soils as well as drainage (Newell 1902; Nash 1968). Expanding water used for irrigation was a Progressive Era imperative. Irrigation began in small settlements located near streams with a reliable flow. Often, farmers cooperated to build weirs and canals to divert river water to individual farm gates. This reliance on the cooperative enterprise of irrigation districts to fund irrigation water systems, combined with the limited year-to-year reliability of stream flows, proved economically untenable. President Theodore Roosevelt, in a 1901 address to Congress, summarized the case for a federal investment program in reservoir construction to serve irrigation:

> The pioneer settlers on the arid public domain chose their homes along streams from which they could themselves divert the water to reclaim their holdings. Such opportunities are practically gone. There still are vast areas of public land which can be made available for homestead settlement, but only by reservoirs and main-line canals impracticable for private enterprise. These irrigation works should be built by the national government ... The distribution of the water, the division of the streams among irrigators, should be left to the settlers themselves, in conformity with state laws and without interference with those laws or with vested rights (as quoted in Newell 1902).

The Reclamation Act of 1902 created the Bureau of Reclamation to lead federal government investments in irrigation. The water storage created and the project operations to use it increased the reliability of water available to irrigators from season to season and within a growing season, fostering the expansion of irrigation throughout the West.

The Progressive conservation argument for water development projects continued in its influence into the New Deal. In 1934, President Franklin Roosevelt's National Resources Planning Board (1934, *237*) declared, "In the interests of national welfare there must be national control of all the running waters of the United States, from the desert trickle that may make an acre or two productive to the rushing flood waters of the Mississippi." Letting water run out to sea without irrigating farms along the way was viewed as a waste of resources, and conservation clearly meant minimizing that waste by investing in engineering control of rivers. By the 1930s, conservation also meant flood control. In the early part of the 20th century, there was limited national attention to controlling frequent floods, perhaps because of a widespread belief that floods were acts of nature beyond the control of human intervention. The federal government, through the U.S. Army Corps of Engineers, had built some flood control levees in the lower Mississippi River and Sacramento River watersheds. The 1936 Flood Control Act initiated a decades-long and national-scale flood control program that constructed not only levees to prevent flood inundation along the rivers but also dams to capture high flows and channels to pass flood flows downstream to areas where damage would be minimal. The reduced vulnerability to flooding allowed vast acreages of land to be used for more intensive agricultural and urban purposes. At the same time these projects, like the Bureau of Reclamation projects, provided hydroelectric power and supported fishing, boating, and swimming. Today, flood damages along rivers still impose a cost on the nation, but as a proportion of national wealth, these costs have remained stable and perhaps declined, even as there have been increases in the benefits realized from floodplain occupancy (Shabman 1988; Pielke 2007).

In 1950 the Truman administration's report *Water in America's Future* included a drawing of an ideally managed river basin where engineering control of water flow secures the economic prosperity of the basin, the region, and also the nation (President's Water Resources Policy Commission 1950). In the upper reaches of the smaller watersheds, cover crops and reforestation on eroded soils slow runoff and control erosion. Downstream, small dams are combined with diversion channels and other conveyance facilities to move water to irrigated farm fields and small communities. Previously wet areas are drained by small ditches leading to larger canals, with the reclaimed land dedicated to cities and farms. On the larger rivers, dams create reservoirs to store water, while levees along the river edges and deepened river channels limit flooding of fertile soils. Cities are located adjacent to flood-protected rivers, and their manufacturing and other commercial facilities along the river edge are served by ports and barge terminals. The water stored in reservoirs irrigates agricultural fields, generates electric power, and provides for other water uses in dry times. That depiction was modeled on the real experience of the Tennessee Valley Authority (TVA), an independent authority with governmental and revenue powers for supporting extensive water development. By the 1950s the TVA experiment was well underway and seemed to be an intuitional model for river basin development. However, no other programs like TVA were ever initiated (Holmes 1972; Goodwin 1983).

The grand vision of the ideally managed watershed was matched by a federal budget commitment. In the early 1950s, nearly 3 percent of the total federal budget was dedicated to water project construction programs of the U.S. Army Corps of Engineers, and it had been as high as 5 percent before World War II; today, that figure is a fraction of 1 percent (NRC 2004b). Other federal agencies, including the Bureau of Reclamation and the Department of Agriculture, had robust water project construction programs. The federal government contributed significant amounts for construction of levees, channels, dams, and reservoirs on the nation's major rivers; meanwhile, state and local governments built thousands of water supply reservoirs, pipes, and open canals and sometimes transferred the stored water over long distances. For example, New York City collects its water in upstate New York and other surrounding watersheds. Water project construction, especially for dams, peaked in the mid- to late 1960s (Graf 1999).

Surface water development was accompanied by increased pumping of groundwater. Initially, access to groundwater was limited to water that emerged through surface springs and reached the surface through artesian pressure or could be extracted from shallow wells. By the late 1930s, new pumping technology had increased effective pumping depth to nearly 300 feet. At this same time, Department of Agriculture price and income support programs for producers of corn, wheat, cotton, and certain other crops, combined with technical and financial assistance for irrigation and land drainage, enhanced the financial returns to crop production. Groundwater use for western irrigation more than doubled after World War II (Frederick 1991). Pumping technology also allowed cities and towns to increase their reliance on groundwater for public water systems.

Today, tens of thousands of groundwater wells, some deeper than 300 feet, withdraw water for many uses. Twenty-five percent of all freshwater withdrawal is from aquifers. Dams, locks, levees, and channels and diversions of water that are the legacy of past investment are pervasive, visible features on the landscape. The water management infrastructure includes more than 80,000 dams of varying sizes; more than

25,000 miles of inland and intracoastal navigation channels supported by some 200 navigation locks and dams; and millions of miles of drainage ditches and canals, pipes and tunnels (Frederick 1991).

The national investment in wells, pumps, storage reservoirs, diversion works, and channel modifications has transformed a natural water supply that varied unpredictably across watersheds, with the season, and between years into a reliable water source for all users in all regions of the nation. The high- and low-flow extremes of the natural hydrograph rarely interfere with normal uses of water or with the use of land adjacent to rivers and streams. In 1963, when dedicating the Whiskeytown Dam on the Trinity River in California, President Kennedy reflected on the history of national water development and traced it back to the Progressives' conservation vision (Kennedy 1963).

> I have come across the United States in the last 5 days, starting at Milford, Pa., which was the home of Gifford Pinchot, who was, with Theodore Roosevelt, the first great conservationist in this country. Imagine how small their country was, how few the people, and yet how dangerous it was in the early part of this century. How great was that danger, that this great natural inheritance of ours given to us by nature, given to us by God, would be wiped away, the forests ruined, the streams destroyed, wasted for the people, water going to the sea unused. And because of the dedicated work of … Pinchot, Theodore Roosevelt, and later Franklin Roosevelt—[a] great national effort was made to realize our resources, to make them useful.
>
> With the Trinity division completed and the upper reaches of the Sacramento now harnessed, Shasta County and its neighbors are assured of water and power. They can enjoy new chances for recreational use, and new access to open space. And of great importance, the flow of two watersheds can now be regulated for the benefit of the farms and cities in the lower valley. For too long this water ran unused to the sea. For too long surplus water in one area was wasted, while there was a deficit nearby. Now, by diverting these waters to the eastern slope, we can irrigate crops on the fertile plains of the Sacramento Valley and supply water also for municipal and industrial use to the cities to the south.
>
> And while running their course, these waters will generate millions of kilowatts of energy and help expand the economy of the fastest growing State in the Nation. In these ways, Whiskeytown Reservoir and the Trinity division will add to our natural beauty and will show that man can improve on nature, and make it possible for this State to continue to grow.

Confronting the Conservation Vision: From Preservation to Sustainability

John Muir (1838–1914) argued for the preservation of places of special beauty. Moved by Muir's vision, the nation made its initial commitment to the creation of national parks (Nash 1968). Muir's advocacy for the preservation of certain special places occasionally created tension between advocates for conservation over preservation, as is illustrated by Muir's debate with Gifford Pinchot over the merits of a water supply dam in the Hetch-Hetchy Valley of California. Muir's opposition to the dam was poetic, as befits the argument being made. "These temple destroyers, devotees of ravaging commercialism, seem to have a perfect contempt for nature, and instead of lifting their eyes to the God of the Mountain, lift them to the Almighty Dollar" (Nash 1968, 74). Pinchot's response reflects the Progressive conservation view of the necessity of capturing the benefits from water development: "As to my attitude regarding the proposed use of Hetch Hetchy by the City of San Francisco … I am fully persuaded that … the injury … by substituting a lake for the present swampy floor of the valley … is altogether unimportant compared with the benefits to be derived from a reservoir" (Nash 1968, *161*).

Over the following decades the conservation vision dictated that the most accessible dam sites be developed. However, by mid-20th century, proposals to build dams in places that had been slated for preservation renewed the latent tension between conservation and preservation. Preservationists challenged river control on aesthetic grounds and in specific places. Opponents of dam construction argued, as had John Muir, that future generations' welfare would be diminished, not enhanced, by locating such projects in places of great natural beauty. In fact, the Sierra Club, which had been founded by Muir, led the opposition to these projects (Leydet 1968).

In 1967 John Krutilla published *Conservation Reconsidered,* in which he argued that the welfare of future generations depended not only on the benefits of water used for hydroelectric power, navigation, and irrigation, but also on the benefits from the preservation of natural places. Conservation should be reconsidered, in his view, to include preservation. Water project development opponents enlisted the support of economists such as Krutilla who questioned the value to the nation of building ever more water projects to control river flows and found a receptive audience for that argument among national water policy leaders (National Water Commission 1973).

Today, advocates for "sustainable river management," or what some have termed "river naturalization" (Rhoads et al. 1999; Frothingham et al. 2002), challenge water withdrawal and river control projects on a broad basis and in all watersheds across the nation. Beginning in the 1970s, and coincident with the tapering off in water project construction, maintenance of minimum in-stream flows to support fish and wildlife increasingly was recognized as a beneficial water use, along with the traditional water uses, such as irrigation and public water supply (U.S. WRC 1978). Over time the condition of aquatic ecosystem habitat was linked to variability in river flows as well as to minimum flows (NRC 1992).

Maintaining and restoring flow and variability of flow in rivers is frequently equated with sustainable water management. "The ultimate challenge of ecologically sustainable water management," according to one effective advocate for flow variability as a measure of sustainability (Richter et al. 2003, *207*),

> is to design and implement a water management program for human purposes in a manner that does not cause affected ecosystems to degrade or simplify. This quest for balance necessarily implies that there is a limit to the amount of water that can be withdrawn from a river and a limit in the degree to which the shape of a river's natural flow patterns can be altered … A river's flow regime is now recognized as a "master variable" that drives variation in

many other components of a river ecosystem, e.g., fish populations, flood plain forest composition, nutrient cycling, in both direct and indirect ways. The extraordinary species richness and productivity characteristic of fresh-water ecosystems is strongly dependent upon, and attributable to, the natural variability of their hydrologic conditions.

The focus on restoration of historic flow patterns is widely accepted as a way to manage rivers in the future (NRC 1992, 1999a, 2002b, 2004b, 2007a; Stanford et al. 1996; Van Herick 2000; Koel and Sparks 2002).

That flow as well as flow variability is a fundamental premise of sustainable water management is illustrated by how the term *sustainability* is applied to groundwater pumping. In the conservation tradition, the amount of water pumped from aquifer storage was supposed to be restricted to long-term aquifer recharge. Definitions of sustainable groundwater use recognize the link between aquifer pumping and surface water conditions. Sustainable groundwater use means restricting pumping to minimize the adverse effects on surface water in rivers, streams, and lakes hydrologically connected to the aquifer (Sophocleous 2000; Alley and Leake 2004; Alley 2006).

Ecologically sustainable water management seeks to secure the "ecological health" or "integrity" of watersheds, terms that have been incorporated into the language used by federal and state agencies. However, if integrity and health define sustainable surface water and groundwater management, then the terms will need operational definition (Holland 2000; Lackey 2001). Many definitions of integrity and health are based on a reference condition that "approximates natural, un-impacted conditions for a waterbody. Since undisturbed or minimally disturbed conditions may be difficult or impossible to find, least disturbed conditions, combined with historical information, models or other methods may be used to approximate reference condition as long as the departure from natural or ideal is understood" (U.S. EPA 2007a).

By this definition, the predisturbance hydrograph is one possible definition for river integrity or health, even though historical flow regimes cannot be achieved if other water uses are also going to be met. In fact, the consequences of river modification are not always detrimental. "Water management for human uses necessarily alters a river's natural flow regime in various ways." However, Richter et al. (2003, *207*) acknowledge, "there is some degree and types of alteration that will not jeopardize the viability of native species and the ability of an ecosystem to provide valuable products and services for society ..."

The problem for water management decisionmaking is the limited understanding of how flow regime changes affect aquatic communities. As a result, there are few analytic procedures for evaluating the consequences of different water flow regimes on aquatic communities. A recent National Research Council committee recommended "characterize[ing] environmental flows in rivers by developing quantitative models that link changes in ecologic structure and function of river ecosystems (aquatic and riparian) to management scale changes in river flow regimes" (NRC 2007b, 75). Without a means to define and then quantify river naturalization as a new water use, it is not possible to compare the relative need for water for naturalization and the more traditional water uses. Over time, methods for predicting how flow volume and flow variability affect the condition of the aquatic environment will be developed.

The predisturbance hydrograph as a reference condition is now used as the starting point, if not the end point, for defining sustainable water management (Stanford et al. 1996; Koel and Sparks 2002; Poff et al. 2003). This reference condition of the minimally altered watershed logically suggests two sustainable water management principles. First, the water withdrawn from streams should be minimized so that the natural hydrograph is minimally disturbed or an already-altered stream is not further changed. Demand reduction, accomplished through adoption of technologies and practices that reduce water use, is the first option, especially if demand is increasing in an area. And it follows that water control and transfer projects should be built as a last resort. Second, sustainable water use calls into question the conservation tradition of river control and opens up the possibility of relaxing the controls that dams, channels, levees, and dikes have imposed on river flows. Meanwhile, sustainable water management principles that call for minimizing human disturbance of river flow regimes have found their way into water law and regulation.

Water Law, Regulation, and Sustainable Use

The United States has two dominant water law systems, the riparian (common law) and prior appropriation doctrines (Getches 1997), which developed in different ways in different states. Under the common law, the right to access a water source is assigned to landowners adjacent to a water body (a riparian landowner) or overlying a water source (in the case of groundwater). The volume of water allowed by the water right is limited to what is needed for beneficial uses, as long as the volume used does not impose an economic loss (harm) on other water users. If a claim of harm is recognized by a court, the court can order the water use to cease or require financial compensation equal to documented economic damage. A similar logic and limitation apply to groundwater rights. In areas where riparian law dominates, water to meet withdrawal uses and maintain navigation and hydroelectric power production is abundant, so harm is difficult to claim and rarely if ever proved (Cox and Shabman 1984). To the west, where rainfall is less abundant, states rely on the prior appropriation doctrine, although there are many situations where common law doctrine applies. The prior appropriation doctrine assigns rights to individuals who register their intention to withdraw a certain amount of water from a defined water body for a beneficial use. User priorities are based on the order in which rights were recognized. The first claim to a defined volume of water withdrawal has priority over subsequent claims. The prior appropriator's right must be met before a subsequent appropriator may take water from the river. Under low-flow conditions, a "junior" appropriator may have access to little or no water. In fact, the return flows (the water that is withdrawn and not consumed) from more senior appropriators may be the only source of water for those with more junior rights. The 20th-century water development programs enhanced the value of water use rights of the more junior appropriators by increasing the reliability of flows and access to water. Also, the ability to store and transfer water to serve multiple users reduced the likelihood of competing claims to water during low-flow periods in all states.

Many states have replaced all or some part of their common law or prior appropriation rights structures with administrative permits. A water withdrawal permit defines the amount of water a permit holder may withdraw, the times that the withdrawal may occur, and the ability to transfer the permit to another user. In the 1970s, for example, Florida replaced its riparian water rights structure with a system of withdrawal permits. Arizona and other arid states have modified their water laws in ways that incorporate permitting (Bloomquist et al. 2004). Virginia, exemplifying a less extensive change, replaced common law groundwater rights with a permit system in designated areas.

The states' water rights systems coexist with other legal and regulatory regimes (Getches 1997). In the West, there are water rights that accrue to Native American tribes and to the federal government. Intergovernmental compacts are written among states and governments to govern the sharing of water in rivers that touch on state political boundaries. A multistate compact allocates water from the Colorado River. Florida has a water-sharing treaty giving the Seminole Nation specific claims to water on its lands. In addition, case law rulings frequently interpret and then reinterpret state water laws.

Over time, states modify their water rights systems to resolve conflicts between uses deemed beneficial to society; these have included in-stream uses for power production and navigation and withdrawal uses for public supply, irrigation, and industrial applications. Most recently, states have modified the rights systems to better reflect the states' priorities for the use of water, especially to recognize in-stream "environmental flow" as a beneficial water use. For example, Texas, as it prepares to provide public water for an expected doubling of its population, has incorporated into its state water plan a requirement to provide for a "sound ecological environment" (NRC 2005). Almost all states now recognize some in-stream flow for environmental purposes as a beneficial water use.

Federal environmental protection laws passed in the late 1960s and early 1970s parallel states' water law changes in recognizing stream flow for environmental purposes as a beneficial use. The regulations implementing these laws, as well as court rulings, have limited the exercise of water rights to serve traditional purposes in riparian, prior appropriation, and permit-based systems. Two examples stand out, the Endangered Species Act of 1973 (ESA) and the Federal Water Pollution Control Act Amendments of 1972 (now the Clean Water Act, CWA).

The ESA prohibits actions that harm the habitat of a species identified as endangered or threatened. Because river flows fall within the definition of habitat, the ESA has had the effect of constraining the construction of new water storage and transfer projects, limiting new water withdrawals, and mandating water reallocations away from historically established water users. Water projects built years ago are being operated in new ways that dedicate storage releases to river flows and reduce the water in storage dedicated to the current withdrawals or in-stream uses, such as hydroelectric power generation and navigation. For example, on the Missouri River, declines in endangered fish populations and other adverse environmental conditions have been ascribed to the ways that maintenance of navigation significantly alters flow patterns and bottom profiles of the river. The ESA has been interpreted as requiring more frequent exposure of riverbeds to mesh with the life-cycle stages of resident fish and wildlife species—for example, sandbars should be seasonally available for bird nesting habitat, and reservoirs cannot be operated only to ensure reliable channel depth to support barge navigation (NRC 2002b). Along the Klamath River, the ESA has been applied to require reduced off-stream irrigation water use with a dedication of more water to maintaining patterns of stream flow to support salmon migration and spawning (Tarlock and Doremus 2003). In the East, compliance with ESA protections to be afforded to Gulf sturgeon and mussels in the Apalachicola River and Bay of Florida has been one constraint on the management of Lake Lanier as a water supply source for Atlanta (Leitman 2005; U.S. FWS 2006).

The CWA calls for reducing the discharge of chemical pollutants to the nation's waters at their source. Progress on achieving this goal has been made, although challenges remain (NRC 2002a). More broadly, the act (Section 108) includes the national goal of "restoring the chemical, physical and biological integrity of the nation's waters." The passing years have brought a scientific consensus that this goal of restoration will require more than controlling the discharge of pollutants; it will include restoration of river flows to mimic predisturbance hydrologic variability, with its attendant effects on sediment movement and deposition and biological conditions (NRC 1992). Restoration requires protection of riparian areas along rivers and the remaining wetlands in the landscape (NRC 2002c). One provision of the CWA that has been used to advance restoration is the permitting requirement authorized by Section 404. This section requires the Corps of Engineers and the Environmental Protection Agency to issue permits for putting fill material into the waters of the United States, broadly understood as wetlands, riparian areas, and streams. States also have developed laws and supporting regulations with a similar purpose (Shabman and Cox 2004).

Today, permit reviewers are expected to apply a decision logic called sequencing when evaluating a permit application for a water project, such as a dam, a water intake for a pump, or a pipeline, whenever any part of the project is in navigable water. Sequencing first requires the applicant to avoid any disturbance to the aquatic environment. If avoiding disturbance is not possible in the view of the permitting agency, then the applicant must minimize the effects of the project to the satisfaction of the agency. The effects that remain if the permit is issued must be offset by mitigation actions that return the aquatic environment to some prepermit condition (Shabman and Cox 2004). There is a strong parallel between the permit review logic of sequencing and sustainable water management principles to minimize disturbance to the natural flow regime, to riparian areas, and to wetlands.

The Section 404 permit review logic, the ESA, and the changes being made to state water law all reflect a national trend toward recognizing sustainability, defined as river naturalization, as a beneficial water use when making water investment and allocation decisions. The challenges of incorporating sustainable water management principles into the water conservation tradition are now evident in water management decisionmaking and will continue for the near future.

Sustainability and the Future of Water Management

Water withdrawals have declined since 1980 for all uses except public water supply. However, the volume of water withdrawn for public water supply relative to other uses is (and will remain) small, and it is unlikely that significant numbers of new dams or other water control projects will be built to serve traditional water uses. For the near future, sustainable water management will focus on two challenges. The first is how to manage existing infrastructure to serve river naturalization.[4] The second is how to maintain and restore river flow regimes where municipal water utilities, especially in coastal and arid areas, want a reliable water supply system for growing customer numbers.

Managing the Built Infrastructure

River naturalization can be achieved by removing small mill and power dams that have outlived their intended purpose (Aspen Institute 2002; Graf 2003). In other places, changes to the water release schedule of larger dams can be accomplished with no loss of project benefits (The Nature Conservancy 2007), or an agreement to revise a water release schedule can be readily negotiated with current beneficiaries of the project. For example, water flows are managed in some western streams to support recreationally valuable fish populations that would not exist under natural flow conditions. Water releases are now being made to mimic the predam flow patterns, with limited detrimental effects on either the recreational fish species or other project purposes (NRC 1999a). Where riparian zones and wetlands have been artificially isolated from streams and rivers in a watershed, the detrimental effects on the life-cycles of fish and wildlife species can be reversed by breaching old levees (U.S. FWS 2004).

However, government agencies and the courts face difficult choices if water is going to be allocated to naturalization. In some places, historic and still used public water supply sources may be replaced. For example, the debate between Muir and Pinchot over the use of the Hetch-Hetchy Valley for water supply has begun anew (Null and Lund 2006). Across the nation the Federal Energy Regulatory Commission (FERC), when it renews a license to operate a dam, has found itself in the midst of disputes over changes to operating rules that yield more natural river flows and less hydroelectric power. FERC has instituted new evaluation and decisionmaking procedures to manage these disputes (Stephenson 2002). The fate of the salmon populations in the Columbia River system has become a well-publicized example of the difficulty of managing the built infrastructure. The diminished state of the recreational and commercial salmon populations in the Pacific Northwest, and their replacement with other species, can be attributed in part to alterations to the rivers made by dams built years ago by the Corps of Engineers, the Bureau of Reclamation, and private power companies. Dams can be removed or operated in different ways, and the hydroelectric and navigation benefits of those dams could be forgone or secured in other ways. Irrigation water use from pools behind the dams can be cut back, and either crop production can be reduced or water-saving technologies that have their own cost can reduce water usage. A public debate now more than 20 years old has been accompanied by federal and state legislation and court rulings related to the ESA and CWA, all in an effort to discern what benefits the region and the nation are willing to forgo in order to restore more natural flow regimes and help rehabilitate salmon populations (Lackey et al. 2006).

The call for sustainable water management not only can spawn conflict but also can require significant financial outlays. Perhaps the nation's most ambitious naturalization effort is the Comprehensive Everglades Restoration Program (CERP). For decades the vast wetlands of South Florida were drained and the water that used to flow slowly south across the width of the state to the Florida Keys was captured, diverted into channels, and discharged along the coasts. This flow modification to the so-called "river of grass" created vast areas of dry land for urban and agricultural development. The CERP goal for restoration has been summarized as "getting the water right" (Sklar et al. 2005), meaning reestablishing the timing, pattern, and direction of water flows in the areas of South Florida that have not already been converted to intensive land use, as well as controlling the discharge of pollutants. To "get the water right," the CERP plans include modifying operations of water supply projects, removing canal and channel projects that provide flood control, and building new water storage and distribution systems to capture water that now flows to the sea, both to provide water for a growing population and to increase water flow in the remnants of the natural system. The Everglades program is expected to cost in excess of $12 billion, and future cost increases are likely (NRC 2006) as the scope of the required effort becomes clearer. Programs that stress naturalization programs are being considered across the nation and may have similar budget requirements (Working Group 2006).

Funds for project modifications may need to be augmented by funds to compensate adversely affected water users who can block changes in project operations. For example, in Washington State, to accommodate the opposition to removing two dams on the Elwha River in Olympic National Park, Congress authorized funds to compensate the dam owners, who had to purchase replacement power (Gowan et al. 2006) And in the arid West, where water control infrastructure increased the year-to-year reliability of water for irrigation and thus increased the value of appropriators' water rights, recent efforts to restore more natural flows now make the water rights less valuable and spark opposition; the resulting conflicts can extend for years (Tarlock and Doremus 2003).

Programs to purchase or rent water rights might minimize opposition to reallocating irrigation water to naturalization of flow. Water banking is a program whereby holders of water use rights can rent any rights that they do not intend to exercise in a particular year to a public or nongovernmental entity; that water can then be dedicated to flow restoration. Another approach might be for a public or nongovernmental entity to enter into a multiyear contract with a rights holder for "on-demand" water. Under the contract, the rights holder makes a fixed payment each year and can call on the water in any year when the flows in the river are below some contract-specified threshold. Such programs need both buyers with access to funds and willing sellers of the water-use rights, plus some form of quantification and enforcement to ensure that the increased flows that were purchased remain in the river and are not withdrawn by other appropriators. There are numerous examples of programs of this nature (Tarlock 2003; Idaho Water Board 2007; Oregon Water Trust 2007).

Water for Growing Populations

Municipal water utilities describe the capacity to reliably deliver water to their customers as "safe yield." The calculation begins by defining a minimum flow from a raw water source, determining normal water use by customers (including households, public service providers such as fire departments, and businesses), and establishing the acceptable frequency of required reductions in normal water use (service disruption).

When water is withdrawn from a stream without surface water storage, the yield is the available flow during a chosen low-flow period, after accounting for water users who have competing or prior water rights. The chosen flow might be the lowest flow during a defined period (say, 60 days) that will be equaled or exceeded some percentage of the time. Reliability of the system (the safe yield) is the ability to meet customers' normal water use levels during the low-flow period. If the chosen yield is the flow that is exceeded 95 percent of the time, then the system will fail to meet normal customer uses 5 percent of the time. If the chosen yield is a flow that will be exceeded 90 percent of the time, then the system will fail to meet normal water use 10 percent of the time. When normal water use cannot be met, withdrawals would be restricted or emergency water sources would be tapped.

When reservoirs are part of the water system, withdrawal of water, plus releases from storage to ensure some downstream flow, may sometimes exceed the flow into the reservoir, drawing down the volume of stored water. At other times water uses and downstream releases are less than inflows, and the reservoir fills. The safe yield of a reservoir is the number of days of normal water use that can be met during a chosen low-flow period if the reservoir is full at the start of the dry period. If the source of supply is an aquifer, the maximum short-term yield is given by pump capacity, and over a longer period, the annual yield is equal to the estimated average annual rate of recharge (Shabman and Cox 2004).

Projections of future water use are compared with the yield of the system (river flows plus surface water and groundwater storage) to identify a possible gap between a yield of the system and projected normal water use. If a gap is identified, a water capacity expansion plan and investment strategy are developed. Projections of water use can be made in several ways (Shabman 1990; NRC 2002a), but the projections always include judgments about what uses are deemed beneficial and should be served by the utility. For example, is the use of water in Las Vegas fountains a beneficial use of water in the desert as long as the casinos cover the utility's cost of securing and delivering the water? Generally, a utility will respect customers' choices for using the water that they pay for.

Utilities' predictions of future use are necessarily uncertain. Different scenarios for population and economic growth, household water use, lawn irrigation, number of commercial and industrial establishments, and other variables might lead to high, moderate, and low projections. Utilities must choose what scenario they will use for making the safe yield calculation. Given the difficulty of securing new supplies and the uncertainties in any projection, the tendency has been to plan for moderate or high growth and to overbuild rather than underbuild (Shabman 1990).

If a deficit is anticipated, the utility identifies alternatives for restoring the safe yield for the system into the future. Alternatives considered may include new reservoir storage, additional well fields, new river intake structures, pipelines to move water from other areas to the service area, water demand management, desalination of saline water, coordination of water supply systems with other areas, reuse of wastewater, and perhaps other options. Different plans that are combinations of the different alternatives are developed, and the plans are judged by how well they serve different utility objectives. Customer satisfaction with drinking water quality (taste, odor, and perceptions of safety) is another consideration.

Costs for storage facilities, pipelines, wells and pumps, the acquisition of water rights, and environmental compliance for capital projects can be significant. To minimize costs and keep customer water rates low, a utility can stretch its capacity during a low-flow period, or choose a more frequent low-flow event to measure yield, but emergency reductions would then be required more frequently. Finally, the utility will try to minimize effects on the aquatic environment (flow regime, riparian areas, and wetlands), if only to avoid legal challenges, political opposition or regulatory barriers, mostly as part of environmental impact reviews.

Safe yield calculations and capacity planning are a mix of data analysis and policy judgments that in the past were the sole responsibility of municipal water utilities. Historically, the first response to projected growth in demand was to build more storage capacity, drill more wells in outlying areas, and transfer the water across watershed and political boundaries to the utility's customers. Now, however, because of sustainable water management principles—limiting water withdrawals and alterations to the volume and patterns of stream flow—water development and transfer are no longer the first response to a deficit. Today, sustainable water management principles are reflected in the permit review processes of Section 404 permitting of the CWA and related laws and regulations. Utilities must carefully define safe yield and balance different objectives, and when they apply for permits for new storage or transfers, they bear the burden of proof in showing that the water supply plan first avoids and then minimizes disturbance to the aquatic environment. Multiple permit processes and legal challenges in the courts now question judgments made by a utility as it has defined safe yield and balanced different objectives in proposing its water supply plan for permitting. The result is a tension of competing authorities between the permitting processes and the municipal water utility, often extending the water supply planning and investment process for decades (Shabman and Cox 2004).

Sustainable water management principles are profoundly affecting planning practice in areas of population growth—in the arid West and along the coasts, and in the expanding suburbs around older cities across the nation. For example, utilities' water supply plans are expected to include reductions in normal water use that will increase the safe yield of the system, reduce the need to build new capacity, and thereby avoid effects on existing wetlands and river flows. Permits for new supply development are rarely issued unless the utility promulgates codes that require new buildings to use low-flush toilets, low-flow shower heads, and water-efficient clothes washers. Developers may need to minimize lawn area and use native plants that can survive in the local climate without supplemental watering (Hank and Davis 2006). Water pricing structures and education programs may be designed to discourage water use, especially for outdoor applications, and the response of water use to price might be accompanied by consumer education programs that encourage water-saving behavior (Gleick et al. 2003; Bell 2007; Keeny et al. 2007). In addition to reducing normal water usage, the utility may be expected to have a program that restricts usage during droughts. Given the ecological importance ascribed to maintaining stream flow in dry years, drought management is said to yield significant environmental benefits. Clearly defined triggers for drought restrictions (such as reservoir levels or other hydrologic measures) will also help extend the defined safe yield of a system. Water utility managers will accept (and may have already implemented) demand management programs when there is the offsetting benefit of delaying the costs for investment in new capacity. However, some demand reduction programs—for example, landscape design limits—may be viewed as inappropriate interference with their customers' decisionmaking. In the case of drought-triggered mandatory reductions, utilities are concerned over how frequently such restrictions will be accepted and heeded by customers. If the safe yield of the system is such that emergency water restrictions need to be applied on a frequent basis, then customer dissatisfaction could increase and compliance with such restrictions might decline over time.

The demand reduction alternatives in a plan, if accompanied by regional water sharing, can further reduce the need to increase water withdrawals or alter river flows or wetlands and riparian areas in a watershed. Under regional water sharing, when it is dry in some places, water transferred from wetter places can be use as a source of supply. A successful application of regionalization is found in the Washington, DC, metropolitan area, where Maryland, Virginia, and the District of Columbia share the Potomac River as a basic supply source but also have their own sources inside their jurisdictions. Coordination, achieved through a regional water management authority, is designed to get the maximum yield from the joint use of all the facilities without regard to where the water is being delivered (Interstate Commission on the Potomac River Basin 2007).

However, utilities in some places resist regionalization because of possible breakdowns in management coordination, jurisdictional antagonisms unrelated to water, or reluctance to forgo revenue from the sale of water to other localities (Shabman and Cox 1986).

Sustainable water management principles call on the utilities to consider and invest in nontraditional water supply sources. For example, the large quantities of water withdrawn for public water supply are returned to watersheds as treated wastewater, but this water might also be reused. And coastal areas on bays and estuaries and large areas of the midsection of the country lie over deep aquifers holding massive quantities of saline water, which might be desalinized. The technology to remove salts and impurities is becoming less costly, making saline water and wastewater possible additions to the yield of a water system, and many cities have incorporated these water sources in their definition of system yield (South Florida Water Management District 2007). However, the technologies are still developing (NRC 2004a; Cooley et al. 2006), and customer acceptance and technical requirements of water reuse make utilities reluctant to rely on these water sources (NRC 1998).

Sustainable water management also implies enhanced coordination of groundwater and surface water storage to increase the defined yield of a water system, as well as to prevent undesired effects on stream flows. Termed conjunctive management, the storage available in aquifers can be managed like a reservoir and substitute for surface water storage. During periods of low surface flow, the aquifer would be drawn upon and groundwater levels would fall, to be replenished by recharge during wetter periods when surface water is used to supply the utility's customers. Such coordinated management might require new wells and pumps and even include a system for intentional aquifer storage and recovery (ASR). ASR uses surface water from high flows in the wet season (and wastewater) to accelerate recharge to groundwater aquifers that were drawn down during dry periods (Eden et al. 2007). ASR is already in use in some places and figures in the supply plans in other locations, such as South Florida (NRC 1999b, 2001). Despite its promise, however, ASR remains a new technology, and a utility's interest in this approach will be tempered by the challenges and costs of gaining access to existing or new well fields outside its service area and the possible need to acquire water rights. Moreover, aquifers discharge water to surface streams and lakes and then recharge in ways that are not completely understood, making storage in aquifers less than certain and the effects of groundwater withdrawal on surface water a possible limit on groundwater use (Alley et al. 2002). For example, Las Vegas is considering drilling well fields outside the city; how pumping might affect aquatic habitat and users of surface water in those areas has yet to be determined (USGS 2007).

Some alternatives that increase yield by withdrawing more surface water will have limited effect on river flow regimes. For example, a storage reservoir might be constructed in a valley or low area with no perennial stream flow and filled with water pumped from the main river during high flows. These projects are not without environmental concerns, because they still require reduction of flows during high-flow periods that might, for example, affect fish spawning runs. Disagreement between the utility and a permitting authority over the duration or volume of pumping may reflect different decisionmaking objectives. The utility might not agree to adopt a plan whose sole purpose is to protect aquatic habitat or particular species. For example, a utility might change the location or operation of water intakes to protect a migrating fish species, but at some point the need to minimize costs and ensure reliability might take precedence over additional prospective harm to fish (Shabman and Cox 2004).

Population and economic growth will be so significant in some places that new water storage and water transfer projects for municipal water supply will be planned and perhaps permitted and built (Archibold and Johnson 2007). Water transferred from watersheds or aquifers outside the utility's political boundaries is a fully consumptive use in the watershed of origin and can have significant localized stream flow effects. For that reason, these projects inevitably generate opposition. The State Water Plan in California, for example, required an amendment to the state constitution to allow the water to be transported outside its county of origin (Hundly 1992).

In the humid East, proposals for water transfers over short distances and between small watersheds generate opposition, and the resolution of such conflicts may take decades (Shabman and Cox 1986). However water transfers will continue to be proposed to serve growing populations, especially in the more arid regions of the nation, after demand reduction programs and nontraditional alternatives are pursued. The highly consumptive use of water for irrigation in those arid regions suggests that municipal water demands can be met through water transfer from agriculture while also restoring river flows in the originating watershed. Even a small reduction in irrigation water use can significantly expand the safe yield of a water utility.

Consider how both river naturalization and water supply might be served by a water rights transfer from irrigation to municipal use outside the watershed through a water bank or other marketlike institution. For purposes of illustration, assume that the consumptive use of withdrawn irrigation water is 50 percent. Suppose a utility purchased an irrigator's water withdrawal rights but was permitted to transfer less than 50 percent of the acquired water to its customers and had to leave the rest of the water in the stream. Under this permit condition, local watershed flows would increase as a result of the purchase and transfer alternative. The municipality's cost for water acquisition would increase by twofold because it would need to buy twice as many rights as its water requirement. Then the water would need to be moved to the population area. Water is expensive to transport in large quantities because a pipeline must be built. So the cost of this new water from irrigation will include the cost of the water right, the pipeline or other transfer costs, plus the cost to assure that the water left for in stream flow is not withdrawn from the river by other appropriators. However, urban dwellers' willingness and ability to pay for water is high, and the utility may be willing and able to accept these costs.

Looking Ahead

There has been a longstanding national concern about whether water availability and water project investments are adequate to serve the many uses made of water, and the adequacy of the nation's water supply and investment remains a focus for public discussion. However, in that discussion, the historical presumption that water supply adequacy is secured by storing water behind dams, drilling deep wells, and then transferring water to points of use is being challenged by the principles of sustainable water use. This said, any discussion and assessment of the adequacy of the nation's water supply must begin with an understanding of the hydrologic conditions and water use now and in the future (Barlow et al. 2004), but such an assessment of future water uses and supply will be confounded by uncertainty (Anderson and Woosley 2005).

Just before water use began to decline after 1980, experts were projecting dramatically higher water consumption through the year 2005 and well into the future. In hindsight, we see that the predictions made in the 1970s failed to anticipate changes in technology, population settlement patterns, and the nature of the nation's economic output (Shabman 1990). This lesson about the uncertainty of water use projections, combined with recent concerns over climate change and energy supply, suggests caution in predicting future water uses. Volatile prices and unreliable supplies of oil and the adverse environmental consequences of fossil fuel production and consumption have heightened interest in fuels produced from corn, sugar cane, and grass crops. Although most of the water needed to grow these bio-mass fuels will come from rainfall, some might require irrigation—perhaps even on newly irrigated land—or increased use of water for processing. This new water use might compete with demand in growing urban areas and with desires to maintain river flows. In the end, whether this form of fuel becomes commercially viable and in turn affects water uses is a matter for speculation. Likewise, energy security and climate concerns might lead to an increased reliance on electricity from hydroelectric dams and nuclear power plants. If so, river flow management for naturalization might be challenged by increases in hydroelectric generation and by increases in withdrawal and consumptive water in nuclear power plant operations.

Future water supply is also uncertain. The data used to estimate future supply for any watershed are based on the historical record from stream flow gauges and aquifer monitoring wells. In some places the record may be more than 100 years long, but in other locations it is far shorter, and even a 100-year record may not be adequate to reflect climatic variation. Recent analysis of tree growth rings to identify droughts that occurred before flow data measurements began suggests that the existing flow record for the Colorado River may not describe the full range of flow variation in that river (NRC 2007a). But the possibility of climate shifts and resulting changes in rainfall or runoff pattern may make historical data an imperfect guide to future water availability (Gleick 2000). For example, winter snowpack serves as a form of storage in many western states, but if the snow begins to melt earlier each season, these changes will render historical flow records a poor guide to future water supply availability and reliability; new surface storage or enhanced use of aquifer storage and recovery would be necessary. Moreover, dramatic relocations of economic activity and population settlement may occur.

Looking ahead, future water uses and supplies are uncertain, but what can be predicted with certainty is that the coming decade will bring a continuation of the public debate seeking to reconcile the conservation tradition of water control with the principles of sustainable water management. The nation's long conversation about water supply adequacy—a conversation that began in the Progressive Era—is not about to end.

In 1999 the National Research Council's Board on Sustainable Development observed that the "quest for sustainability will necessarily be a collective, uncertain, and adaptive endeavor in which society's discovering of where it wants to go and how it might try to get there will be inextricably intertwined" (NRC 1999c, 17). This observation will describe the national discussion about water supply adequacy. Sustainable water management will be discovered through decisions about how water is going to be used over time and in specific places. We will learn from the consequences of the decisions we make and adjust our laws, regulations, and investment practices, just as we have learned about the consequences of past water control projects and are now making adjustments to how those projects are operated. Sustainable water management is a journey of discovery, and not a destination.

Notes

1. Appreciation is expressed to Carl Bauer, Hal Cardwell, Will Graf, Jeffrey Jacobs, and John Schefter for their critical and insightful reviews of early drafts of this chapter.

2. Chapter 2 of this book includes a discussion of the history and interpretations of the concept of sustainability. This chapter reviews the specific application of sustainability in the literature on water use and management. However, papers and reports on sustainability of water use include concerns and issues that are broader than what is considered here. For example, water that is free of chemical contaminants is often associated with sustainable water use. Equitable access to safe drinking water to prevent disease outbreaks from water contamination might be described as an imperative of sustainable water use (Loucks and Gladwell 1999; Solanes and Gonzalez-Villarreal 1999). At times *sustainability* has been used to describe the way that water utilities should set prices for cost recovery at their capital facilities (U.S. EPA 2007b). These water use and management concerns require serious and continuing attention by the nation. However, in the United States, laws and derivative programs were operating to address these issues long before the popular assignment of the term sustainability to describe these needs. The particular focus for this chapter is on how sustainability fundamentally changes the ways in which the nation assesses water availability and use (Barlow et al. 2004).

3. Throughout this chapter, data on water use, unless otherwise noted, are from Hutson et al. (2004). The limitations in their accuracy (NRC 2004b) are recognized, but they are the best available for national and regional assessments.

4. The water control infrastructure is aging, and expenditures for maintaining and rehabilitating it are increasing. For example, well over half of the Corps of Engineers budget is now dedicated to operations and maintenance. Waterways and ports must be continually dredged to maintain their capacity to handle traffic, but costs to dredge the same amount of sediment are increasing each year. Most of the nation's locks and dams are more than 50 years old. At the same time, levees for flood protection are in need of renewal and repair, and the nation is undertaking a massive levee assessment study in the aftermath of Hurricane Katrina. Water supplies of people in some of the nation's oldest and largest cities depend on antiquated delivery systems. In this chapter, *sustainability* has been reserved for discussing use of water resource itself, but the term has been employed to describe the challenge of maintaining the benefits from this aging investment portfolio (American Society of Civil Engineers 2007).

References

Alley, W.M. 2006. Tracking U.S. Ground Water. *Environment* 48(3): 10–25.

Alley, W.M., and S.A. Leake. 2004. The Journey from Safe Yield to Sustainability. *Ground Water* 42(1): 12–16.

Alley, W.M., R.W. Healy, J.W. LaBaugh, and T.E. Reilly. 2002. Flow and Storage in Groundwater Systems. *Science* 296: 1985–90.

American Society of Civil Engineers. 2007. Report Card for America's Infrastructure—2005. http://www.asce.org/reportcard/2005/index2005.cfm (accessed May 20, 2007).

Anderson, M.T., and L.H. Woosley Jr. 2005. *Water Availability for the Western United States—Key Scientific Challenges.* Circular 1261. Reston, VA: U.S. Geological Survey.

Archibold, R., and K. Johnson. 2007. *No Longer Waiting for Rain, an Arid West Takes Action.* http://www.iht.com/articles/2007/04/04/america/web-0404west.php (accessed May 20, 2007).

Aspen Institute. 2002. *Dam Removal: A New Option for a New Century.* Queenstown, MD: Aspen Institute Publications Office.

Barlow, P.M., W.M. Alley, and D.N. Myers. 2004. Hydrologic Aspects of Water Sustainability and Their Relation to a National Assessment of Water Availability and Use. *Water Resources Update* 127 (February): 76-86.

Bell, C. 2007. Water Conservation Initiatives: Western States Take Action. *The Water Report* 38 (April 15): 1–8.

Bloomquist, W., E. Schlager, and T. Heikkila. 2004. *Common Waters, Diverging Streams: Linking Institutions and Water Management in Arizona, California, and Colorado.* Washington, DC: Resources for the Future.

Brown, T.C. 1999. *Past and Future Freshwater Use in the United States: A Technical Document Supporting the 2000 USDA Forest Service RPA Assessment.* Fort Collins, CO: Rocky Mountain Research Station.

Central Kansas Water Bank Association. 2007. Water banking will promote water conservation and the wise use of the groundwater resources and provide increased flexibility for the water users within the banking area. http://www.gmd5.org/Water_Bank/index.htm (accessed May 20, 2007).

Collier, M., R.H. Webb, and J.C. Schmidt. 1996. *Dams and Rivers: Primer on the Downstream Effects of Dams.* Reston, VA: Circular 1126. U.S. Geological Survey.

Cooley, H., P. Gleick, and G. Wolff. 2006. *Desalination with a Grain of Salt: A California Perspective.* Oakland, CA: Pacific Institute for Studies in Development, Environment and Security.

Cox, W., and L. Shabman. 1984. Virginia's Water Law: Resolving the Inter-jurisdictional Transfer Issue. *Virginia Journal of Natural Resources Law* 3(2): 181–234.

Eden, S., J. Gelt, S. Megdal, T. Shipman, A. Smart, and M. Escobedo. 2007. Artificial Recharge: A Multipurpose Water Management Tool. Arroyo, Tucson: University of Arizona.

Frederick, K.D. 1991. Water Resources: Increasing Demand and Scarce Supplies. In *America's Renewable Resources: Historical Trends and Current Challenges,* edited by Kenneth D. Frederick and Roger A. Sedjo. Washington, DC: Resources for the Future, 23–78.

Frothingham, K.M., B.L. Rhoads, and E.E. Herricks. 2002. Profile: A Multiscale Conceptual Framework for Integrated Ecogeomorphological Research to Support Stream Naturalization in the Agricultural Midwest. *Environmental Management* 29(1): 16–33.

Getches, D.H. 1997. *Water Law in a Nutshell.* St. Paul, MN: Thompson-West.

Gleick, P.H. 2000. Water: The Potential Consequences of Climate Variability and Change for the Water Resources of the United States. Report of the Water Sector Assessment Team of the National Assessment of the Potential Consequences of Climate Variability and Change. Oakland, CA: Pacific Institute for Studies in Development, Environment and Security.

Gleick, P.H., D. Haasz, C. Henges-Jeck, V. Srinivasn, G. Wolff, K.K. Cushing, and A. Mann. 2003. *Waste Not, Want Not: The Potential for Urban Water Conservation in California.* Oakland, CA: Pacific Institute for Studies in Development, Environment and Security.

Gollehon, N., and W. Quinby. 2006. *Irrigation Resources and Water Costs.* http://www.ers.usda.gov/publications/arei/eib16/chapter2/2.1/ (accessed May 20, 2007).

Goodwin, C.D. 1983. The Valley Authority Idea—The Fading of a National Vision. In *TVA: Fifty Years of Grass-roots Bureaucracy,* edited by E.C. Hargrove and P.K. Conkin. Urbana and Chicago: University of Illinois Press, 263–96.

Gowan, C., K. Stephenson, and L. Shabman 2006. The Role of Ecosystem Valuation in Environmental Decision Making: Hydropower Relicensing and Dam Removal on the Elwha River. *Ecological Economics* 56: 508–23.

Graf, W.L. 1999. Dam Nation: A Geographic Census of American Dams and Their Large Scale Hydrologic Impacts. *Water Resources Research* 35(4): 1305–11.

———. (ed.). 2003. *Dam Removal Research: Status and Prospects.* Washington, DC: Heinz Center.

Hank, E., and M. Davis. 2006. Lawns and Water Demand in California. *California Economic Policy* 2(2): 1–22.

Heinz Jr., H.T. 2004. Applying the Concept of Sustainability to Water Resources Management. *Water Resources Update* 127 (February): 6–10.

Holland, A. 2000. Ecological Integrity and the Darwinian Paradigm. In *Ecological Integrity: Integrating Environment, Conservation, and Health,* edited by D. Pimentel, L. Westra, and R.F. Noss. Washington, DC, and Covelo, CA: Island Press, 45–59.

Holmes, B.H. 1972. *A History of Federal Water Resources Programs, 1800–1960.* Miscellaneous Publication 1233. Economic Research Service. Washington, DC: U.S. Department of Agriculture.

Hundly, N., Jr. 1992. *The Great Thirst: Californians and Water, 1770s–1990s.* Berkeley: University of California Press.

Hutson, S.S., N.L. Barber, J.F. Kenny, K.S. Linsey, D.S. Lumia, and M.A. Maupin. 2004. *Estimated Use of Water in the United States in 2000.* Circular 1268. Reston, VA: U.S. Geological Survey.

Idaho Water Board. 2007. *Idaho Water Supply Bank.* http://www.idwr.idaho.gov/waterboard/water%20bank/waterbank.htm (accessed May 20, 2007).

Interstate Commission on the Potomac River Basin. 2007. Co-op history. http://www.potomacriver.org/water_supply/co-op.htm (accessed May 20, 2007).

Keeny, D., C. Goemans, B. Klein, J. Lowrey, and K. Reidy. 2007. Residential Water Demand Management in Aurora: Learning from the Drought Crisis. *Colorado Water* 25(1): 14–16. http://wwa.colorado.edu/resources/water_demand_and_conservation/WaterDemandAurora.pdf (accessed May 20, 2007).

Kennedy, J.F. 1963. Remarks at the Dedication of the Whiskeytown, California, Dam and Reservoir. September 28. http://www.presidency.ucsb.edu/ws/print.php?pid=9441 (accessed May 20, 2007).

Koel, T.M., and R.E. Sparks. 2002. Historical Patterns of River Stage and Fish Communities as Criteria for Operations of Dams on the Illinois River. *River Research and Applications* 18: 3–19.

Kramer, R., and L. Shabman. 1993. The Effects of Agricultural and Tax Policy Reform on the Economic Return to Wetland Drainage in the Mississippi Delta Region. *Land Economics* 69(3): 85–126.

Krutilla, J.V. 1967. Conservation Reconsidered. *American Economic Review.* September: 777–86.

Lackey, R.T. 2001. Values, Policy, and Ecosystem Health. *BioScience* 51(6): 437–43.

Lackey, R.T., D.H. Lach, and S.L. Duncan (eds.). 2006. *Salmon 2100: The Future of Wild Pacific Salmon.* Bethesda, MD: American Fisheries Society. http://inr.oregonstate.edu/salmon2100/book.htm (accessed May 20, 2007).

Leitman, S. 2005. Apalachicola-Chattahoochee-Flint Basin: Tri-state Negotiations of a Water Allocation Formula. In *Adaptive Governance and Water Conflict: New Institutions for Collaborative Planning,* edited by John T. Scholz and Bruce Stiffel. Washington, DC: Resources for the Future, 74–88.

Leydet, F. 1968. *Time and the River Flowing: Grand Canyon,* edited by David Brower. Sierra Club. New York: Ballantine Books.

Loucks, D.P., and J.S. Gladwell (eds.). 1999. *Sustainability Criteria for Water Resource Systems.* Cambridge: Cambridge University Press.

Loucks, D.P., E.Z. Stakhiv, and L.R. Martin. 2000. Sustainable Water Resources Management. *Journal of Water Resources Planning and Management* 126(2): 43–47.

Nash, R. 1968. *The American Environment: Readings in the History of Conservation.* Boston: Addison Wesley.

———. 2001. *Wilderness in the American Mind,* 4th edition. New Haven: Yale University Press.

National Research Council (NRC). 1992. *Restoration of Aquatic Ecosystems.* Washington, DC: National Academy Press.

———. 1998. *Issues in Potable Water Reuse: The Viability of Augmenting Drinking Water with Reclaimed Water.* Washington, DC: National Academies Press.

———. 1999a. *Downstream: Adaptive Management of Glen Canyon and the Colorado River.* Washington, DC: National Academies Press.

———. 1999b. *New Strategies for America's Watersheds.* Washington, DC: National Academies Press.

———. 1999c. *Our Common Journey: A Transition toward Sustainability.* Washington, DC: National Academies Press.

———. 2001. *Aquifer Storage and Recovery in the Comprehensive Everglades Restoration Plan.* Washington, DC: National Academies Press.

———. 2002a. *Estimating Water Use in the United States: A New Paradigm for the National Water-Use Information Program.* Washington, DC: National Academies Press.

———. 2002b. *The Missouri River Ecosystem: Exploring the Prospects for Recovery.* Washington, DC: National Academies Press.

———. 2002c. *Riparian Areas: Functions and Strategies for Management.* Washington, DC: National Academies Press.

———. 2004a. *Review of the Desalination and Water Purification Technology Road Map.* Washington, DC: National Academies Press.

———. 2004b. *U.S. Army Corps of Engineers Water Resources Project Planning: A New Opportunity for Service.* Washington, DC: National Academies Press.

———. 2005. *Science of Instream Flows: A Review of the Texas Instream Flow Program.* Washington, DC: National Academies Press.

————. 2006. *Progress toward Restoring the Everglades: The First Biennial Review.* Washington, DC: National Academies Press.

————. 2007a. *Colorado River Basin Management: Evaluating and Adjusting to Hydroclimatic Variability.* Washington, DC: National Academies Press.

————. 2007b. *River Science at the U.S. Geological Survey.* Washington, DC: National Academies Press.

National Resources Planning Board. 1934. *Report on Planning and Public Works in Relation to Natural Resources and Including Land Use and Water Resources.* Washington, DC: U.S. Government Printing Office.

National Water Commission. 1973. *Water Policies for the Future: Final Report to the President and to the Congress of the United States.*

The Nature Conservancy. 2007. Pioneering Effort to Restore Green River is Extended. http://www.nature.org/initiatives/freshwater/press/press2982.html (accessed May 20, 2007).

Newell, F.H. 1902. *Irrigation in the United States.* New York: Thomas Y. Crowell & Co.

Null, S.E., and J.R. Lund. 2006. Reassembling Hetch Hetchy: Water Supply without O'Shaughnessy Dam. *Journal of AWRA* 42(2): 395–408.

Oregon Water Trust. 2007. Cooperative Solutions, Healthy Streams. http://www.owt.org/ (accessed May 20, 2007).

Osborn, C.T., J. Schefter, and L. Shabman. 1986. The Accuracy of Water Use Forecasts: Evaluation and Implications. *Water Resources Bulletin* 21(1): 101–109.

Pielke, R. 2007. Flood Damage in the United States, 1926–2003: A Reanalysis of National Weather Service Estimates. http://www.flooddamagedata.org/contact.html (accessed May 20, 2007).

Poff, N.L., J.D. Allan, M.A. Palmer, D.D. Hart, B. Richter, A.H. Arthington, K.H. Rogers, J.L. Meyer, and J.A. Stanford. 2003. River Flows and Water Wars: Emerging Science for Environmental Decision Making. *Frontiers in Ecology* 1(6): 298–306.

President's Water Resources Policy Commission. 1950. *A Water Policy for the American People* (vol. 1). Washington, DC: Government Printing Office.

Rhoads, B.L., D. Wilson, M. Urban, and E.E. Herricks. 1999. Interaction between Scientists and Nonscientists in Community-based Watershed Management: Emergence of the Concept of Stream Naturalization. *Environmental Management* 24(3): 297–308.

Richter, B.D., R. Mathews, D.L. Harrison, and R. Wigington. 2003. Ecologically Sustainable Water Management: Managing River Flows for Ecological Integrity. *Ecological Applications* 13(1): 206–24.

Select Committee on National Water Resources. 1961. *Water Resources Activities in the United States.* United States Senate. Washington, DC: Government Printing Office.

Shabman, L. 1988. The Benefits and Costs of Flood Control: Reflections on the Flood Control Act of 1936. In *The Flood Control Challenge: Past, Present, and Future,* edited by H. Rosen and M. Reuss. Chicago: Public Works Historical Society, 109–23.

————. 1990. Water-use Forecasting—Benefits and Capabilities. In *National Water Summary, 1987.* Reston, VA: U.S. Geological Survey, 117–22.

Shabman, L., and W. Cox. 1986. Costs of Water Management Institutions: A Study of Southeastern Virginia. In *Scarce Water and Institutional Change,* edited by Ken Frederick. Washington, DC: Resources for the Future, 134–70.

————. 2004. Urban Water Supply Planning and the Environment: Extending the Reach of Section 404 of the Clean Water Act. *Virginia Journal of Environmental Law* (Spring).

Sklar, F.H., M.J. Chimney, S. Newman, P. McCormick, D. Gawlik, S. Miao, C. McVoy, W. Said, J. Newman, C. Coronado, G. Crozier, M. Korvela, and K. Rutchey. 2005. The Ecological-societal Underpinnings of Everglades Restoration. *Frontiers in Ecology* 3(3):161–69.

Solanes, M., and F. Gonzalez-Villarreal. 1999. *The Dublin Principles for Water as Reflected in a Comparative Assessment of Institutional and Legal Arrangements for Integrated Water Resources Management.* TAC Background Paper 3. Stockholm: Development Cooperation Agency.

Sophocleous, M. 2000. From Safe Yield to Sustainable Development of Water Resources—The Kansas Experience. *Journal of Hydrology* 235: 27–43.

South Florida Water Management District. 2007. Alternative Water Supply Funding. https://my.sfwmd.gov/portal/page?_pageid=1874,4164635,1874_13062096&_dad=portal&_schema=PORTAL (accessed May 20, 2007).

Stanford, J.A., J.V. Ward, W.J. Liss, C.A. Frissell, R.N. Williams, J.A. Lichatowich, and C.C. Coutant. 1996. A General Protocol for Restoration of Regulated Rivers. *Regulated Rivers: Research & Management* 12: 391–413.

Stephenson, K. 2002. Taking Nature into Account: Observations about the Changing Role of Analysis and Negotiation in Hydropower Relicensing. *William and Mary Environmental Law and Policy Review* 25(2): 473–98.

Subcommittee on Water Availability and Quality. 2004. *Science and Technology to Support Freshwater Availability in the United States.* National Science and Technology Council Committee on Environment and Natural Resources. Washington, DC: Office of Science and Technology Policy.

Tarlock, A.D. 2003. The Creation of New Risk Sharing Water Entitlement Regimes: The Case of the Truckee-Carson Settlement. *Ecology Law Quarterly* 25(4): 674–91.

Tarlock, A.D., and H. Doremus. 2003. Fish, Farms, and the Clash of Cultures in the Klamath Basin. *Ecology Law Quarterly* 279.

U.S. Army Corps of Engineers. 2007. Navigation Data Center. http://www.iwr.usace.army.mil/ndc/wcsc/wcsc.htm (accessed May 20, 2007).

U.S. Department of the Interior. 2005. Water 2025: Preventing Crises and Conflict in the West. http://www.doi.gov/water2025 (accessed May 20, 2007).

U.S. Environmental Protection Agency (U.S. EPA). 2007a. Ecoregions, Reference Conditions, and Index Calibration. http://www.epa.gov/bioindicators//html/chapter5_acronyms_definitions.html (accessed May 20, 2007).

———. 2007b. Sustainable Infrastructure for Water and Wastewater. http://www.epa.gov/water-infrastructure/ (accessed May 20, 2007).

U.S. Fish and Wildlife Service (U.S. FWS). 2004. *Management Plan for Endangered Fishes in the Yampa River Basin.* http://www.r6.fws.gov/crrip/doc/yampa/ExecutiveSummary.pdf (accessed May 20, 2007).

———. 2006. Questions and Answers. Biological Opinion on U.S. Army Corps of Engineers' Interim Operations Plan (IOP) for Jim Woodruff Dam and Associated Releases to the Apalachicola River. http://www.fws.gov/panamacity/species/ACF%20BO%20updated%20QA%209-11.pdf (accessed May 20, 2007).

U.S. General Accounting Office (U.S. GAO). 1982. *Water Issues Facing the Nation: An Overview.* Gaithersburg, MD.

U.S. Geological Survey (USGS). 2002. Concepts for National Assessment of Water Availability and Use. Report to Congress. Circular 1223. Denver: U.S. Geological Survey.

———. 2007. Basin and range carbonate and aquifer system study. http://nevada.usgs.gov/bar-cass/ (accessed May 20, 2007).

U.S. Water Resources Council (U.S. WRC). 1978. The Nation's Water Resources: 1975–2000. Second National Water Assessment. Washington, DC: Government Printing Office.

Van Herik, R. 2000. The Natural Flow Regime: An Organizing Principle for Great Lakes Ecosystem Restoration. In *State of the Great Lakes: 2000 Annual Report.* Lansing: Michigan Department of Environmental Quality, 8–11.

Wollman, N., and G.W. Bonem. 1971. *The Outlook for Water: Quality, Quantity, and National Growth.* Washington, DC: Resources for the Future.

Working Group for Post Hurricane Planning for the Louisiana Coast. 2006. A new framework for planning the future of coastal Louisiana after the hurricanes of 2005. http://www.umces.edu/la-restore/ (accessed May 20, 2007).

CHAPTER 6

Wildlife

Sustainability and Management

Dean Lueck

*A*T THE TIME EUROPEANS began to explore and settle North America, the native populations were primarily hunters and gatherers who had relatively little impact on wildlife populations.[1] In many ways, the wildlife populations in North America were pristine around 1600, or had at least settled into an equilibrium in which most populations were relatively stable and large. In Europe, however, long-established and widespread human civilizations had dramatically reduced many wild populations (e.g., bears, elk, deer, wildfowl, bison, and wolves).

This chapter examines the pattern of use and conservation of wildlife—and their implications for the sustainability of wildlife—from the time of European contact to the present. During these past four centuries, human activities have directly exploited and conserved wildlife populations and have directly and indirectly altered habitats. Some populations and species have been driven to extinction (e.g., passenger pigeon) or the brink of extinction (e.g., bison and ivory-billed woodpeckers), and some have thrived (e.g., white-tailed deer, coyotes, and crows). It is customary to characterize this history (e.g., Harrington 1991) as comprising three distinct periods: (1) little impact; (2) dramatic decline because of overexploitation and habitat destruction, and (3) recovery. Table 6-1 shows that this has been the case for many species, yet there is substantial variation in the timing and causes of decline and the degree of recovery.

The information in Table 6-1 cannot usefully be examined without an understanding of several other major historical trends. Foremost among these are the changes in land use over time and the implications of these changes for wildlife habitat. Table 6-2 shows how population growth, urbanization, and agriculture have changed the landscape since the time of European contact. These land use changes have had the most impact on the Great Plains, the eastern forests,[2] and the coastal

Table 6-1. *U.S. Wildlife and Human Populations, 1700–2000*

Species	1700	1800	1900	2000	Sources
Bison	40,000,000	25,000,000	1,000	400,000	Shaw (1995)
White-tailed deer	30,000,000	13,000,000	350,000	26,000,000	McCabe and McCabe (1984), Demarais and Krausman (2000), Demarais et al. (2000)
Mule deer	7,500,000	4,000,000	500,000	5,000,000	Kie and Czech (2000)
Elk	10,000,000	5,030,000	60,000	700,000	Wisdom and Cook (2000)
Wild turkey	25,000,000	12,515,000	30,000	7,000,000	National Wild Turkey Federation (2005)
Gray wolf	500,000	350,000	200,000	65,000	Hampton (1997)
Pronghorn antelope	30,000,000	15,000,000	15,000	650,000	Yoakum and O'Gara (2000)
Gray whale	19,500	10,000	5,000	26,600	NOAA (2002)
Bald eagle	250,000	100,000	NA	11,000	U.S. FWS (1999), American Eagle Foundation (2001)
Whooping crane	1,500	1,000	50	450	U.S. FWS (2004), Whooping Crane Operation Migration (2005)
Passenger pigeon	5,000,000,000	2,200,000,000	0	0	
Humans	2,250,000	4,500,000	75,994,575	281,422,426	U.S. Census Bureau (1960, 2000) Thornton (1987) and http://www.britannica.com/eb/article-77693/United-States

(*Note:* these figures include the Native American population figures which are then added to the U.S. Census data for the respective years)

zones. The dramatic land use changes have reduced the habitat for some species but favored others.

Another important trend to understand when studying wildlife is the substantial role taken by government (both state and federal) in the management of wildlife. Today, state wildlife agencies are the primary government actor involved in wildlife, by regulating hunting, fishing, and trapping; by providing law enforcement; by conducting research; and by educating the public. The federal government is also heavily involved, primarily as a major landowner and in endangered species conservation.

During the first 200 years of American history, wildlife was viewed primarily either as a source of food (or related products, such as hides and furs) or as pests. During the latter part of the 19th century and throughout much of the 20th century, wildlife became more important as a source of recreation through hunting and fishing. State wildlife agencies arose to address these demands. As Table 6-3

Table 6-2. *U.S. Land-Use Trends, 1800–2000*

	1800	1850	1900	1950	2000
Land (thousands of acres)	568,839	1,915,358	1,934,328	1,934,328	2,428,213
Population	5,308,483	23,191,876	75,994,575	150,697,361	281,422,426
Density (pop./acre)	0.93	1.21	3.93	7.79	11.59
Population in urban areas (%)	6.1	15.4	39.6	59.6	75.2
Farms	NA	1,449,000	5,737,000	5,648,000	2,172,000
Farmland, in thousands of acres (%)	NA	29,3534 (15.3)	838,583 (43.4)	1,158,565 (59.9)	943,090 (38.8)
Cropland, in thousands of acres (%)	<20,000 (3.5)	113,000 (5.9)	319,000 (16.5)	409,000 (21.1)	343,000 (14.1)
National forest area, in thousands of acres (%)	0	0	75,352 (3.9)	181,205 (9.4)	192,335 (7.9)
National parks and federal refuges, in thousands of acres (%)	0	0	3,289 (.2)	12,238 (.6)	142,326 (5.9)

Sources: U.S. Census Bureau, *Historical Statistics of the U.S.: Colonial Times to 1957*, Washington, DC, 1960, U.S. Census Bureau, *Statistical Abstract of the United States: 2002*, 122nd edition, Washington, DC, 2002; Fedkiw 1989; Greenwalt 1978.

Table 6-3. *Hunting, Fishing, and Wildlife-Related Activities*

Participants	1955	1980	2001
Hunters	10,700,000	17,400,000	13,034,000
Anglers	19,000,000	42,000,000	34,067,000
Wildlife watchers	NA	28,800,000	66,105,000

Sources: Clawson and Van Doren 1984; U.S. FWS (1988, 2002).

shows, the relative importance of hunting and fishing has declined, and in its place wildlife-based recreation tied to viewing or "watching" has risen.[3]

A final important trend in wildlife management has been the emergence of private interest groups involved in wildlife conservation and management. Table 6-4 shows some of the most important of these groups. Many are focused on a singles species, and several are explicitly linked to hunters and anglers who want to maintain harvestable populations. Other groups, however, are not linked to hunting or fishing (and may even be openly hostile toward these activities) and instead are interested in preservation of natural environments in which certain species are found.

This chapter examines the history of wildlife management in the United States and its economic underpinnings. In doing so, the question of the sustainability of wildlife is addressed. The term wildlife has tended to refer to mammals, birds, and fish, so this chapter will focus on these groups of species and will not generally consider the broader issue of biodiversity.[4]

What does sustainability mean for wildlife? The most widely accepted definition of sustainability was developed by the Brundtland Commission (WCED

Table 6-4. *U.S. Wildlife Interest Groups*

Organization	Issues	Year Founded	Members (2005)
General wildlife interest groups			
National Audubon Society	Conservation and restoration of natural ecosystems, focusing on birds.	1905	550,000
Izaak Walton League of America	Conservation and protection of natural resources, focusing on wetlands, streams, and fish.	1923	50,000
National Wildlife Federation	Protection of wildlife and habitat through conservation, land stewardship, and water resources programs.	1936	4,000,000
Defenders of Wildlife	Protection of wild animals and plants, focusing on ecosystem preservation and predator conservation.	1947	480,000
Center for Biological Diversity	Prevention of biodiversity loss.	1989	13,000
Species-based wildlife interest groups			
American Bison Society	Protection and enhancement of the U.S. bison population; disbanded in 1930 after meeting goals.	1905	—
Ducks Unlimited	Protection and enhancement of waterfowl populations and their habitat.	1937	778,000
National Wild Turkey Federation	Improvement of wild turkey habitat, management, and hunting.	1973	525,000
Peregrine Fund	Conservation of birds of prey.	1970	3,700
Foundation for North American Wild Sheep	Promotion and enhancement of wild sheep populations.	1977	6,000
Rocky Mountain Elk Foundation	Restoration of natural elk habitats and promotion of elk conservation, hunting, and management.	1984	132,000

Sources: Clawson and Van Doren (1984), U.S. FWS (1988, 2002).

1987), which stated, "development is sustainable when it meets the needs of the present without compromising the ability of future generations to meet theirs."[5] Many have noted the vagueness of this concept (see Chapter 1, this volume), yet in the forestry, fisheries, and wildlife fields, the idea of sustainable yield predates our more current focus on sustainability as defined by the Brundtland Commission's report. The concept of sustained yield dictates that harvesting must not exceed growth rates, or the natural stocks will decline and the amount of products flowing from these stocks must also necessarily decline. Heal (1998, 2000) has done the most to add analytical economic rigor to the concept of sustainability.[6] In particular, Heal stresses that ecosystems and stocks of natural resources generate value by providing services beyond those derived from resource harvest or extraction. For wildlife, this means that important values can come from nonconsumptive uses of wildlife, including viewing, genetic information, and contributions to ecosystem services and seed dispersal. Heal also stresses the importance of resource values that come in the very long run—say, more than 50 or 100 years. When these concerns are incorporated into economic models, sustainability tends to mean that it can be efficient to hold relatively larger resource stocks (i.e., wildlife populations) than implied by simpler economic models.[7]

Yet, even within Heal's framework, sustainability remains an elusive empirical concept, so the focus in this chapter will be on explaining how wildlife management institutions have affected wildlife populations and how economic forces have in turn shaped these management institutions. Importantly, however, the chapter will examine how wildlife management institutions have responded to increases in the values of wildlife stocks, as suggested by Heal.

Economics and Wildlife

Before examining the economics of wildlife, it is important to clarify what is meant by wildlife and how wildlife differs from other biological resources. What distinguishes wild species (or individual animals) from domestic? The answer lies in the property rights associated with various species. The distinction is important, as it focuses on ownership as a key to understanding wildlife institutions and therefore the size and sustainability of these populations.

A population or stock of animals is completely wild only when there are no exclusive rights to the stock—that is, when "open access" exists.[8] Similarly, a stock is fully domestic only when property rights to the stock are perfectly defined and enforced. Because ownership is costly, domestication is never complete (e.g., cattle break fences and escape).[9] Similarly, because open access dissipates wealth, wildness is also unlikely to be absolute. The completeness of ownership varies widely across species both over time and across places. Ownership can take place over populations (e.g., a herd of caribou) or over individuals (e.g., a trained circus elephant), though in this chapter the focus will be on ownership of populations and other aggregations of individuals.

One can also consider wild versus domestic in terms of the animals' habitat. Wild animals have "natural" habitat while domestic animals have "human-made" habitat. The more natural the habitat, the more wild the animals are. In everyday usage "wild" implies something about both ownership and habitat, probably because people implicitly recognize that the establishment of property rights to animals usually—maybe always—requires some modification of habitat, such as building fences or controlling predators. It also follows that ownership affects animal behavior (and ultimately biology) by altering the natural parameters faced by the animals (Geist 1994). It is also true that humans affect a population even without ownership because open-access exploitation can lead to overharvest and other impacts, thus implicating the question of sustainability.

The Benefits and Costs of Wild Populations

The potential value and costs associated with wildlife are crucial in determining the ownership and use of a population or stock. Because these benefits and costs are connected to different characteristics of wildlife, so will ownership rights be connected with different characteristics. For example, for stocks that generate valuable pelts, ownership will be specified in terms of trapping rights. If, on the other hand, a stock is most important for the costs it imposes on livestock owners, ownership is expected to be specified in terms of rights to eradicate the stock.[10] In turn, the realized net benefits depend on the system of ownership that governs the stock.

The net value of a wild population is determined by the gross value it generates and by the costs of generating them. A stock of wildlife is valued for products derived from its carcass, which requires killing individuals, and for services derived from living animals, including ecosystem services. Costs arise, in the form of damage to other resources, because animals consume resources in their day-to-day lives. Ducks and geese feast on small grains, elk and deer forage in hay fields, and mountain lions attack sheep, pets, and even children.

Animal products such as feathers, flesh, hides, and pelts are valuable commodities for which well-established markets often exist. For a market transaction to occur, property rights to at least some of the attributes of the commodity must be well specified, as is true for hides and pelts. Live animals are valuable because not only can they provide these products at a future date, but also during their lifetime they periodically provide antlers, manure, power, or wool, and they can also produce aesthetic value from activities like viewing or photographing or simply from "existence." In addition, wild populations can potentially provide a wide variety of ecosystem services (Daily 1997).[11] These latter considerations are important because of the growth in the demand for these nonconsumptive uses. In turn, institutions have developed in recognition of these types of uses, and they tend to focus on habitat management rather than on managing the harvest of individuals.

Recognizing Biological Forces

Wildlife populations are renewable or sustainable biological resources, and some basic elements of population dynamics are important for understanding the effects of various uses on populations. The two panels in Figure 6-1 show the basic features of biological growth common to nearly all living things. The top panel shows that when plotted against time, a wild population tends to grow slowly at first, then more rapidly before ultimately slowing down as it reaches its maximum level, or its "carrying capacity" (often called K) for a given habitat.[12] The bottom panel simply displays the same information by plotting the size of the population against the rate of growth of the population. It shows that when the stock is zero or when it is at the carrying capacity, there is no growth. Typically, the growth is largest (MSY) when the population is of some medium size. When the population growth rate is largest (see Point A), it is said to be at maximum sustainable yield level. This means that at that population (X_{MSY}), the largest possible level of harvest could indefinitely be sustained because growth would exactly offset it. At a carrying capacity population, however, the sustainable harvest is zero because the net growth rate is also zero. Thus the simple features of biological growth indicate that population levels must be reduced from carrying capacity to increase sustainable harvest. The term old-growth, as used by foresters, simply means a stock of trees old enough to have a total biomass at the level of carrying capacity and that these trees must be cut to induce new growth. The same idea holds for the animal species that we typically think of as wildlife, although the timeframe is much shorter than for forest species.

Panel A. The Time-Stock Relationship

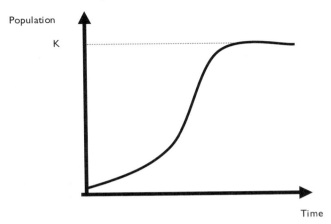

Panel B. The Stock-Growth Relationship

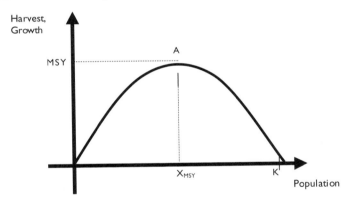

Figure 6-1. *Biological Production Function*

The economically optimal use of a wild population must not only recognize these biological forces but also take into account both the net benefits of associated with various populations and the property rights to the population or to individuals within a population. In some cases (e.g., mosquitoes) it might be optimal for the population to be eradicated, or nearly so.[13] The economic problem is to determine the optimal time to harvest or whether to harvest; that is, how long should the population be allowed to grow? Property rights are important in determining effort, harvest (or preservation), stock size, and wealth generated from the stock. If secure property rights to a population exist, the typical outcome is for the owner to harvest an entire cohort at the same time and then restock the habitat with another population.[14] This would be the case for domestic cattle as well as for aquaculture. In addition to this, strong property rights also give the owner a strong incentive to invest in habitat (changing K) or changing population dynamics (e.g., growth rates) themselves through animal husbandry (e.g., selective breeding, medicine).

The alternative to a regime in which management is based on optimal harvest timing is a regime in which harvesting is done continually and the new economic problem is to determine the optimal number of animals to harvest each time.[15] This kind of regime can be found in situations where populations are owned, or where there is open access. If property rights are secure, the owner will choose the optimal amount of harvest each period.[16] Regardless of whether an owner chooses to continually harvest or to periodically harvest an entire cohort, the owner will earn a rent from optimal management, and the total value of the stock will be the discounted present value of this stream of rents.

If, however, the population is open access, the level of harvest will be excessive because each user does not bear the cost of his harvest on the size or productivity of the population.[17] If harvest costs are low, open access can lead to extreme reductions in population and even extinction.[18] Indeed, open-access exploitation is a dominant cause of many dramatic population reductions and extinctions. In addition, the value of the rent (and its present value equivalent) will be dissipated in the process of overexploitation. Thus, not only is the wildlife resource damaged, but little or no economic value is generated from its presence.

When nonconsumptive values (i.e., values from the living stock, not harvest) dominate, a private owner may optimally choose to limit harvest or not harvest at all. However, because many such uses (e.g., viewing, scientific research) are public goods, a private owner will have to overcome free-riding problems, and this may depend on the owner's ability to enforce his property right. For example, to restrict access to a herd of elephants for photographic safaris, an owner might need to acquire additional land to have a buffer to reduce the ability of neighbors to view the animals at no charge. Public parks face the same problem of enforcement. If open access prevails and there is consumptive value of individuals aside from the nonconsumptive value of the stock, then overexploitation will reduce the value of the wildlife by reducing the size of the population and its value for various nonconsumptive uses. Only when consumptive uses are limited and harvest costs are high will open access sustain wild populations, and even in that situation, alternative land use might lead to overexploitation of wildlife.

Ownership of Land and Wildlife

Ownership of a wildlife population is costly to establish because the ownership patterns of land do not always coincide with the habitat requirements of wildlife populations.[19] Land ownership patterns tend not to be determined by wildlife use but rather by such uses as agriculture (e.g., farms, ranches), mining, and commercial forestry. If a wildlife population were the only valuable resource tied to a parcel of land, then the value of the land would be maximized when landownership coincided with the population's territory. In this situation, a landowner would implicitly own the wildlife population and have incentive to maximize its value by choosing the optimal level of use and population size. Wildlife would then be quite similar economically to domestic animals, although the habitat would still be "natural." In the usual case, however, wildlife is not the only valued use of land, and the analysis is not so straightforward.

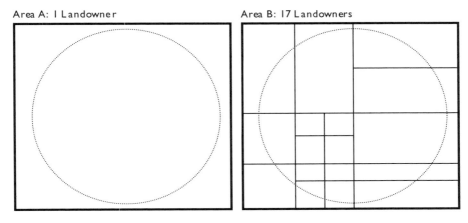

PROPERTY BORDER

WILDLIFE TERRITORY

Figure 6-2. *Wildlife and Land Ownership Patterns*

Figure 6-2 shows two possible scenarios that illustrate the fundamental issues. Both panels show a square piece of land that encompasses a circular area of wildlife habitat. For simplicity, assume the wildlife equally use all portions of the habitat. In the left panel (A), there is a single landowner. In the right panel (B) there are 17 landowners with tracts of various sizes. It is easy to see that in panel A, the landowner accrues all costs and benefits that come from the wildlife (except for nonlocal values, such as existence value). In panel (B), however, no single landowner faces the full costs and benefits, and each will have an incentive to harvest animals that occupy his own tract before they move on; thus no one will have a strong incentive to invest in habitat improvement or enforcement.

Consider a more specific example. If deer require 10,000 acres and the optimal plot size for agriculture is at least 10,000 acres, then the agricultural landowner would de facto own the deer population. If the optimal plot size is only 1,000 acres, then the landowner's (or another agent's) ability to own the "deer population rights" will depend on the cost of transacting and enforcing an agreement among 10 1,000-acre landowners. These contracting costs among landowners may eliminate the potential gains they could acquire from specifying their rights to the wildlife.

Sometimes wildlife values dominate agricultural and other land-use values and determine the ownership pattern of land (e.g., aboriginal hunting grounds, a wildlife refuge). If wildlife is the most valued attribute of the land, the game manager would be the most efficient landowner. A similar case describes the governing property rights for many aboriginal hunting and gathering societies (Lueck 2002). Property rights were designed to protect valuable wild populations that required greater territories than did agriculture.

In principle, the landowners can make a contract to jointly manage the wildlife, thus solving the problem of how to establish ownership to wildlife populations whose habitat encompasses many landowners. The ability of landowners to establish rights to wildlife on their property depends on the incentive they have to resolve the conflict between the territorial requirements of a wild population and the optimal tract size of land used for other purposes. Generally, it is more likely that private landowners will find it in their interest to assert rights to wildlife where wildlife values are highest, where the land is more productive (or of a better quality) for wildlife, where land holdings are large, and where the territorial requirements of wildlife are small. Accordingly, where these conditions are not met, it is more likely that government will assert control over wildlife.

Government Wildlife Agencies as Contractual Solutions

Because it may simply be too costly for wildlife ownership to be established via private contracting, alternative institutions may emerge to govern wildlife. In particular, government wildlife departments can be seen as agents that have contracted with landowners for control of the wildlife attributes of their land where the costs of contracting with other private landowners are relatively high (Lueck 1991; Lueck and Parker 2007).

The creation of a game department that acts as a wildlife owner may aid in overcoming the often prohibitive costs of private contracting for ownership of wildlife populations. It is important to realize, however, that the nature of the game department carries with it certain limitations that restrict its efficiency. A game department will be unable to effectively control land uses that affect wildlife, and it will also be driven by various inefficiencies common to all government bureaucracies (these flaws will be further discussed below). Since it is costly to enforce property rights to wildlife, this trade-off cannot be avoided. These costs depend not only on traditional economic variables but also on the character of the wild populations themselves (Diamond 1997). For example, zebras are the same genus as the domestic horse but are notoriously more difficult to control.

The History of American Wildlife Management

Table 6-5 shows the broad historical development of American wildlife management institutions, which have varied widely among regions, across species, and over time.

Origins: Pre-Columbian North American and English Game Laws

Prior to white settlement, American Indian tribes specified rights to live wildlife stocks by protecting hunting and fishing territories. The ownership of game among Native Americans had an uncanny resemblance to current American institutions. Indian tribal societies, much like state agencies, controlled wildlife stocks by enforcing the rights to hunting and fishing territories and restricting the time and method of harvest by tribal members.[20] Native Americans found it difficult, if not impossi-

Table 6-5. *History of U.S. Wildlife Management Institutions*

Period	Institution
Pre-1492	Native American tribal territories.
1700	Demise of tribal territories; some open access.
1800	Open access; some early game laws.
1865	Development of game laws.
1896	Constitutional support for state game regulations in *Geer v. Connecticut*.
1900	Emergence of state game departments and federal control over migratory species via the Lacey Act.
1916	Migratory bird treaty.
1973	Endangered Species Act, giving broad power to the federal government and lessening state authority.
1990	Federal control over endangered species. Development of private institutions for hunting and preservation.

Source: Lueck (1998).

ble, to enforce their property rights to these regions as whites introduced agriculture and industry to the New World, causing the relative value of the wildlife attributes of the land to decline drastically (Cronon 1986; Lund 1980). During this period of open access, "market hunting" flourished and many wildlife populations in the United States plummeted. There were well-established rights and markets for game products, such as meat and hides, but rights to live wildlife stocks were practically nonexistent (Trefethen and Corbin 1975; Tober 1981; Harrington 1991).

American wildlife law, which frames management institutions, has origins in English common law, but for wildlife, present-day American and English law differ sharply (Lueck 1998). In the United States, the law places most control of wildlife in the hands of government, primarily the states. In Great Britain, the law places nearly all control in the hands of private landowners.

The English common law of property distinguished between domestic and wild animals. For domestics animals (e.g., cattle), property rights were nearly absolute, and rights were retained even when the animals strayed from the owner's property. Wild animals were generally considered an open-access resource; however, landowners had important rights to game on their own property. In addition to the common law rules, from 1369 to 1831, Parliament restricted access to wildlife through the Game Laws, which basically limited wildlife access to landowners. Sanctions for violators were often severe, with poachers sometimes being punished by death. After the qualification statutes were abolished in 1831, landowners acquired explicit ownership of wildlife stocks that inhabited their land. Today, British landowners still control a preponderance of rights to game and fish and routinely charge for hunting and fishing privileges (sporting rights) for deer, gamebirds, and trout. The government is still present, having a role in protecting certain nongame species, regulating game markets, and enforcing poaching laws, but compared with the United States, government regulation of wildlife is minimal. Statutes determine the length of open seasons for taking game, but the owners of the sporting rights determine bag limits and actually own the game when it is killed.[21]

Government Control in the United States

By the mid-19th century, English law explicitly recognized that wildlife owner-ship rested principally with landowners. During this same period, however, Amer-ican law evolved quite differently (Lund 1980; Bean 1983; Lueck 1998). As noted earlier, the rapid growth of white civilization severely damaged existing property rights institutions among American Indians. These tribal institutions were largely replaced by state restrictions on takings (or harvest), beginning in the early 1800s. The earliest state controls simply restricted the time of year during which it was legal to kill game. When these restrictions were contested, numerous court deci-sions bolstered the states' authority to regulate the taking and trading of wildlife (Lueck 1998). Courts consistently upheld state wildlife regulations.[22]

Today, states have the dominant regulatory authority over wildlife control and use, typically vested in a state fish and game department or wildlife agency (Lund 1980; Tober 1989; Musgrave and Stein 1993). The critical components of modern game laws and regulations, administered and enforced by game departments, include seasonal restrictions (and sometimes prohibitions) on taking wildlife, bans or severe restrictions on game trade, licensing requirements for legal taking of game, and restrictions on the methods by which animals can be taken. Game departments also administer state wildlife refuges and undertake research (e.g., population sur-veys, restocking programs).

The federal government's role in wildlife regulation developed at the start of the 20th century, with the Lacey Act of 1900,[23] the first major piece of federal wildlife legislation. The act prohibited the interstate transportation of wild game killed in violation of state laws and prohibited the importation of certain animals known to cause damage to agricultural or horticultural assets. The federal govern-ment's second major action on wildlife conservation was the 1916 treaty with Great Britain (on behalf of Canada) to protect migratory birds.[24]

In the first half of the 20th century, three pieces of federal legislation involved raising revenue to support wildlife protection. The Pittman-Robertson Act (1937),[25] which taxes arms and ammunition, and the Dingell-Johnson Act (1950),[26] which taxes fishing equipment, provide federal funds for state wildlife programs. The Migratory Bird Hunting Stamp Act (1934) requires waterfowl hunters to pur-chase a "duck stamp" in addition to a state license.[27] More recently, the federal gov-ernment began protecting both endangered species and nongame wildlife.

Today, the federal government, concurrently with the states, regulates the tak-ing of certain species, manages wildlife on federal land, conducts animal damage programs, enforces international treaties and environmental legislation relating to wildlife, regulates wildlife commerce, and operates wildlife research programs. The Fish and Wildlife Service within the Department of the Interior is the primary fed-eral agency involved in wildlife issues.

When the first game laws were enacted, the local law enforcement authorities were charged with their enforcement. Because these local officials were reluctant to enforce the new laws—often violently resisted by locals who were used to open-access hunting and fishing (Warren 1997; Jacoby 2001)—there arose a demand for specialized and separately funded enforcement. Game wardens or conservation officers (the modern term) became these "game police." The first state game wardens appeared in Maine, in 1843 for fish and in 1852 for moose.[28] Since warden positions were created before the formation of agencies and before hunting and fishing licenses, they were not salaried agency employees; rather, they were generally paid a share of the fines they collected from the apprehension and prosecution of game law violators. In 1890, for instance, Washington State established an office of game wardens with four-year terms in which wardens kept one-half of the collected fines from their arrests.

The beginnings of the modern game agency came in 1878, when the first game commissions were established in California and New Hampshire. By 1900, 17 states had game commissions. These commissions were, and still are, the governing bodies of the state game department, with the legislative authority to implement game regulations that will be carried out by the bureaucrats in the agencies. Commissioners have usually been unpaid appointees of the governor of each state.

The first state resident hunting license was implemented by New York, in 1864, as a permit to hunt deer. In 1875, the first nonresident license ($25) was established in Florida, and in 1879 Missouri banned all nonresident hunting. By 1900, roughly 20 states had some form of licensing system, which both limited access to wildlife and generated funds that gave the wildlife agencies the ability to enforce the game laws.[29] By 1904, 31 (of 45) states had nonresident fees, and by 1912, all 46 states had such licenses (Palmer 1912). From their inception, nonresident licenses have been substantially more expensive than resident licenses. For example, Reynolds (1913) found that the typical resident licenses were $1 per year, while nonresident licenses tended to be at least 10 times higher. This discriminatory pricing has been challenged in court many times by nonresidents as a violation of the privileges and immunities clause of the Constitution (Art. IV, sec. 2). These challenges have been defeated at all levels, including the Supreme Court, and higher-cost licenses for nonresidents are found in all states today.[30]

By the 1930s, state game commissions and their agencies were well established and operating in a manner quite similar to what we now observe. As noted, in 1937, the Pittman-Robertson Federal Aid in Wildlife Restoration Act directed existing federal excise taxes on guns and ammunition to state agencies for the protection and restoration of wildlife.[31] However, this federal revenue was available only on the condition that each state dedicated all of its hunting license revenue to state wildlife management programs. Pittman-Robertson allocates federal funds to states (after deducting 8 percent for administration) using a formula based on state land area and state hunter numbers. The Dingell-Johnson Act similarly allocated federal tax dollars on fishing equipment to states for fisheries programs.[32]

The impact of federal tax support on state wildlife agencies has been substantial. First, it consolidated the political constituency for wildlife agencies to hunting and fishing groups.[33] As Lund (1980, 86) notes, "Prior to the federal tax act many states diverted game license revenues to programs unrelated to game production, such as the funding of highway agencies or school budgets … Wildlife agency revenues thereafter became proportional to the sale of hunting and fishing licenses and equipment." Second, federal funds have provided a large fraction of state agency revenues, currently around 25 percent of agency budgets. More than $6 billion in federal funds has been allocated to the states since the programs began, and annual appropriations to states exceed $350 million today.[34]

The Economic Structure of Wildlife Management

The structure of wildlife management can be best understood by focusing on property rights, population biology, and political economy. This section examines the various facets of wildlife management, including the distinctions between England and America, the major changes in American management over time, and differences across the 50 states.

England and America: The Rationale for State Control

A comparison of the differences between England and America is a useful way to understand the American reliance on state control. To explain this difference, simply compare the ecological character of wildlife and the pattern of landownership in Great Britain and the United States during the crucial period of the 1800s when wildlife institutions in both countries were solidifying (Lueck 1989). Private landholdings in the United States in the 1800s were small and scattered. In England, landholdings were relatively large and concentrated, and the government held little land (Lueck 1989).

The wildlife stocks that inhabit the two countries also differ in important respects. For example, North American waterfowl typically nest during the summer in Alaska and northern Canada, migrating to Mexico and the southern states for the winter. By contrast, most British waterfowl are not migratory, even though the types of species present are nearly identical. North America is inhabited by many relatively large herbivores, such as bison, deer, elk, moose, mountain goats, and pronghorn antelope, and by carnivores, such as bear, cougar, coyotes, and wolves—all of which require rather large territories. Except for the red deer, wide-ranging herbivores and carnivores are not currently present in Great Britain. Many of the large mammalian species native to Great Britain (and the rest of Europe) became extinct before modern nations emerged.

The assignments of property rights to wildlife in England and the United States reflect the disparity in landownership and wildlife ecology between the two countries.[35] During the 19th and 20th centuries, English landowners had a comparative advantage in wildlife ownership not found in the United States. Vesting ownership in the states during the 19th century can be viewed as a second-best solution because of the costs of organizing many small and geographically scattered landowners.

Government Contracting and Geographical Jurisdiction

In the United States, government agencies with large geographical jurisdictions tend to control wildlife with large territories, while private parties or local governments tend to control those with small territories. Control of migratory waterfowl, such as ducks and geese, lies with the federal government in cooperation with the governments of Canada and Mexico via a 1916 treaty.[36] The federal government also has responsibility for whales and other marine mammals; many of these species are controlled by international treaty, many are migratory, and all inhabit territory that is not expressly controlled by states.

The regulation of migratory waterfowl hunting is guided by several flyway councils composed of agencies from the appropriate states and provinces. In their semiannual migrations, North American waterfowl populations use "flyways" that support distinct populations, and their control roughly corresponds with this distinction. Many animals do not use the territory controlled by more than one state, but they still require territory larger than most private landholdings. States uniformly control upland game birds, such as quail and grouse, which have relatively small territories and do not migrate. Big game mammals, which include ungulates such as deer and elk as well as large predators like bears and cougars, are ordinarily controlled by state governments. Mammals with even smaller territories, such as foxes and bobcats, are usually controlled by states, but in some cases they are unprotected and thus effectively controlled by landowners.

When a stock of wildlife inhabits an area controlled by two or more governments, agreement for unified control leads to better management. In general, the nature of the arrangement depends on the interest each government agency has in the particular stock. International control of wildlife is likely when a valuable population—such as migratory waterfowl, certain whales, halibut, salmon, northern fur seals, and polar bears—does not live completely within one national boundary. The first international game treaty, for the northern fur seal, was signed in 1911 by the United States, Great Britain, Russia, and Japan.[37] The United States and Canada entered into treaties for migratory birds in 1916 and Pacific halibut in 1953.[38] More recently, there have been treaties for such species as polar bears (1973)[39] and caribou (1987).[40] International wildlife treaties assign property rights to wildlife in a way that is closely linked to the species' territory. By strengthening property rights, these treaties can increase the value of wild populations. A species need not be migratory for there to be contracting gains between two parties in control of different areas; it is sufficient that the species reside in or habitually range through an area under the jurisdiction of different parties. For example, the polar bear, which is not migratory but extremely nomadic, lives on the polar ice pack controlled by the United States, Russia, Canada, Denmark, and Norway.

Management of Wildlife Damage

Damage by wildlife creates similar incentives and contracting problems. When a single landowner does not face the full costs of the damage, he will not have the incentive to undertake optimal damage control unless he can contract for control of the stock with the neighboring landowners. If the territory required for farming is coincident with the territory of the population causing the damage, the farmer-landowner will have the incentive to optimally reduce the wildlife population so as to maximize the value of the land. But if the offending wildlife population inhabits the territory of many farmers, then each farmer will tend to free-ride on the others' damage control, unless they can form a contract to coordinate the activity and share associated costs and benefits. Private damage control efforts are most likely to be present for relatively large landowners. Indeed, large private landowners have long hired hunters and trappers to reduce the stocks of undesired animals such as bears, beavers, and coyotes (Lueck 1989; Yoder 2002).

The same private contracting difficulties present for valued wildlife have been common for undesirable wildlife. Since private landholdings are often small and scattered compared with the large territorial requirements of damaging wild populations, government agencies are predicted to emerge to coordinate efforts to reduce wildlife damage. Indeed, "animal damage control" programs have been a part of game departments since their inception (Lund 1980; Musgrave and Stein 1993). Government actions have included bounties for undesired animals, hired hunters, and compensation of individuals for documented losses from wildlife damage (Musgrave and Stein 1993). In addition to state and federal actions, localized county programs, financed by taxes or donations, have often been the vehicle for government action for control of predators, such as coyotes (Lund 1980).

Regulation of Hunting by State Game Agencies

Excluding habitat, state wildlife departments own most attributes of wildlife. Most prominently this includes the right to kill or "take" animals by hunting or trapping which is governed by state issued licenses and attendant regulations on season closures, bag limits, and weapons. Hunters can harm others by shooting other hunters, shooting livestock or protected wildlife, and damaging roads or other property. State regulations reduce the losses from these externalities by prohibiting hunters from using fire, explosives, or bait, destroying nests or dens, shooting from vehicles or from roads, hunting while intoxicated, and using certain weapons.

State regulations vary with the ability of a landowner to establish hunting rights to wildlife and the relative value of wildlife as an attribute of the land. For example, shotgun requirements for big game hunters and Sunday hunting prohibitions limit the impact of hunting on nonhunters. Lueck (1991) found that states with larger private landholdings less often restrict big game hunters to shotguns (because errant shots from rifles are more likely to cause injuries) or ban hunting on Sundays. For example, there are shotgun requirements and no Sunday bans in areas where agricultural property values are high, such as Iowa and Indiana. Neither restriction is found in western states, where landholdings are large and wildlife values are relatively high. Densely populated states more often require residents to use shotguns. Greater population densities indicate that the relative value of the land for wildlife is low compared with other uses such as horseback riding and hiking. Similarly, more densely populated states tend to outlaw Sunday hunting.

Laws also vary within states for the same reasons. This is especially true of larger states that have considerable variation in wildlife habitat and land uses within their borders. Geographical "hunting areas" are the most conspicuous examples of such variation. State regulations for season lengths and bag limits typically are divided into relatively homogeneous geographic units. Most western states have hundreds of distinct elk-hunting areas, each with different season dates, bag limits, and rules on taking cows versus bulls. Some states require shotguns for hunting big game in certain regions where landholdings are smaller and the likelihood of hunter accidents and property damage would be higher if rifles were used.

State laws classify species into such categories as big game and small game, migratory and upland game birds, fur-bearers, predators, non-game animals, and endangered species. For most of these categories, killing is restricted, but for nongame animals and predators, restrictions are few or nonexistent. All states consider deer, elk, geese, and pheasants to be game, but bobcats, coyotes, foxes, and porcupines are not treated uniformly. States also recognize that game species may cause damage and routinely grant landowners the right to kill specific animals that damage property. Coyotes, for instance, are valued for their pelts,[41] but they also impose costs, mostly by killing domestic sheep. Lueck (1991) found that states with valuable sheep stocks are less likely to protect coyotes and more likely to treat them as predators. Lueck also found that states where coyote pelts were more highly valued were more likely to protect them as fur-bearing animals.

Regulating the Game Trade

An important and common component of wildlife institutions is restrictions and prohibitions on market activity. Prohibitions on market hunting (i.e., hunting to sell game products) and game trade emerged around the turn of the century in state wildlife law and persist to this day (Lund 1980). Since this time, it has often been illegal to sell animal parts even if they are legally taken (Musgrave and Stein 1993).[42] The Lacey Act, passed in 1900, added federal enforcement authority by prohibiting the interstate and international sale of wildlife and wildlife products obtained in violation of state (and federal) laws. More recently, both the Endangered Species Act and the Convention on International Trade in Endangered Species (CITES) restrict trade in endangered species and their products.

In the United States and in other countries, the efficacy of game trade is a prominent issue in current environmental policy.[43] One view, often held by conservationists, is that market forces wreak havoc on wildlife by increasing the (financial) incentives for poaching and can lead to such catastrophes as the near-extinction of the American bison. By this view, profit from game is destructive.[44] The minority, opposing view is that market forces provide incentives to protect wildlife and are compatible with healthy populations, as evidenced by the thriving wild alligator population in Louisiana. From this perspective, profit from game is protective.[45]

Economists tend to view restrictions on trade as limits on the creation of wealth. Recognition of the often substantial costs of enforcing property rights to wild populations suggests that the traditional economic view must be made conditional on the property rights system governing a particular population (Lueck 1989). For wildlife populations under open access, trade restrictions can secure ownership of wildlife stocks by reducing the gains from poaching. With these restrictions in place, poachers have no smoothly functioning game market in which to sell, and ownership of the wildlife stocks is enhanced because enforcement costs are reduced. This is an example of a case with two limitations on efficient markets—trade barriers and weak property rights—and removing only one can reduce total wealth.

Organization and Behavior of Wildlife Agencies

The days in which game wardens are paid a commission based on their collected fines from game law violators are long gone. Like other natural resource agencies, state wildlife agencies are modern hierarchical bureaucracies. The wildlife commissions are composed of political appointees, and the agencies are staffed by career civil servants paid by salaries that are only loosely connected to the "output" of the agency. On average, a state wildlife agency sells 750,000 fishing licenses and 600,000 hunting licenses each year, has an operating budget of more than $50 million, and manages thousands of acres of wildlife habitat as refuges (Lueck and Parker 2007). The earliest laws were uniform, statewide restrictions on taking wildlife; the current system is a complex mix of season dates, bag limits, and other regulations. The first hunting licenses entitled one to hunt all legal game within a state; the current system is a complex menu of licenses and permits that vary by species (and sometimes sex), region, and method of allocation. Montana, for example, sells bird, deer, and elk licenses over the counter to residents, but licenses for resident antelope, bighorn sheep, and nearly all nonresident big game are available only by lottery, and a few (e.g., for trophy bighorn sheep) are even auctioned to the highest bidder. Moreover, the state sells various combinations of licenses (e.g., a "sportsman's" license allows one to hunt deer, elk, and upland birds). All told, there are more than 20 types of Montana hunting licenses.

In one form or another, all state agencies are involved in the following activities: (1) setting season closures to limit access to wildlife, (2) setting bag limits on daily and seasonal take, (3) administering license sales (with discriminatory prices for nonresidents), (4) restricting the methods by which wildlife can be taken, (5) using salaried game wardens to enforce the game laws, (6) hiring agency biologists to undertake research programs, (7) managing a system of wildlife refuges, (8) protecting nongame and endangered species, and (9) administering education programs that include the publication of a monthly magazine (e.g., *Montana Outdoors*).[46]

The first agencies were independent game and fish departments, reflecting an exclusive concern with species valued by sportsmen and species considered to be pests or vermin. Many agencies still retain this focus, but other types of agencies also exist. Some are independent agencies and some are part of larger natural resource agencies that also have regulatory jurisdiction over state parks, state forest, and environmental policy.[47]

Each state agency is responsible to a commission, made up of appointed commissioners. The commission has the final authority to promulgate regulations (e.g., hunting seasons) but routinely ratifies the recommendation of the agency on these matters. Simultaneously, the agency is aware of the demands and concerns of the commission and typically tailors its policy so that the commission endorses it. The size of the commission and the requirements for commissioners vary across states. Some states require an even mix of members from the major political parties, and many states require that certain groups be represented (e.g., landowners, organized sportsmen's groups). Some states also require that commissioners represent specific regions of the state.

The funding for these agencies still comes mostly from hunters and anglers. Nationwide, nearly 35 percent of all wildlife agency funds come from licenses.

License revenue has been the primary source of funding since the establishment of game agencies. Since Pittman-Robertson, federal funds have been added as an important source of funds for agencies. Nationwide, federal funds account for nearly 30 percent of all agency revenue. Agencies also receive funding from interest income on deposited funds, tax check-off programs, lotteries (Colorado, Maine), wildlife license plates (Maine, New Jersey, Wisconsin), dedicated taxes (e.g., cigarette taxes), and miscellaneous fees (e.g., refuge entry fees). In recent years, "dedicated taxes" have become more common as a source of funds from outside traditional hunting and fishing groups. Missouri is an outlier, with more than 60 percent of the agency budget coming from general tax sources. No other state general fund contributes more than 50 percent, and only five other states contribute more than 30 percent. Missouri's constitution has earmarked 1/8 of 1 percent of its sales and use tax for conservation purposes, and these funds go to the Department of Conservation.

In principle, a game department can solve the problem of open access to wildlife through a well-designed system of seasons, bag limits, and other restrictions on human behavior. In practice, however, the game department will be limited in its successes. Indeed, the political and bureaucratic characteristics that make a game agency a viable institution—that full agreement among all landowners (and other related parties) is not required for binding game management policy—also limit its performance. Two general limits are worth noting. First, because the property rights within the agency are not precise, individual agency personnel will not act simply to maximize the value of the wildlife. Game wardens, refuge managers, and research biologists are salaried employees whose compensation does not closely depend on their day-to-day behavior. Second, interest groups may also be able to influence agency behavior in ways that will tend not to maximize the value of the wildlife. For example, hunters might successfully push for regulations that adversely affect nongame species. Similarly, landowners might succeed in obtaining regulations that limit game populations but reduce damage to crops. A third limitation arises because the agency does not generally own or lease land.[48] Because of this, the agency cannot directly control agricultural and other uses of land that can affect the land's value as wildlife habitat. For instance, farmers might drain marshes and sloughs (ideal waterfowl habitat) to increase wheat production.

The mere presence of a game department cannot completely solve the open-access problem. If state policies are uniform across the state, inefficiencies will arise because locally specific costs and benefits are not accounted for. For example, deer may be plentiful in one region and scarce in another, and thus uniform season and bag regulations would lead to excessive harvest in one area and too little harvest in another. The agency can, instead, implement diverse regionally tailored regulations, but this entails greater effort in the collection of information and the enforcement of regulations. Salaried game agents, however, have limited ability to collect detailed population data (they do not own land and cannot monitor regularly) and limited incentive to collect it even when able. All policies are imperfect because of the bureaucrat's incentives and because of enforcement costs.

State game departments are affected by federal policies in two important ways. First, Pittman-Robertson tax policy limits state discretion of license revenue.

Because the act allocates federal tax revenues according to a formula based on state hunter numbers, each agency has an incentive to increase these numbers.[49] It can most easily do so by lowering license fees and selling more licenses. Second, federal endangered species law can impose wildlife policies on a state and alter the agency's agenda. For example, a state might have to alter its hunting or fishing regulation to prevent a federally endangered species from being inadvertently taken. State agencies may be required to study and monitor endangered populations. Both federal tax and endangered species policies are likely to have substantial effects on state agencies and should be examined.

The organization and funding of state agencies also shape incentives (Lueck and Parker 2007). Independent agencies tend have narrow constituencies and may behave in ways more conforming to an agency capture model. When, however, a game department is part of a larger agency with jurisdiction over state parks and other natural resource issues, the agency will be subjected to political pressure from constituencies beyond those associated with hunting and fishing. It is likely then, that independent agencies will devote more resources to the management of game species and the enforcement of laws regarding these species. The structure of agency funding has similar effects on agency incentives. The more traditional agency, with no general fund support, will cater entirely to the desires of the hunting and fishing groups. Agencies with substantial general funding will face demand from nongame wildlife interests and are expected to devote resources to their management. Environmentalists and nongame groups have recently been pressing to alter the funding and structure of wildlife agencies, arguing that since the public demand for nongame wildlife is increasing, this segment of the public should contribute more to the budget of the agency charged with the management of wildlife.[50] If increased budgets come to agencies at the expense of added interest group pressures, traditional wildlife groups may find themselves worse off (Madsen 1999).

Changes in land use and landownership are also affecting wildlife agencies. Farms and ranches are getting larger, enabling more landowners to establish fee hunting and fishing programs in which wildlife become increasingly governed by private management plans. As the gains from fee operations have increased, landowners have lobbied for more liberal game regulations that allow them greater control over season and bag limits for the wildlife on their land.[51] States like Texas and New Mexico have long granted extensive management authority to landowners, but in recent years, more states have implemented policies toward this end. Leal and Grewell (1999) have studied the rapid growth in wildlife "ranching" programs, in which a landowner gets regulatory flexibility (which he can convert into more revenue from fee hunting) and the agency gets additional habitat management. These kinds of programs seem to be growing and are signaling a slow shift toward private management of game populations.

Private Wildlife Management

Although government agencies tend to dominate wildlife institutions, the role of private parties is important and perhaps growing. The significant private sector presence in wildlife management indicates both the limits of bureaucratic wildlife management and the ability of landowners to contract for ownership and control of wildlife populations.[52]

From an economic perspective, landowners typically control a well-specified set of rights to wildlife. One of the longest standing landowner rights is the legal authority to kill animals that damage crops and livestock (Lund 1980; Musgrave and Stein 1993). For many species, landowners are not required to purchase a license for hunting on their own land, and often they have a greater bag limit than other licensed hunters. In recent years, large landowners have been given wider authority for setting season and bag limits for certain big game animals. Owners of large holdings are more likely to completely control a population's territory and thus be an optimal owner in terms of game management.[53]

Landowners can establish partial ownership and control of wildlife (and thus gain from habitat provision and enhancing) by enforcing rights to their land for hunting, fishing, or trapping.[54] For example, as the size of a landholding increases, it is more likely that hunting rights will be sold, because larger landowners face lower costs of establishing rights to wildlife stocks. This implies that owners of larger holdings will control access to more species and, therefore, will lease access rights more frequently than small landholders. Because the size of agricultural holdings has increased, especially in the past 50 years, the amount of fee hunting on private lands is predicted to have increased. Journalists and wildlife biologists have presented abundant evidence that fee hunting has increased dramatically. In some cases, contracts are used to bind separate landholdings together, placing hunting rights to a large area under unified ownership. These contracts might be used by businesses (such as guides or hunting companies), hunting clubs, state agencies, or local farm cooperatives.[55]

Private rights for fishing, hunting, and trapping are mechanisms by which private landowners are able to capture a portion of the value from wild populations that inhabit their land. For wildlife values characterized as public goods, private action would seem to be limited because of potential free-riding. Despite the free-rider incentives, the provision of nonconsumptive wildlife values by private action is substantial and growing (see Table 6-3). Groups like The Nature Conservancy, Ducks Unlimited, and the National Audubon Society own and manage millions of acres of wildlife habitat. Land is obtained through outright purchase or through conservation easements.

One of the most innovative approaches to private wildlife preservation is the Greater Yellowstone wolf program of Defenders of Wildlife (Fischer 1989).[56] The reintroduction of the gray wolf into Yellowstone National Park in 1995 generated strong opposition from adjacent landowners and stockmen, who feared stock depredation by wolves migrating out of the park. Defenders of Wildlife soothed these fears by using market payments both to encourage private landowners to protect wolf populations and to compensate stockmen for depredation from wolves. To date, Defenders of Wildlife has paid some $500,000 to more than 400 ranchers for the loss of 565 cattle and 1,378 sheep. A similar program for grizzly bear depredation was established in 1997 and has made more than $100,000 in payments to 150 ranchers for 153 cattle, 157 sheep, and numerous other animals.

Endangered Species and Biodiversity Protection

Biological diversity, or biodiversity, refers to the richness of life on earth, between and within species and among ecosystems. The term *biodiversity* was coined in the mid-1980s and has since become a major focus of conservation policy since the United Nations Convention on Biological Diversity in Rio de Janeiro in 1992 (Jeffries 1997). In the United States, the Endangered Species Act (ESA) of 1973 is the most important institution regarding biodiversity.[57] The ESA fundamentally changed the role of the federal government in wildlife issues. Not only did the act expand the federal authority beyond its traditional role of regulating trade and managing migratory species, it also dramatically changed the way in which endangered species would be managed.

Prior to the ESA, federal policy authorized the secretary of the Interior, through the Fish and Wildlife Service,[58] to "list" species considered to be in peril and to foster protection by banning the "taking," or killing, of such species, prohibiting trade in endangered species, encouraging federal agencies to protect habitat, and establishing a federal fund for habitat acquisition. The ESA broadened and deepened this policy. It expanded protection to a much larger set of species and populations, including invertebrates and plants. It broadly defined *take* to (ultimately) include alteration of a species' habitat.[59] And it extended federal species protection to private lands.

The ESA had almost no impact during its first few years, partly because the full force of the act's language was not clear in the law. Starting in 1978, with the famous snail darter case, *Tennessee Valley Authority v. Hill*,[60] a series of federal court decisions and administrative rulings transformed the ESA into perhaps the most authoritative and wide-reaching federal environmental law. The court said the ESA required that construction of TVA's nearly completed federal dam be halted to save habitat for an endangered minnow (the snail darter) and issued its famous mandate: "The plain intent of the statute was to halt and reverse the trend toward species extinction, whatever the cost."

Although many of the high-profile conflicts over the ESA have involved public land management, the majority of endangered and candidate species reside on private land. The ESA made it unlawful to take any endangered species within the jurisdiction of the United States and defined *take* to mean "harass, harm, pursue, hunt, shoot, wound, kill, trap, capture, or collect." In 1975, the secretary of the Interior went on to define *harm* as[61] "an act or omission which actually injures or kills wildlife, including acts which annoy it to such an extent as to significantly disrupt essential behavioral patterns, which include, but are not limited to, breeding, feeding, or sheltering; significant environmental modification or degradation which has such effects is included within the meaning of harm." By the mid-1980s, a combination of administrative and court rulings combined to make habitat modification a violation of the ESA.[62] Thus, under the ESA, it is not only illegal to destroy an endangered species, but it is also illegal to damage its habitat.[63]

Species conservation policy can be usefully divided into two basic types. The first type is the ESA approach, which utilizes land-use restrictions in an attempt to lock in existing habitat and penalize landowners for adverse alterations. The second method, used before the ESA and for species not governed by the ESA, is pay-to-protect programs in which landowners are compensated for habitat provision. A pay-to-protect system retains the basic system of rights to land but generates a market for wildlife habitat, whereas the ESA substantially alters the system of property rights to land and the incentives of many people and institutions, most notably environmentalists, private landowners, the Fish and Wildlife Service, and public land agencies. Private conservation organizations such as The Nature Conservancy, of course, use pay-to-protect methods themselves.

Environmentalists: Claiming Rights to Land

The ESA alters the property rights of a landowner when an endangered species is present or when there is a positive probability that a species will inhabit the land. Under the ESA, the Fish and Wildlife Service essentially controls wildlife (at least listed species) by virtue of its authority to enforce the ESA. Once a species has been listed, the ESA is in force, and land that provides habitat for that species is governed by the ESA. A landowner thus finds that a portion of his rights to the use and income of the land essentially are transferred to the Fish and Wildlife Service and those who are able to influence it through political or legal avenues.

Because the ESA allows citizen lawsuits, environmental groups can sue for listing and implementation of the ESA and thus "claim" land (public or private) by removing it from nonwildlife uses. Also, because the ESA places no limits on the number of species that can be listed or the number of acres affected and does not require that landowners be compensated for their losses, there is a weaker budget constraint than with a habitat acquisition program. In principle, a group can claim large areas by seeking and obtaining the listing of a species that inhabits this land and thus impeding those land-use actions that harm the species. The ESA can also lead to land claims on public lands.

For environmentalists, the ESA offers a mechanism to affect land use by changing policy on public land, halting private development, and eliminating what are seen to be pork barrel subsidies that allow certain public agencies to thrive at the expense of environmental quality. Environmentalists can force the Fish and Wildlife Service to act by showing that federal agencies' or private land use harms listed species. They also can encourage the listing of a new species that inhabits land for which they desire to change existing or planned land use. The record of extensive litigation under the ESA indicates that environmentalists have successfully used the citizen lawsuit provision to invoke and strengthen the ESA.[64] The interpretation of the ESA by the Supreme Court in the snail darter case resulted from a lawsuit brought by environmentalists interested in stopping the Tennessee Valley Authority's Tellico Dam. Starting with that case, environmentalists have been successful in forcing federal agencies—the Bureau of Reclamation, the Corps of Engineers, the Forest Service, the Bureau of Land Management, the Park Service, and the military services—to alter their land management to comply with the ESA. In the process, millions of acres of federal land have become refuges for listed species. Litigation has also expanded federal authority over interests formerly governed by the states and has broadened the definition of *take*. One strategy is to use lawsuits to force the listing of species that are widely distributed geographically so that the ESA can govern enormous expanses of land, both public and private.

The listing of the northern spotted owl is perhaps the environmentalists' greatest success in terms of diverting land use towards an endangered species. The owl inhabits the old-growth conifers of the Pacific Northwest, from northern California to British Columbia, and individuals require a home range of 1,000 to 8,000 acres. By the early 1980s, environmentalists had begun to pressure federal forest managers in the Forest Service and the Bureau of Land Management to limit harvest of old-growth forests. Environmentalists challenged both agencies under a variety of federal environmental laws for failing to consider how proposed timber sales would affect the spotted owl. Ultimately, the Fish and Wildlife Service was forced to list the spotted owl as a threatened species throughout its range in 1990. As a result of these lawsuits and the settlements that followed, nearly 11 million acres of federal land in California, Oregon, and Washington is now considered critical habitat and thus off-limits to logging. This acreage represents a substantial fraction (as much as 50 percent in Oregon and Washington) of public forests in these three states. By invoking the ESA (and related environmental legislation), environmentalists have dramatically altered land uses on public forestland in the Pacific Coast states.

In recent years, environmentalists have become more open about the use of the ESA as a land management tool. For example, in July 1998, after the National Wildlife Federation led a successful petition to force the Fish and Wildlife Service to list the black-tailed prairie dog, the federation's president, Mark Van Putten, stated, "This is the best possible use of the Endangered Species Act … If we can help the prairie dog, we'll be saving grasslands that benefit all sorts of wildlife, and people too."[65] In another example, the Center for Biological Diversity (Lemann 1999) has extensively used the ESA throughout the desert Southwest and currently is trying to get more than 100 new species listings or critical habitat designations in California. In 1995, it obtained a one-year injunction on all logging on national forests in Arizona and New Mexico by forcing critical habitat designation for the Mexican spotted owl.

Landowners: Reclaiming Rights to Land

Even under the ESA, a landowner maintains important influence over the land by virtue of his control over nonwildlife uses. Because of the information advantage the landowner has over the Fish and Wildlife Service, he may be able to take action to prevent the administration of the ESA. If the ESA can be avoided, then the landowner has successfully reclaimed his rights to wildlife habitat. There are several means by which a landowner can frustrate the implementation of the ESA. First, if the species is already present but unknown to the agency, he may secretly (and illegally) kill all listed species inhabiting the property—"shoot, shovel, and shut up"—thus rendering ESA regulations moot on his land.[66] Second, if the species is not yet present but the potential for inhabitance is high, he may destroy habitat to preempt ESA regulations. Preemptive habitat destruction might be active (e.g., bull-dozing junipers that provide habitat for endangered warblers) or passive (e.g., stopping understory burning that would maintain pine forest habitat for endangered woodpeckers). Such preemption not only removes the potential for costly regulations, it also and necessarily reduces the habitat for the endangered species. On public land, the ESA creates different incentives because land managers and land users do not have effective control over land use as do private landowners.

The possibility of preemptive habitat destruction has been noted by numerous journalists and scholars.[67] Anecdotes and case studies abound.[68] In Texas, landowners have cleared and overgrazed juniper habitat for the golden-cheeked warbler and the black-capped vireo. Forest owners have clearcut old-growth Douglas fir stands in the Pacific Northwest to avoid logging restrictions designed to protect the northern spotted owl. Farmers in California have switched crops to eliminate habitat for kangaroo rats. The National Association of Home Builders actually advises preemption, or what it calls scorched-earth management.[69]

The evidence of preemption is strongest for the red-cockaded woodpecker.[70] This woodpecker is a nonmigratory, territorial species that resides exclusively in longleaf pine ecosystems ranging from Virginia to Arkansas. It was listed as an endangered species in 1970, before the ESA was enacted, making it one of the longest listed species. A woodpecker clan requires 100 to 250 acres of mature pine forest for nesting and foraging, and Fish and Wildlife Service guidelines recommend parcels ranging between 60 and 300 acres. At roughly $2,000 per acre of forgone timber, these regulations are potentially costly land-use restrictions that can stimulate preemption. Lueck and Michael (2003) use detailed data on forest ownership and management coupled with the locations of known colonies of red-cockaded woodpeckers to examine how the potential for ESA regulation affects the probability that a particular forest plot will be harvested. Controlling for other economic factors, such as timber prices and stand quality, they find that increases in the proximity of a plot to woodpeckers increases the probability that the plot will be harvested and decreases the age at which the forest is harvested. For the 1984–1990 period, the probability of harvesting a 50-year-old stand of pine increases between 5 and 25 percent when there are woodpeckers within 5 to 15 miles of a site. Of a total pine acreage of 960,000 acres in North Carolina, they find that between 12,000 and 70,000 additional acres were harvested between 1984 and 1990 because of the potential of ESA regulations. These findings are the first evidence of systematic preemptive habitat destruction; they confirm the preemption model and help explain the observation that red-cockaded woodpecker populations have been declining on private land under the ESA.

In the public sphere, landowners may form interest groups and lobby for changes in the ESA or its implementation by the Fish and Wildlife Service. Indeed, the emergence of the so-called property rights movement in the early 1990s came as a response to ESA regulations. In some cases, existing groups such as the American Farm Bureau Federation and the Forest Products Association were ready to champion the causes of landowners affected by the ESA. In other cases, new organizations were formed to explicitly address the concerns of landowners with the ESA. In 1994, this property rights movement gained supporters in the Republican-led 104th Congress, which generated numerous bills to amend the ESA, as well as anti-takings bills that would require compensation to landowners if some portion of land value were lost. None of these bills became law, though as of February 2006, a new and similar bill in Congress was being considered.[71]

More importantly the political pressure that emerged from the preemption incentives inherent in the ESA led to the development of policies—called No Surprises and Safe Harbor[72]—designed to mitigate these effects. One of the major environmental groups responsible for these policy changes was Environmental Defense (formerly the Environmental Defense Fund), which publicized some of these incentives to the environmental community and the public (Wilcove et al. 1996). Under safe harbor agreements, established by the Fish and Wildlife Service in 1995, the agency promises not to prosecute a private landowner for taking an endangered species so long as he maintains a baseline population on his property. This allows the landowner to develop parts of his land as long as other parts of the land are enhanced enough to maintain the population. In this way, safe harbor agreements do not create an incentive to preemptively destroy habitat. Currently, more than 325 landowners have enrolled some 3.6 million acres in 17 states in 32 safe harbor agreements.[73] Still, as Thompson (2005) notes, these agreements only remove the landowner's disincentive; they do not reward landowners for habitat preservation or enhancement. Candidate conservation agreements are a related policy tool designed to prevent an ESA listing from occurring at all. A candidate conservation agreement is struck between the Fish and Wildlife Service and other parties (private and public) to develop a plan to enhance habitat for a species with the goal of avoiding a listing and the regulatory burden that accompanies it.[74] Thompson (2005) counted 110 candidate conservation agreements as of November 1, 2003.

The ESA's Record

From an economic perspective, the ESA's record should be assessed by comparing the benefits of species conservation with the costs of doing so. This task is, however, overwhelming and has not even been partly attempted. The estimation of both benefits and costs would be daunting. On the benefit side, the task would be to impute the value that consumers (i.e., citizens) place on reducing the probability of extinction or of maintaining a certain level of species diversity and the associated natural environments. Because market data would generally not be available, such a study would have to rely on contingent valuation methods, which are controversial even among economists. On the cost side, the task would be to tally up the explicit resource costs of implementing and enforcing the ESA and monitoring populations and the implicit opportunity costs of land uses that are forgone because of the ESA's regulatory reach. Even for a single species, the data requirements would be substantial.

At this date, there are no benefit-cost studies of the ESA or even of a single species governed by the ESA. Economists have, however, examined some of the incentive effects inherent in the act (e.g., Brown and Shogren 1998; Innes et al. 1998; Lueck and Michael 2003), and there are studies that examine the behavior of the Fish and Wildlife Service. For example, Ando (1999) finds that listing decisions depend on the power of interest groups affected by the potential decisions. In another study, Metrick and Weitzman (1998) find that Fish and Wildlife Service listing and expenditure behavior depends on the size of an individual member of the species (e.g., bears fare better than frogs), its taxonomic types (e.g., mammals and birds fare better than reptiles and amphibians), and importantly, not on a measure of "endangerment."[75] Metrick and Weitzman conclude that the agency disproportionately spends its resources on "charismatic megafauna" rather than on a program that would maximize biodiversity. Given these limited findings and the difficulty of even defining an objective function inherent in the ESA (Metrick and Weitzman 1998), I examine the ESA's record primarily in terms of its record on species recovery and how it compares with non-ESA conservation policies.

Many of the species driven to distressingly low numbers in the late 19th century have now recovered. For example, white-tailed deer fell to less than half a million by 1900 but are now estimated at 26 million and are often considered a pest. The pronghorn antelope, present in large numbers throughout the Great Plains during the Lewis and Clark expedition, had been reduced to 26,600 by 1924 in the United States. By 1964, just 40 years later, populations had increased more than 10-fold steadily approaching 650,000 today. Similar recoveries have occurred for bison, bighorn sheep, and elk. The bluebird, turkey, and wood duck have all experienced population recoveries at least as dramatic as the big game species noted above.

For all of those cases of recovery, similar forces were at work. Season closures were enforced and game trade was restricted. Habitat was often enhanced through refuges, especially for migratory waterfowl. Animals were live-captured in the wild and reared in captivity before being transplanted to extinct or depleted areas. The cooperation of private landowners to develop and protect habitat was important. For example, conservation groups built nesting boxes for wood ducks and bluebirds on private land. In New Mexico, landowners consented to the reintroduction of elk and pronghorn on the condition of being able to influence hunting once populations increased. In most cases, narrow interest groups, such as Ducks Unlimited and the National Wild Turkey Federation, have helped steer restoration by raising revenue and negotiating with wildlife agencies and landowners. As Table 6-4 suggests, it has been relatively uncommon for groups to organize around the protection of a single nongame species.

The evidence for ESA-based recoveries thus far does not suggest any dramatic recoveries like those mentioned above. Of the more than 1,200 domestic species that have been listed as endangered or threatened, only 40 had been "delisted" as of September 2005.[76] Of these, 9 were extinct and 16 were delisted because of "data error," indicating that the original listing was based on mistaken population estimates. The remaining 15 species were considered "recovered," although there is debate over the ESA's role here, too. More specifically, mammals, birds, and fish accounted for 243 listed species, and of these, 18 have been delisted, and of these, 7 have covered, 7 are extinct, and 4 were cases of data error.

One study that examined Fish and Wildlife Service reports contends that none of these recoveries are the result of the ESA (Gordon et al. 1997).[77] For example, the improving status of the bald eagle is now mostly attributed to the ban on DDT and enforcement against poaching, neither of which are uniquely ESA-based policies.[78] Thus far, the ESA's success record is still limited, compared with the impressive restorations that occurred without the ESA. No dramatic species recovery can be claimed; indeed, such long-listed species as the red-cockaded woodpecker (35 years) have had declining populations during much of this period. Perhaps the two greatest successes are the grizzly bear and the gray wolf, both of which (particularly the wolf) have seen increasing populations. Here the reasons for population increases seem to be both restrictions on hunting (a pre-ESA tool, as noted below) and land-use changes on public lands that provide critical habitat. It is also worth noting that both of these species are thriving in Canada and Alaska, so from a biodiversity perspective, the rather large expenditures on these two species may not be cost-effective. In both of these cases, too, the compensation program of Defenders of Wildlife may have been important in mitigating landowners' and ranchers' opposition and preemptive action.[79]

Wildlife restoration policy before the ESA used season closures and game trade restrictions to limit open-access killing. Moreover, it used pay-to-protect methods to enhance wildlife habitat, by either purchasing or leasing land for refuges. Unlike the regulations inherent in the ESA, landowners were never penalized for altering habitat. Thus the preemption incentive was completely absent. Under the ESA, the prohibition on taking amounts to a season closure, so along with game trade restrictions, the ESA has features equivalent to pre-ESA approaches. It is the broad definition of *take*, which includes harm to habitat, that makes a crucial difference. Because of this, the ESA creates the incentive for preemption and also limits the potential for using the land market to allocate habitat. The main distinction between the two approaches is how each alters the incentives of landowners to provide and enhance habitat. Under a pre-ESA policy, the landowner has an incentive to both provide and enhance habitat. Under the ESA, the landowner instead has an incentive to eliminate habitat. Thus, the ESA will be most successful where habitat development is not important or where the landowner's ability to manipulate habitat is limited.

When enacted in 1973, the ESA had the nearly unanimous support of the Congress and the president, yet it has become one of the most controversial environmental laws in the United States. It has been lauded by environmentalists and vilified by landowners. Congressional authorization for the ESA expired in 1992, and gridlock has ruled since. All students of the ESA recognize that it was a major shift in federal wildlife law, dramatically altering the property rights to habitat that sustain endangered species. In the nearly 35 years that have passed, there have been so many adjustments to and investments in the ESA property regime that strong vested interests have been established. So the current gridlock is not a surprise.

The current dissatisfaction with the ESA suggests that some of the incentive problems with the current ESA are still important, even with safe harbor and candidate conservation agreements. Although property owners tend to be uniformly opposed to the ESA (unless they can be sure they will avoid its force), the ESA has been a double-edged sword for environmental groups. On one hand, it has given environmentalists great influence in the use and management of public lands and helped them challenge large-scale federal development projects.[80] On the other hand, habitat is being destroyed and species are losing ground on private land. These combined forces seem to be generating pressure to change the ESA, especially as it affects private landowners. Indeed, the Fish and Wildlife Service has recently implemented more flexible policies for private landowners.

Two lessons can be drawn. First, a focus on the property rights to land clarifies the issues and the motives of various groups in supporting or opposing various policies. Specific attention to the incentives of landowners, both private and public, is important for understanding the performance of wildlife preservation policies. Second, because of the discretion of agencies and courts' deference to them, the passage of seemingly benign legislation can evolve into a set of institutions largely unintended. Along the way, the institutions may become quite permanent, regardless of their merits, as vested interests also evolve to take advantage of the new regime.

Case Studies

To this point, this chapter has examined general trends in the history of American wildlife management and examined aggregate statistics, where available. This section examines several cases that illustrate the range of outcomes that have been part of this history. In each case, close attention is paid to the property rights to the wild populations, the ownership of the land, the use of the land (i.e., the habitat), the territorial requirements and behavior of the species in question, and the market for wildlife products. Table 6-6 summarizes the cases in terms of these issues.

Table 6-6. *Case Studies in Wildlife Conservation*

Species	Biological characteristics and habitat range	Habitat: land use	Market(s)	Law, politics	Outcome
Passenger pigeon	Continental migration	Eastern forests: forest clearing	Meat	Open access, few (unenforced) hunting regulations	Extinct
American bison	Nomadic, large range	Central Plains: livestock and agriculture	Hide	Open access, protection	Near extinction and recovery
White-tailed deer	Local, non-migratory	Open woodland, urban fringes, residential	Meat, hide	Open access, protection through controlled harvest	Decline and dramatic recovery
Mule deer	Seasonal migratory	Open woodlands, rangeland, canyons, mountains, sagebrush basins	Meat, hide	Open access, protection through controlled harvest	Decline and dramatic recovery
Wolf	Large territory, predator	Forests and grassland: livestock	Fur	Open access, great effort to eradicate, protection and reintroduction	Dramatic reduction near livestock, now preserved in large parks

Sources: See text.

Extinction: Passenger Pigeon[83]

Prior to its extinction in 1914, the passenger pigeon *(Ectopistes migratorius)* was thought to be the most abundant bird in North America (Schorger 1955). Its population has been estimated to have been between 3 billion and 5 billion, and it may have accounted for as much as 40 percent of all birds in North America (Schorger 1955).[84] The passenger pigeon inhabited mixed hardwood forests from Canada (Ontario, Québec, Nova Scotia) to the Gulf states (Texas to Florida). Their main spring nesting areas were in the Great Lakes states, and in the winters they migrated to the southern reaches of their habitat. The migrations were said to be so large that the flocks blackened the skies as they passed overhead. One nesting area in Wisconsin was reported to cover 850 square miles and contain perhaps 136 million birds.

Native Americans hunted the pigeon for meat and used its oil and fat for cooking but had little impact on their populations. It was during the latter half of the 19th century that habitat conversion (clearing the hardwood forests for farmland) and open-access market hunting caused the species' rapid decline and extinction. The passenger pigeon's abundance and nesting behavior made it easy to kill. First-hand accounts detailing hunting methods used by market hunters describe how hunters could simply walk close to a nesting and shower the sky with shotgun pellets as the birds and their young flew up in confusion. The passenger pigeon served as an important food source for many settlers, but when the railroads connected the Midwest to the Northeast in the 1850s, the market dramatically expanded, along with the rate of killing. Concurrently, the pigeon's habitat was severely reduced as settlers cleared the hardwood forests to create cropland. From this point forward, the decline in population was precipitous and ultimately irreversible. By the late 1870s, the large nestings were gone, and by the early 1890s, they were rare; there are no reported wild sightings after 1900. The last known pigeon, "Martha," died in 1914 at age 29 in the Cincinnati Zoo.

The extinction of the passenger pigeon occurred because of open-access market hunting and large-scale habitat conversion. The migratory nature of the birds required control of large landscapes to protect habitat. Incentives for private conservation action were missing, and there was little government action. Some states passed laws protecting eggs or restricting the distance hunters could be from a nest when shooting, but these laws were rarely enforced and also did not effectively control the necessary territory. Information may have also been a problem. Because of the widespread range of the pigeon and the relatively primitive communication, the overall population levels were not well known until it was too late.

Near Extinction and Recovery: The American Bison[85]

The American bison *(Bison bison)* was nearly as ubiquitous as the passenger pigeon. Prior to European settlement, bison were widespread throughout North America, with a population estimated at 25 million to 40 million. Apart from the Pacific Coast, they were found throughout the continent but thrived on the grasslands of the Great Plains. Bison are nomadic, social animals that require large territories and are known for their aggressive behavior, especially by the older bulls. These two factors ultimately led to the demise of the bison: it was prohibitively costly to control large expanses of habitat, and they could not be easily domesticated.[86] Bison survived in large numbers until the mid-1800s but ultimately diminished in dramatic fashion in the presence of a national hide market combined with open-access hunting on the Great Plains.

Until the middle of the 19th century, the tribal societies that lived on the Great Plains had relatively secure common property rights to bison-hunting territories, and populations were quite stable despite hunting for food and hides. But the U.S.–Indian wars and settlement pressure broke down the tribal system of property rights and led to open-access hunting just as the hide trade emerged in the 1870s. The coincidence of these two events led to the near extinction of the Great Plains herds. Open access prevailed because white encroachment broke down tribal territories and because wild bison were extremely costly to own, given their intractable disposition. In addition, the conversion of the plains into private agricultural land reduced the value of the herds by significantly altering their habitat.

By 1890, only those few small and scattered bison herds that were too far removed from white settlement remained; essentially, they were too costly to find and kill. The best estimates indicate that the population was roughly 1,000. On a few occasions during the hide-hunting era, wild bison calves were live-captured and reared in confinement, establishing private herds of bison. Some of the progeny of these captives were later sold to public refuges established in the early 20th century at the behest of the American Bison Society, which raised funds for their purchase. In the past 50 years, bison numbers have increased dramatically, mostly as private entrepreneurs have established and expanded herds and developed a market for bison and bison products. The costs of fencing and herd monitoring as well as assembly of large contiguous tracts of rangeland are now low enough that private ownership of bison is no longer prohibitive. In effect, the property rights to the bison evolved from common property to open access to, finally, private property. Although the current bison herds are substantially lower than they were in the 1700s, their present population[87] reflects their limited compatibility with contemporary land use and their high cost relative to their close substitute, domestic cattle.

Like the passenger pigeon, the bison was subject to market hunting under open access, yet the bison survived. The reason is not clear but three forces seem important.[88] The large and powerful bison may have had enough "charisma" to generate more conservation demand than a small nondescript bird could muster. Also, some small groups of bison inhabited extremely isolated and rugged terrain, thus making hunting very costly. And finally for bison, but not pigeons, there was also the allure of profits from some partial domestication.

Overexploitation to Overabundance: Deer[89]

The deer population in the United States has gone through different stages since European settlement.[90] Deer were thought to have numbered 37.5 million before 1700. In the next two centuries, the population fell to as few as 850,000 (Demarais, 2000; Kie and Czech, 2000). This decrease has been largely attributed to overexploitation by market hunters, which occurred because of low harvest cost coupled with open-access rights.[91] The effects of overharvesting were also somewhat exacerbated by habitat modification due to changing land use. By 1900, the restorative effects of game laws (e.g., season closures, bag limits) were observable (McCabe and McCabe 1984). During the 1900s the deer population grew rapidly, reaching 31 million by 2000. In recent decades, urbanization has encouraged populations of an ungulate that adapts well to urban fringes and forages in lawns and gardens. Moreover, its new habitat is devoid of predators, thus further increasing the populations.[92] In many urban areas now, counties and municipalities have instituted culling programs to reduce populations (Rondeau and Conrad 2003).

Although the protection and restoration of the U.S. deer population can be seen as a success in many ways, the large deer population also provides a challenge to wildlife managers. A charismatic species loved by many, the deer is a pest to many others, especially in the suburban environments to which deer are now strongly attracted. Additionally, population control is becoming a growing concern because hunting is declining across the country and other methods, such as capture, sterilization and cullling, are costly and socially controversial. This begs the question of whether it is desirable to try to return all wildlife populations to their pre-Columbian level.

From Scourge to Exotic Amenity: Wolves

The gray wolf (Canis lupus) was once widely distributed throughout North America, stretching from the Arctic to the middle of Mexico. Since European settlement, the population of wolves is estimated to have dropped from 500,000 to 65,000 (Hampton 1997). As a territorial predator, wolves threatened the safety of European settlers, preyed on their livestock, and competed for game animals. Consequently, wolves were widely pursued and hunted voraciously, and great collective effort was made toward eradication. Many states offered bounties for wolves, and Wyoming even imposed a penalty for removing a wolf from a trap. At the same time that many species came under protection of state, and later federal, game laws, great collective effort was taken to eradicate the wolf because it imposed costs upon livestock owners. By the middle of the 20th century, the wolf was essentially extinct in the contiguous United States but for a few hundred individuals in northern Minnesota and a smaller number in the northern Rocky Mountains. In Canada and Alaska, however, wolf populations remain well over 60,000.

In the past half-century, however, changing public sentiment has transformed the wolf from a pest to an amenity. Many state bounty programs were repealed in the 1950s and 1960s. In 1973, the wolf came under the protection of the Endangered Species Act. At this time the northern Rocky Mountains' "distinct population segment" was listed as endangered, and the Western Great Lakes as threatened. The wolf and other large predators, such as the mountain lion (cougar) and grizzly bear, have reached a symbolic status such that they have a high marginal value, especially in parks and other public areas. As wildlife viewing continues to rise as a national activity, the value of the wolf will most likely rise accordingly.

Wolves have been reintroduced into Yellowstone National Park and are now thriving and moving well beyond the park borders.[93] Since the 1995–1996 release of 31 Canadian wolves into Yellowstone Park in 1995 and 1996, the number in the northern Rockies has grown to more than 1,200. The Great Lakes population is now nearly 4,000.[94] In fact, on January 29, 2007, the Fish and Wildlife Service announced that it was delisting the Great Lakes population and proposing to delist the northern Rockies segment.[95] In terms of population recovery, it is clear that the wolf program has been a success. In the absence of data on the cost of the program and some estimate of the benefits, an overall economic assessment is not available.[96]

Sustainability and the Future: Summary and Discussion

Are wildlife populations sustainable in America? The question itself is rife with ambiguity. The answer is yes if the question is: Can we expect to have large and relatively stable populations of the species most people think of as wildlife—namely mammals, birds, and fish? However, if the sustainability question is whether we can expect to support and sustain populations at pre-Columbian levels, the answer is no. The population history of deer usefully calls into question the use of sustainability as a guide to wildlife management policy. Under open access, deer populations plummeted. Under protection and with habitat changes, they have become a pest. Sustainability offers no guide for determining what a desirable or optimal deer population should be. The answer to such a question depends on human valuation of deer and its habitat and the costs of providing and protecting both. There is every reason to think that these values will change over time and that so will deer populations. The same can be said for bison, wolves, and red-cockaded woodpeckers. Given the limits of sustainability as a guide, this chapter has instead sought to develop a framework to explain the population history of American wildlife and reveal lessons for successful conservation and management.

The course of American history has seen widespread and spectacular changes in wildlife populations. Some species have been extinguished, some have nearly been. Others have made dramatic recoveries—some so much that they have largely become pests. Still others have been little affected by the events of the past 500 years.

Numerous species are largely unstudied and of little concern to wildlife managers, simply because they confer few benefits to people or their presence imposes little or no cost. A wide range of so-called nongame wildlife fit this category, including such ubiquitous species as robins and garter snakes. However, it is possible that with the increasing emphasis on biodiversity within the scientific community, more attention will be granted to species that were previously either despised or unnoticed.

As noted in the beginning of the chapter, other dramatic changes have occurred. Human populations have increased by 20- or 30-fold since European contact. Land use has dramatically shifted toward agriculture and urban development, affecting wildlife habitat in many ways. Government agencies have arisen as dominant forces in wildlife management, and private interest groups have formed to fund wildlife management and influence public policy.

The structure of wildlife management institutions shows a basic economic logic. Because of the difficulty of owning wild populations that inhabit the small and scattered holdings of private landowners, government wildlife agencies have assumed control to limit open-access exploitation. This control is primarily manifested in hunting and fishing regulations, which are administered and enforced by bureaucrats. Because of the weak performance incentives inherent in bureaucracies, these regulations are necessarily rigid and often inefficient compared with an ideal system. Private parties have developed markets that are tied to these regulations in the form of access and guide fees for the right to hunt and fish. For species whose numbers are deemed to be sufficiently low, more severe limits on killing and habitat modification have been imposed, though in some cases the latter seem to have created counterproductive incentives (as for red-cockaded woodpeckers).

There are some famous success stories in wildlife conservation, but what can be said about the recipes for success? The American bison were on the brink of extinction but now thrive and are in no danger.[97] Deer and waterfowl are now so plentiful as to often be pests. Elk and antelope thrive in huntable numbers in the western states. Successful restoration has been accomplished when there has been a focused interest group that stands to directly benefit from increases in a particular species. With the exception of bald eagles, most dramatic recoveries have been driven by groups interested in maintaining populations for recreational hunting and fishing. In these cases, groups have been able to raise funds to compete in the marketplace for habitat and to compete in the public sector for policies and public funds. The record of success for less charismatic species has been less positive. The prospects for species without a specific constituency may even be poorer because of incentives within the ESA.

The lessons, then, from this chapter are that economic forces—the forces of human values and opportunity cost—explain how people exploit and conserve wildlife. It can be reasonably stated, though empirically hard to verify, that for the most part, the species people want to save or sustain are in fact saved. Some species do go beyond the brink and are lost forever. Whether they might have been saved with minor adjustments in policy or institutions is hard to assess.

The basic problem of wildlife conservation is the difficulty of establishing property rights to live populations. Because it is costly to coordinate the actions of various landowners (private and public) who provide habitat, wild populations often are managed as open-access resources, predictably leading to overexploitation (hunting, fishing, trapping) and destruction of habitat. This lack of ownership makes it difficult for landowners to benefit from either habitat provision or species protection. The challenge ahead is to design institutions that capture the net benefits of nonconsumptive value in wild stocks and that provide the right incentives to landowners, land users, and governments.

Notes

1. Some Pleistocene extinctions, however, are now thought to be human caused (Smith 1975 and Martin and Klein, 1984). More generally, there is evidence that Native Americans had a sig-

nificant impact on the natural environment, particularly through their use of fire (Cronon 1986; Mann 2005).

2. See Sedjo (Chapter 3, this volume) on forestlands.

3. There are no reliable data on market hunting or subsistence hunting during the 19th century, though the practice was widespread and its impact was likely enormous.

4. The focus here, however, is on terrestrial wildlife, with only a limited discussion of fisheries and marine life. Siikamäki and Chow (Chapter 7, this volume) explicitly examine biodiversity.

5. In 1987, the World Commission on Environment and Development, which had been set up in 1983, published a report entitled *Our Common Future*. The document came to be known as the Brundtland Report, after Gro Harlen Brundtland, the committee's chairwoman. See www.brundtlandnet.com/bruntlandreport.net.htm.

6. See also Stavins et al. (2002) for analysis of these issues.

7. Specifically, Heal (1998) develops dynamic models that incorporate value generated from resource stocks and that do not significantly discount benefits coming in the distant future.

8. "Open access" is the preferred term for what Hardin (1968) called "the commons." Open access means there is no owner (as opposed to common property with communal management structures).

9. Indeed, there are often important but subtle biological factors that influence the cost of ownership of animals (Diamond 1997). For example, Indian elephants have been domesticated, but African elephants have not. See also Sauer (1953), Zuener (1963), and Clutton-Brock (1981) on the domestication of wild populations. It might be argued that for complete wildness, there must be not just open access but no human interaction at all.

10. The problem of invasive species is of this type, though the issues are not specifically examined here, partly because some of the dominant species are weeds, pests, and pathogens not typically considered wildlife. See Perrings et al. (2000) for a summary and analysis of the issues.

11. Many of these issues are examined by Siikamäki and Chow (Chapter 7, this volume, on biodiversity).

12. Modern biologists are often critical of the idea of a deterministic carrying capacity, but as a general point about resource constraints, it is useful. A more realistic and more complex population model would incorporate uncertainty.

13. Even a small population of mosquitoes, however, is likely to be valuable for genetic and biodiversity reasons.

14. This is what economists call an optimal timing problem, and it is the framework that describes everything from timber cutting to grain harvest.

15. Of course, the optimal number need not be constant over time because conditions change.

16. This would include cases in which the population provided public goods because perfect property rights would still allow the owner to exclude.

17. Another possible case of suboptimal use occurs when investment is required for harvest; in this case an open-access regime can lead to underexploitation. This has been a problem in oil production but has not been the case in wildlife exploitation (Bohn and Deacon 2000).

18. It is not essential that $X = 0$ when the growth rate is zero; there may be a "minimum viable stock size" required to ensure positive growth rates, which makes extinction more likely. Note, however, that extinction of a single stock is not the same as biological extinction of a species, which is composed of many stocks.

19. The problem of game ownership is analytically similar to oil and gas reservoirs, in which wildlife resemble "above-ground" oil reservoirs. See Libecap and Wiggins (1984) and Lueck (1995).

20. Most often, rights to game were held as common property among members of relatively small tribal units (see Demsetz 1967; Cronon 1986; Johnsen 1986). Bailey (1992) finds similar arrangements for tribal groups outside North America.

21. Not surprisingly, there is a thriving market in game meat in Great Britain, and landowners routinely penalize (through fines) those hunters who damage meat by careless shooting.

22. See, for example, *Geer v. Connecticut*, 161 U.S. 519 (1896).

23. Act of 1900 Ch. 553, §§ 1–5, 31 Stat. 187 (current version at 16 U.S.C. §§701, 3371–3378 (1988 & Supp. IV 1993) and 18 U.S.C. §§ 42–44 (1988 & Supp. IV 1993)).

24. Convention for the Protection of Migratory Birds, August 16, 1916, United States–Great Britain (on behalf of Canada), 39 Stat. 1702, T.S. No. 628.

25. Federal Aid in Wildlife Restoration (Pittman-Robertson) Act of 1937, Ch. 899, 50 Stat. 917 (codified at 16 U.S.C. § 669 (1988)).

26. Federal Aid in Fish Restoration (Dingell-Johnson) Act of 1950, Ch. 658, 64 Stat. 430 (codified at 16 U.S.C. § 777 (1988)).

27. Migratory Bird Hunting Stamp (Duck Stamp) Act of 1934, Ch. 71, 48 Stat. 451 (codified at 16 U.S.C. § 718b (1988 & Supp. 1992).

28. Palmer (1912) also reports deer wardens in Massachusetts in 1739 for the state deer reserve.

29. In many states, recently arrived poor immigrants were singled out for their disregard of the game laws. For example, in 1903 Pennsylvania prohibited all hunting by resident aliens.

30. The final case upholding this practice was *Baldwin v. Fish and Game Commission* 436, U.S. 371 (1978). A recent federal case, however, enjoined Arizona's policy of limiting elk hunting licenses to nonresidents and ordered the state to modify its nonresident regulations. See *Conservation Force Inc. v. Manning* 301 F.3d 985 (9th Cir. August 20, 2002). More than 20 state agencies filed an appeal to the U.S. Supreme Court, but the court chose not to hear the case.

31. 16 U.S.C § 669.

32. Federal Aid in Fish Restoration and Management Projects Act, 16 U.S.C. § 777. This program was expanded in 1984 by the Wallop-Breaux amendments.

33. In modern parlance these groups are often known as "cast and blast" or "hook and bullet."

34. States also receive federal funds from the sale of federal duck stamps, which allow one to hunt migratory waterfowl. This system developed as a result of the Migratory Bird Treaty Act of 1918.

35. The regulation of fisheries in the two countries is also supportive. In the United States, the government generally controls fisheries, but state laws ordinarily grant private control of fish in small lakes and private ponds. In Great Britain, however, private fishing rights are very common on the numerous and rather small streams in the countryside. At the same time, the Crown has long controlled the fisheries in open seas, navigable rivers, and the foreshore.

36. 16 U.S.C. § 17b.

37. Treaty for the Preservation and Protection of Fur Seals, July 7, 1911, 37 Stat. 1542, T.S. No. 564.

38. Convention for the Preservation of the Halibut Fishery of the North Pacific Ocean and the Bering Sea, March 2, 1953, United States–Canada, 5 U.S.T. 5, T.I.A.S. No. 2900.

39. Agreement on the Conservation of Polar Bears, November 15, 1973, T.I.A.S. No. 8409.

40. Agreement on the Conservation of the Porcupine Caribou herd, with annex, July 17, 1987, T.I.A.S. No. 11259. Lueck (1989) discusses international treaties protecting wildlife.

41. Coyotes of course may have nonuse values, and as these values become more important, one would expect more protection of these stocks.

42. Also, no state allows the private sale of hunting licenses. The taking and sale of live animals is also severely restricted by state law.

43. The issue is perhaps no more important than in Africa, where two arguments are currently being made about the ivory trade. In Zimbabwe and southern Africa, the ivory trade is revered as an important source of revenue used to maintain and husband elephants, while in Kenya and east Africa it is scorned as the cause of severe poaching (Simmons and Kreuter 1989).

44. Lund (1980, *105*) articulates the mainstream view: "Prohibition of commercial dealing in wildlife was the ingenious solution American law devised to the problem of limiting takers." See also Geist (1988).

45. Goldstein (1991) and Simmons and Kreuter (1989). Lund (1980) notes how some government-sponsored bounties designed to eradicate undesirable species actually led to the protection of certain populations.

46. These publications are directly linked to Pittman-Robertson funds.

47. The Wildlife Management Institute (1997) report shows four basics types: independent agencies (20), independent agencies with state parks (7), agencies in the second tier of a bigger agency (20), and agencies in the third tier (4).

48. Even though agencies do own and lease habitat for refuges, the vast majority of wildlife populations occur on private land.

49. Allocation is also based on a state's land area.

50. In some cases, management of game and nongame species are aligned, and it is likely that interest groups will form a coalition to foster this kind of management.

51. Landowners have also increasingly limited access to local sportsmen, causing a political backlash from resident hunters who want free access to private lands.

52. Within the United States, Indian tribes have jurisdiction over wildlife management and have their own management systems. These systems vary widely but are often akin to private hunting and fishing operations. For a summary, see the website of the Native American Fish and Wildlife Society (http://www.nafws.org/index.html). Some tribes, such as the White Mountain Apache in Arizona, have developed sophisticated game management programs that generate substantial revenues for the tribes. See their recognition for these achievements at http://www.ksg.harvard.edu/hpaied/hn/hn_2000_rec.htm.

53. Large landowners have also dominated state game commissions, which oversee the activities of the state game agencies. Their presence in the game bureaucracy strongly supports view of the game department as a contractual institution.

54. Indeed, hunting rights severable from the land have ancient origins (Lueck 1998).

55. Anderson and Hill (1995) document the widespread nature of private hunting, but perhaps the easiest way to see its extent is to simply conduct an online search.

56. Details can also be found at http://www.defenders.org/wildlife/new/facts/faq.html (accessed February 21, 2006).

57. Siikamäki and Chow (Chapter 7, this volume) examine biodiversity thoroughly.

58. The National Marine Fisheries Service administers the ESA for marine species.

59. Thompson (1997, 2005) examines these issues in detail.

60. 437 U.S. 153 (1978). *TVA* is the most important case for federal lands and federal agencies because it established the unilateral authority of the ESA to control the actions of federal agencies.

61. 40 Fed. Reg. 44412, 44416 (1975).

62. This policy was further solidified by the Supreme Court in 1995 in *Babbitt v. Sweet Home Communities for a Greater Oregon* 515 U.S. 687.

63. Thompson (2005) notes, however, that modification of "potential habitat" is not forbidden, and it is also true that under Section 10, permits can be granted to take species and thus allow some development.

64. Rohlf (1998) finds more than 40 federal cases by 1988. From 1973 to 1998, the *Environmental Law Reporter* (various issues) shows that 24 cases reached the Supreme Court, 360 reached a federal appellate court, and 488 reached a federal district court.

65. Quoted in "NWF Seeks Prairie Dog Listing: Action Will Save Wildlife and Grassland Habitat," http://www.nwf.org/grasslands/prairied.html. After six years of litigation and study, the Fish and Wildlife Service decided not to list the prairie dog in 2004.

66. The compensation program of Defenders of Wildlife was established to mitigate this sort of behavior by ranchers faced with depredation of livestock by bears and wolves.

67. The idea of preemption in the face of pending costly regulations (e.g., getting development permits before fees rise, making income and investment decisions before tax laws change) is well known among economists and legal scholars. See Dana (1995) for a study of preemption and natural resources.

68. See Mann and Plummer (1995), Wilcove et al. (1996), Thompson (1997), Goble et al. (2005, *239, 257*).

69. "[T]he highest level of assurance that a property owner will not face an ESA issue is to maintain the property in a condition such that protected species cannot occupy the property. ... *This is referred to as the 'scorched earth' technique*" (National Association of Homebuilders 1996, *109*).

70. List et al. (2006) also find similar preemptive effects for desert habitat of the pygmy owl in Arizona.

71. In fall 2005, the U.S. House passed the Threatened and Endangered Species Recovery Act, which did not become law.

72. Thompson (2005) discusses these in detail.

73. See the Fish and Wildlife Service Web site, http://www.fws.gov/endangered/ and http://www.fws.gov/endangered/recovery/harborqa.pdf (accessed February 21, 2006).

74. See http://www.fws.gov/endangered/landowner/CCAAs%20(Non-Federal).pdf (accessed February 21, 2006).

75. The authors use a measure of endangerment published by The Nature Conservancy.

76. For details see http://www.fws.gov/endangered/wildlife.html#Species (accessed September 13, 2005).

77. Gordon et al. (1997) uses Fish and Wildlife Service biannual reports, annual species spending reports, individual species recovery plans, and all *Federal Register* notices to delist or reclassify species.

78. The point here is not that the bald eagle did not recover under the ESA but that the conservation policies unique to the ESA were not critical in the recovery. The bald eagle recovered under policies used before the ESA—namely, restrictions on killing and the prohibition on toxic pesticides. Habitat maintenance was not particularly important.

79. "Taylor et al. (2005) use Fish and Wildlife Service data to statistically examine the correlation between recovery categories (the agency uses "stable", "improving", "declining" and unknown") and such ESA outcomes as listing and critical habitat designation. They find a positive correlation between recovery status and ESA protection. Schwartz (1999) calculates that the ESA has prevented 185 species from becoming extinct. This relies on the assumption that 67 percent of "endangered" species will go extinct in 100 years. Since, during the first 25 years of the ESA, only 7 of the 1,143 listed species have gone extinct (instead of the "expected" 192), the ESA is said to have saved 185 species."

80. See, for example, comments by Michael Bean (chair of Environmental Defense's Wildlife Program) in remarks on the 25th anniversary of ESA: http://www.environmentaldefense.org/content.cfm?contentID=1081 (accessed April 21, 2008).

81. See the Smithsonian Institute website, http://www.si.edu/resource/faq/nmnh/passpig.htm (accessed February 16, 2007).

82. This magnitude is striking. Compare, for example, the estimates of some 35 million ducks in North America. See http://www.environmentaldefense.org/content.cfm?contentID=1081

84. Diamond (1997) notes that relatively few mammals have been domesticated by humans, and nearly all originated in Europe and/or Asia.

87. It is true, however, that most of the current bison populations have some genetic material from domestic cattle, so their numbers overstate the state of the conservation of genetic material.

88. There may also be differences in population dynamics that explain the pigeon's demise. Pigeons seem to have a critical minimum population, but bison do not appear to have such limits.

89. Waterfowl are very similar to deer in the circumstances of their decline and have also significantly rebounded in numbers. Once decimated, ducks and geese are now populous generally and often pests in urban and suburban areas. See http://www.fws.gov/waterfowlsurveys/ (accessed February 27, 2006).

90. I am lumping white-tailed and mule deer together, though most of the discussion is about whitetails *(Odocoileus virginianus),* which are much more widespread in the lower 48 states. Mule deer *(Odocoileus hemionus)* tend to be found only in the 17 western states and in much lower numbers. Table 6-1 shows population estimates over time.

91. It is likely that early white settlers also killed large numbers of deer for personal consumption, but this has not been documented to my knowledge.

92. The situation for mule deer is different, however, where urbanization tends to decrease habitat (primarily by limiting winter range), and in recent years many western states have seen decreasing mule deer populations. Even this is somewhat simplistic, since in many western state predators—especially coyotes and sometime cougars—are now thriving in urban and suburban areas. This human-predator conflict promises to be an issue in the near future.

93. For more information, see http://www.nps.gov/yell/nature/animals/wolf/wolfrest.html.

94. See http://www.fws.gov/home/feature/2007/gray_wolf_factsheet_populations.pdf (accessed February 19, 2007).

95. See http://www.fws.gov/news/NewsReleases/showNews.cfm?newsId=6F1726CD-952D-6E23-9A79F5D44DBC2637 (accessed February 19, 2007).

96. I was unable to find Fish and Wildlife Service budget data on the Northern Rockies program.

97. As noted above, however, there are relatively few bison with pure DNA.

References

Ando, A. 1999. Waiting to be Protected under the Endangered Species Act: The Political Economy of Regulatory Delay. *Journal of Law and Economics* 42(1): 29–60.

American Eagle Foundation. 2001. Bald eagle protection and recovery status. http://www.eagles.org/status.html.

Anderson, T.L., and P.J. Hill. 1995. *Wildlife in the Marketplace*. Lanham, MD: Rowman & Littlefield.

Bailey, M. 1992. Approximate Optimality of Aboriginal Property Rights. *Journal of Law and Economics* 35(1): 183–98.

Bean, M.J. 1983. *The Evolution of National Wildlife Law*. New York: Praeger.

Bohn, H., and R.T. Deacon. 2000. Ownership Risk, Investment, and the Use of Natural Resources. *American Economic Review* 90(3): 526–49.

Brown, G.M., and J. Shogren. 1998. Economics of the Endangered Species Act. *Journal of Economics Perspectives* 12(3): 3–20.

Clawson, M., and C.S. Van Doren (eds.). 1984. *Statistics on Outdoor Recreation*. Washington, DC: Resources for the Future.

Clutton-Brock, J. 1981. *Domesticated Animals from Early Times*. London: British Museum.

Cronon, W. 1986. *Changes in the Land: Indians, Colonists, and the Ecology of New England*. New York: Hill and Wang.

Daily, G. (ed.). 1997. *Nature's Services: Societal Dependence on Natural Ecosystems*. Washington, DC: Island Press.

Dana, D. (1995) *Natural Preservation and the Race to Develop*. 143, University of Pennsylvania Law Review. 655–708

Demarais, S., and P.R. Krausman (eds). 2000. *Ecology and Management of Large Mammals in North America*. New Jersey: Prentice-Hall.

Demarais, S., K.V. Miller, and H.A. Jacobson. 2000. White-tailed Deer. In *Ecology and Management of Large Mammals in North America,* edited by S. Demarais and P.R. Krausman. New Jersey: Prentice-Hall, 601–19.

Demsetz, H. 1967. Toward a Theory of Property Rights. *American Economic Review* 57(2): 347–59.

Diamond, J. 1997. *Guns, Germs and Steel: The Fates of Human Societies*. New York: W.W. Norton.

Fedkiw, J. 2004. Sustainability and the Pathway Hypothesis. In *Pathway to Sustainability,* edited by J. Fedkiw, D. MacCleery, and V.A. Sample. Durham, NC: Forest History Society, 7–24.

Fischer, H. 1989. Restoring the Wolf: Defenders Launches a Compensation Fund. *Defenders of Wildlife* 64(1): 9–10.

Geist, V. 1988. How Markets in Wildlife Meat and Parts, and the Sale of Hunting Privileges, Jeopardize Wildlife Conservation. *Conservation Biology* 2(1): 15–26.

———. 1994. Wildlife Conservation as Wealth. *Nature* 368 (April 7): 491–92.

Goble, D.D., J.M. Scott, and F.W. Davis (eds.). 2005. *The Endangered Species Act at Thirty*. Washington, DC: Island Press.

Goldstein, J.H. 1991. The Prospects for Using Market Incentives to Conserve Biological Diversity. *Environmental Law* 21(3): 985–1014.

Gordon, R.E., J.K. Lacy, and J.R. Streeter. 1997. Conservation under the Endangered Species Act. *Environment International* 23(3): 359–419.

Greenwalt, L A. 1978. The National Wildlife Refuge System. Wildlife and America. H.P. Brokaw, editor. Council on Environmental Quality.

Hampton, B. 1997. *The Great American Wolf*. New York: Henry Holt and Company.

Hardin, G. 1968. The Tragedy of the Commons. *Science* 162: 1243–48.

Harrington, W. 1991. Wildlife in the United States. In *America's Renewable Resources*, edited by R.A. Sedjo and K.D. Frederick. Washington, DC: Resources for the Future, 205–46.

Heal, G.M. 1998. *Valuing the Future: Economic Theory and Sustainability*. New York: Columbia University Press.

———. 2000. *Nature and the Marketplace*. Washington, DC: Island Press.

Innes, R., S. Polasky, and J. Tschirhart. 1998. Takings, Compensation, and Endangered Species Protection on Private Lands. *Journal of Economics Perspectives* 12(3): 35–52.

Jacoby, K. 2001. *Crimes Against Nature: Squatters, Poachers, Thieves and the Hidden History of American Conservation*. Berkeley: University of California Press.

Jeffries, M.J. 1997. *Biodiversity and Conservation*. London and New York: Routledge.

Johnsen, D.B. 1986. The Formation and Protection of Property Rights among the Southern Kwakiutl Indians. *Journal of Legal Studies* 15(1): 41–67.

Kie, J.G., and B. Czech. 2000. Mule and Black-tailed Deer. In *Ecology and Management of Large Mammals in North America*, edited by S. Demarais and P.R. Krausman. New Jersey: Prentice-Hall, 629–48.

Leal, D.R., and J.B. Grewell. 1999. *Hunting for Habitat: A Practical Guide to State-landowner Partnerships*. Bozeman, MT: Political Economy Research Center.

Lemann, N. 1999. No People Allowed. *The New Yorker* November 22: 101–13.

Libecap, G.D., and S.N. Wiggins. 1984. Contractual Responses to the Common Pool: Prorationing of Crude Oil Production. *American Economic Review* 74(1): 87–98.

List, J.A., M. Margolis, and D.E. Osgood. 2006. Is the Endangered Species Act Endangering Species? Working paper 12777. National Bureau of Economic Research.

Lueck, D. 1989. The Economic Nature of Wildlife Law. *Journal of Legal Studies* 18(2): 291– 324.

———. 1991. Ownership and Regulation of Wildlife. *Economic Inquiry* 29(2): 249–60.

———. 1995. Property Rights and the Economic Logic of Wildlife Institutions. *Natural Resources Journal* 35(3): 625–70.

———. 1998. Auctions, Markets, and Spectrum Ownership: Comment on Moreton and Spiller. *Journal of Law and Economics* 41(2): 717–25.

———. 2002. The Extermination and Conservation of the American Bison. *Journal of Legal Studies* 31(2): 609–52.

Lueck, D., and J.A. Michael. 2003. Preemptive Habitat Destruction under the Endangered Species Act. *Journal of Law and Economics* 46(1): 27–60.

Lueck, D., and D. Parker. 2007. Contracting, Organization and Public Bureaucracy. Working paper. Tucson: University of Arizona.

Lund, T.A. 1980. *American Wildlife Law*. Berkeley: University of California Press.

Madsen, C. 1999. Brave New World: Hunters and Wildlife Managers in the Next Century. *Wing & Shot: The Magazine for Upland Bird Hunters* October/November: 63–65.

Mann, C.C. 2005. *1491*. New York: Knopf.

Mann, C.C., and M.L. Plummer. 1995. *Noah's Choice: The Future of Endangered Species*. New York: Knopf.

Martin, P. S. and Klein, R. G. (1984) "Quaternary Extinctions: A Prehistoric Revolution". Tucson, AZ. University of Arizona Press.

McCabe, R.E., and T.R. McCabe. 1984. Of Slings and Arrows: A Historical Retrospection. In *White-tailed Deer: Ecology and Management*, edited by L.K. Halls. Harrisburg, PA: Stackpole Books, 19–72.

Metrick, A., and M.L. Weitzman. 1998. Conflicts and Choices in Biodiversity Preservation. *Journal of Economics Perspectives* 12(3): 21–34.

Montana State University. 1986. 1986 Montana Fee Hunting Survey. Bozeman: Montana State University.

Musgrave, R.S., and M.A. Stein. 1993. *State Wildlife Laws Handbook*. Rockville, MD: Government Institutes.

National Association of Homebuilders. 1996. Developer's Guide to Endangered Species Regulation. Washington, DC.

National Oceanic and Atmospheric Administration (NOAA). 2002. Stock Assessment Reports: Gray Whale. http://www.nmfs.noaa.gov/prot_res/PR2/Stock_Assessment_Program/Cetaceans/Gray_Whale_(Eastern_N._Pacific)/AK02graywhale_E.N.Pacific.PDF.

National Wild Turkey Federation. 2005. Wild turkey conservation. http://www.nwtf.org/about_us/tukeycons/.

Palmer, T.S. 1912. Chronology and Index of the More Important Events in American Game Protection 1776–1911. Bulletin 41. Biological Survey. Washington, DC: U.S. Department of Agriculture.

Pelton, M.R. 2000. Black Bear. In *Ecology and Management of Large Mammals in North America,* edited by S. Demarais and P.R. Krausman. New Jersey: Prentice-Hall, 389–402.

Perrings, C., M. Williamson, and S. Dalmazzone (eds.). 2000. *The Economics of Biological Invasions.* Cheltenham, UK: Edward Elgar Publishing.

Reynolds, C.B. 1896. *The Game Laws in Brief.* New York: Forest and Stream Publishing Co.

———. 1913. *Game Law Blue Book and Directory of Guides.* New York: Game Law Publishing Co.

Rohlf, D.J. 1998. *The Endangered Species Act: A Guide to Its Protections and Implementation.* Stanford, CA: Stanford Environmental Law Society.

Rondeau, D., and J.M. Conrad. 2003. Managing Urban Deer. *American Journal of Agricultural Economics* 85(1): 266–81.

Sauer, C.O. 1953. *Agricultural Origins and Dispersals.* American Geographic Society. Cambridge, MA: MIT Press.

Schorger, A.W. 1955. *The Passenger Pigeon: Its Natural History and Extinction.* Madison: University of Wisconsin Press.

Schwartz, M.W. 1999. Choosing the Appropriate Scale of Reserve for Conservation. *Annual Review of Ecology and Systematics* 30: 83–108.

Seton, E.T. 1927. *Lives of Game Animals* (vol. 3, part I). Garden City, NJ: Doubleday, Page, and Co.

Shaw, J.H. 1995. How Many Bison Originally Populated Western Rangelands? *Rangelands* 17(5): 148–50.

Simmons, R.T., and U.P. Kreuter. 1989. Herd Mentality: Banning Ivory Sales Is No Way to Save Elephants. *Policy Review* 50: 46–49.

Smith, V.L. 1975. The Primitive Hunter Culture, Pleistocene Extinction, and the Rise of Agriculture. *Journal of Political Economy* 83(4): 727–55.

Stavins, R.N., A.F. Wagner, and G. Wagner. 2002. Interpreting Sustainability in Economic Terms: Dynamic Efficiency Plus Intergenerational Equity. Washington, DC: Resources for the Future. www.rff.org/Documents/RFF-DP-02-29.pdf (accessed March 28, 2006).

Taylor, M.F.J., K.F. Suckling, and J.J. Rachlinski. 2005. The Effectiveness of the Endangered Species Act: A Quantitative Analysis. *BioScience* 55(4): 360–67.

Thompson, B.H. Jr. 1997. The Endangered Species Act: A Case Study in Takings and Incentives. *Stanford Law Review* 49(2): 305–80.

———. 2005. Managing the Working Landscape. In *The Endangered Species Act at Thirty,* edited by D.D. Goble, J.M. Scott, and F.W. Davis. Washington, DC: Island Press.

Thornton, R. (1987) "American Indian Holocaust and Survival: A Population History Since 1492". Norman, OK. University of Oklahoma Press.

Tober, J. 1981. *Who Owns the Wildlife? The Political Economy of Conservation in Nineteenth Century America.* Westport, CT: Greenwood Press.

———. 1989. *Wildlife and the Public Interest: Nonprofit Organizations and Federal Wildlife Policy.* New York: Praeger Publishers.

Trefethen, J.B., and P. Corbin. 1975. *An American Crusade for Wildlife.* New York: Winchester Press.

U.S. Census Bureau. 1960. *Historical Statistics of the U.S.: Colonial Times to 1957.* Washington, DC.

———. 2002. *Statistical Abstract of the United States: 2002,* 122nd Edition. Washington, DC.

U.S. Fish and Wildlife Service (U.S. FWS). 1988. 1985 National Survey of Fishing, Hunting, and Wildlife–associated Recreation. U.S. Department of the Interior. Washington, DC: Government Printing Office.

———. 1999. News release: The Bald Eagle Is Back! http://www.fws.gov/r9extaff/eaglejuly2.html.

———. 2002. 2001 National Survey on Hunting, Fishing, and Wildlife–associated Recreation. http://training.fws.gov/library/nat_survey2001.pdf.

———. 2004. Species Accounts: Whooping Crane. http://www.fws.gov/species/species_accounts/bio_whoo.html.

Vaughn, M.R., and M.R. Pelton. Black Bears in North America. National Biological Service. http://biology.usgs.gov/s+t/noframe/c286.htm.

Warren, L.S. 1997. *The Hunter's Game: Poachers and Conservationists in Twentieth Century America*. New Haven: Yale University Press.

Whooping Crane Operation Migration. 2005. Population Tables. http://www.operationmigration.org/Whooping_Crane_Count.html.

Wilcove, D.S., M.J. Bean, R. Bonnie, and M. McMillan. 1996. *Rebuilding the Ark: Toward a More Effective Endangered Species Act on Private Lands*. New York: Environmental Defense Fund.

Wildlife Management Institute (WMI). 1997. Organization, Authority and Programs of State Wildlife Agencies. Washington, DC: WMI.

Wisdom, M.J., and J.G. Cook. 2000. North American Elk. In *Ecology and Management of Large Mammals in North America*, edited by S. Demarais and P.R. Krausman. New Jersey: Prentice-Hall, 694–726.

World Commission on Environment and Development (WCED). 1987. *Our Common Future*. New York: Oxford University Press.

Yoakum, J.D., and B.W. O'Gara. 2000. Pronghorn. In *Ecology and Management of Large Mammals in North America*, edited by S. Demarais and P.R. Krausman. New Jersey: Prentice-Hall, 559–74.

Yoder, J.K. 2002. Estimating Aggregate Wildlife-Inflicted Crop Damage with Self-selected Data. *Land Economics* 78(1): 45–59.

Zuener, F.E. 1963. *History of Domesticated Animals*. New York: Harper and Row.

CHAPTER 7

Biodiversity in the United States

Juha Siikamäki and Jeffrey Chow

THE UNITED STATES has an exceptionally rich natural heritage. The vast size of the nation and the extensive variation of climate, topography, and biota across different regions all contribute to this richness. Subtropical Florida, arctic Alaska, the Great Plains, the northwestern temperate rain forests, the southwestern deserts, and the southeastern wetlands, among numerous other biomes, exemplify the ecological and biological diversity of the United States.

Biological diversity, or biodiversity, denotes the wealth and variety of all living things. Although there is a long history of naturalists' examining and classifying animals, plants, fungi, and other organisms, the term biodiversity, meaning the total variability of life, dates only from the 1980s (Lovejoy 1980; Wilson 1985). The concept was quickly popularized. The importance of biodiversity was widely recognized by the late 1980s, it became a subject to international agreements in the early 1990s, and today, protection of biodiversity is a part of everyday public discourse, politics, and business.

This chapter provides an overview of biodiversity, including its definitions, ecological and economic meanings, and current preservation efforts, especially through regulatory approaches. We focus almost exclusively on U.S. terrestrial and freshwater biodiversity; although they are clearly important, marine and international issues related to biodiversity generally are not covered in this text.

Our general objective is to highlight relevant issues by summarizing existing literature and policy.[1] We begin by reviewing the various definitions of biodiversity, the measurement of biodiversity, and the role of biodiversity in ecosystem processes. Thereafter, we discuss the current status of biodiversity in the United States as well as the number of species in the various regions of the country. Then, we discuss biodiversity loss, summarizing current knowledge about species endangerment and extinction, and their causes. We next review the economic literature on biodiversity as a source for values related to human welfare, as well as summarize estimated values for rare, threatened, and endangered species and habitat. Subsequently, we explain the protection of biodiversity in the United States, a discussion that revolves around the Endangered Species Act but considers the increasingly important role of other approaches to biodiversity conservation, including public protected areas, land trusts, and forest certification programs. A discussion concerning the relationship between sustainability and biodiversity concludes the chapter.

What Is Biodiversity?

Biodiversity refers to the overall biological variety of life, which is a complex notion with several definitions. Often, statements of biodiversity refer to the number of species in a geographical area. However, biodiversity occurs at other levels of organization, including genetic variation among different individuals or populations within a particular species. The range of ecosystems, such as forests, agricultural areas, wetlands, mountains, lakes, and rivers, and differences between and within geographical landscapes, regions, countries, and continents are also important dimensions of biodiversity.

Definitions

Biodiversity typically is considered at three levels: species diversity, genetic diversity, and ecosystem diversity. *Species diversity* is the variety and abundance of species in a geographical area. The number of species in a given area, known as species richness, is the simplest and arguably most commonly used measure of biodiversity. Species are the central unit in biodiversity studies and conservation, at least in part because ecosystems are hard to delimit and genes have until recently been difficult to count and identify. A species is the basic unit of organism classification. It is typically defined as a group of similar organisms that interbreed in nature or share a common, genetically distinct lineage of descent. However, each species consists of subspecies (i.e., geographical races), populations, and individuals, each possessing its own levels of genetic distinctiveness. A population is a geographically distinct group of individuals of a particular species. An evolutionarily significant unit (ESU) is a population or group of populations that is substantially reproductively isolated and is sufficiently genetically unique from other populations to make it an important evolutionary component of the species. Although biodiversity is often measured using species richness, practical species management and conservation efforts often target populations and ESUs rather than entire species.[2]

Genetic diversity refers to genetic variation within species, both among distinct populations and among the individuals within a population. Genes are the chromosomal units that code for the unique morphological and biochemical characteristics of an organism and are passed down along generations of organisms. Variation arises from mutations in genes, and natural selection of these characteristics within a population is the primary mechanism of biological evolution. In sexually reproducing species, genetic diversity also comes from recombination that occurs when genes are exchanged.

Ecosystem diversity refers to the variation within and between communities and their associations with the physical environment. A biological community is the collection of species populations that exist and interact in a particular location. The number of different ecological systems within an area also is sometimes called systems diversity. Species play different functions within their communities; some species are functionally substitutable, whereas others (keystone species) play determinant roles in the food web and cannot be removed from the system without fundamentally altering the species composition of the community. Ecosystem diversity also relates to landscape diversity, which denotes the diversity and connectivity of ecosystems within large geographical areas.

Ecological systems have three primary attributes—composition, structure, and function—which contribute to biodiversity. *Composition* denotes the identity and variability of different elements, such as genes, individuals and populations. *Structure* is the physical organization, pattern, and complexity of elements at different organizational scales (habitat, ecosystem, landscape). *Function* consists of ecological and evolutionary processes of elements, such as "nutrient cycling," disturbance, or gene flow. Although each primary attribute of biodiversity is potentially important, interest in biodiversity tends to concentrate around composition, chiefly species diversity.

Biodiversity and Ecosystem Processes

Ecologists generally consider that species diversity increases ecosystem productivity, stability, and resilience (e.g., McCann 2000). Results from long-term field experiments (e.g., Tilman and Downing 1994; Tilman et al. 2001) indicate that although species richness and the resulting interspecies competition may cause fluctuations in individual species populations, diversity tends to increase the productive stability of an ecosystem as a whole. This concept is similar to the portfolio theory in economics, which suggests that diversification of stock portfolios can effectively reduce stock-specific risks on returns. Like stocks, the returns (i.e., biomass) generated by different species are not perfectly correlated. Rather, changes in the biomass production by some species are associated with dissimilar changes in the biomass production by other species. In other words, a high number of species acts as a buffer against productivity reductions within any single species, and ecosystems with greater numbers of species experience fewer fluctuations in aggregate biomass production.

Diverse ecosystems also generally have relatively high rates of ecosystem processes and produce more biomass than less diverse systems. However, increases in the rates of ecosystem processes are not constant and seem to plateau at relatively low levels of species richness. Cardinale et al. (2006) present a meta-analysis of more than 100 field, greenhouse, and laboratory experiments that manipulate species diversity to examine the effects on ecosystem function. Their results confirm that, on average, a decrease in species richness reduces biomass generation. The magnitude of the effect depends on the species removed from the system, suggesting that some species have a much greater impact on ecological processes than others. However, predicting in advance of extinction the level of impact by different species is problematic. Experimental analyses also suggest that functional groups—that is, sets of species serving different ecosystem functions such as decomposition, production, and nutrient recycling—are important to the role of biodiversity in ecosystems (e.g., Holling et al. 1995). Therefore, the distribution of species within and between functional groups also is an important determinant of ecosystem functions. Differential responses by various species and functional groups give rise to ecosystem stability (McCann 2000).

Ecosystem resilience has two meanings in ecology. First, resilience can be defined as the magnitude of disturbance that can be absorbed by the ecosystem before it changes to another equilibrium state. Second, resilience is the rate at which the ecosystem returns to equilibrium after a disturbance. Species diversity may play important roles in this process. For example, recent research suggests that diverse communities may have a capacity to resist invasions by exotic, nonnative species that are a major threat to biodiversity[3] (e.g., Kennedy et al. 2002; Tilman 2004).

Several components of species diversity determine its effects within actual ecosystems. These include the number of species, the relative abundances of species, the particular species present, the interactions among the species present, and the spatial and temporal variations of these components. Current knowledge about the consequences of biodiversity loss in actual ecosystems is quite limited, particularly when considering large ecosystems and substantial changes in biodiversity. Present information about how ecosystem functions relate to diversity comes from mostly simple ecosystems with only few species, reflecting small variations in species composition and relative abundance.

Although examining biodiversity functions in simplified settings helps keep experiments manageable and facilitates identification of relevant relationships, it also limits the generality of the findings. Critics note that real ecosystems may be structured quite differently and operate under rather different processes than those in experimental studies (e.g., Grime 1997). Consequently, questions about the role of biodiversity within actual ecosystems remain somewhat unanswered. Because of the complexity of ecosystems, no simple, *ex ante* relationship between diversity, stability, and resilience in actual ecosystems likely even exists. Therefore, empirical research at different ecological scales is necessary to help identify the functions of biodiversity in actual ecosystems.

Measuring Biodiversity

Two major approaches to the quantification of biodiversity exist. The economics literature focuses on measures of biodiversity based on joint dissimilarity among a set of species, whereas the ecological literature emphasizes measures of biodiversity based on relative abundance of species within ecological communities (Polasky et al. 2005a).

Joint dissimilarity of species can be determined from a phylogenetic tree, which describes the evolutionary interrelationships among various organisms and their common ancestors. Two species separated by shorter branch distances are more closely related than species separated by longer branches. For example, in Figure 7-1, species E is a closer relative of species F than is species A.

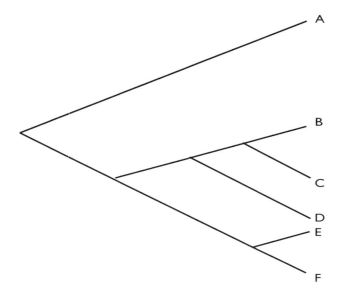

Figure 7-1. *Phylogenetic Tree Schematic*

Vane-Wright et al. (1991) propose measuring the diversity of a collection of species based on the phylogenetic tree connecting them. Weitzman (1992) formalizes the measurement problem and formulates the following conditions that the proposed measure should satisfy: first, diversity should not reduce by the addition of species to a group; second, diversity should not increase by the addition of identical species; and third, diversity should increase by the addition of species dissimilar to species already in the collection. For the simplest case in which all distances between species are equal, the total length of the tree determines the level of biodiversity.

Although the joint dissimilarity of species is helpful for describing species diversity, its usefulness for conservation decisions is limited. Most conservation efforts deal with habitats rather than species; thus habitat-based measures of biodiversity are needed for assessing and designing alternative conservation strategies. The joint dissimilarity of species also does not necessarily indicate the value of biodiversity. Brock and Xepapadeas (2003) show that just a slightly more diverse ecosystem can be much more valuable even though the increase in dissimilarity is almost zero. It also is not clear how well joint dissimilarity of species relates to functional diversity, which is essential to considering how changes in biodiversity affect the stability of ecosystems.

In the ecological literature, the most common characterizations of biodiversity are based on the relative abundance of species within ecological communities. Mathematical indices of biodiversity quantify species diversity at three geographical scales. *Alpha diversity* is the number of species in a certain community and can be used to compare the diversity of different locales or ecosystem types. *Gamma diversity* is the species richness of a wide geographical area that encompasses multiple ecosystems, such as a country or continent. *Beta diversity* measures the variability of species composition over an environmental or geographical gradient; it is sometimes calculated as the ratio of gamma diversity to alpha diversity.

Biodiversity indicators are measures of ecological end points, selected based on their perceived importance to biodiversity. Examples of such end points include species richness and the number of extinct, endangered, and threatened species within an ecological community or geographical area. Repeated measurements of different endpoints help evaluate how biodiversity changes over time and how it is influenced by human activities, such as land use and management, as well as biodiversity conservation efforts.

Biodiversity indicators should be simple enough to be routinely monitored yet capable of capturing the complexity of ecosystems. Specifically, biodiversity indicators should be sensitive to environmental change, convenient to monitor, widely applicable, capable of assessing a wide range of stress, relevant to significant ecological phenomena, and related to changes that can be addressed by management actions, and they should have known and steady responses to disturbance over time (Dale and Beyeler 2001). Rather than a single indicator, biodiversity often is estimated using several complementary measures.

Different indicators must be specified for particular ecosystems to reflect their unique characteristics. In the *National Report on Sustainable Forests*, the Forest Service describes 9 indicators for biodiversity conservation in forest ecosystems, as well as another 58 indicators of other dimensions of sustainability (USDA Forest Service 2004). Ecosystem diversity is addressed by multiple indicators that measure the extent of fragmentation, the number of forest types, the successional stages, and the age classes of forests and protected areas. Other biodiversity indicators include the number of forest-dependent species, the percentage of species at risk, the number of species that occupy a small portion of their original range, and the population levels of representative species from diverse habitats. Several of these indicators cannot be currently monitored because the data are insufficient. Their use also reflects a broader trend: measurements of biodiversity are often based on simple species counts because more complicated measures that take into account species and habitat dynamics often are impractical.

Status of Biodiversity

Many basic questions related to the current status of biodiversity remain unanswered. For instance, the total number of species in the world is unknown. Estimates vary from a few million to more than a hundred million species, with current consensus around 14 million species (Table 7-1). The species counts and their precision vary considerably across different taxonomic groups, and only the best-known taxonomic groups—plants and animals—have species counts with narrow bounds of agreement. For all other groups of organisms, the precision of the estimated species counts is generally considered poor or moderate.

Globally, the number of actually recognized and described species is fewer than 2 million. The animal kingdom is the taxonomic group with the largest number—about

Table 7-1. *Estimated Number of Species, U.S. and Globally*

Kingdoms	Described USA	World	Estimated Total World
Bacteria	-	4,000	1,000,000
Protists (algae, protozoa, etc)	-	80,000	600,000
Animals	149,000	1,320,000	10,600,000
Fungi	>37,800	72,000	1,500,000
Plants	18,400	270,000	320,000
Total	> 200,000	1,746,000	Ca. 14,000,000

Source: U.S. estimates: Wilcove and Master (2005), Stein et al. (2000a, 2000b). Global estimates: Hawksworth and Kalin-Arroyo (1995).

1.3 million—of described species. Of all known animal species, the vast majority—almost 1.1 million—are insects and other arthropods. Vertebrates and plants have been catalogued quite comprehensively, and their estimated numbers are not expected to change dramatically as information increases over time. Viruses, bacteria, and fungi are the major groups of organisms with the most undescribed species. New species are regularly identified in all taxonomic groups; every year, about 10,000 new species are catalogued globally (Purvis and Hector 2000; Hawksworth and Kalin-Arroyo 1995).[4] Although these new species are mostly insects and other inconspicuous animals, a few new vertebrate species are also typically found every year, mostly in the tropics.

Most species that live in the United States are well known and have been catalogued, especially macrobiotic ones. Recent estimates report that the total count of species in the United States exceeds 200,000 (Stein et al. 2000a, 2000b). However, this figure excludes two entire kingdoms, bacteria and protists (algae, protozoa, etc.) because of the inherent difficulty in finding and describing microscopic species. Because new species are catalogued constantly, the actual number of U.S. species is expected to be substantially higher. Around 140,000 U.S. species are currently described from the well-studied taxonomic groups (Figure 7-2), including more than 96,000 insects, some 15,000 flowering plants, almost 10,000 crustaceans, over 1,100 fishes, over 500 birds, and over 400 mammals.

Within the United States, biodiversity tends to be greater in southern areas and decreases gradually toward the north. This pattern is particularly true for flowering plants, but it applies also to vertebrate diversity. A similar longitudinal gradient is observed in global biodiversity; species richness increases from the poles to the equator (Gaston 2000).

Larger states with boundaries that encompass a diverse array of ecosystems tend to contain a greater number of species. Hence, California, Texas, Arizona, New Mexico, and Alabama are the five states with the most species richness (Table 7-2; Stein 2002). States with the fewest species are geographically small, such as Hawaii (1,418 species) or have relatively uniform ecosystems, such as North Dakota (1,889 species). Despite its vast landmass, Alaska has fewer than 2,000 known species.

Endemic species are those that exist only within a limited region or location. Regions with high levels of endemism often constitute a wealth of unique biodiversity, making them particularly attractive for biodiversity conservation. Generally, states

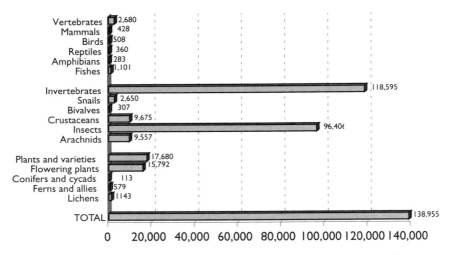

Figure 7-2. *Known Species of Vertebrates, Invertebrates, and Plants and Varieties (including lichens)*

with distinct geographical features that are sufficiently isolated from surrounding areas are likely to have many endemic species. Isolation of habitats allows unique paths of divergent evolution to take place, resulting in distinctive species. California, with almost 1,300 endemic species, has the most species that are unique to one state. The small but geographically isolated Hawaiian Islands have an exceptional amount of endemic species. More than 1,000 of Hawaii's 1,418 known species are endemic. In addition to California and Hawaii, Texas, Florida, and Utah also have large numbers of endemic species.

Ecosystem diversity, characterized here simply as the number of distinct ecosystem types found within each state, also varies across the United States. Oregon and

Table 7-2. *Ranking of States According to Biological Diversity*

Rank	Species Diversity	Species	Endemism	Species	Ecosystems	Ecosystems types
1	California	6,717	California	1,295	Oregon	117
2	Texas	6,273	Hawaii	1,011	California	111
3	Arizona	4,759	Texas	340	Texas	96
4	New Mexico	4,583	Florida	269	Washington	83
5	Alabama	4,533	Utah	182	Nevada	79
46	Delaware	2,224	Delaware	0	Connecticut	23
47	Rhode Island	2,078	Iowa	0	Kansas	20
48	N. Dakota	1,889	Kansas	0	Delaware	16
49	Alaska	1,835	New Jersey	0	Iowa	12
50	Hawaii	1418	N. Dakota	0	Rhode Island	11

Note: Species and endemic species: data from Stein (2002). Ecosystems: data from, Ecological Systems Database 1.02, NatureServe (2003).

California each have more than 100 ecosystem types (Table 7-2), whereas the number in Texas, Washington, and Nevada ranges from about 80 to 100. Ecosystem diversity follows different patterns than species diversity, but generally, coastal and southern states contain more ecosystems than the central states. The characterization of ecosystem diversity across the United States is instructive, but it must be emphasized that ecosystems are more difficult to classify than species. No commonly accepted classification of ecosystems exists for the United States. Compared with species, ecosystems are considered short-lived, ambiguous, artificial, and intangible (Noss and Cooperrider 1994).

Although more species are found in the tropics than in the temperate zone, where most of the United States lies, several species groups, such as freshwater fish, mussels, and snails, have globally significant levels of biodiversity. For example, about 30 percent of all the world's freshwater mussel species, as well as over 60 percent of all crayfish species, are from the United States. There are also other species groups for which the United States has global significance, but by and large, the richness of U.S. freshwater biota is especially high (Stein et al. 2000a, 2000b).

Biodiversity Loss

Extinctions and Endangerment

Extinction of a species is an especially concrete example of biodiversity loss. By definition, a species becomes extinct when its last member dies. When only a few individuals of a species exist, a species may become functionally extinct, meaning that the reproduction and the long-term survival of that species become impossible. A species becomes extinct in the wild when the only living individuals belonging to that species are maintained in unnatural environments, such as zoos. A species is ecologically extinct if it persists at numbers so low that it has no substantial impact on the other species in its community and, therefore, no longer plays a functional role in the ecosystem.

Ecological theory suggests several factors that contribute to the vulnerability of certain species to extinction. Species that are most susceptible to extinctions include (1) large organisms; (2) species high on the food web; (3) species with small population ranges or population sizes; (4) species that have evolved in isolation; (5) species with little evolutionary experience of disturbances; (6) species with poor dispersal or colonization abilities; (7) migratory species; and (8) colonially nesting/reproducing species (Barbault and Sastrapradja 1995). Many island and locally endemic species share several of the above characteristics.

The World Conservation Union (IUCN),[5] characterizes endangered species as vulnerable (i.e., high risk), endangered (i.e., very high risk), or critically endangered (i.e., extremely high risk). All species in these three threat categories rely on conservation measures for their continued existence. The degree of species endangerment is determined by using multiple criteria, including population size, population range, and the rates at which they are decreasing.

According to the IUCN, 1,143 species in the United States—903 animals and 240 plants—are classified from vulnerable to critically endangered (hereafter, endangered). In addition, IUCN lists another 292 animals and 27 plants that are either conservation dependent or near threatened. The 903 endangered animal species include 342 vertebrates: 40 mammals, 71 birds, 27 reptiles, 50 amphibians, and 154 fishes. Taking into account the known 52 extinct vertebrates, almost 15 percent of all known U.S. vertebrates, or 393 of 2,680 species, are either extinct or endangered (Table 7-3).

Endangered invertebrates consist of 561 species, including 261 snails and other mollusks. Because the total number of invertebrates is considerably higher than that of vertebrates, the percentage of endangered or extinct invertebrates of all known invertebrates is relatively low. Nonetheless, some invertebrates, such as freshwater mussels, are among the species groups that have experienced the most endangerment and extinctions (Stein et al. 2000a).

The United States has 150 tree species listed as endangered by IUCN. In the continental United States, 6 tree species are critically endangered, 6 are endangered, 19 are vulnerable, and 18 are at a lower risk of endangerment. The remaining species occur in Hawaii and include 48 critically endangered, 41 endangered, and 30 vulnerable species. About half of all known Hawaiian tree species are listed at some level of endangerment or extinction, exacerbated by its small geographic area and high levels of endemism.

Extinctions are difficult to verify, and the number of known extinctions in the United States varies depending on the source. According to IUCN, a total of 255 species are known to have gone extinct in the United States (Table 7-4). Twelve more species are extinct in their natural habitat, but some individuals remain in captivity. IUCN also lists another 266 species as critically endangered—in other words, in extreme danger of extinction.

Table 7-3. *Extinctions and Species Endangerment in the United States, IUCN Classification*

Taxonomic group	Extinct, or equal	Critically endangered, endangered, vulnerable	Known species[a]
Vertebrates, total	52	342	2,680
Mammals	4	40	428
Birds	27	71	508
Reptiles	1	27	360
Amphibians	3	50	283
Fishes	17	154	1,101
Invertebrates, total[b]	185	561	>119,500
Mollusks, snails	134	261	7,500
Other invertebrates	51	300	>112,000
Plants[c]	30	240	17,680
TOTAL	267	1,143	>139,860

Note: Compiled from the IUCN database (accessed Nov. 10, 2005).

[a] Sources: USFWS, WRI (vertebrates); Stein et al. 2000b (invertebrates); and NatureServe 2003 (plants and invertebrates).
[b] Includes only the five invertebrate groups considered here.
[c] Known species include only the flowering plants, conifers and cycads, ferns and allies, and lichens.

Table 7-4. *Recorded Extinctions in the United States*

Kingdom	Phylum	Class	Extinct	Extinct in the Wild	Extinct, Total
Animal	Arthropods	Crustaceans	2	1	3
		Insects	47	1	48
	Chordata	Fish (ray-finned)	17		17
	(vertebrates, tunicates, and lancelets)	Amphibians	2	1	3
		Birds	26	1	27
		Mammals	3	1	4
		Reptiles	1		1
	Mollusks	Bivalves	26		26
		Gastropods	108		108
Plant	Vascular plants	Angiosperms	23	7	30
and		Total	255	12	267
Varieties					

Source: Compiled from the IUCN database.

Extinction rates are best known for mammals and birds because these species are large and well studied. Extinct species include three mammals[6] and 26 bird species.[7] Snails have been particularly vulnerable to extinctions; altogether, 108 gastropods have gone extinct. Known extinctions also include 47 insects and 26 bivalves.

Recorded extinctions in the United States include 15 tree species; another 2 tree species are listed as extinct in the wild. Almost all of the extinct tree species (15 of 17) are Hawaiian. Excluding Hawaii, 2 of the 833 tree species in the continental U.S. have gone extinct.

NatureServe[8] categorizes extinctions using slightly different criteria than IUCN[9] and lists a total of 100 U.S. species that are presumed extinct and another 439 species that are possibly extinct. Of these extinct species, 40 species are vertebrates, 49 are invertebrates, and 11 are vascular plants.

Summarizing the two sources of information on extinctions, IUCN lists 267 species as extinct or extinct in the wild in the United States, plus 260 species as critically endangered, whereas NatureServe lists 539 species as extinct or possibly extinct. The dissimilarity between these estimates is due to the differing criteria and data used to generate them, not to mention the difficulty of documenting extinctions.

Such difficulty is demonstrated by the possible rediscovery of the ivory-billed woodpecker, which has long been considered extinct. This species once ranged through the southeastern and lower Mississippi valley states but declined because of the loss of bottomland hardwood forest, its preferred habitat. After its last official sighting in 1944, serious field expeditions to locate it again largely failed to verify the anecdotal sightings that sporadically occurred. However, in 2005 a group of reputable ornithologists reported a sighting of the ivory-billed woodpecker in the Big Woods area of eastern Arkansas (Fitzpatrick et al. 2005). Although possible additional sightings have also been reported, it is not known how many, if any, individual birds may be left. Several scientists also remain skeptical whether the sighted birds were actually ivory-billed woodpeckers rather than similar-looking but common pileated woodpeckers (Collinson 2007). The inaccessible nature of the ivory-bill's habitat, combined with a potential ability to persist in very low densities, makes confirming its continued existence or extinction particularly problematic.

Extinction records generally are conservative. They typically underestimate actual extinctions and focus on well-known species, which often are more widely dispersed and abundant, and consequently less vulnerable to extinction than less studied, more isolated species. According to records of known species extinctions, approximately 0.2 to 0.4 percent of all described U.S. species have gone extinct. Within certain taxonomic groups, such as vertebrates, extinction rates are considerably higher. For example, about 5 percent of all known bird species in the United States are extinct.

Extinctions have been recorded in every state, but the Hawaiian Islands are the unambiguous hotbed of extinctions. Hawaii constitutes only a small fraction (<0.2 percent) of the total land area of the United States but accounts for about 30 percent of extinctions and 50 percent of possible extinctions.[10] In addition, 31 percent of all endangered species in the United States are Hawaiian (USFWS 2004a). The loss of Hawaiian species is linked with landscape alteration from agriculture, urbanization, resort development, recreation, and particularly the introduction of nonnative species. Historically, the Hawaiian Islands were covered by a variety of native vegetation types; today, the native vegetation is found only sparsely.

The remaining extinctions in the United States have taken place mostly across the southern part of the country, especially in California and Alabama. The number of extinctions follows the general patterns of species richness: more species have gone extinct where more species occur. However, other patterns also emerge; extinctions are also correlated with habitat alteration, historical exploitation, and introduction of exotic species (Stein et al. 2000a).

Some extinction occurs naturally (Box 7-1). A critical question is therefore how the current extinction rate compares with natural or background extinction rates. Geologists, by examining the fossil record, estimate a natural underlying global extinction rate of approximately 0.1 to 1 species per million species per year. During the past 400 years, around 400 invertebrate and 300 to 350 vertebrate extinctions have been recorded globally. The number of plant extinctions is not well known but is believed to be several hundred. Among birds, mammals, and amphibians, the taxa for which extinction records are most reliable, the estimated current average extinction rate is about 50 to 500 times the background extinction rate. Including possible but unconfirmed extinctions, the current extinction rate is about 100 to 1,000 times the geological extinction rate (IUCN 2004).

Although extinctions have become more common because of human activities, considerably fewer species have gone extinct than predicted in some widely publicized—and criticized (e.g., Simon and Wildawsky 1984)—scenarios from the 1980s. At the time, it was predicted that as many as 15 to 20 percent of all species on earth would go extinct within the next 20 years, equivalent to a loss of tens to hundreds of thousands of species annually (Global 2000 Report). Yet the IUCN's 2004 Red List reports that only 27 species are known to have gone extinct worldwide during the past 20 years. Though by all accounts biodiversity loss is a serious problem, and humans unequivocally cause extinctions, we fortunately have not wit-

Box 7-1. Mass Extinctions of the Past

The record of life on earth during the past 600 million years (the Phanerozoic Eon) consists almost entirely of species gone extinct. Using fossil records, scientists have identified distinct eras that are known as mass extinctions. The causes of past mass extinctions are not known for certain, but they are generally thought to have been major physical events, such as climate change, to which many species were not able to adapt.

Mass extinctions typically were not sudden events, at least according to the scale of human lifetimes, but took place across hundreds, thousands, or even tens of thousands of years. Collisions between earth and celestial objects and the resulting massive species losses may be exceptions to this rule. Intervals between extinctions do not follow any discernible pattern. Regardless of their causes or timelines, the five major mass extinctions resulted in enormous change:

- The first mass extinction took place about 440 millions years ago and caused the extinction of some 25 percent of families of marine life (the only form of life, land species not yet having appeared). Climate change involving severe and sudden global cooling is considered the cause of this earliest known mass extinction.

- The second major extinction took place some 70 million years later, or about 370 million years ago, during the Devonian Period. Approximately 20 percent of taxonomic families were lost.

- The third major extinction happened around 245 million years ago. This, the greatest mass extinction, caused the loss of more than half of all existing families.

- The fourth major extinction took place around 210 million years ago, at the end of the Triassic Period, shortly after dinosaurs and mammals had first evolved. More than 20 percent of species were lost.

- The fifth mass extinction, the most well known, took place about 65 million years ago. It wiped out terrestrial dinosaurs, in addition to contemporary flora and other fauna, and 17 percent of families were lost. The causes of this extinction involve possibly multiple collisions between earth and asteroids or comets. Volcanic activity may have added to the disruption of ecosystems.

Scientists debate whether another major extinction is currently underway. If so, this event would be the first one caused by biotic (i.e., human) rather than abiotic factors.

---

nessed the apocalyptic extinction rates that were once predicted. Regardless, though actual extinction rates have remained low relative to the worst predictions, in many species groups, 10 to 20 percent of all known species are endangered and require intervention to avoid extinction.

Extinctions are irreversible events that permanently remove a unique constituent of biodiversity. In addition to the disappearance of a species, extinctions also eliminate the speciation potential of a distinctly evolving lineage. However, since genetic information is often shared among members of related species, there is not necessarily a one-to-one relationship between extinctions and the loss of evolutionary information. Even an extreme mass extinction that eliminated 95 percent of all species would allow the surviving species to maintain most of the underlying evolutionary information (Nee and May 1997). This does not mean that extinctions are insignificant events; extinctions can have a potentially large impact on the structure and dynamics of communities and ecosystems. The idea is simply that species share significant amounts of genetic information, and different species substitute as carriers of this information.

Conservation importance assigned to a species is not necessarily proportional or even closely related to the amount of evolutionary information it represents. Nevertheless, competing alternative conservation strategies may be evaluated not only by how many species they protect but also by how effectively they preserve evolutionary history (e.g., Mace et al. 2003). For example, each species in the phylogenetic tree in Figure 7-1 possesses both unique and shared evolutionary history. Extinction of any one species leads to the loss of some unique evolutionary history, the magnitude of loss varying by species. The extinction of species A is the most serious reduction in evolutionary information, whereas the extinction of species B, E, or F causes only moderate losses. Using preservation of evolutionary history for assessments of alternative conservation plans is difficult in practice because it requires obtaining detailed information on the evolutionary history of different species via genetic sequencing and phylogenetic analysis. Furthermore, determining *ex ante* what evolutionary information would be most valuable for preservation is challenging, to say the least.

Threats to Biodiversity

The level of biodiversity in a particular area is the outcome of opposing processes that generate heterogeneity (increasing diversity) and homogeneity (decreasing diversity). Factors that favor heterogeneity create ecological niches and opportunities for many species to thrive in a single area. These include spatial heterogeneity in the form of environmental gradients (e.g., moisture, temperature, and climatic gradients), ecological patches that are distinct from surrounding habitat, as well as community dynamics, such as competition, predation, and ecological succession. Periodic natural disturbances and episodic events, such as tree falls and flooding, also contribute to spatial and biotic heterogeneity.

Homogenizing factors, on the other hand, reduce the opportunities for different species to exist in an area and reduce biotic heterogeneity. Human activities that have a homogenizing effect are considered threats to biodiversity. The leading threats to biodiversity in the United States are habitat loss and degradation, invasive non-indigenous species, pollution, and overexploitation of species (Figure 7-3). Most threatened species face two or more of these threats simultaneously. For example, freshwater fauna in the United States is experiencing a decline because of a combination of habitat deterioration due to sediment loading and organic pollution from land-use activities, toxic contaminants from municipal and industrial sources, stream fragmentation by dams, canalization and dredging projects, and interactions with increasing numbers of exotic species (Ricciardi and Rasmussen 1999).

Human land-use patterns can have significant consequences for biological diversity. The primary cause of contemporary biodiversity decline is habitat destruction

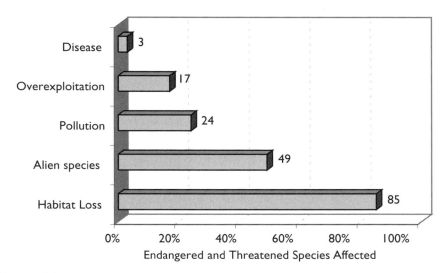

Figure 7-3. *Leading Threats to U.S. Biodiversity*

Source: Wilcove et al. 2000.

and degradation, driven by the expansion of human populations and activities. It is a major cause of endangerment for 85 percent of the species listed under the Endangered Species Act (Wilcove et al. 2000). Habitat loss takes several forms: habitat can be completely converted to another land cover (e.g., to urban development), become degraded (e.g., from pollution of wetlands), or become fragmented by small-scale encroachment (e.g., by urban sprawl). Though human activities may alter relative abundances of habitat types and increase local species varieties by increasing habitat types, the end result is often a reduction of suitable habitat for native species.

Species loss caused by habitat loss and fragmentation is related to the study of island biogeography, a fundamental concept in ecology that helps explain the determining factors of species diversity within a community. In this context, *island* refers not only to an oceanic island, but also to any relatively disconnected and distinct patch of habitat. Examples of habitat islands include montane habitats surrounded by desert, lakes within a continuum of dry land, and forest fragments within an urbanized landscape. According to the theory of island biogeography (MacArthur and Wilson 1967), the number of species supported on an island is determined by the extinction rate and immigration rate at equilibrium. Extinction rates on habitat islands are determined by their size, with greater extinction rates in smaller patches than in larger ones. Hence, larger areas of contiguous habitat support a greater number of species, with the number of sustainable species increasing proportionately with habitat size. The increase in biodiversity via immigration of species into a habitat island is determined by its distance or connectivity to other patches of habitat. The closer the island is to another patch, the greater the likelihood that species from one will colonize the other.

Therefore, according to this framework, conversion and fragmentation of natural habitats affect biodiversity in two major ways. First, they decrease the size of habitats, allowing them to support fewer species overall. Second, they decrease the connectivity among patches, preventing species from recolonizing patches where localized extinctions have occurred and exacerbating species survival at the landscape level. Habitat conversion, particularly into urban uses, also has other effects that affect species survival, such as by causing pollution, creating habitat edge effects, and introducing invasive species.

After habitat loss, invasive nonindigenous species are the second leading cause of species endangerment. Also called transplanted, exotic, introduced, or alien species, these are organisms moved beyond their natural range by human activities. Pathways by which invasive species are introduced can be intentional, such as the importation of ornamental plants, livestock, and game species. Nonindigenous species are also unintentionally introduced, traveling, for example, via ballast water, potted soil, or freight containers. Tolerance of a wide range of environmental conditions, high rates of reproduction and dispersal, and lack of natural predators within the new community are characteristics that help nonnative species thrive in the new habitat.

Nonnative species can cause a loss of biodiversity through predation, competition, or other modification of the ecosystem to which native species cannot adapt. For example, predation by the unintentially introduced brown tree snakes on Guam causing the extinction of five bird species and the significant decline of many other species (Savidge 1987). Zebra mussels, native to freshwater lakes in Russia, arrived in North America via the ballast water of seafaring vessels. Since their establishment, they have contributed to the sharp decline of native mollusks throughout the United States by decreasing attachment space and food availability for other filter feeders, increasing light penetration, and dramatically altering the habitats they invade.

Invasive species are found in every state, although their numbers vary substantially. In the mainland United States, the share of nonnative species of all species is particularly high in the Northeast, southern Florida, California, and the rest of the Pacific Coast. In these regions, more than 25 percent of all species can be nonnative. Oceanic island habitats, populated with endemic biota lacking defenses against nonnative species, are especially vulnerable to exotic invasions. The Hawaiian Islands have the nation's highest rates of nonindigenous invasions and native species extinctions, and a large share of current flora consists of nonnative species (see Box 7-2).

Introduction of nonnative species also has important economic effects. For example, in addition to the harm to native species and ecosystems, zebra mussels create a nuisance by attaching in large numbers to docks, boats, anchors, and pipelines, sometimes to the extent that they block water intakes used for power generation or water supply. The U.S. Office of Technology Assessment (1993) estimated that nonnative species caused approximately $5 billion in annual losses to the U.S. economy. Later estimates put the losses significantly higher. Pimentel et al. (2000) suggest that the losses from invasive species may exceed $100 billion annually, although this estimate is generally considered speculative (Polasky et al. 2005a).

Box 7-2. Invasive Species: *Miconia calvescens* in Hawaii

Oceanic island ecosystems, such as those found in Hawaii, are especially susceptible to damage caused by introduced nonnative organisms. Native oceanic island biota typically has evolved few defenses against opportunistic invasive species. Predation and competition from nonnative species are now the main cause of biodiversity loss in Hawaii.

Miconia calvescens, an invasive tree from Central and South America, is perhaps the most invasive and damaging nonnative plant in Pacific island forests. In Tahiti, it has formed single-species stands on over a quarter of the island's forest ecosystem. Introduced to Hawaii as an ornamental in the 1960s, the tree has been naturalized on Oahu, Hawaii, Maui, and Kauai islands. Because the Hawaiian Islands have very similar climate, topography, and biota, this species could potentially completely shade out many native plants and threaten endangered plant species, including the Hawaiian state flower, *mao hau hele.*

Miconia calvescens thrives in Hawaiian conditions, gaining dominance by creating a tall, thick canopy and a deep shade beneath it that few species can tolerate. A typical tree can produce 30,000 fruit and three million seeds two or three times a year, generating a dense and persistent soil seed bank that is widely dispersed by birds. The seed bank is viable for years, and regeneration often occurs when, ironically, mechanical or herbicidal removal of adult *M. calvescens* creates canopy openings that stimulate mass germination.

M. calvescens has high management priority in Hawaii because of its potential impacts on biodiversity. Its containment and eradication may still be feasible through identification and mechanical and chemical removal of infestations, as well as continuous reconnaissance to eliminate regeneration.

Besides biological contamination, human activities also cause chemical pollution and contamination of natural systems. Pollution that affects biodiversity can come from agricultural, industrial, and urban sources and can have individual or aggregated effects. For instance, the bioaccumulation of the agricultural pesticide DDT in the tissues of North American birds of prey once led to the sharp decline of peregrine falcons, ospreys, and bald eagles in the United States. In contrast, human sewage, agricultural fertilizers, household detergents, and industrial processes often release large amounts of nitrates and phosphates into aquatic systems, where they may cause algal blooms that choke oxygen and shade other species. Once released into the environment, contaminants are distributed in water, air, soil, and sediment, potentially affecting biota long distances from their sources.

The regulation of toxic pollutants in the United States has lowered concentrations of many industrial pollutants from point sources (e.g., factories) to the lowest levels since measurements began. With traditional contaminant sources regulated, future reductions in environmental concentrations will come from the control of more diffuse sources. These include agricultural soil erosion, urban runoff, and the atmospheric and waterborne transport of contaminants from artificial and natural sinks, such as industrial and mining waste disposal sites, landfills, and contaminated sediments.

Another threat to biodiversity, overexploitation, occurs when hunting or other harvesting of a particular species exceeds its ability to regenerate, leading to a decline in population. Excessive hunting helped drive two bird species in the continental United States, the passenger pigeon and the Carolina parakeet, to extinction. In both cases, overexploitation, combined with habitat loss, reduced breeding populations to below the critical depensation level; despite later hunting reductions, the populations dwindled to the point of functional extinction, making their disappearance inevitable. Currently, however, because of bans and regulations on the hunting or harvesting of sensitive species, overexploitation is more relevant to marine species than the terrestrial and freshwater species addressed here.

Global climate change, caused by the atmospheric accumulation of human-generated greenhouse gases, may drive substantial biodiversity loss. Although species have the capacity to adapt to environmental change, climate change likely will occur more rapidly than most previous, natural climate shifts. Alteration of temperature and precipitation regimes could potentially have numerous impacts on biodiversity, including shifts in migration and breeding patterns; expansions or contractions of natural species ranges; rise in sea level, water temperature, and carbonic acidification; increase in disease transmission and pest infestations; and unpredictable fluctuations in populations and habitat conditions. The adaptive power of some species will likely be overwhelmed by these new pressures, especially if combined with fragmentation, decreased connectivity of habitats, and other stresses that may create additional barriers to adjustment (Thomas et al. 2004; Pounds et al. 2006). The polar bear, threatened by the loss of sea ice, is a widely publicized example of a species potentially harmed by climate change.

Economic Values for Biodiversity

Humans derive economic value from biodiversity through the structure and function of ecosystems and their components. Many commodities essential to human well-being, such as food, feed, fiber, wood, and pharmaceutical products, originate from and are continually supplemented by biodiversity. Nature provides resources for many economically important activities, such as the genetic material for breeding new plant varieties and the organisms for development of biological control and remediation methods. In addition to these assets, ecosystems provide many valuable services, such as watershed protection, nutrient storage and cycling, pollution breakdown and absorption, replenishment of soil fertility, erosion prevention, climate stability, and recovery from unpredictable events, to name just a few examples. Furthermore, nature and biodiversity generate benefits that are important for recreation and tourism, research and education, and culture and tradition.

Economic valuation of biodiversity and its preservation is sometimes controversial and, to some, even fundamentally objectionable. Disagreements are especially common when economic arguments are used to address species protection and, alternatively, extinctions. The concept of economic value should not be confused with the ethical values commonly referred to as "values" in everyday parlance or other disciplines, such as philosophy or psychology (Simpson 2000). Economic valuation deals with the relative utility (i.e., usefulness) of goods and services, commonly expressed in dollar terms. Economic values are not rigid but conditional on the availability of other goods and services.

Fundamentally, economics is about assessing alternatives for resource allocation. Rather than taking it for granted that biodiversity should or should not be preserved, economists try to systematically assess the various trade-offs involved in decisions regarding biodiversity preservation. For example, when determining how much land should be reserved for habitat and species conservation in a certain region, economists may estimate the conservation benefits achieved from allocating land for protection and compare them with the benefits of using the same land for other purposes, such as agriculture or forestry. Depending on the relative benefits and costs, an economic analysis may suggest that all, none, or just a fraction of the land should be devoted to conservation. Analytical results may vary greatly by location, depending on the unique economic (e.g., profitability) and natural (e.g., species richness) characteristics. Although economic analyses are not definitive because of limited knowledge and imperfect methods in both economics and ecology, they provide information that, in the context of other considerations, can help decisionmakers identify practical conservation choices.

In many conservation problems, a certain conservation budget exists and the question is merely how best to use it. Economic tools such as cost-effectiveness analyses help evaluate how best to design conservation reserve networks for endangered species when conservation budgets or targets are fixed (e.g. Polasky et al. 2001; Siikamäki and Layton 2007a). By comparing the costs and effectiveness of alternative scenarios, cost-effectiveness analyses help determine the most efficient strategy for achieving conservation objectives, such as target species abundances. One can also view these analyses as efforts to determine how to achieve the greatest biological benefits within a given budget. Cost-effectiveness analyses do not directly address the broader rationale for conservation, but they help improve practical conservation decisions.

Polasky et al. (2005a) review the economics literature on the biodiversity valuation and suggest the following broad study categories: the use and existence values of individual species, biological prospecting, and ecosystem services. Adapting from Polasky et al. (2005a), we expand this review of biodiversity valuation. We also draw from other literature reviews, including a meta-analysis of existence values for imperiled species by Loomis and White (1996), as well as a review of valuation studies by Nunes and van den Bergh (2001). We summarize, modify, and update parts of these reviews to fit the theme of this chapter and to reflect recent economics literature.

Use and Existence of Species

Humans have always used nature as a source for food, fiber, wood, and other products. Although wild species have become less essential for nutrition, they are increasingly important for other purposes, such as for viewing and recreational hunting and fishing. Methods for assigning the use value to such benefits examine the trade-offs revealed in the behavior and choices of hunters, anglers, hikers, and other recreational users of nature. For example, researchers may examine which fishing sites anglers prefer and the distance they are willing to drive to reach sites with different characteristics. Observing many anglers and sites, one can then predict the values anglers assign to different lake characteristics, such as catch rate or water quality. Economists use these values to estimate the benefits to anglers of environmental goods and services that also bolster biodiversity, such as water quality.

Wildlife-associated outdoor recreation is very popular. The U.S. Fish and Wildlife Service regularly surveys people participating in outdoor recreation activities and estimates that more than 30 million people in the United States are regular anglers, about 13 million people participate annually in hunting, and some 18 million people per year make trips specifically for bird watching (USFWS 2004b). Estimated values associated with various recreational uses of nature are substantial. For example, salmon fishing has been estimated to be worth on average from $14 to more than $110 per day to an angler, depending on the location and type of salmon. A day of hunting has been estimated to be worth on average about $30 to $45 per hunter, depending on the game species (Phaneuf and Smith 2005). Given that many participants spend several days per year in outdoor activities, these estimates suggest that overall benefits from wildlife-associated recreation are substantial.

The value of biodiversity is often related not to personal usage but rather to the intrinsic worth of its existence, especially that of imperiled species and habitats (e.g., Krutilla 1967). Such nonuse values are difficult to measure because they are not captured in market data on purchase decisions. Nonuse values also often are insufficiently discernible by the travel cost method (discussed above) and other approaches that examine observable behavioral signals commonly used for economic valuation. Although indications of nonuse values may be observed in how people decide to join environmental organizations, these observations do not necessarily fully reflect the nonuse value. Because nonuse benefits from the preservation of biodiversity are public, those who do not contribute to conservation can nonetheless benefit from the efforts of those who do. The sum of individual contributions therefore does not correspond to the full value of nonuse benefits.

This problem has given rise to the development of nonmarket valuation methods that use surveys to elicit preferences for public goods, such as protection of threatened and endangered species. Because these methods are based on eliciting and examining stated rather than actual preferences, they also are broadly categorized as stated preference (SP) methods (e.g., Louviere et al. 2000, Siikamäki and Layton 2007b). The contingent valuation (CV) method, in particular its referendum (dichotomous choice) format, is the most commonly applied SP method for valuing biodiversity. The CV method involves developing and administering surveys in which the respondent is presented with a scenario with specified environmental outcomes and cost to the respondent. The respondent is asked to indicate approval or disapproval of the proposed scenario and suggested payment. Researchers vary the proposed costs across different survey respondents and use the approval data to estimate how much, on average, people are willing to pay for different biodiversity conservation scenarios.

Another leading SP method is the choice experiment (CE), also known as conjoint analysis. In this method, survey respondents are asked to identify their preferences from two or more scenarios. Each scenario is described as a bundle of attributes, such as the environmental outcomes and monetary cost of each policy alternative, and these attributes are varied across different respondents. Again, by examining respondents' choices, researchers estimate how people compare and trade off the different attributes of proposed scenarios. When scenario attributes include several environmental outcomes and at least one monetary attribute (e.g., cost), discrete choice data help reveal, through econometric methods, how people trade off personal income and environmental quality, thus providing implicit estimates of the willingness to pay (WTP) for environmental quality.

Different valuation problems call for different valuation methods. The CV method is particularly well suited for estimating WTP for specified policy programs to improve ecosystem services. The CE method focuses on identifying the trade-offs and substitution patterns between different attributes of the proposed programs rather than on predicting WTP for one specific program (though CE results can be readily applied to predict WTP for specific programs). As such, CE also facilitates benefit transfers, in which values for environmental changes at a certain location are predicted using valuation results from another area.

Table 7-5 summarizes a number of studies published about willingness to pay for specific rare, threatened, or endangered species in the United States. This table, which adapts and updates information from Loomis and White (1996), summarizes values for 29 species examined in one or more CV studies. These studies generally

Table 7-5. *Estimated Willingness-to-Pay ($2005) Values for Rare, Threatened, or Endangered Species in the United States*

	Low	High	Avg.	Reference(s)	Sample
Studies reporting annual WTP					
Striped shiner*			$8	Boyle and Bishop 1987	Wisconsin
Atlantic salmon*	$10	$11	$10	Stevens et al. 1991	Massachusetts
Florida manatee*			$11	Solomon et al. 2004	Citrus County, Florida
Squawfish*			$11	Cummings et al. 1994	New Mexico
Red-cockaded woodpecker	$9	$20	$13	Reaves et al. 1994, 1999	Varies (South Carolina and U.S.)
Bighorn sheep	$17	$40	$28	Brookshire et al. 1983; King et al. 1988	Varies (Wyoming hunters, Arizona households)
Riverside fairy shrimp*	$27	$31	$29	Stanley 2005	Orange County, California
Gray whale	$23	$42	$32	Loomis and Larson 1994	California
Bald eagle*	$21	$44	$32	Boyle and Bishop 1987; Stevens et al. 1991	Varies (Wisconsin, New England)

(Continued)

Table 7-5. *Estimated Willingness-to-Pay ($2005) Values for Rare, Threatened, or Endangered Species in the United States (Continued)*

	Low	High	Avg.	Reference(s)	Sample
Silvery minnow*	$31	$36	$34	Berrens et al. 1996, 2000	New Mexico
Sea otter*			$39	Hageman 1985	California
Gray whale	$31	$47	$39	Larson et al. 2004	California
Grizzly bear			$49	Brookshire et al. 1983	Wyoming hunters
Mexican spotted owl*	$49	$58	$53	Loomis and Ekstrand 1997; Giraud et al. 1999	Varies (Arizona, Colorado, Utah, Northwest)
Whooping crane*	$43	$67	$55	Bowker and Stoll 1988	Varies (Texas, U.S.)
Northern spotted owl*	$30	$128	$64	Rubin et al. 1991; Hagen et al. 1992	Varies (Washington, U.S.)
Pacific salmon and steelhead	$42	$118	$80	Olsen et al. 1991	Pacific Northwest (anglers and households)
Steller sea lion	$69	$99	$84	Giraud et al. 2002; Giraud and Valcic 2004	U.S.
Coho salmon	$23	$137	$87	Bell et al. 2003	Oregon, Washington
Studies reporting lump-sum WTP					
Sea turtle*			$17	Whitehead 1991, 1992	North Carolina
Cutthroat trout*			$17	Duffield and Patterson 1992	Visitors
Arctic grayling			$23	Duffield and Patterson 1992	Visitors
Peregrine falcon			$35	Kotchen and Reiling 2000	Maine
Shortnose sturgeon*			$36	Kotchen and Reiling 2000	Maine
Timber wolf	$54	$56	$55	Heberlein et al. 2005	Minnesota
Gray wolf	$5	$157	$67	Duffield 1991, 1992; Duffield et al. 1993; USDOI 1994; Chambers and Whitehead 2003	Varies (Minnesota, U.S., visitors)
Monk seal*			$160	Samples and Hollyer 1989	Hawaii
Humpback whale*			$231	Samples and Hollyer 1989	Hawaii
Bald eagle	$239	$341	$290	Swanson 1993	Washington

Source: Adapted, updated, and expanded from Loomis and White 1996.

Note: * indicates that the study estimates WTP for avoiding the loss of species. Other studies typically estimate WTP for an increase in population size or chance of survival. Samples are typically households, if not otherwise indicated.

estimate the WTP on the part of the general public for avoiding loss of a species, increasing species abundance, or improving species population size or viability. Studies that do not value the protection of a species based on existence values include, for example, the Brookshire et al. (1983) study, which elicits Wyoming hunters' WTP for the hunting of grizzly bears. Although this estimate likely does not reflect the full societal benefits from protecting the grizzlies, we include it to illustrate the values that various members of the public may have for different species.

The estimates suggest substantial variation in the willingness to pay for rare, threatened, and endangered species. Bell et al. (2003) estimate that the WTP for the protection of coho salmon can surpass $100 per year per household, and Giraud et al. (2002) and Giraud and Valcic (2004) predict that U.S. households are willing to pay $69 to $99 for the protection of Steller sea lions in Alaska, whereas the WTP of Wisconsin households for the protection of striped shiner (Boyle and Bishop 1987) and that of Massachusetts households for the protection of Atlantic salmon (Stevens et al. 1991) are both roughly $10. Hence, preferences vary across locations and species. Often, visceral characteristics (e.g., among so-called charismatic megafauna) elicit more favor from the public, not to mention public officials, than the relative rarity or imperilment of a species.

The estimates of WTP reported here and elsewhere are illustrative, but at least three caveats should be kept in mind regarding their generality. First, they are not representative of most rare, threatened, or endangered species. Most valuation efforts have focused on species of significant publicity, such as the bald eagle, spotted owl, Pacific salmon, or whooping crane, and many less publicized yet susceptible species have not been valued by any studies. Second, surveyed populations vary remarkably across studies. We list the geographical sample underlying the value estimates to underscore the variation between different studies that make systematic comparisons difficult. Third, past studies must be evaluated relative to the survey and estimation methods, because such techniques continually evolve.

The validity of using surveys to value a public good like environmental quality is sometimes questioned.[11] For instance, Diamond and Hausman (1994) argue that people do not have well-defined preferences for the types of goods and services environmental CV studies consider. Hanemann (1994) is more optimistic and argues that despite the challenges, the ability to place an economic value on environmental quality is essential for environmental policy and a cornerstone of the economic approach to the environment. Nevertheless, because SP methods are based on what people say, not what they do, the credibility of the results is often questioned. For this reason, SP researchers, following the lead of an expert panel of the National Oceanic and Atmospheric Administration that reviewed the highly publicized studies valuing damages from the *Exxon Valdez* oil spill, often build into their surveys a series of validity tests, such as testing for the sensitivity of WTP to the scope of resource being valued (Arrow et al. 1993).

Finally, we have intentionally not explained or reviewed in detail the different valuation methods related to biodiversity and environmental quality. Instead, we refer interested readers to sources devoted specifically to explaining these methods and their application. For example, a recent volume of the *Handbook of Environmental Economics* (Mäler and Vincent 2005) is dedicated to this topic.

Natural Habitat

We summarize several studies evaluating the benefits from different types of natural habitat in Table 7-6. Most of these studies estimate the value of specific resources, such as aquatic or forest habitat, in a specific geographical area. For example, Holmes et al. (2004) estimate the value of riparian restoration along the Little Tennessee River in western North Carolina; Kealy and Turner (1993) and Banzhaf et al. (2006) value the preservation of aquatic systems in the Adirondack region; Smith and Desvousges (1986) estimate benefits from the preservation of water quality in the Monongahela River; and Hoehn and Loomis (1993) estimate the value of wetlands and habitat in the San Joaquin Valley in California.

As an alternative to scrutinizing finely defined natural habitats, some studies estimate values of broadly specified resources. For example, Mitchell and Carson (1984) estimate the benefits from preserving water quality in all rivers and lakes of the

Table 7-6. *Valuation Estimates of U.S. Habitats ($2005)*

Author(s)	Study	Mean WTP estimates (per household)
Holmes et al. 2004	Riparian restoration along the Little Tennessee River in western North Carolina	$0.69–$40.89 per year
Loomis 1989	Preservation of the Mono Lake, California	$4–$11
Silberman et al. 1992	Protection of beach systems, New Jersey	$9.26–$15.1
Kealy and Turner 1993	Preservation of the aquatic system in the Adirondack region, U.S.	$12–$18
Smith and Desvousges 1986	Preservation of water quality in the Monongahela River Basin	$21–$58 (for users), $14–$53 (for non users)
Walsh et al. 1984	Protection of wilderness areas in Colorado	$32
Diamond et al. 1993	Protection of wilderness areas in Colorado, Idaho, Montana, and Wyoming	$29–$66
Boyle 1990	Preservation of the Illinois Beach State Nature Reserve	$37–$41
Loomis and Gonzales-Caban 1998	Fire management plan to reduce burning of old growth forests in California and Oregon	$56 per year
Larson and Siikamaki 2006	Removal of surface water quality impairment in California	$67–$133 per year
Loomis et al. 1994	Fire management plan to reduce burning of old growth forests in Oregon	$90 per year
Hoehn and Loomis 1993	Enhancing wetlands and habitat in San Joaquin Valley in California	$96–$284 (single program)
Richer 1995	Desert protection in California	$101
Mitchell and Carson 1984	Preservation of water quality for all rivers and lakes	$242

Source: Adapted from Nunes and van den Bergh (2001).

United States. In another geographically broad study, Larson and Siikamäki (2006) estimate California households' willingness to pay for regional and state programs designed to improve water quality in surface water bodies. Using a broadly defined resource as the basis of valuation has the benefit of yielding a WTP that reflects the sum of values for subcomponents of an aggregated resource, such as all lakes across a large region. This method, however, yields little information on the value of individual subcomponents, such as a specific lake or group of lakes. In contrast, summing values from disparate studies, each focusing on a single species or a local habitat, may disregard relevant information such as substitutes and scale, resulting in unrealistically high aggregate estimates. For example, Brown and Shogren (1998) note that aggregating the estimates summarized in Loomis and White (1996) implies that the total WTP for less than 2 percent of endangered species exceeds 1 percent of U.S. gross domestic production (GDP), which appears suspiciously high.

Bioprospecting

Biodiversity conservation preserves options for utilizing unique organisms in the future, especially those with unforeseen and untapped potential to benefit human society. Bioprospecting is the collecting of wild biological samples to use their genetic and biochemical information as sources of new or improved pharmaceutical and industrial products and applications. Pharmaceutical uses of biological material receive much attention, but the variety of potential uses of biological organisms is vast. In addition to the food, agricultural, and pharmaceutical industries, pulp and paper production, oil drilling, and textile manufacturing use natural enzymes. Biotechnology, a rapidly growing and multibillion-dollar business, often uses bioprospecting for leads on new products.

Preserving biodiversity for possible pharmaceutical purposes was once touted as one of the principal economic rationales for protecting biodiversity. However, the economic worth of these bioprospecting options alone is unlikely to provide sufficient incentives for the preservation of biodiversity. Simpson et al. (1996) demonstrate that when researchers must analyze an abundance of biological material to locate a single species that yields valuable material, the average incremental value of any one species in an ecosystem is not very high, particularly if several species are close substitutes. The economic returns from bioprospecting per hectare are likely quite modest even in biodiversity hotspots that are rich in endemic species—from $0.20 per hectare in the California Floristic Province to $20.63 in western Ecuador—and even under assumptions that likely overstate their option benefits. Rausser and Small (2000) suggest that prior information (e.g., indigenous knowledge) on which species possess valuable traits can in some circumstances improve the economic returns from bioprospecting. However, Costello and Ward (2006) show that under a consistent set of assumptions, the marginal value of an average species or hectare of land for bioprospecting is low, as Simpson et al. (1996) suggest. For this reason, the potential for new product development alone usually does not provide enough benefits to compel private parties to invest in biodiversity conservation.

Although incremental benefits per species from bioprospecting are on average low, nature is still an important source for new products. Newman et al. (2003) analyze new drugs approved by regulatory agencies over the period 1981–2002 and find that the majority of them have origins in nature. According to this study, 57 to 62 percent of all novel, active substances for treating disease are initially derived from natural biological sources. These include approximately 62 percent of cancer medications and about 65 percent of drugs for treating hypertension. There is some variation across disease categories, but fully synthetic drugs are nevertheless often a minority of new drugs.

Bioprospecting has created disputes over compensation between private bioprospectors and the owners (e.g., private or government entities) of the land on which biological materials are found. Such conflicts have prompted the development of benefit-sharing agreements, which specify how the benefits from bioprospecting are divided between the bioprospector and the country- or landowner-of-origin. Bioprospecting contracts help alleviate at least two problems that result when biodiversity is an open-access resource: the lack of economic incentives to preserve biodiversity because of the inability of the country-of-origin or landowner to appropriate bioprospecting benefits, and second, issues of equity that arise especially when bioprospecting takes place in poor areas. However, despite the initial enthusiasm for benefit-sharing agreements and their use for biodiversity conservation, their success has been meager because of the limitations discussed above.

Although benefit-sharing agreements are most common in the tropics, where much bioprospecting activity is concentrated, domestic examples exist as well. Yellowstone National Park, where hot springs host a unique array of thermophilic biodiversity, has yielded heat-tolerant enzymes worth hundreds of millions of dollars to the biotechnology industry. In 1997, Yellowstone National Park and Diversa Corporation, a biotech company, entered into a five-year term benefit-sharing contract. According to the agreement, Diversa compensates Yellowstone $175,000 for bioprospecting rights, in addition to sharing scientific information and paying a 0.5 to 10 percent royalty for products developed from any biological material obtained from the park.

Biological remediation, or bioremediation, is an industry in which biodiversity is of increasing importance. Bioremediation uses living organisms to decontaminate soil or water—for example, bacteria in wastewater treatment. The processes used to treat wastewater, a mixture of water and dissolved and suspended solids, typically include the removal of dissolved organic matter by utilizing microorganisms, which metabolize organic matter from the sewage. Bioremediation also has shown promise as a cost-effective way to detoxify soil contaminated by oil spills, polychlorinated biphenyls (PCBs), and polyaromatic hydrocarbons (PAHs). New ways of harnessing living organisms to resolving soil and water contamination are continually developed. Therefore, although bioprospecting is not likely to generate large economic values per average species or hectare or by itself generate sufficient incentives to preserve biodiversity, it feeds several industries of considerable ecological and economic importance.

Ecosystem Services

By and large, economic valuation of biodiversity has focused mostly on the contributions of individual biotic elements of ecosystems, such as a population or species, to human well-being. Alternatively, ecosystem services valuation is based on the various benefits generated by the ecosystem as a whole (Polasky et al. 2005a). Ecosystem services are the economically valuable "conditions and processes by which natural ecosystems, and the species that make them up, sustain and fulfill human life" (Daily 1997). These functions can generate both marketed and non-marketed services. Examples include water purification, oxygen creation, maintenance of soil productivity, waste decomposition, nutrient cycling, pest control, flood control, climatic control (e.g., climate moderation, carbon sequestration), pollination of crops and native vegetation, and provision of recreational opportunities. Valuation of ecosystem services considers the environment as a natural capital asset that generates returns to investment in ecosystem protection and management. Ecosystems are productive systems in which various biological and physical factors, as well as their interactions, serve various functions in the production of ecosystem services. Biodiversity is one element of this natural capital that contributes to the stream of benefits from an ecosystem.

Consider, for example, wetlands as a form of natural capital. They serve as flood barriers, soaking up excess water and slowing and preventing floodwaters from spreading uncontrollably. Wetlands help replenish groundwater and improve both ground- and surface-water quality by slowing the flow of water and absorbing and filtering out sediments and contaminants. Wetlands also provide spawning habitat for fish, supporting the regeneration of fisheries. In addition, wetlands provide habitat for many species and support commercial and sport fishing, as well as hunting and recreation. Investing in wetlands protection and preventing their conversion to other land uses can help maintain these benefits.

Given the complexity of ecosystems and the variety of services they provide, the valuation of ecosystem services clearly poses several challenges. The National Academy of Sciences Committee on the Valuation of Ecosystem Services finds that the importance of ecosystem functions and services is often taken for granted and overlooked in environmental decisionmaking. Moreover, the challenge in the valuation of ecosystem services lies in the difficult integration of economic valuation and ecological production theory. This is no straightforward task because many ecosystem goods and services are not quantifiable under current methods, and the application of economic valuation methods may be subject to judgment, uncertainty, and bias (Heal et al. 2005)

Costanza et al. (1997) attempt to estimate the total value of global ecosystem services by deriving and summing value estimates from the existing literature for a wide range of ecosystem services. This study suggests that the total value of global ecosystem services likely ranges from $16 trillion to $54 trillion annually, or roughly one to three times global GDP. The study has been influential and widely quoted and used, especially among scientists and environmentalists, but economists consider it problematic both conceptually and methodologically, especially on the grounds that estimating the total value of global ecosystem services is not meaningful because the global ecosystem is a necessity without which life would not continue (e.g., Toman 1998).

Another well-known example of valuing ecosystem services involves the Catskill Mountains watershed. For years, this watershed has provided New York City with a high-quality water supply requiring no additional filtering. By the late 1980s, however, changing land-use patterns, urbanization, and agricultural practices in the Catskills had degraded the groundwater quality and forced New York City to evaluate alternatives for securing the quality of its drinking water. Constructing and operating a filtration plant was estimated to cost approximately $8 billion to $10 billion. Rather than making this expensive investment, New York City decided to invest $1.5 billion in the preservation of the Catskills rural environment. By preserving the Catskills, the city achieved considerable cost savings relative to constructing and operating a filtration plant. In this example, these cost savings can be considered the value of an ecosystem service—water filtration—by the Catskills (Chichilnisky and Heal 1998). Using this method, called the replacement cost approach, for the valuation of ecosystem services requires the following three conditions: (1) the alternative or replacement service is equivalent in quality and magnitude to the ecosystem service, (2) the replacement is the least-cost approach to replacing the ecosystem service, and (3) people are willing to pay the replacement cost (Shabman and Batie 1978). However, there is no general relationship between the cost of replacement and individuals' valuation of that improvement.

Table 7-7 summarizes several studies that estimate values for ecosystem services that are related to water supply, water quality, and soil erosion control. These analyses use a variety of methods, including contingent valuation (McClelland et al. 1992; Heberlein et al. 2005), averting expenditures (Laughland et al. 1996; Abdalla et al. 1992; Ribaudo 1989a, 1989b), replacement cost (Holmes 1988; Huszar 1989), and production function (Walker and Young 1986; Torell et al. 1990).

Table 7-7. *Valuation Estimates of Selected Ecosystem Services ($2005)*

Author(s)	Study	Measurement method	Estimates
Walker and Young (1986)	Value soil erosion on (loss) agriculture revenue in the Palouse region	Production function	$4 and 6 per acre
McClelland et al. (1992)	Protection of groundwater program, U.S.	Contingent valuation	$7–$22
Torell et al. (1990)	Water in-storage on the high plains aquifer, U.S.	Production function	$9.5–$1.09 per acre-foot
Laughland et al. (1996)	Value of a water supply in Milesburg, Pennsylvania	Averting expenditures	$14 and $36 per household
Heberlein et al. (2005)	Water quality in lakes of northern Wisconsin	Contingent valuation	$107–$260 per household
Abdalla et al. (1992)	Groundwater ecosystem in Perkasie, Pennsylvania	Averting expenditures	$61,313–$131,334
Holmes (1988)	Value of the impact of water turbidity due to soil erosion on the water treatment, U.S.	Replacement cost	$35–$661 million per year
Huszar (1989)	Value of wind erosion costs to households in New Mexico	Replacement cost	$454 million per year
Ribaudo (1989a,b)	Water quality benefits in ten U.S. regions	Averting expenditures	$4.4 billion per year

For an explanation of various techniques for valuing the environment as a factor of production, including averting cost, replacement cost, and production function methods, see, for example, McConnell and Bockstael (2005).

Biodiversity Protection

In this section, we explain the prevailing mechanisms for the protection of biodiversity in the United States. Strategies to protect biodiversity can be broadly categorized into fine-scale methods, which focus on individual species, and coarse-scale approaches, which apply to habitats, landscapes, and regions. The Endangered Species Act (ESA) and the Convention on International Trade in Endangered Species of Wild Fauna and Flora (CITES), both of which prohibit the harm and trade of officially listed imperiled species, are examples of policies that generally mandate fine-scale methods. In contrast, coarse-scale approaches, such as protected areas, land trusts, and biodiversity-sensitive land management practices, can offer protection for more species simultaneously by conserving entire habitats and landscapes. The line between fine-scale methods and coarse-scale approaches is not always entirely clear, and biodiversity policies can have characteristics of both. For example, the ESA, by listing particular species and mandating their protection, is generally a fine-scale approach. However, implementation of the ESA via conservation banking, which aggregates conserved habitat, often offers coarse-scale protection for many species in addition to those listed.

The following sections describe approaches to biodiversity protection undertaken in the United States. We focus on the Endangered Species Act, the primary federal statute governing the protection and management of biodiversity. Beginning with an overview of the legislative history related to endangered species, we explain the ESA and its implementation. We then summarize trends in species listings and government expenditures for their protection, looking not only at the number of species but also at their distribution across taxonomic groups. We also examine other approaches to biodiversity protection by government and private, nongovernmental organizations. The importance of such private actions has increased in recent years and will likely continue to do so.

Legislative History of the Endangered Species Act

The purpose of the Endangered Species Act is to conserve "the ecosystems upon which endangered species and threatened species depend," create programs for the conservation of such species, and meet the obligations of the United States under international treaties concerning biodiversity. The virtually unopposed passage of the 1973 act was the culmination of significant public interest in environmental issues during the 1960s and early 1970s.[12]

Historically, wildlife resources were solely under the jurisdiction of the states, which lacked adequate enforcement and were unable to prevent declining wildlife populations and the extinction of the passenger pigeon, a game species. Early federal wildlife statutes were aimed at protecting traditional game species (see the

Appendix for the legislative timeline). These were followed by legislation, passed in the 1910s to 1930s, designed to protect migratory birds. The federal government continued to expand its authority over wildlife during the next several decades by allowing and funding the acquisition and restoration of wildlife habitat, and also by creating the Fish and Wildlife Service to conduct research and enforce fish and wildlife laws. However, the federal government still lacked systematic and comprehensive authority to protect most imperiled species (Flather et al. 1994).

The 1966 Endangered Species Preservation Act and 1969 Endangered Species Conservation Act provided protection for vertebrate species in danger of extinction, but these laws were limited in their ability to protect biodiversity. The 1969 Endangered Species Conservation Act also called for an international convention on the conservation of endangered species. The Convention on International Trade in Endangered Species of Wild Fauna and Flora then resulted from a resolution by 80 countries in 1973. The Endangered Species Act, passed later that year, ratified CITES and generally strengthened federal authority in protecting species. For example, it made the "taking"[13] of endangered species a federal offense, established categories of endangerment, prohibited any federal action that would jeopardize a listed species or its habitat, created a formal structure for species listing and management, and allowed citizens to sue the federal government for failures to meet its obligations under the act. The overall framework of the ESA has remained essentially unchanged, although Congress has amended it three times.[14] The ESA was due for renewal in 1992, but Congress has yet to pass such legislation.

Current Implementation of the Endangered Species Act

Listing. The U.S. Fish and Wildlife Service and the National Marine Fisheries Service administer the ESA. Terrestrial and freshwater organisms lie within the jurisdiction of the former, and the latter is responsible for marine species. A species is listed under the ESA when it is determined to be at risk of extinction due to destruction, modification, or curtailment of its habitat or range; overutilization for commercial, recreational, scientific, or educational purposes; disease or predation; the inadequacy of existing regulatory mechanisms; or other natural or manmade factors affecting its survival (USFWS 2004a).

Whether a species is listed as endangered or threatened depends on the degree of threat it faces, particularly within the United States. The ESA defines an endangered species as "in danger of extinction throughout all or a significant portion of its range," and a threatened species as "likely to become an endangered species within the foreseeable future throughout all or a significant portion of its range." The meaning of concepts such as "danger of extinction" and "significant portion of range" is determined by case; identifying general rules is difficult because of the uneven characteristics and requirements of different species. Listing a species under the ESA gives the federal government a requirement to protect the species and to prosecute those that harm it or its habitat, and it authorizes the Fish and Wildlife Service or the National Marine Fisheries Service to perform activities such as habitat preservation to protect and recover listed species.

All species of plants and animals native to the United States are eligible for listing except for insect pests. To address conservation of genetic diversity, the ESA defines species broadly to include subspecies, varieties (in the case of plants), and "distinct population segments" or "evolutionarily significant units," as is the case with Pacific salmon (see Box 7-3).

Since 1967, 33 species listed under the ESA have been delisted because of recovery, extinction, or taxonomic reclassification. The 1,311 species listed as of 2007 represent approximately 1 percent of all domestic species in the animal and plant classes listed (Table 7-8). Most listed U.S. species, approximately 78 percent,

Box 7-3. Pacific Salmon: Upstream

Salmon is virtually synonymous with the Pacific Northwest. Settlers of this region some 150 years ago found an abundance of coho, chinook, chum, sockeye, cutthroat, steelhead, and pink salmon. Since then, salmon populations have declined, and many are currently threatened or endangered. Causes for the declines include harvesting, river and stream obstructions such as dams and culverts, change in water flows and temperatures, degradation of spawning habitat, competition and genetic degradation from hatchery populations, and water pollution. Current runs of many Northwest salmon populations are a fraction of their estimated historical levels, and intense efforts are underway to restore them.

Fifty-two evolutionarily significant units (ESUs) of Pacific salmon and steelhead have been identified in Washington, Oregon, California, and Idaho. An ESU is a group of individual populations that share common genetic, ecological, and life history traits and differ in important ways from populations in other ESUs. Since 1989, 26 ESUs of Pacific salmon and steelhead species have been designated as threatened or endangered. In 2000, the National Oceanic and Atmospheric Administration announced critical habitat designations for 19 of the listed populations. Shortly thereafter, the agency's decisions were challenged in court on the grounds that economic impacts were not adequately considered. It then revisited its proposal and in 2004 announced new critical habitat designations that excluded approximately 80 percent of the originally proposed areas. Designating certain watersheds as critical habitat for salmon triggers stricter-than-usual permitting requirements for activities in those areas.

In addition to regulatory approaches such as critical habitat designations, significant federal and state resources are allocated for the protection of Pacific salmon. For example, in 2000–2003, the Pacific Coastal Salmon Recovery Fund used about $350 million in federal funds for some 3,000 projects supporting the protection of salmon. This funding was matched by almost $170 million from the Pacific Northwest states, pushing the total over $500 million in just four years. Most funding is directed toward salmon habitat protection and restoration; watershed planning, assessment, and management; salmon research, monitoring, and assessment; and public outreach and education.

Despite the vast efforts to restore salmon populations in the Pacific Northwest, it is too early to say whether these efforts will be successful. Changing environmental conditions and the sensitivity of salmon to them makes protecting these species particularly challenging. Salmon populations are strongly affected by Pacific Ocean conditions, which tend to follow fairly strong decadal but ultimately unpredictable fluctuations. For example, the record salmon runs observed in 2001 and 2002 may have been attributable to active recovery efforts or simply favorable ocean conditions. Record runs were again expected in 2005 from the offspring of the 2001 and 2002 runs. However, instead of returning in large numbers, the 2005 run was unexpectedly low, demonstrating the unpredictable nature of salmon populations.

Table 7-8. *Domestic Species Listed under Endangered Species Act, December 2006*

Taxonomic group	Endangered number[a]	% of known	Threatened number[d]	Total listed number	Candidate number	Known species number[b]
Vertebrates	247	9.2	123	370	55	2,680
Mammals	69	16.1	13	82	15	428
Birds	76	15.0	15	91	12	508
Reptiles	14	3.9	23	37	5	360
Amphibians	13	4.6	10	23	10	283
Fishes	75	6.8	62	137	13	1,101
Invertebrates[c]	165	0.1	32	197	83	118,595
Snails	25	0.9	11	36	25	2,650
Bivalves[d]	62	20.2	8	70	17	307
Crustaceans	19	0.2	3	22	6	9,675
Insects	47	0.0	10	57	34	96,406
Arachnids	12	0.1	0	12	1	9,557
Plants[e]	598	3.4	146	744	140	17,680
Flowering plants	570	3.6	143	713	135	15,792
Conifers and cycads	2	1.8	1	3	0	113
Ferns and allies	24	4.1	2	26	5	579
Lichens	2	0.2	0	2	0	1,196
TOTAL	**1,010**	**0.7**	**301**	**1,311**	**278**	**138,955**

[a]Source: USFWS.
[b]Sources: WRI (vertebrates); Stein et al. 2000 (invertebrates) and NatureServe (plants and invertebrates).
[c]Includes only the five invertebrate groups considered here.
[d]Includes only freshwater mussels.
[e]Includes only the four plant groups considered here.

are categorized as endangered.[15] The ESA does not limit listings to the U.S. species but allows any species to become listed, regardless of where it exists. Currently, 587 foreign species are listed. Listings of foreign species authorize activities against trade and trafficking and require that the needs of those species be considered when federal activities, such as development assistance programs, are planned and executed.

Critical habitat. The ESA mandates the designation of critical habitat for listed species "to the maximum extent prudent and determinable." Critical habitats include areas of land, water, and air required for the survival and recovery of a listed species but do not constitute a wildlife refuge or wilderness area. Unlike the listing action, a critical habitat designation requires analysis of economic impacts of proposed designation. Areas where the economic benefits of exclusion outweigh the benefits of inclusion may be excluded from critical habitat, but not if this would result in extinction (USFWS 1993). Currently, critical habitat designations cover about 37 percent of all listed species.

Species recovery. The ESA requires that for each listed species, a recovery plan be developed describing the actions needed to restore it to viable population levels. Recovery measures, such as consultations with other federal agencies to avoid harmful impacts, habitat acquisition and restoration, captive breeding and reintroductions (see Box 7-4), and other management and monitoring activities, are executed with the cooperation of federal, state, and local agencies; tribal governments; and private and nongovernmental stakeholders. Many listed species exist on privately owned

Box 7-4. Restoring the Gray Wolf in Yellowstone

The gray wolf *(Canis lupus)* was once plentiful in the United States but had practically disappeared from all 48 lower states by the 1970s. Wolves were considered harmful predators and their eradication in everybody's best interest. Federal and state programs were set up to shoot, trap, and poison wolves. As a result, wolf populations persisted only in northern Minnesota and Isle Royale of Michigan. Today, opinions about wolves are changing, and their importance as the top predator in ecosystems is recognized. After many decades of population decline, wolves are making a comeback in some of their former habitats.

The gray wolf is native to Yellowstone, where the first national park was established in 1872. Fearing that wolves in the area would extirpate elk and moose populations, Congress approved funding to eradicate wolves from Yellowstone in 1914. Wolves were hunted so effectively that by the 1940s, they were rarely observed, and by the 1970s, wolves had disappeared from the entire area. This development slowly reversed in the 1980s, when park officials started planning a reintroduction of wolves to Yellowstone. At the time, wolves had already begun reestablishing themselves in northern Montana and Idaho.

The reintroduction of wolves to one of the most visited national parks did not occur without controversy. But after cautious planning and thorough debate, the National Park Service devised a plan that included capturing wolves in Canada and transferring them to Yellowstone. In 1995, 14 wolves were released into the park. In 1996 and 1997, more wolves were released. After release, wolves were unexpectedly quick to adapt to their new environment, reproducing at higher rates than expected. Currently, tens of wolf packs roam Yellowstone and the surrounding area. Some park visitors have already viewed wolves chasing and killing elk or deer and interacting with other wolves and competing predators such as bears.

Interestingly, deer and elk modified their behavior after wolves reappeared. When wolves were absent, deer foraged in large numbers in riparian areas, removing vegetation and keeping them open. The wolves' presence has caused deer to avoid open areas, where they are most vulnerable. Consequently, with the regrowth of vegetation, riparian habitat for birds and beavers has increased in both quality and extent. Willow, cottonwood, aspen, and other plants that were earlier overgrazed now flourish in the places that elk and deer avoid. The new vegetation provides food for beaver and habitat for songbirds such as yellow warblers, and their populations have increased. Deer and elk carcasses provide food for grizzlies, coyotes, ravens, and other scavengers, which all seem to benefit from the wolves' reintroduction. Even trout regeneration has improved thanks to increased vegetation and its cooling effect on water temperatures in spawning areas. Similar cascading effects in the food web due to the reintroduction of wolves have been observed in Canada.

land, which makes the participation of private landowners in conservation efforts essential. Where species have broad ranges that extend beyond the borders of the United States, the Fish and Wildlife Service collaborates with foreign governments, particularly Canada and Mexico, to implement recovery activities.

Currently, more than 81 percent of listed species have final recovery plans, substantially up from 54 percent in 1995 (NRC 1995; USFWS 2004c). The Fish and Wildlife Service also reports that greater than 50 percent recovery has been achieved for 7 percent of listed species. The vast majority (77 percent) of listed species have reached less than 25 percent recovery (USFWS 2004c).

Downlisting, delisting, and extinction. Downlisting species from endangered to threatened occurs when threats to a species are reduced and population numbers meet criteria specified in the recovery plan. A species can be delisted because of recovery, new information about its status, taxonomic changes, or extinction. Since the inception of the ESA, 19 species or distinct population segments have been delisted because of successful recovery (Table 7-9), and 9 species have been declared extinct.[16]

Takings exemptions. Since the amendments of 1978, development projects can be exempted from restrictions pertaining to species preservation if the cabinet-level Endangered Species Committee decides that the actions meet certain criteria: (1) there are no "reasonable or prudent alternatives"; (2) the benefits of the project are in the public interest and outweigh the benefits of conserving the species; (3) the project is regionally or nationally vital; and (4) the project includes steps to mitigate the impact on the listed species. The committee has been convened only three times to make this decision.[17]

Additional amendments in 1982 further expanded exemptions for takings, particularly when private property rights are involved. These include a provision for experimental populations, such as reintroduced populations, to be governed under special rules.[18] Small landowners (residential properties, properties of five acres or less) also became exempt from prosecution for incidental takings.[19] Most signifi-

Table 7-9. *Recovered Species Delisted (Domestic and Foreign) Under the Endangered Species Act*

Taxonomic group	Common name	Scientific name	Year listed	Year delisted
Mammals	Gray wolf, MN	*Canis lupus*	1967	2007
	Gray wolf, Western Great Lakes	*Canis lupus*	2006	2007
	Grizzly bear, Yellowstone	*Ursus arctos horribilis*	1970	2007
	Columbian white-tailed deer, Douglas County DPS	*Odocoileus virginianus leucurus*	1970	2003
	Eastern gray kangaroo	*Macropus giganteus*	1974	1995
	Red kangaroo	*Macropus rufus*	1974	1995
	Western gray kangaroo	*Macropus fuliginosus*	1974	1995
	Gray whale	*Eschrichtius robustus*	1994	1994
Birds	Tinian monarch	*Monarcha takatsukasae*	1970	2004
	Aleutian Canada goose	*Branta canadensis leucopareia*	1967	2001
	American peregrine falcon	*Falco peregrinus anatum*	1970	1999
	Arctic peregrine falcon	*Falco peregrinus tundrius*	1970	1994
	Palau ground dove	*Gallicolumba canifrons*	1970	1985
	Palau fantail flycatcher	*Rhipidura lepida*	1970	1985
	Palau owl	*Pyrroglaux podargina*	1970	1985
	Brown pelican	*Pelecanus occidentalis*	1970	1985
Reptiles	American alligator	*Alligator mississippiensis*	1967	1987
Plants	Hoover's woolly-star	*Eriastrum hooveri*	1990	2003
	Robbin's cinquefoil	*Potentilla robbinsiana*	1980	2002

cantly, to provide incentives for private landowners to enhance and maintain natural habitat and to discourage practices that may harm listed species, landowners are allowed to obtain permits for incidental takings, provided that mitigation actions take place and the species is protected elsewhere. Incidental takings became authorized via three types of voluntary agreements between private landowners and the federal government: candidate conservation agreements with assurances, habitat conservation plans, and safe harbor agreements.

Candidate conservation agreements with assurances. Restrictions due to ESA create perverse incentives to manage lands in a way that prevents or discourages colonization by candidate species, or even to remove or destroy them. Candidate conservation agreements provide private property owners with guarantees that voluntary efforts to conserve candidate species will not result in additional regulatory obligations. The landowner receives an incidental take permit covering specified activities. Should the target species be listed as threatened or endangered, the landowner would still possess incidental take authorization and would not face regulations beyond those to which the landowner had already voluntarily committed (USFWS 2002b).

Habitat conservation plans. Implementing habitat conservation plans (HCPs) enables private landowners wanting to develop land that is or could be inhabited by listed species to receive an incidental take permit. HCPs integrate conservation activities into the development project to address species conservation goals, such as habitat preservation and restoration, new habitat creation, establishment of buffer areas, or access restrictions.

Like the candidate conservation agreements with assurances, HCPs have a "no surprises" policy to rule out additional future restrictions under unforeseen circumstances. Since 2000, these plans must outline an adaptive management strategy to prescribe actions given a range of potential uncertainties. This requirement increases the complexity of HCPs, but it also increases landowners' flexibility in choosing methods to achieve species and habitat conservation objectives.

Currently, more than 430 HCPs have been approved, with many more in the planning process. Most of the earlier HCPs were for areas of less than 1,000 acres. Now, 10 plans exceed 500,000 acres, and several are larger than 1,000,000 acres.

Safe harbor agreements. Some landowners are willing to undertake management actions that could benefit listed species but avoid doing so given the prospects of regulatory burdens should listed species colonize or increase their numbers on the property. The Safe Harbor Agreement program provides assurances to landowners that conservation activities that may benefit listed species will not result in land-use restrictions. A landowner can also be granted an "enhancement of survival" incidental take permit, which allows the incidental taking of species provided that population levels and habitat conditions do not move below the baseline established prior to the agreement. The Fish and Wildlife Service has issued more than 125 safe harbor agreements, encompassing some 2 million acres.

Conservation banking. A species conservation bank is land containing natural resource values, particularly threatened and endangered species habitat, that is conserved through a conservation easement. The bank can generate credits by acquiring or improving existing habitat, creating new habitat, or managing habitats for specific biological goals. The credits can be sold to private HCP enrollees, who in effect meet their HCP obligations by funding conservation activities off-site.

Banking provides several potential advantages to species conservation activities. First, conservation banks take advantage of market mechanisms to fund and cost-effectively allocate conservation activities. Second, banking provides landowners with incentives to promote species conservation by turning the regulatory liabilities associated with the ESA into potential financial assets. Third, conservation banks utilize potential economies of scale related to habitat conservation. Protecting large contiguous areas through conservation banking can create greater connectivity, fewer edges, and larger areas resulting in higher population viabilities compared with on-site mitigation activities.

Despite its potential, conservation banking is still in its infancy. Of the 76 properties self-identified as conservation banks, only 35 meet the guidelines established by the Fish and Wildlife Service (Fox and Nino-Murcia 2005). These 35 official banks cumulatively cover 15,987 hectares and shelter 22 listed species.

Trends in Species Listing and Recovery Expenditures

Listings. The number of listed domestic species has increased continually from the 63 vertebrates originally covered in the 1966 Endangered Species Preservation Act (Figure 7-4). During the first few years of the ESA, about 25 species were listed annually (Flather et al. 1994). Since then, the number of species listed has ranged from a net addition 128 species in 1994 to only 9 net species between 2002 and

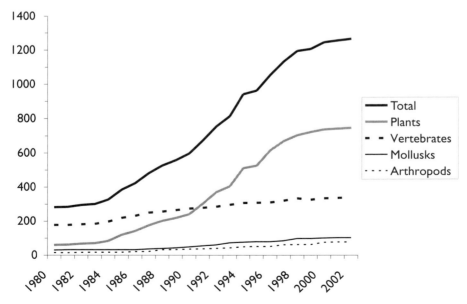

Figure 7-4. *Known Species Listed as Threatened or Endangered, 1980–2002*

2005. The relative inactivity in listings in the late 1970s was at least partly caused by the 1978 amendments mandating that critical habitat designation accompany every listing. The listings increased again after amendments in 1982 and 1988 allowed critical habitat designation to be postponed and codified emergency listings and monitoring of candidate species. These changes helped alleviate the continuing difficulties in managing the number of species petitioned. Listings continued at high rates until April 1995, when Congress enacted a year-long moratorium on new listings and critical habitat designation.

After the moratorium, the Fish and Wildlife Service redefined the system for designating candidate species for listing. Previously, the agency maintained three candidate lists: Category 1 for species with sufficient information to support listing, Category 2 for species yet to be properly evaluated, and Category 3 for species found unsuitable for listing. In practice, protective measures were extended to species in Category 2, even though some were unlikely to become listed. This system was changed to a single list of only those species for which sufficient information exists to warrant listing. This drastically reduced the number of species with federal status, from more than 4,000 candidate species to about 420. However, the Fish and Wildlife Service still maintains a candidate species list, now called Species of Concern.

Listing in the past few years has been at its lowest rate ever, at least in part because of shifts in priorities in ESA implementation. The ESA requires that critical habitat be designated at the time of listing to the maximum extent prudent and determinable. Previously, the Fish and Wildlife Service found that critical habitat designation was "not prudent" for most species because of incomplete knowledge of species' distribution and habitat needs; the agency determined that designating critical habitat generally generated only negligible benefits, given the other protections already afforded by the ESA. Therefore, critical habitat designations were indefinitely postponed for the vast majority of listed species. However, court rulings have ordered the designation of critical habitats for listed species. Consequently, in recent years new listing activity has slowed, while critical habitats have substantially increased.

Vertebrates, mammals and birds in particular, have historically received most of the research, management, and funding associated with the ESA. This reflects both the general state of knowledge about biodiversity and the popular demand for reducing the imperilment of large, conspicuous, well-studied animals (NRC 1995). From the inception of the ESA until 1989, vertebrates accounted for the majority of all federally protected species (Figure 7-4). Currently, about 13 percent of the known vertebrate species in the United States are listed as threatened or endangered (Figure 7-5)—a higher percentage than for any other taxonomic group.

Among vertebrates, fish, mammals, and birds have the greatest number of species listed (Figure 7-6). Recently, the increase in vertebrates listed has been driven largely by the addition of fish species. Though the percentage of known fish species listed is less than that of birds or mammals, there are more fish species listed than any other vertebrate class.

Bivalvia, which includes clams and mussels, is the invertebrate class with the most species listed. Nearly 23 percent of all known bivalves in the United States are federally listed, more than any other class covered by the ESA. This rate reflects

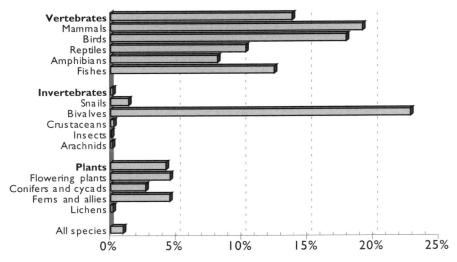

Figure 7-5. *Percentage of All Known Species in the United States Listed as Endangered or Threatened, by Taxonomic Group, December 2006*

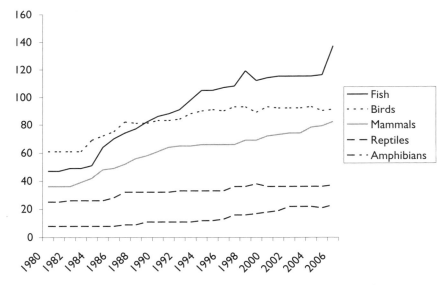

Figure 7-6. *Vertebrate Species Listed as Threatened or Endangered, 1980–2006*

the fact that freshwater bivalves have more imperiled species than any other group and are considered at greatest risk from pollution and habitat loss.

Plants were listed for federal protection in 1977, and since the mid-1980s, they have accounted for most new listings. On average, more than 35 plant species have been added each year, with as many as 107 listed in a single year. As a result, plants have accounted for the majority of listed species since 1994. About 3 percent of the nearly 22,000 known plant species in the United States are now listed under the ESA.

Expenditures for endangered and threatened species protection. Increases in government expenditures for the recovery of endangered and threatened species from 1989 to 2004, shown in Figure 7-7, come almost entirely from increases in federal spending. State spending for species recovery has been nearly flat.[20] In part, aggregate spending increases are due to the growing number of listed species, but also the average annual recovery expenditures per species has increased, from roughly $250,000 in 1989 to about $800,000 in 2004.

Vertebrates on average receive substantially more recovery funding per species than invertebrates or plants (Figure 7-8). Fishes on average receive the greatest expenditures per species among all classes listed, nearly twice the average for all vertebrates, followed by mammals, birds, and reptiles. Among vertebrates, amphibians receive the least funding per species, though still more than the average for invertebrates and for plants. Bivalvia, the invertebrate class with the greatest number of imperiled and federally protected species, receives the greatest recovery expenditure per invertebrate species.

Recovery expenditures concentrate on a few species. Since 1999, the 10 species with the highest reported expenditures have consistently received around 50 percent or more of all species-specific recovery spending. The top-10 list has regularly included the Steller sea lion, steelhead, chinook salmon, coho salmon, sockeye salmon, chum salmon, bull trout, right whale, red-cockaded woodpecker, and West Indian manatee. The five fish species in particular typically account for at least 40 percent of total recovery expenditures. Despite this concentration of expenditures on a handful of species, funding for other species also appears to have increased. For example, even excluding the 10 species with the highest reported expenditures, total recovery spending per species increased from $270,000 in 1999 to $417,000 in 2002.

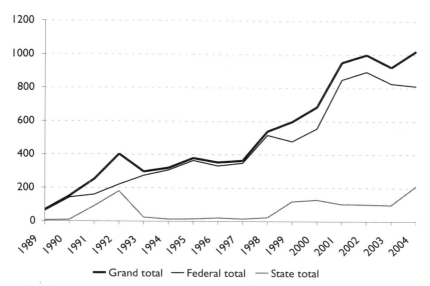

Figure 7-7. *Annual Expenditures on Threatened Species Protection and Recovery, 1989-2004 ($2005)*

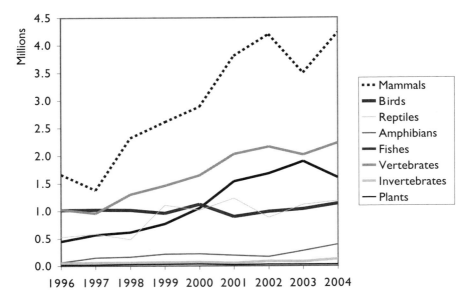

Figure 7-8. *Total Government Recovery Expenditure per Species, 1996-2004 ($2005)*

Criticisms of the Endangered Species Act

Some extinctions have been prevented by the ESA, but controversy exists over whether it effectively facilitates species' recovery (NRC 1995). Criticism of ESA ranges from economic and scientific concerns to its fundamental approach to biodiversity preservation (see Lueck in Chapter 6 of this volume).

Economic concerns. Though economic factors are considered in critical habitat designation and the voluntary agreement programs address concerns about economic efficiency and incentives, the overall approach of the ESA still explicitly ignores costs and other economic considerations by prohibiting any activity that causes net harm to listed species populations. Effectively, this puts a very large or even infinite value on avoiding extinction (Polasky et al. 1997; Brown and Shogren 1998). Implicitly, the ESA assumes that conserving species nearly always provides net benefits, placing the ESA largely beyond decisions reflecting economic trade-offs.

Although the government bears the burden of proof to determine that a listed species occurs on private land, constitutional rights prevent unwarranted searches and hinder investigations to confirm listed species existence or absence on private property. Moreover, the potential costs of species' protection create perverse incentives for the landowner to withhold information on the listed species and to manage his property so that they are not discovered (Polasky and Doremus 1998). Landowners may also preemptively develop their properties to avoid regulation (Lueck and Michael 2003). Essentially, landowners have clear incentives to manipulate decisions under their control, such as investing in development or not disclosing information on listed species, to capture the full development value of their land rather than be left with regulatory costs imposed by the ESA. Such patterns of behavior are confirmed by both anecdotal (e.g., Bean and Wilcove 1997) and empirical (Lueck and Michael 2003) evidence. Therefore, supplementary measures—such as those included in the voluntary agreements between private landowners and the federal government—are necessary to reduce perverse incentives for landowners.,

Scientific concerns. In 1991, Congress charged an independent research group with the task of evaluating the scientific validity of the ESA. The National Research Council (1995) found that although the scientific basis of the act was sound, there was room for improvement. For instance, listing decisions revealed some scientifically invalid implementation. Although distinct population segments were eligible for protection, only those for vertebrates had been listed. No scientific reason existed to justify the exclusion of evolutionarily significant units of plants and invertebrate animals. Studies also suggested that visceral characteristics, such as physical size and the degree to which species were considered higher forms of life, influenced listing decisions and overshadowed such scientific qualifications as taxonomic uniqueness and the degree of threat (Metrick and Weitzman 1996, 1998). Ando (1999) found that public opposition or support could substantially slow or hasten the progress of the listing process.

Spending decisions also indicated a bias toward charismatic megafauna. Vertebrates have received substantially more recovery spending per species than invertebrates or plants, and some studies suggest that spending decisions are strongly influenced by not only visceral characteristics, but also whether the protection of a species is in conflict with development activities (e.g., Metrick and Weitzman 1996, 1998). Though species in conflict are supposed to receive only a tiebreaking preference in the priority ranking, in practice, species in conflict have tended to receive disproportionately greater attention and spending. Researchers have yet to establish that recovery expenditures are driven by science—the only allowable criterion under the ESA (Brown and Shogren 1998).

The National Research Council (1995) review also found that several habitat-related aspects of the ESA were scientifically invalid. For instance, the ESA restricts the incidental take, such as via habitat modification, of listed animals but prohibits only the direct removal or malicious destruction of endangered plants, even though plants require intact habitat for survival to the same degree that animals do. The National Research Council also reported that different standards were used for determining "jeopardy," "survival," or "recovery," depending on whether the listed species occurred on public or private land. The biological and physical requirements for species survival obviously do not vary depending on the ownership of their habitat, so such differences in standards are scientifically indefensible. The review criticized the limited role that biologically explicit, quantitative models for risk assessment have played in ESA implementation. It suggested that these models play a more central role, especially as tools to evaluate management decisions and assess the need for protection before the risk of extinction becomes too high.

Concerns related to public–private agreements. The growing role of public–private conservation agreements, such as habitat conservation plans, candidate conservation plans, and safe harbor agreements, also has been controversial. HCPs are promoted as a way to protect imperiled species by engaging private and state landowners, but critics contend that many agreements are approved without sufficient scientific or public oversight. Another fear is that landowners take advantage of overburdened government agencies susceptible to political compromises and use these agreements to avoid conservation (Innes et al. 1998).

Environmental groups have been concerned that HCPs permanently establish long-term habitat management plans without proper long-term biological monitoring. The No Surprises policy, in particular, hinders adaptive management strategies that could address future changes in natural conditions and scientific knowledge. HCPs and other public–private conservation plans, which effectively seek no net loss of listed species, are also criticized for the absence of requirements to contribute to the recovery of listed species Moreover, these agreements are not subject to independent scientific review and receive only limited public review, and the cumulative impacts of multiple plans are not analyzed. Some of these criticisms have been addressed by recent changes in HCP policy, which now requires new plans to outline measurable biological goals, include monitoring and adaptive management provisions, and increase public comment periods. However, the new rules do not provide for independent scientific review.

Concerns regarding fundamental approach. Critics argue that the species-specific approach of the ESA is a fundamentally flawed policy, one that is unwieldy and slow and ignores the dynamics of ecological systems (Flather et al. 1994). Moreover, the ESA calls for action only after a species population has dwindled to near-extinction, when protection and recovery may be especially expensive and difficult. In addition, recovery goals established after listing may still leave the species at high risk of extinction (NRC 1995).

The National Research Council's scientific assessment reports that the ESA is deficient as a comprehensive policy for protecting biodiversity. However, as a safety net to prevent extinction, the ESA performs more adequately. To sustain biodiversity in the long term, the ESA must be part of a wider set of habitat-level biodiversity conservation policies, utilize new cooperative approaches, and maintain viable populations of species, thereby precluding new listings.

The ESA is often criticized for imposing excessive regulatory burdens on landowners and businesses. Recent proposals suggest shifting responsibility from landowners to regulators so that, for example, the regulator would have to provide more timely decisions in response to landowners' requests for them. There have also been proposals for greater cost-sharing for conservation activities, which currently is limited to government grants to develop and support HCPs. These proposals would change the current ESA considerably, but it is yet too early to say which proposed changes would be supported in the legislative process.

Areas Protected by Federal, State, Tribal, and Local Governments

Governments at the federal, state, tribal, and local levels have set aside land they own, regulating access and usage to achieve a variety of goals. The Department of the Interior manages most federally protected areas through the National Park

Service, the Forest Service, the Bureau of Land Management, and the Fish and Wildlife Service. The Department of Agriculture and the Department of Defense also control some protected lands. Additionally, every state manages a system of state parks, and counties, municipalities, soil conservation districts, and other units manage local parks.

These areas receive various levels of protection, depending on their designation and the agency in charge of their management. Most protected areas are set aside for direct human uses. For instance, national parks and historical landmarks are managed for the purpose of their enjoyment by present and future generations, typically restricting uses to recreation. In contrast, the Bureau of Land Management and the Forest Service each manage a network of federal lands that allow multiple uses, such as hunting, grazing, and timber and mineral extraction. Including all nonmarine areas, the United States has around 7,500 protected areas covering almost 16 percent of the total land area.

Although the Endangered Species Act restricts activities on government land that harms listed species or their habitat, only some protected areas are designated specifically for conserving diverse ecosystems and their native species. The national Wildlife Refuge system, managed by the Fish and Wildlife Service, encompasses 38 million hectares comprising more than 535 refuges and more than 3,000 breeding and nesting areas for small waterfowl (USFWS 2002a). These refuges provide habitat for 250 threatened and endangered species, in many cases constituting the only protected habitat for a particular species, such as the Florida panther and the desert bighorn sheep.

Nongovernmental Biodiversity Protection

Environmental organizations, the forest products industry, and private landowners have become increasingly proactive and important in the management and preservation of biodiversity. Although they often operate in cooperation with state and federal conservation agencies, many of their actions are driven not by regulatory requirements, such as the ESA, but by the conservation and business interests of the involved parties. Two important nongovernmental approaches to conservation are forest certification by sustainable forestry programs and land conservation by private land trusts.[21]

Forest certification. Forest certification uses a set of environmental, social, and economic sustainability standards—often developed collaboratively by foresters, conservationists, and scientists—to assure consumers that the forest from which timber products are derived is managed according to environmentally and socially sound practices. Forest owners, wood manufacturers, and retailers who meet the program's criteria may earn certification.

Several forest certification programs currently exist, each adopting different criteria. The Sustainable Forestry Initiative (SFI) is the largest U.S. program. It is an independent organization, established in 1994 by the American Forest and Paper Association. Approximately 50 million acres of forestland in United States are enrolled in this program. The Forest Stewardship Council (FSC) is the second major U.S. forest certification program. This program, which is promoted especially by environmental groups, has certified nearly 20 million acres in the United States. Some landowners participate in both programs; for example, nearly 4.8 million acres of forest managed by the Minnesota Department of Natural Resources is certified by both SFI and FSC.

Although forest certification is continuously expanding, critics argue that it is no substitute for biodiversity conservation. Forest certification is limited by the wood producer's inclination to participate voluntarily, which is in turn limited by consumers' demand and willingness to pay a premium for certified products. Environmental groups also argue that the standards of certification programs may not be sufficient to protect biodiversity and seek adoption of stricter environmental requirements. Despite these potential weaknesses, on the whole, forest certification programs have established multiobjective forest management criteria that a growing number of consumers and businesses require and that forest owners and managers follow. Chapter 3 in this book discusses forest certification; we refer interested readers to it for a more detailed description.

Conservation land trusts. Conservation land trusts are nonprofit and nongovernmental organizations that acquire and protect land with threatened habitat through donations and purchases. Though the earliest land trusts were established in the 1800s,[22] they have recently emerged as central actors in land conservation. They obtain land to maintain working farms, forests, and wilderness and for other uses that often help sustain biodiversity. Private land trusts also protect land to preserve open space, agricultural land, or historically important areas, but protecting wildlife and nature is the leading goal (LTA 2006). Land trusts obtain real estate from landowners who sell or donate conservation easements (i.e., deed restrictions on land uses), or by outright purchases of property. Although conservation land trusts can include large organizations such as The Nature Conservancy and the Audubon Society, many are formed by relatively small organizations operating at community, state, or regional levels (hereafter, local).

According to the Land Trust Alliance (2006),[23] a total of 1,667 local land trusts operated in the United States in 2005. About one-third (581) of local land trusts operate in the Northeast, where they protect more than 3.5 million acres (Figure 7-9). Local land trusts conserve about 2 million acres in the Southwest and about 1.7 million acres in the Mid-Atlantic and Pacific regions each.

The number of local land trusts has increased gradually, nearly doubling during the past 10 years (Figure 7-10). The land area protected has increased yet more rapidly, from about 6 million acres in 2000 to 12 million acres in 2005 (Table 7-9)— nearly the size of Maryland.

Much of the recent increase in the area protected comes from the growing use of easements and other contractual arrangements rather than through direct land purchases. Currently, only about 14 percent of the total area under conservation by local land trusts is in their ownership; other areas are conserved either under easements (53 percent) or by acquisition by other organizations or agencies or other means (33 percent) (Table 7-9). Between 2000 and 2005, the land acquired by non-purchase means increased by 1.6 million acres, whereas land purchases added only about 0.5 million protected acres.[24]

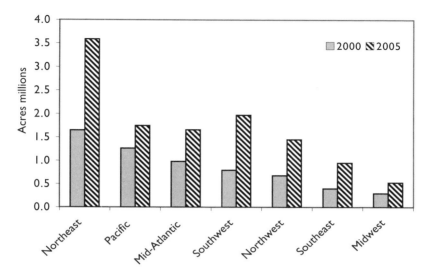

Figure 7-9. *Acres Protected by Local, State, and Regional Land Trusts, 2000 and 2005*

Source: Land Trust Alliance 2006.

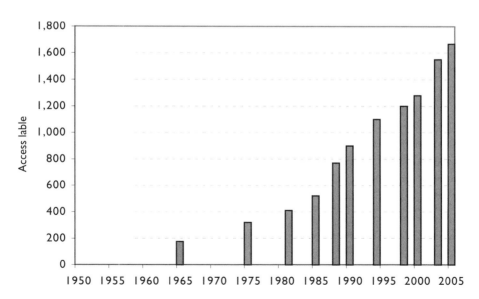

Figure 7-10. *Land Trusts, 1950–2005*

Source: Land Trust Alliance 2006.

Table 7-10. *Total Acres Conserved by Local, State, and Regional Land Trusts in 2000 and 2005, by Method of Conservation*

Conservation Method	2000 Acres	%	2005 Acres	%	Increase 2000-2005 Acres	%
Ownership	1,219,632	20%	1,703,212	14%	483,580	40%
Easements	2,514,545	42%	6,245,969	53%	3,731,424	148%
Other means	2,322,447	38%	3,940,928	33%	1,618,481	70%
Total	6,056,624	100%	11,890,109	100%	5,833,485	96%

Source: Land Trust Alliance (2006).

In addition to the local land trusts included in the above estimates, several national private land trusts also operate. The Nature Conservancy, the largest, protects some 15 million acres in the United States. The second-largest private land trust, the Conservation Fund, conserves more than 5 million acres. Ducks Unlimited, which manages and restores wetlands for waterfowl conservation, has preserved about 3.5 million acres. The Trust for Public Land, another major national land trust, has conserved more than 2 million acres. To put these numbers in perspective, these four private land trusts together conserve some 25 million acres, which is more than the total area of national parks outside Alaska,[25] or roughly 2.5 times the size of Massachusetts.

Biodiversity and Sustainability

We have so far described the status and protection of biodiversity in the United States without placing them in the broader context of sustainability, the theme of this book. Unlike some of the other resources covered in this volume, biodiversity is unique in that it can only partly recover after being degraded and thus is not renewable in the traditional sense. Stocks of traditional renewable resources, such as timber, game, and freshwater, can replenish themselves with new units functionally indistinguishable from those consumed. In contrast, though populations and habitats can recover under the right circumstances, extinction of species is permanent: evolution is unlikely to produce it again. Because its loss is irreversible, biodiversity is an exhaustible resource (Heal 1998).

The often-cited statement by the Brundtland Commission (WCED 1987) describes sustainable development as "development that meets the needs of the present without compromising the ability of future generations to meet their own needs." From the perspective of biodiversity conservation, sustainable development calls for the current generation to obtain needed resources from the environment without degrading the ecosystems and biological diversity required by future generations. Therefore, two issues important in considering the sustainability of economic activities are the placement of adequate value on the long-run future, as well as the recognition of all sources of value from biodiversity (Heal 1998).

Because the effects of biodiversity loss accrue in the long run, economic activities that deplete biodiversity impose a cost, or negative externality, on future generations. Because of incentives for free-riding, private conservation actions are unlikely to completely ameliorate this externality and provide socially optimal levels of biodiversity, particularly across generations. The underprovision of biodiversity protection by the market can be partly resolved through government action, such as legislation protecting endangered species and the establishment of protected areas. However, such policies may fail to capture intergenerational conservation provision because governments do not necessarily respond to the needs of future generations.

Although scientific consensus indicates that human activities are causing a biodiversity decline orders of magnitude faster than background extinction rates, vast gaps remain in the understanding of ecological complexity and its relationship with the long-term sustainability of ecosystems. In experimental or simplified settings, biodiversity tends to contribute positively to the stability, productivity, and resilience of natural ecosystems. The presence of specific functional groups also is necessary in all ecosystems to maintain their overall functionality. However, knowledge concerning the importance of biodiversity in controlling ecological processes in more complex processes and at larger scales of time and space is limited at best.

In determining the appropriate long-term policy for biodiversity, one certainty is that economic trade-offs are unavoidable. Much of economics literature concentrates on estimating the benefits from biodiversity conservation and the pressing methodological challenges in the valuation of nonmarket benefits for setting priorities in the research agenda. However, when valuation results are used for policy analysis and decisionmaking, both benefit and cost estimates are necessary to determine the efficiency or effectiveness of policy alternatives.

Systematically assessing alternative biodiversity policies requires difficult comparisons between biodiversity and the well-being of current and future generations, especially when species have significant nonuse values and cannot be treated purely as productive capital. A substantial, mainly conceptual literature exists on intergenerational equity and efficiency,[26] but applying the rigorous principles developed in this literature to evaluate present policies requires daring assumptions regarding discounting, uncertainty, and other variables. Difficulties in determining present-day trade-offs related to biodiversity loss are magnified when the relevant comparative benefits and costs must be projected decades or centuries into the future.

Successful strategies to preserve biodiversity will likely approach human and natural systems from an integrative perspective, and several areas of research currently pursue this vein. Bioeconomics is a field of resource economics that examines interactions between biological resources and human activities. These studies investigate human activities (e.g., fishing, hunting, land management) and species abundance over time and space and analyze their linkages. Another example of integrated economic and ecological research is systematic conservation planning. This research, developed at the interface of ecology, conservation biology, operations research, and environmental economics, aims to identify the most cost-effective conservation strategies for achieving specific conservation goals. The early studies focused on optimization methods for determining the configuration of reserve networks. Recent research seeks to better address the many complexities that arise in actual conservation decisions, such as balancing species preservation with other land-use objectives. Incorporating the dynamic and spatial aspects of conservation decisions is also a high priority in the current research agenda (Williams et al. 2004).

Because most biodiversity in the United States occupies working landscapes rather than reserves, examining alternative management strategies for multiple-use areas is centrally important to conservation (e.g., Polasky et al. 2005b). Understanding landowners' preferences and behavior relative to alternative biodiversity conservation policies will be helpful in identifying cost-effective approaches to protecting biodiversity. For example, protecting biodiversity in working landscapes using easements may be achieved inexpensively compared with full preservation through acquisition or prohibitive regulation (e.g., Siikamäki and Layton, 2007a). Augmenting regulatory approaches, such as the ESA, with economic incentives to protect biodiversity may therefore prove both economically and ecologically more sensible than relying solely on regulation.

Finally, the role of economists and ecologists is not to set policies but to help societies make informed decisions about biodiversity conservation. Ecological study is vital to understanding the role biodiversity plays in ecosystem functions; economics can help assess how these functions, as well as other less tangible benefits, contribute to human well-being. The integration of both fields of knowledge is necessary to determine how various policy mechanisms can achieve their conservation goals.

Appendix. Timeline of Species Protection Legislation

1894: Yellowstone Game Protection Act

Prohibited the hunting, wounding, or capturing of any animal, including birds, within Yellowstone National Park and restricted allowable fishing methods. Also gave the Department of the Interior rulemaking authority to protect all plants, animals, and minerals within the park.

1900: Lacey Act

Outlawed interstate traffic in birds and other animals illegally killed in their state of origin. Later amendments have prohibited all trafficking and commerce in fish, wildlife, and rare plants taken or possessed illegally.

1918: Migratory Bird Treaty Act

Implemented the 1916 Convention between the United States and Great Britain (for Canada), prohibiting the hunting, trafficking, sale, and purchase of migratory birds listed in the treaty. Later amendments implemented conventions with Mexico, Japan, and the Soviet Union (now Russia).

1929: Migratory Bird Conservation Act

Created the Migratory Bird Conservation Commission to approve areas of land or water recommended by the secretary of the Interior for acquisition as reservations for migratory birds.

1934: Migratory Bird Hunting and Conservation Stamp Act

Required use of a migratory bird stamp for hunting and raised funds from stamp sales for the conservation of migratory waterfowl.

1937: Federal Aid in Wildlife Restoration Act (Pittman–Robertson Act)

Provided funding for the selection, restoration, rehabilitation, and improvement of wildlife habitat, wildlife management research, and the distribution of information produced by such projects.

1940: Bald Eagle Protection Act

Prohibited the taking, possession, and commerce of the bald eagle and the golden eagle, except under certain specified conditions.

1956: Fish and Wildlife Act

Mandated the development by the secretary of the Interior of policies and procedures necessary for executing fish and wildlife laws, as well as research and reports on fish and wildlife. Also created the Fish and Wildlife Service within the Department of the Interior.

1966: Endangered Species Preservation Act

Authorized the secretary of the Interior to list endangered domestic fish and wildlife and allowed the Fish and Wildlife Service to buy habitat for listed species. The Departments of the Interior, Agriculture, and Defense were to protect listed species and preserve their habitats.

1969: Endangered Species Conservation Act

Expanded the Endangered Species Preservation Act to include foreign species, prohibiting their U.S. imports and sales. Called for an international convention on endangered species protection.

1969: National Environmental Policy Act

Required that all federal agencies prepare detailed environmental impact statements for any federal action that could affect the environment.

1972: Marine Mammal Protection Act

Mandated a moratorium on the taking and importation of marine mammals, as well as products taken from them, and established procedures for waiving the moratorium and transferring management responsibility to the states. Also created the Marine Mammal Commission under the National Oceanic and Atmospheric Administration with specific advisory and research duties related to the protection of marine mammals.

1973: Convention on International Trade in Endangered Species of Wild Fauna and Flora

Outlawed international commerce in plant and animal species believed to be actually or potentially harmed by trade. Entered into force in 1975.

1973: Endangered Species Act

Strengthened and expanded federal authority granted from preceding species protection legislation, as well as distinguished "endangered" and "threatened" species, made plants and invertebrates eligible for protection, established taking prohibitions, provided federal matching funds for states with cooperative agreements, and enacted U.S. implementation of the Convention on International Trade in Endangered Species of Wild Fauna and Flora.

1978: Endangered Species Act (amendments)

Allowed exemptions for takings by federal agencies if approved by a cabinet-level committee; required critical habitat to be designated concurrently with species listing while taking into consideration economic and other impacts of designation; and directed the secretaries of the Interior and Agriculture to develop a program for conserving fish, wildlife, and plants. Also expanded protection to "distinct population segments" of vertebrates.

1982: Endangered Species Act (amendments)

Required status designations to be based on biological and trade information, without any consideration of economic effects; mandated determination of species status within one year following its proposal; created provisions for experimental populations to be subject to different treatment than other populations; and prohibited removing listed plants from federal land. Allowed private landowners to receive permits for incidental takings, given that mitigation actions are in place and the species is protected elsewhere.

1988: Endangered Species Act (amendments)

Mandated the monitoring of candidate and recovered species; allowed emergency listing when evidence of significant risk exists; enacted new procedures for recovery plans; required a report of all reasonably identifiable government expenditures for recovery on a species-by-species basis; extended protection for endangered plants to include destruction on federal land and other taking when it violates state law; and established a "cooperative endangered species conservation fund" to provide matching funds to states for conservation projects.

Notes

1. The authors would like to acknowledge extremely helpful comments by Christopher Costello, Dean Lueck, Roger Sedjo, and David Simpson to early sketches and drafts of this chapter. The authors also gratefully acknowledge Thomas Lovejoy and Robin O'Malley from the Heinz Center and John Heissenbuttel and Nadine Block from the American Forest and Paper Association for particularly helpful discussions and suggestions during the planning stages of this chapter.

2. For example, Pacific salmon has over fifty distinct ESUs, which are the basis for their management and conservation (NOAA 2005).

3. Exotic species that establish themselves in nonnative habitats may displace native species through competition for natural resources, predate upon native species to extinction, or alter habitat to the point that native species can no longer persist.

4. Regardless of what the exact number of current species may be, scientists believe that it is more than at any other point in the Earth's history. However, current species represent only a fraction of all species ever that existed, which is estimated at around 5 billion species. An estimated 95% of species ever that existed are now extinct.

5. IUCN stands for the International Union for the Conservation of Nature and Natural Resources, the full name of the World Conservation Union.

6. These include the Steller's sea cow, Caribbean monk seal, and sea mink.

7. These include the passenger pigeon, Carolina parakeet, Labrador duck, Hawaiian black crow, and other, mostly Hawaiian, birds.

8. NatureServe is a nonprofit conservation organization that maintains a network of natural heritage programs and produces scientific information about rare and endangered species and threatened ecosystems. NatureServe's natural heritage program represents an international network of biological inventories operating in all 50 U.S. states, Canada, Latin America, and the Caribbean.

9. The IUCN and NatureServe classify some species differently, but their assessments of species status are strongly correlated (O'Grady et al. 2004).

10. The Hawaiian Islands have lost over 50% of their native bird species, 50% of their plants, and 90% of their native land snails.

11. For a thorough review of the history, current practices, and different methods of contingent valuation, see Carson and Hanemann (2005).

12. It took place amidst other seminal events in environmental governance, such as the formation of the EPA in 1970 and the passage of the 1969 National Environmental Policy Act, 1970 Clean Air Act, and the 1977 Clean Water Act.

13. The ESA defines a "take" as "to harass, harm, pursue, hunt, shoot, wound, kill, trap, capture, or collect, or to attempt to engage in any such conduct." "Harm" includes "significant habitat modification or degradation where it actually kills or injures wildlife by significantly impairing essential behavioral patterns, including breeding, feeding, or sheltering."

14. The first amendment came in 1978, after the Supreme Court ordered a stop to construction on the Tellico Dam in order to preserve habitat of the endangered snail darter (*Tennessee Valley Authority v. Hill*). The ruling reasoned that because the intent of the ESA was to prevent any action that threatened listed species, the ESA mandated species protection regardless of economic cost. Congress responded by creating an Endangered Species Committee that could exempt activities from the ESA, if it determined that their benefits outweigh the damage from jeopardizing listed species. The second amendment took place in 1982, after a developer bulldozed a population of the San Diego mesa mint following its proposed listing, rather than allow it to jeopardize a federal loan guarantee. Congress recognized that the ESA created perverse incentives to harm rare species and amended the ESA to allow landowners to prepare habitat-conservation plans (HCPs), which allow landowners to take endangered species if they provide its protection elsewhere. The third amendment of the ESA in 1988 included requirements for monitoring candidate and recovered species and codified rules for public notice (NRC 1995).

15. The Fish and Wildlife Service reports that currently 30 percent of listed species are stable, 6 percent are improving, and 21 percent are declining. The status of 39 percent of listed species is presently uncertain because additional information on species population numbers and

threats is needed. Additionally, one percent of listed species are found only in captivity and three percent are presumed extinct (USFWS 2004c).

16. Species delisted due to extinction include four bird species (Guam broadbill, Mariana mallard, Dusky seaside sparrow, and Santa Barbara song sparrow), four fish species (Longjaw cisco, Blue pike, Tecopa pupfish, and Amistad gambusia) and one clam species (Sampson's pearlymussel).

17. The first was the Tellico Dam decision described earlier. The second committee decision, in 1983, allowed the Gray Rocks Dam in Nebraska to operate while expanding the nesting areas for the endangered whooping crane. In 1992, the committee permitted logging in public forestlands that serve as habitat for the endangered Northern spotted owl. A court order later prevented logging from occurring.

18. These rules were enacted to mitigate the concern that reintroductions might bring new restrictions on private land use.

19. Incidental takings are those that occur only in the course of otherwise legal activities, such as habitat modification due to property development.

20. Since the 1988 Amendments, the ESA has required the FWS to annually report government expenditures for recovery. The most recent report available in January 2007 covers expenditures up until 2004.

21. Certification and ecolabeling according to various biodiversity and sustainability criteria is important also outside forestry. For example, the Marine Stewardship Council (founded in 1997) is an international labeling program aimed at promoting sustainable fisheries.

22. For example, The Trustees of Reservations in Massachusetts was founded in 1891 "for the purposes of acquiring, holding, maintaining and opening to the public…beautiful and historic places…"

23. The LTA represents local, state, and regional land trusts, providing technical assistance, and tracking of the amount of land preserved.

24. During this period, purchased land increased by 40% while the area under easements increased by nearly four times that rate, 148%.

25. The National Park System as a whole comprises more than just national parks, covering almost 400 areas and over 84 million acres, including national parks, monuments, battlefields, military parks, historical parks, historic sites, lakeshores, seashores, recreation areas, and scenic rivers and trails. National parks alone cover about 51.9 million acres, out of which about 32.5 million acres are in Alaska (www.nps.gov).

26. See, for example, Toman (1994) and Pezzey (1997) for more on sustainability.

References

Abdalla, C.A., B.A. Roach, and D.J. Epp. 1992. Valuing Environmental Groundwater Changes Using Averting Expenditures: An Application to Groundwater Contamination. *Land Economics* 68: 163–69.

Ando, A. 1999. Waiting to be Protected under The Endangered Species Act: the Political Economy of Regulatory Delay. *Journal of Law and Economics* 42: 29–60.

Arrow, K., R. Solow, P.R. Portney, E.E. Leamer, R. Radner, and H. Schuman. 1993. Report of the NOAA Panel on Contingent Valuation, *Federal Register* 58(10) (January 15): 4601–14.

Banzhaf, H.S., D. Burtraw, D. Evans, and A.J. Krupnick. 2006. Valuation of Natural Resources in the Adirondacks. *Land Economics* 82(3): 445–64.

Barbault, R., and S. Sastrapradja. 1995. Generation, Maintenance, and Loss of Biodiversity. In *Global Biodiversity Assessment,* edited by V.H. Heywood. UN Environment Programme.

Bean, M.J., and D. Wilcove. 1997. The Private Land Problem. *Conservation Biology* 11(1): 1–2.

Bell, K.P., D. Huppert, and R.L. Johnson. 2003. Willingness to Pay for Local Coho Salmon Enhancement in Coastal Communities. *Marine Resource Economics* 18: 15–31.

Berrens, R.P., A.K. Bohara, C.L. Silva, D. Brookshire, and M. McKee. 2000. Contingent Values for New Mexico Instream Flows: With Tests of Scope, Group-size Reminder and Temporal Reliability. *Journal of Environmental Management* 58: 73–90.

Berrens, R.P., P. Ganderton, and C.L. Silva. 1996. Valuing the Protection of Minimum Instream Flows in New Mexico. *Journal of Agricultural and Resource Economics* 21: 294–309.

Bowker, J.M., and J.R. Stoll. 1988. Use of Dichotomous Choice Nonmarket Methods to Value the Whooping Crane Resource. *American Journal of Agricultural Economics* 70(2): 372–81.

Boyle, K.J. 1990. Dichotomous Choice, Contingent Valuation Questions: Functional Form Is Important. *Northeastern Journal of Agriculture and Resource Economics* 19: 125–31.

Boyle, K.J., and R.C. Bishop. 1987. Valuing Wildlife in Benefit-cost Analyses: A Case Study Involving Endangered Species. *Water Resources Research* 23 (May): 943–50.

Brock W.A., and A. Xepapadeas. 2003. Valuing Biodiversity from an Economic Perspective: A Unified Economic, Ecological, and Genetic Approach. *The American Economic Review* 93(5): 1597–614.

Brookshire, D., L. Eubanks, and A. Randall. 1983. Estimating Option Prices and Existence Values for Wildlife Resources. *Land Economics* 59: 1–15.

Brown, G.M., Jr., and J.F. Shogren. 1998. Economics of the Endangered Species Act. *Journal of Economic Perspectives* 12(3): 3–20.

Cardinale, B.J., D.S. Srivastava, J.E. Duffy, J.P. Wright, A.L. Downing, M. Sankaran, and C. Jousseau. 2006. Effects of Biodiversity on the Functioning of Trophic Groups and Ecosystems. *Nature* 443: 989–92.

Carson, R.T., and M.W. Hanemann. 2005. Contingent Valuation. In *Handbook of Environmental Economics* (vol. 2), edited by K.-G. Mäler and J.R. Vincent. Elsevier, Chapter 17.

Chambers, C.M., and J.C. Whitehead. 2003. A Contingent Valuation Estimate of the Benefits of Wolves in Minnesota. *Environmental and Resource Economics* 26: 249–67.

Chichilnisky, G., and G. Heal. 1998. Economic Returns from the Biosphere. *Nature* 391: 629–30.

Collinson, J.M. 2007. Video Analysis of the Escape Flight of Pileated Woodpecker *Dryocopus pileatus:* Does the Ivory-billed Woodpecker *Campephilus principalis* Persist in Continental North America? *BMC Biology* 2007, 5:8 (March 15) doi:10.1186/1741-7007-5-8.

Costanza, R., et al. 1997. The Value of the World's Ecosystem Services and Natural Capital. *Nature* (May 15): 253–60.

Costello, C., and M. Ward. 2006. Search, Bioprospecting and Biodiversity Conservation. *Journal of Environmental Economics and Management* 52: 615–26.

Cummings, R., P. Ganderton, and T. McGuckin. 1994. Substitution Effects in CVM Values. *American Journal of Agricultural Economics* 76: 205–14.

Daily, G.C. (ed.). 1997. *Nature's Services: Societal Dependence on Natural Ecosystems.* Washington, DC: Island Press.

Dale, V.H., and S.C. Beyeler. 2001. Challenges in the Development and Use of Ecological Indicators. *Ecological Indicators* 1: 3–10.

Diamond, P.A., and J.A. Hausman. 1994. Contingent Valuation: Is Some Number Better Than No Number? *Journal of Economic Perspectives* 8(4): 45–64.

Duffield, J. 1991. Existence and Non-consumptive Values for Wildlife: Application of Wolf Recovery in Yellowstone National Park. W-133/Western Regional Science Association Joint Session, Measuring Non-Market and Non-Use Values. Monterey, CA.

———. 1992. An Economic Valuation of Wolf Recovery in Yellowstone: Park Visitor Attitudes and Values. In *Wolves for Yellowstone?* edited by J. Varley and W. Brewster. National Park Service, Yellowstone National Park.

Duffield, J., and D. Patterson. 1992. Field Testing Existence Values: Comparison of Hypothetical and Cash Transaction Values. Benefits and Costs in Natural Resource Planning, 5th Report. W-133 Western Regional Research Publication, compiled by B. Rettig. Department of Agricultural and Resource Economics. Corvallis: Oregon State University.

Duffield, J., D. Patterson, and C. Neher. 1993. Wolves and People in Yellowstone: A Case Study in the New Resource Economics. Report to Liz Claiborne and Art Ortenberg Foundation. Department of Economics. Missoula: University of Montana.

Fitzpatrick, J.W., M. Lammertink, M.D. Luneau, et al. 2005. Ivory-billed Woodpecker *(Campephilus principalis)* Persists in Continental North America. *Science* 308: 1460–62.

Flather, C.H., L.A. Joyce, and C.A. Bloomgarden. 1994. Species Endangerment Patterns in the United States. General Technical Report RM-241. Washington, DC: USDA Forest Service.

Fox, J., and A. Nino-Murcia. 2005. Status of Species Conservation Banking in the United States. *Conservation Biology* 19(4): 996–1007.

Giraud, K.L., J.B. Loomis, and R.L. Johnson. 1999. Internal and External Scope in Willingness-to-Pay Estimates for Threatened and Endangered Wildlife. *Journal of Environmental Management* 56: 221–29.

Giraud, K., and B. Valcic. 2004. Willingness-to-Pay Estimates and Geographic Embedded Samples: Case Study of Alaskan Steller Sea Lion. *Journal of International Wildlife Law and Policy* 7: 57–72.

Giraud, K., B. Turcin, J. Loomis, and J. Cooper. 2002. Economic Benefit of the Protection Program for the Steller Sea Lion. *Marine Policy* 26: 451–58.

Gaston, K.G. 2000. Global Patterns in Biodiversity. *Nature* 405: 220–27.

Grime, J.P. 1997. Biodiversity and Ecosystem Function: The Debate Deepens. *Science* 277: 1260–61.

Hageman, R. 1985. Valuing marine mammal populations: benefit valuations in a multi-species ecosystem. Administrative Report LJ-85-22. Southwest Fisheries Center. La Jolla, CA: National Marine Fisheries Service.

Hagen, D., J. Vincent, and P. Welle. 1992. Benefits of Preserving Old-growth Forests and the Spotted Owl. *Contemporary Policy Issues* 10: 13–25.

Hanemann, W.M. 1994. Valuing the Environment Through Contingent Valuation. *Journal of Economic Perspectives* 8(4): 18–44.

Hawksworth, D.L., and M.T. Kalin-Arroyo. 1995. Magnitude and Distribution of Biodiversity. In *Global Biodiversity Assessment,* edited by V.K. Heywood. UN Environment Programme.

Heal, G. 1998. *Valuing the Future: Economic Theory and Sustainability.* New York: Columbia University Press.

Heal, G.M., E.B. Barbier, K.J. Boyle, et al. 2005. Valuing Ecosystem Services: Toward Better Environmental Decision Making. Washington, DC: National Academies Press.

Heberlein, T.A., M.A. Wilson, R.C. Bishop, and N.C. Schaeffer. 2005. Rethinking the Scope Test as a Criterion for Validity in Contingent Valuation. *Journal of Environmental Economics and Management* 50: 1–22.

Hoehn, J.P., and J.B. Loomis. 1993. Substitution Effects in the Valuation of Multiple Environmental Programs. *Journal of Environmental Economics and Management* 25: 56–75.

Holling, C.S., D.W. Shindler, B.W. Walker, and J. Roughgarden. 1995. Biodiversity in the Functioning of Ecosystems: An Ecological Synthesis. In *Biodiversity Loss: Economic and Ecological Issues,* edited by C. Perrings, K.-G. Mäler, C. Folke, C.S. Holing, and B.-O. Jansson. Cambridge: Cambridge University Press, Chapter 2.

Holmes, T.P. 1988. The Offsite Impact of Soil Erosion on the Water Treatment Industry. *Land Economics* 64: 356–66.

Holmes, T.P., J.C. Bergstrom, E. Huszar, S.B. Kask, and F. Orr III. 2004. Contingent Valuation, Net Marginal Benefits, and the Scale of Riparian Ecosystem Restoration. *Ecological Economics* 49: 19–30.

Huszar, P.C. 1989. Economics of Reducing Off-site Costs of Wind Erosion. *Land Economics* 65: 333–40.

Innes, R., S. Polasky, and J. Tschirhart. 1998. Takings, Compensation and Endangered Species Protection on Private Lands. *Journal of Economic Perspectives* 12(3): 35–52.

IUCN. 2004. The Red List of Threatened Species. www.iucnredlist.org.

Kealy, M.J., and R.W. Turner. 1993. A Test of the Equality of the Close-Ended and the Open-Ended Contingent Valuation. *American Journal of Agricultural Economics* 75: 311–31.

Kennedy, T.A., S. Naeem, K.M. Howe, J.M.H. Knops, D. Tilman, and P. Reich. 2002. Biodiversity as a Barrier to Ecological Invasion. *Nature* 417: 636–38.

King, D., D. Flynn, and W. Shaw. 1988. Total and Existence Values of a Herd of Desert Bighorn Sheep. Benefits and Costs in Natural Resource Planning, Interim Report. Western Regional Research Publication W-133. Davis: University of California Press.

Kotchen, M.J., and S.D. Reiling. 2000. Environmental Attitudes, Motivations, and Contingent Valuation of Nonuse Values: A Case Study Involving Endangered Species. *Ecological Economics* 32: 93–107.

Krutilla, J.V. 1967. Conservation Reconsidered. *American Economic Review* 57(4): 777–86.

Land Trust Alliance (LTA). 2006. 2005 National Land Trust Census Report. Washington, DC: Land Trust Alliance.

Larson, D., and J. Siikamäki. 2006. Valuing Surface Water Quality in California: A Mixed Panel Logit Model Using a 2?-bounded CVM. Third World Congress of Environmental and Resource Economics, Kyoto, July 3–7.

Larson, D.M., S.L. Shaikh, and D.F. Layton. 2004. Revealing Preferences for Leisure Time from Stated Preference Data. *American Journal of Agricultural Economics* 86: 307–20.

Laughland, A.S., W.N. Musser, J.S. Shortle, and L.M. Musser. 1996. Construct Validity of Averting Cost Measures of Environmental Benefits. *Land Economics* 72: 100–12.

Loomis, J.B. 1989. Test-retest Reliability of the Contingent Valuation Method: A Comparison of General Population and Visitor Responses. *American Journal of Agriculture Economics* 71: 76–81.

Loomis, J., and E. Ekstrand. 1997. Economic Benefits of Critical Habitat for the Mexican Spotted Owl: A Scope Test Using a Multiple-Bounded Contingent Valuation Survey. *Journal of Agricultural and Resource Economics* 22(2): 356–66.

Loomis, J.B., and A. Gonzales-Caban. 1998. A Willingness-to-Pay Function for Protecting Acres of Spotted Owl Habitat from Fire. *Ecological Economics* 25: 315–22.

Loomis, J., and D. Larson. 1994. Total Economic Values of Increasing Gray Whale Populations: Results from a Contingent Valuation Survey of Visitors and Households. *Marine Resource Economics* 9: 275–86.

Loomis, J.B., and White, D.S. 1996. Economic Benefits of Rare and Endangered Species: Summary and Meta-analysis. *Ecological Economics* 18: 197–206.

Loomis, J.B., A. Gonzales-Caban, and R. Gregory. 1994. Do Reminders of Substitutes and Budget Constraints Influence Contingent Valuation Estimates? *Land Economics* 70: 499–506.

Louviere, J.J., D.A. Hensher, and J.S. Swait. 2000. *Stated Choice Methods: Analysis and Application.* Cambridge: Cambridge University Press.

Lovejoy, T.E. 1980. Changes in Biological Diversity. In *Global 2000 Report to the President* (vol. 2).

Lueck, D., and J.A. Michael. 2003. Preemptive Habitat Destruction under the Endangered Species Act. *The Journal of Law and Economics* 46: 27–60.

MacArthur, R.H., and E.O. Wilson. 1967. *The Theory of Island Biogeography.* Princeton: Princeton University Press.

Mace, G.M., J.L. Gittleman, and A. Purvis. 2003. Preserving the Tree of Life. *Science* 300: 1707–709.

Mäler, K.-G., and J.R. Vincent. 2005. *Handbook of Environmental Economics* (vol. 2, *Valuing Environmental Changes*). Amsterdam: Elsevier North-Holland.

McCann, K.S. 2000. The Diversity-Stability Debate. *Nature* 405: 228–33.

McClelland, G.H., W.D. Schultze, J.K. Lazo, D.M. Waldman, J.K. Doyle, S.R. Elliot, and J.R. Irwin. 1992. Methods for Measuring the Non-use Values: A Contingent Valuation Study of the Groundwater Cleanup. Draft report to the U.S. EPA, Center for Economic Analysis. Boulder: University of Colorado.

McConnell, K.E., and N.E. Bockstael. 2005. Valuing the Environment as a Factor of Production. In *Handbook of Environmental Economics* (vol. 1), edited by K.-G. Mäler and J.R. Vincent. Elsevier, North-Holland, Chapter 14.

Metrick, A., and M.L. Weitzman. 1996. Patterns of Behavior in Endangered Species Preservation. *Land Economics* 72(1): 1–16.

———. 1998. Conflicts and Choices in Biodiversity Preservation. *Journal of Economic Perspectives* 12(3): 21–34.

Mitchell, R.C., and R.T. Carson. 1984. Willingness to Pay for National Freshwater Improvements. Draft report to U.S. EPA. Washington, DC: Resources for the Future.

National Oceanic and Atmospheric Administration (NOAA). 2005. Endangered and Threatened Species; Designation of Critical Habitat for Seven Evolutionarily Significant Units of Pacific Salmon and Steelhead in California: Final Rule. *Federal Register* 70(170): 52488-52586, Friday, September 2, Rules and Regulations.

National Research Council (NRC). 1995. *Science and the Endangered Species Act.* Washington, DC: National Academies Press.

NatureServe. 2003. Ecological Systems Database, version 1.02. Arlington, VA: NatureServe.

Nee, S., and R.M. May. 1997. Extinction and the Loss of Evolutionary History. *Science* 278: 692–94.

Newman, D.J., G.M. Cragg, and K.M. Snader. 2003. Natural Products as Sources of New Drugs over the Period 1981–2002. *Journal of Natural Products* 66(7): 1022–37.

Noss, R.D., and A.F. Cooperrider. 1994. *Saving Nature's Legacy: Protecting and Restoring Biodiversity.* Defenders of Wildlife. Washington, DC: Island Press.

Nunes, P.A.L.D., and J.C.J.M. van den Bergh. 2001. Economic Valuation of Biodiversity: Sense or Nonsense? *Ecological Economics* 39: 203–22.

O'Grady, J., M.A. Burgman, D.A. Keith, L.L. Master, S.J. Andelman, B.W. Brook, G.A. Hammerson, T. Regan, and R. Frankham. 2004. Correlations among Extinction Risks Assessed by Different Systems of Threatened Species Categorization. *Conservation Biology* 18(6): 1624–35.

Olsen, D., J. Richards, and D. Scott. 1991. Existence and Sport Values for Doubling the Size of Columbia River Basin Salmon and Steelhead Runs. *Rivers* 2: 44–56.

Pezzey, John C.V. 1997. Sustainability Constraints Versus "Optimality" Versus Intertemporal Concern, and Axioms Versus Data. *Land Economics* 73(4): 448–66.

Phaneuf, D.J., and V.K. Smith. 2005. Recreation Demand Models. In *Handbook of Environmental Economics* (vol. 2), edited by K.-G. Mäler and J.R. Vincent. Elsevier, Chapter 15.

Pimentel, D., L. Lach, R. Zuniga, and D. Morrison. 2000. Environmental and Economic Costs of Nonindigenous Species in the United States. *Bioscience* 50(1): 53–67.

Polasky, S., and H. Doremus. 1998. When the Truth Hurts: Endangered Species Policy on Private Land with Imperfect Information. *Journal of Environmental Economics and Management* 35(1): 22–47.

Polasky, S., H. Doremus, and B. Rettig. 1997. Endangered Species Conservation on Private Land. *Contemporary Economic Policy* 15(4): 66–76.

Polasky, S., J. Camm, and B. Garber-Yonts. 2001. Selecting Biological Reserves Cost Effectively: An Application to Terrestrial Vertebrate Conservation in Oregon. *Land Economics* 77(1): 68–78.

Polasky, S., C. Costello, and A. Solow. 2005a. The Economics of Biodiversity. In *Handbook of Environmental Economics* (vol. 3), edited by K.-G. Mäler and J.R. Vincent. Elsevier, Chapter 29.

Polasky, S., E. Nelson, E. Lonsdorf, P. Fackler, and A. Starfield. 2005b. Conserving Species in a Working Landscape: Land Use with Biological and Economic Objectives. *Ecological Applications* 15(4): 1387–401.

Pounds, J.A., M.R. Bustamante, L.A. Coloma, et al. 2006. Widespread Amphibian Extinctions from Epidemic Disease Driven by Global Warming. *Nature* 439 (January 12): 161–67.

Purvis, A., and A. Hector. 2000. Getting the Measure of Biodiversity. *Nature* 405 (May 11): 212–19.

Rausser, G., and A. Small. 2000. Valuing Research Leads: Bioprospecting and the Conservation of Genetic Resources. *Journal of Political Economy* 108(1): 173–206.

Reaves, D.W., R.A. Kramer, and T.P. Holmes. 1994. Valuing the Endangered Red-cockaded Woodpecker and Its Habitat: A Comparison of Contingent Valuation Elicitation Techniques and a Test for Embedding. Contributed paper, American Association of Agricultural Economics annual meeting, San Diego, CA, August.

———. 1999. Does Question Format Matter? Valuing an Endangered Species. *Environmental and Resource Economics* 14: 365–83.

Ribaudo, M.O. 1989a. Water Quality Benefits from the Conservation Reserve Program, Agricultural Economics Report. Washington, DC: Economic Research Service.

———. 1989b. Targeting the Conservation Reserve Program to Maximize Water Quality Benefits. *Land Economics* 65: 320–32.

Ricciardi, A., and J.B. Rasmussen. 1999. Extinction Rates of North American Freshwater Fauna. *Conservation Biology* 13(5): 1220–22.

Richer, J. 1995. Willingness to Pay for Desert Protection. *Contemporary Economic Policy* 13: 93–104.

Rubin, J., G. Helfand, and J. Loomis. 1991. A Benefit-cost Analysis of the Northern Spotted Owl. *Journal of Forestry* 89: 25–30.

Samples, K., and J. Hollyer. 1989. Contingent Valuation of Wildlife Resources in the Presence of Substitutes and Complement. In *Economic Valuation of Natural Resources: Issues, Theory, and Application,* edited by R. Johnson and G. Johnson. Boulder, CO: Westview Press.

Savidge, J.A. 1987. Extinction of an Island Forest Avifauna by an Introduced Snake. *Ecology* 68: 660–68.

Shabman, L., and S. Batie. 1978. The Economic Value of Natural Coastal Wetlands: A Critique. *Coastal Zone Management Journal* 4(3): 231–47.

Siikamäki, J., and D.F. Layton. 2007a. Potential Cost-effectiveness of Incentive Payment Programs for the Protection of Non-industrial Private Forests. *Land Economics* 83(4): 95-116.

Siikamäki, J., and D.F. Layton. 2007b. Discrete Choice Survey Experiments: A Comparison Using Flexible Methods. *Journal of Environmental Economics and Management* 53: 122–39.

Silberman, J., D.A. Gerlowski, and N.A. Williams. 1992. Estimating Existence Value for Users and Nonusers of New Jersey Beaches. *Land Economics* 68: 225–36.

Simon, J.L., and A. Wildawsky. 1984. On Species Loss, the Absence of Data, and Risks to Humanity. In *The Resourceful Earth: A Response to "Global 2000,"* edited by J.L. Simon and H. Kahn. Oxford: Blackwell.

Simpson, R.D. 2000. Economic Perspectives on Preservation of Biodiversity. In *Conserving Nature's Diversity: Insights from Biology, Ethics, and Economics,* edited by G.C. van Kooten, E.H. Bulte, and A.R.E. Sinclair. Aldershot, UK: Ashgate.

Simpson, R.D., R. Sedjo, and J. Reid. 1996. Valuing Biodiversity for Use in Pharmaceutical Research. *Journal of Political Economy* 104(1): 163–85.

Smith, V.K., and W.H. Desvousges. 1986. Measuring Water Quality Benefits. Dordrecht, Netherlands: Kluwer Nijhoff Publishing.

Stanley, D.L. 2005. Local Perceptions of Public Goods: Recent Assessments of Willingness-to-Pay for Endangered Species. *Contemporary Economic Policy* 23: 165–79, Table 7-5.

Stein, B.A. 2002. States of the Union: Ranking America's Biodiversity. Arlington, VA: NatureServe.

Stein, B.A, J.S. Adams, L.M. Master, L.E. Morse, and G.A. Hammerson. 2000a. A Remarkable Array: Species Diversity in the United States. In *Precious Heritage: The Status of Biodiversity in the United States,* edited by Stein et al. Oxford: Oxford University Press.

Stein, B.A., L.S. Kutner, and J.S. Adams (eds.). 2000a. *Precious Heritage: The Status of Biodiversity in the United States.* Oxford: Oxford University Press.

Stevens, T., J. Echeverria, R. Glass, T. Hager, and T. More. 1991. Measuring the Existence Value of Wildlife: What Do CVM Estimates Really Show? *Land Economics* 67: 390–400.

Swanson, C. 1993. Economics of non-game management: bald eagles on the Skagit River Bald Eagle Natural Area, Washington. Ph.D. dissertation. Department of Agricultural Economics. Columbus: Ohio State University, Table 7-5.

Thomas, C.D., A. Cameron, R.E. Green, et al. 2004. Extinction Risk from Climate Change. *Nature* 427: 145–48.

Tilman, D. 2004. Niche Tradeoffs, Neutrality, and Community Structure: A Stochastic Theory of Resource Competition, Invasion, and Community Assembly. Proceedings of National Academy of Sciences 101: 10854–61.

Tilman, D., and J.A. Downing. 1994. Biodiversity and Stability in Grasslands. *Nature* 367: 363–65.

Tilman, D., P.B. Reich, J. Knops, D. Wedin, T. Mielke, and C. Lehman. 2001. Diversity and Productivity in a Long-term Grassland Experiment. *Science* 294: 843–45.

Toman, M.A. 1994. Economics and "Sustainability": Balancing Trade-offs and Imperatives. *Land Economics* 70(4): 399–413.

———. 1998. Why not Calculate the Value of the World's Ecosystem Services and Natural Capital. *Ecological Economics* 25: 61–65.

Torell, L.A., J.D. Libbin, and M.D. Miller. 1990. The Market Value of Water in the Ogallala Aquifer. *Land Economics* 66: 163–75.

U.S. Council on Environmental Quality and Department of State. 1980. *Global 2000 Report to the President* (vol. 2).

USDA Forest Service. 2004. National Report on Sustainable Forests: 2003. Washington, DC: Department of Agriculture.

U.S. Fish and Wildlife Service (USFWS). 1993. Placing Animals and Plants on the List of Endangered and Threatened Species. Washington, DC: Department of the Interior.

———. 2002a. America's National Wildlife Refuges. Washington, DC: Department of the Interior. http://www.fws.gov/refuges/generalInterest/factSheets/FactSheetAmNationalWild.pdf.

———. 2002b. Candidate Conservation Agreements with Assurances for Non-federal Property Owners. Washington, DC: Department of the Interior.

————. 2004a. Listing a Species as Threatened or Endangered, Section 4 of the Endangered Species Act. Washington, DC: Department of the Interior.

————. 2004b. Participation trends: addendum to the 2001 National Survey of Fishing, Hunting, and Wildlife-Associated Recreation (Report 2001-5).

————. 2004c. Recovery Report to Congress, Fiscal Years 2001–2002. Washington, DC: Department of the Interior.

U.S. Office of Technology Assessment. 1993. Harmful Nonindigenous Species in the United States. Technical Report. Washington, DC: U.S. Congress.

Vane-Wright, R.I., C.J. Humphries, and P.H. Williams. 1991. What to Protect? Systematics and the Agony of Choice. *Biological Conservation* 55: 235–54.

Walker, D.J., and D. L. Young. 1986. The Effect of Technical Progress Erosion Damage and Economic Incentives for Soil Conservation. *Land Economics* 62: 83–93.

Walsh, R.O., J.B. Loomis, and R.A. Gillman. 1984. Valuing Option, Existence, and Bequest Demands for Wilderness. *Land Economics* 60: 14–29.

Weitzman, M.L. 1992. On Diversity. *Quarterly Journal of Economics* 107(2): 363–405.

Whitehead, J. 1991. Economic Values of Threatened and Endangered Wildlife: A Case Study of Coastal Nongame Wildlife. Transactions of the 57th North American Wildlife and Natural Resources Conference. Washington, DC: Wildlife Management Institute.

————. 1992. Ex ante Willingness to Pay with Supply and Demand Uncertainty: Implications for Valuing a Sea Turtle Protection Programme. *Applied Economics* 24: 981–88.

Wilcove, D.S., D. Rothstein, J. Dubow, A. Phillips, and E. Losos. 2000. Leading Threats to U.S. Biodiversity: What's Threatening Imperiled Species? In *Precious Heritage: The Status of Biodiversity in the United States,* edited by B. Stein et al. Oxford: Oxford University Press.

Williams, J.C., C.S. ReVelle, and S.A. Levin. 2004. Using Mathematical Optimization Models to Design Nature Reserves. *Frontiers in Ecology and the Environment* 2: 98–105.

Wilson, E.O. 1985. The Biological Diversity Crisis. *BioScience* 35: 700–706.

Index